CHILD ABUSE
AND NEGLECT
A Medical Reference

CHILD ABUSE AND NEGLECT
A Medical Reference

Edited by
Norman S. Ellerstein, M.D.

Assistant Professor of Pediatrics
State University of New York at Buffalo School of Medicine
Director, Child Abuse and Neglect Program
The Children's Hospital of Buffalo
Buffalo, New York

A WILEY MEDICAL PUBLICATION
JOHN WILEY & SONS
New York • Chichester • Brisbane • Toronto

614.1
C 536 e

Library of Congress Cataloging in Publication Data:

Ellerstein, Norman S., 1945–
  Child abuse and neglect.

  (A Wiley medical publication)
  Includes index.
  1. Battered child syndrome.   2. Child abuse.
I. Title.   II. Series: Wiley medical publication.

[DNLM: 1. Child abuse. WA 320 C534013]
RA1122.5.E43   614'.1   81-2978
ISBN 0-471-05877-7   AACR2

Printed in the United States of America

10 9 8 7 6 5 4 3 2 1

Contributors

Joseph E. Bernat, D.D.S.
Associate Professor of Pedodontics
State University of New York at Buffalo School of Dentistry
Buffalo, New York

Douglas J. Besharov, J.D., Ll.M.
Federal Executive Fellow
The Brookings Institution
First Director
U.S. National Center on Child Abuse and Neglect
Washington, D.C.

J. William Canavan, M.D.
Clinical Instructor of Pediatrics
State University of New York at Buffalo School of Medicine
Buffalo, New York

Norman S. Ellerstein, M.D.
Assistant Professor of Pediatrics
State University of New York at Buffalo School of Medicine
Director, Child Abuse and Neglect Program
The Children's Hospital of Buffalo
Buffalo, New York

Robert J. Ford, R.B.P. (Registered Biological Photographer)
Photographer–Illustrator
Sierra Research Corporation
Former Senior Medical Photographer
The Children's Hospital of Buffalo
Buffalo, New York

J. Allen Gammon, M.D., M.P.H.
Assistant Professor of Ophthalmology
Emory University School of Medicine
Chief of Ophthalmology
The Henrietta Egleston Hospital for Children
Atlanta, Georgia

Jane D. Gray, M.D.
Assistant Clinical Professor of Pediatrics
University of Colorado School of Medicine
Denver, Colorado

Reid F. Holbrook, J.D.
Attorney at Law
Partner, Holbrook and Ellis, P.A.
Kansas City, Kansas

Theodore C. Jewett, Jr., M.D.
Professor of Surgery and Pediatrics
State University of New York at Buffalo School of Medicine
Surgeon-in-Chief
The Children's Hospital of Buffalo
Buffalo, New York

David M. Klein, M.D.
Associate Professor of Neurosurgery
State University of New York at Buffalo School of Medicine
Head, Department of Neurosurgery
The Children's Hospital of Buffalo
Buffalo, New York

James J. Kresel, M.S.
Director, Pharmacy Services
Mary Hitchcock Memorial Hospital
Assistant Director
New Hampshire Poison Center
Instructor of Community and Family Medicine
Dartmouth Medical School
Hanover, New Hampshire

Jerald P. Kuhn, M.D.
Professor of Radiology and Associate Professor of Pediatrics
State University of New York at Buffalo School of Medicine
Head, Department of Radiology
The Children's Hospital of Buffalo
Buffalo, New York

Hunter C. Leake III, M.D.
Clinical Associate Professor of Pediatrics
University of Kansas College of Health Sciences and Hospital
Former Director of Ambulatory Pediatrics
University of Kansas Medical Center
Kansas City, Kansas

Frederick H. Lovejoy, Jr., M.D.
Associate Professor of Pediatrics
Harvard Medical School
Senior Associate in Medicine and Clinical Pharmacology
The Children's Hospital Medical Center
Director, The Massachusetts Poison Control System
Boston, Massachusetts

Harold P. Martin, M.D.
Associate Professor of Pediatrics and Psychiatry
University of Colorado School of Medicine
John F. Kennedy Child Development Center
Denver, Colorado

Carolyn Moore Newberger, Ed.D.
Instructor in Psychiatry (Psychology)
Harvard Medical School
Staff Psychologist
Judge Baker Guidance Center
Boston, Massachusetts

Eli H. Newberger, M.D.
Assistant Professor of Pediatrics
Harvard Medical School
Director, Family Development Study
The Children's Hospital Medical Center
Boston, Massachusetts

Barton D. Schmitt, M.D.
Associate Professor of Pediatrics
University of Colorado School of Medicine
Director, Child Protection Team
University of Colorado Health Sciences Center
Denver, Colorado

Brian S. Smistek
Senior Medical Photographer
The Children's Hospital of Buffalo
Buffalo, New York

Leonard E. Swischuk, M.D.
Professor of Radiology and Pediatrics
University of Texas Medical Branch
Director, Division of Pediatric Radiology
Child Health Center
Galveston, Texas

Charles F. Whitten, M.D.
Professor of Pediatrics and Associate Dean for Curricular Affairs
Wayne State University School of Medicine
Detroit, Michigan

Preface

There are many books available that deal with child abuse and neglect. To reflect the multidisciplinary nature of child maltreatment, the majority of books address, in a single volume, issues facing several disciplines such as social work, law, medicine, criminal justice, and community issues. As a pediatrician working with abused children, I needed a reference concentrating on the medical issues of maltreated children. *Child Abuse and Neglect: A Medical Reference* is an exhaustive presentation of the medical issues involved in cases of abused and neglected children. If a parent does not give his child the medicine for asthma, is that medical neglect? Does gonorrhea in a 6-year-old girl mean that she was sexually abused? What should a physician do if he is called to testify in court? How can an intentional burn be differentiated from an accidental one? These are the types of issues that are addressed in this book.

Physicians, as a group, have been criticized for not being as active as they could be as child advocates. In particular, clinicians have been accused of underreporting abuse and neglect cases. This lack of involvement has a variety of causes, one of which has been cited as an underemphasis of biosocial topics in medical education. This book contains detailed data on medical issues that confront clinicians dealing with children who might be abused or neglected. Any physician who cares for children, as a primary practitioner or specialist, should find this information useful. However, the book should also appeal to child protection workers, attorneys, judges, law enforcement officials, and other nonhealth professionals who deal with medical issues in their professional capacities.

I have been fortunate to have assembled a group of contributors who collectively represent a broad and profound experience in the area of child maltreatment. The information herein was gleaned from thousands of scientific articles and years of personal experience of each of the contributors. This reference should prove useful when the clinician is making a decision as to whether his patient has been maltreated, when medical testimony must be given in court, and when planning for the long-term care and rehabilitation of the child. The majority of chapters deal with specific organ system manifestations of abuse and neglect and how to evaluate and treat these problems. The chapters on medical testimony, photography, and legal issues offer valuable supportive information to the clinician to which he is not usually exposed. Several chapters, such as those addressing etiology and prevention, offer scholarly discussions of broad issues. Although this volume is intended as a medical reference, most of the text and the majority of the figures should be understandable to the nonhealth professional. Therefore, anyone seeking specific medical facts or a general discussion of abuse- or neglect-related issues should benefit from this text. I hope that the children whom we all serve will be the ultimate beneficiaries.

N.S.E.

Acknowledgments

It is traditional to list the people who were helpful to an editor or author in the preparation of a book. I have learned why this practice is so common; it would have been a much more difficult and less enjoyable pursuit without the aid of certain people.

My family, friends, and colleagues encouraged me to accept the opportunity to create this book. I hope that those who use the book will agree that their advice was correct.

Two friends and teachers were particularly helpful during the time this book was being written. Elliot F. Ellis, M.D., Professor and Chairman of the Department of Pediatrics at the State University of New York at Buffalo School of Medicine, has been very supportive of my professional and personal interests. I consider myself fortunate to work for a man with such integrity, compassion, and insight. The second person is Professor Erwin Neter, also of the medical school and The Children's Hospital of Buffalo. Dr. Neter is a constant source of advice and friendly criticism. He has selflessly helped many young authors, investigators, and clinicians; I am lucky to be one of them.

Only through the care of children have I gained experience and developed an interest in maltreated children. Therefore, I am indebted to other physicians who send me their patients and to parents who allow me to care for their children. I hope that the past experience of these silent sufferers will serve to prevent tomorrow's children from a similar fate.

Dr. T. Dennis Sullivan, a colleague at The Children's Hospital of Buffalo, helped me as consultant grammarian and knowledgeable critic.

Nancy Moen and Kathleen Harding had the courage to serve as my secretaries for this book. Their help went far beyond their typing and clerical skills.

My parents are a constant help to me by their example of self-confidence, hard work, and faith in times of adversity.

I dedicate this book to my wife, Ellen, and son, David, in recognition of their continuing support and love.

N.S.E.

Contents

CHILD ABUSE
AND NEGLECT
A Medical Reference

1
The Role
of the Physician

Norman S. Ellerstein

Child maltreatment (abuse and neglect) is one of the major problems affecting children today. Although no exact statistics are available, approximately 1 to 3% of children in the United States are abused or neglected. Child maltreatment causes more physical and psychological morbidity than does most pediatric illnesses. Approximately 4,000 children per year die from child abuse in the United States (1); this is more than the number of children who die from leukemia annually. Even though child maltreatment is not solely a medical problem, the physician is in a key position to help reduce the number of children who suffer abuse and neglect.

The maltreatment of children has existed since recorded time and has taken many forms (2). Infanticide was practiced because of ritual belief, illegitimacy, population control, and greed for power and money. Abandonment, which frequently led to the death of the infant, was occasionally caused by religious beliefs, but was more commonly the result of illegitimacy. Children were mutilated for a variety of reasons. Circumcision, foot and head binding, and castration were all accepted at various times in history. Deformities were intentionally inflicted on children to arouse pity, thereby making them more convincing beggars. Beating or whipping children was commonly considered an acceptable form of punishment to maintain discipline and encourage more productive work. In the 17th century in Connecticut and Massachusetts, laws were passed imposing the death penalty on unruly children (3). Urbanization and the industrial revolution increased the exploitation of children as laborers and led to the death of many through occupational diseases, malnutrition, beatings, and suicides.

It was not until the second half of the 20th century that the medical profession became seriously involved in the problem of child abuse. In the 1940s and 1950s descriptions of battered children appeared in the medical literature (4–6); but it was not until the publication in 1962 of an article by Dr. C. Henry Kempe and his colleagues (7) that major attention of the medical profession was drawn to the problem of child abuse and neglect. Since that time, physicians and other health professionals have become increasingly involved in many aspects of child

1

protection. In this chapter, the various roles and responsibilities of the physician in the area of child maltreatment are presented.

PHYSICIAN'S BASIC RESPONSIBILITIES

The first step in becoming involved in suspected child maltreatment cases is to acknowledge that the problem exists. Some physicians refuse to believe that parents have injured their own children. This idea seems so abhorrent to the physician that he puts it out of his mind and, therefore, feels that he does not have to deal with it. Once the physician acknowledges that abuse and neglect occur, he must maintain a high index of suspicion for cases of abuse and neglect. The nature of the problem is such that parents do not suggest maltreatment as a possible cause of their child's condition; therefore, the physician must constantly consider the diagnosis. If the physician is confronted with a child who manifests some of the classic features of abuse or neglect, the recognition is easier. However, many times the physical evidence is not blatant and a careful interview with the child and his parent will point out inconsistencies between the historical and objective data. The physician must then make a medical judgment as to whether the physical signs and symptoms are plausibly explained by the history offered. The physician's consideration of abuse or neglect should not be swayed by the economic, educational, or occupational level of the parents.

The next step that the physicians must take is to discuss with the parents the fact that child maltreatment is in the differential diagnosis of their child's problem. This is probably one of the most difficult duties of the child's physician.

This is the time when the physician must be aware of his own feelings so that he can deal with them and, thereby, communicate effectively with the parents. The physician may feel hostility toward the parents because they may have injured their child. He has fear of confronting the parents with this fact because they may become angry with the physician. He must maintain his objectivity, control his hostility, and be honest with the parents so that he does not alienate them at this pivotal point in initiating diagnostic and therapeutic modalities. The physician cannot be accusatory or judgmental in his interaction with the parents. Frequently it is helpful to explain to the parents the facts as they appear to the physician: that is, the injuries cannot be explained by the history; therefore another mechanism must be present. Instead of saying, "One of you must have injured the child," it is less alienating to say, "The child could not have injured himself; this was not accidental; therefore, some other person must have been instrumental in causing the injury." It is when the physician confronts the parents with the possible diagnosis that many parents are alienated from the physician and the medical profession in general. If the physician tries to cover-up the diagnosis or reports the suspected case to the child protection agency without telling the parens, the parents may generalize their distrust and avoid contact with the medical profession in the future. If handled properly, the parents can be informed of the suspected diagnosis, will cooperate with the recommendations of the physician, and will probably cooperate with the initial investigation by the appropriate child protection agency. If the parents offer an argument or accuse the physician of falsely persecuting them, the physician can defend himself by stating that his diagnosis was based on the medical facts, his report to the child protection authorities is mandated by law, and he would be breaking the law or be accused of professional negligence if he did not report the case as he saw it.

The physician's next responsibility is to protect the child. This may be done initially by admitting him to a hospital and contacting an agency that handles child protection matters in his community. All states have laws mandating the reporting of child maltreatment cases, and most are accessible through a 24-hour telephone number. Once the child is in the hospital and is at least temporarily protected from his parents, an appropriate evaluation of the child's physical and developmental problem is necessary. If the physician who initially recognized the child as being possibly maltreated is not able to offer the necessary evaluation himself, he is obligated to seek appropriate consultations. In major pediatric institutions there is usually a physician particularly interested in child abuse who can serve as a consultant. Furthermore, evaluation by the social service and behavioral science departments will aid in clarifying the family dynamics. Consultations from surgeons, ophthalmologists, orthopedists, psychiatrists, psychologists, and radiologists may be necessary as indicated to evaluate and document individual physical and psychological manifestations of the maltreatment. During this evaluation procedure it is essential that everything be documented in the medical chart. This is important in all medical cases, but especially in suspected abuse and neglect cases in which the medical record may be reviewed by attorneys and may be admitted into evidence in a juvenile or family court.

The physician must be aware that his input into a case of suspected child maltreatment should be limited to that of a physician. Attorneys, judges, social workers, and others involved in child protection issues all have thier roles to play; the physician should not think that he can perform all the necessary functions in the evaluation and treatment of a child and his family. Because child abuse is such a multidisciplinary problem, the physician may get caught up in the nonmedical aspects of the case. In doing so he may forget that the child has physical and psychological problems secondary to his maltreatment. Therefore, the physician must attend to the child's acute medical needs as well as arranging for continued medical care. It should not be assumed that just because the child is followed by the appropriate social agency or is being placed in a foster home that his medical care will be properly arranged. The physician involved should specifically set up outpatient medical care after the child's hospitalization. Maltreated children have many more medical and psychological problems than nonabused children and, therefore, need more extensive evaluation and treatment.

PHYSICIAN'S RELUCTANCE TO BECOME INVOLVED IN CHILD ABUSE AND NEGLECT

Several authors (8–10) have discussed the multiple reasons for why physicians do not get involved in child maltreatment cases. Helfer, in his 1975 article (8), points out that medical schools do not adequately train students in subjects related to child abuse and neglect. Deficiencies existed in subjects such as normal and abnormal family dynamics, interviewing skills, and the ability to work with nonhealth professionals from disciplines such as social work, psychology, and law enforcement. However, since 1975 many medical schools have added courses on interviewing and interpersonal skills and specific courses dealing with child maltreatment.

The rewards for dealing with cases of abuse and neglect are few. The time necessary to deal appropriately with the abused child and his family is not financially compensated adequately by medical insurance or other means of payment. The parents are infrequently appreciative of what the physician is doing for their family. In fact, in the early stages of working with the family, they are frequently hostile and angry with the physician for recognizing the family as abusive. Therefore, there is a great outlay of emotion and little positive feedback for the physician; he develops a "negative emotional balance." This is a state in which the physician is emotionally underrewarded for his efforts; anxiety, frustration, and a feeling of helplessness are common manifestations.

From dealing with child abuse cases or other problems requiring community agency cooperation, the physician may have become frustrated with the community services' inadequacies. Because of these failures of the system, the physician may choose not to refer cases to them. He may also be fearful that the community will take a punitive approach to the parents and involve the police and criminal court system. In relation to this fear, the physician may also be reluctant to get involved because of his fear of testifying in court. Because of the prevalence of malpractice litigation and other legal entanglements, physicians appear to be reluctant to raise any issues that might embroil them in a court case.

Schmitt and Kempe (9) feel that some physicians are reluctant to report abuse because they are ignorant of the seriousness of the problem. They further suggest that the physician may be trying to identify the abuser. However, in at least 50% of child abuse cases, it is impossible to determine who actually caused the child's injuries. The physician may feel that if he is unable to determine who injured the child, then he should not report it; this, of course, is a dangerous policy. Finally, the physician may be fearful of liability from his actions. This fear is unwarranted; the law requiring the physician to report also protects him from liability if his suspicions are unfounded.

ADDITIONAL ROLES FOR THE PHYSICIAN

The physician can be instrumental in the prevention of abuse and neglect. He can provide prenatal and postnatal family counseling, identify problems in child rearing and parenting, and offer advice about family planning and birth control. Since the possibility of child maltreatment is increased with additional stress within the family, the physician can help reduce the potential for abuse by keeping stress factors caused by medical problems to a minimum. Children with chronic diseases, handicapping conditions, and frequent illnesses can themselves be additional stress factors that bring a family closer to an abusive situation. If the physician adequately manages the family's health problems, he may reduce the likelihood that illness will be one of the potentiating causes of maltreatment.

The physician can be an influential child advocate. Physicians are frequently held in high esteem in their community. Their advice is frequently sought and well received. It is the physician's duty to promote the importance of children. He should be active in school systems, child welfare groups, parents' groups, and local medical societies. It is hoped that he would encourage charitable organizations to assign a high priority to funding for children's services.

Physicians, especially those interested in child protection issues, can serve as the primary educators in the field of child abuse and neglect. Physicians involved in medical education must infuse biosocial issues, such as child abuse, into curricula for medical students and residents. Physicians should also participate in the education of nonhealth professionals and laymen to increase their awareness of child maltreatment.

A physician may serve as a child abuse consultant. These are usually full-time hospital-based physicians, who are usually pediatricians, but may be surgeons, orthopedists, or other people experienced in dealing with child abuse cases. These physicians can serve as consultants to other physicians to help decide whether a child has been intentionally injured or not. The child abuse consultant may report suspected child abuse cases for the primary physician. A similar, but not identical, role is that of the child protection team physician. The multidisciplinary child protection team is a useful approach in handling the evaluation and management of suspected child maltreatment cases. Usually a variety of disciplines, including social work, law, child development, and medicine, are represented on the team. It is desirable to have a physician on the team to explain the medical aspects of the case and to help plan the child's future medical, developmental, and psychological rehabilitation. Child protection team physicians need not be hospital based; many are in the private practice of pediatrics.

Even though all physicians should be familiar with the subject of child abuse and neglect, some physicians should have a more profound knowledge than others. Primary care physicians (pediatricians, family practitioners, internists, and obstetricians) who daily come in contact with children and their families should be well versed, not only in the recognition of the abused child, but also in the various preventative measures that may be taken. Emergency room physicians and others who see trauma cases should be acutely sensitive to the nonaccidental causes of childhood trauma. Ophthalmologists, radiologists, and orthopedists should become familiar with the manifestations of abuse likely to be seen in their specialty. Neonatologists can be instrumental in the prevention of child maltreatment if they are aware of the causes of the increased incidence of abuse in the patients whom they treat.

COMMONLY ASKED MEDICAL QUESTIONS ABOUT ABUSE AND NEGLECT

In the hospital where I work, I am frequently asked questions by house officers, medical students, social workers, or nurses about possibly abused children.

Many times these people do not want a list of journal articles and directions to the library or a long and inconclusive answer. More frequently they are searching for a yes or no answer with which they can dispatch the problem at hand. Therefore, I have assembled a list of questions that I have been frequently asked, and I have attempted to give short, direct answers. For a more in-depth discussion of most of these issues, references to other chapters in the book are provided.

Question. Are all prepubertal children with venereal disease, such as gonorrhea, sexually abused?

Answer. With rare exceptions, it is wisest to assume that a child with venereal disease has been sexually abused. There is no substantial evidence to show that venereal diseases can be acquired in any way other than a sexual mode. Some authors have suggested that close-personal contact, such as sleeping in the same bed, can lead to the acquisition of a venereal disease by a child. However, this possibility has not been substantiated in any well-controlled experiments. Therefore, it is recommended to report as suspected sexual abuse all children who have venereal disease. Gonorrhea is the most common venereal disease in children. In summary, it can be said that children with venereal diseases have been sexually abused; however, future research may teach us that some children may acquire diseases that are usually transmitted sexually through other modes. (See Chap. 13.)

Question. What is the risk of radiation from a skeletal survey as compared to the potential benefit of this study? Aren't many x-ray films taken of children suspected of being abused compared to the number of old or new fractures found on these films?

Answer. It is unknown what percentage of skeletal surveys reveal suspicious fractures. However, the minimal radiation exposure risks are probably worthwhile considering the fact that physical child abuse is potentially fatal if undetected. Therefore, the risk-benefit ratio of skeletal surveys is favorable. (See Chap. 14.)

Question. Isn't it common for children to fall off beds or couches and sustain head trauma?

Answer. Accidentally falling off of a couch or bed is a common household occurrence; but sustaining some serious injury from this is extremely unlikely. Children who fall short distances may sustain simple linear skull fractures; but a skull fracture by itself is not a dangerous injury. It has never been shown that a child will sustain brain injury from a short fall. The skull is designed to protect its contents and does its job very well. Therefore, the skull may absorb the impact and crack leaving the underlying brain undamaged. A child who has a brain injury probably received a force to the head that was significantly greater than could be acquired by a fall of 30 in. (See Chap. 5.)

Question. Don't most children who fail to grow have something wrong with them?

Answer. Yes, but what is wrong with them is most likely not an organic disease. Several studies have shown that the majority of children who fail to thrive do not suffer from an organic condition but rather are the victims of nonorganic failure-to-thrive, which is caused by maternal deprivation. (See Chap. 11.)

Question. Isn't it common for an infant to get his arm or leg caught in crib slats and accidentally break it?

Answer. No, this probably does not happen. There is no reason to believe that an infant or child has enough strength to break his own limb. Since this does not occur in older children or adults, there is no reason to believe that it can occur in infants or young children. There may be special circumstances that are the exception to this rule. Children with bone diseases, such as osteogenesis imperfecta or advanced osteoporosis, have bones that are more easily broken than those of normal children. However, to assume that an otherwise normal child became entangled in his own crib or bed clothing and therefore sustained a fracture or other serious injury would lead to missing many physically abused children. Unfortunately, it is difficult to do the kind of research that would offer definitive answers to these questions.

Question. Aren't parents who are noncompliant with medical instructions, such as administering prescribed medicines, neglecting their children?

Answer. Some parents are not given enough instruction about what the physician wants to be done for the child. Other parents need significant education in order to follow the physicians prescribed treatment or medicines. However, there are some parents who, despite adequate understanding, neglect to give their children needed medicines. Some of these children, such as asthmatics or diabetics, will unquestionably suffer without receiving their prescribed medication. If a parent, after being carefully counseled and educated as to the seriousness of their child's illness, still refuses to administer the prescribed medicines, then there is reason to believe that medical neglect is present. Situations in which the child's health is seriously endangered from the lack of medication warrant a report for medical neglect. (See Chap. 16.)

Questions. Aren't parents who let their child get burned neglecting them?

Answer. No. Not all accidents are preventable. If a child is repeatedly in a dangerous situation and incurs multiple preventable accidents, such as burns, ingestions, or falls, then the possibility of supervisional neglect exists. (See Chap. 16.)

Question. Is an infant born to a drug- or alcohol-abusing mother necessarily abused or neglected?

Answer. No, but the incidence of abuse and neglect is higher in this type of family. Therefore, it is advised that this child be followed more closely, both medically and socially, than an infant born to a mother without these particular problems. (See Chaps. 2, 4, and 17.)

Question. Are there any physical findings that are pathognomonic for child abuse or neglect?

Answer. Even though most injuries seen in abused and neglected children can also be caused accidentally, there are some pathognomonic findings. These include loop marks (see Chap. 12), venereal disease in prepubertal children (see Chap. 13), certain burns (see Chap. 10), most human bite marks (see Chap. 8), and multiple fractures of varying ages (see Chap. 14). Nonorganic failure-to-thrive is pathognomonic of maternal deprivation, which is manifestation of severe parenting difficulty (see Chap. 11).

Question. Is it legal to photograph suspected abuse cases without parental consent?

Answer. In most states, yes. In fact some states mandate that photographs must be taken of suspected abusive injuries. In some states the photographer is reimbursed by the agency investigating the case. (See Chaps. 3 and 18.)

Question. Do retinal hemorrhages always mean abuse?

Answer. No. Retinal hemorrhages are seen in cases of physical abuse and are commonly associated with intentional head trauma, but accidental head trauma may also cause hemorrhages in the retina. (See Chaps. 5 and 7.)

Question. If a child dies and abuse and neglect are suspected but not proven, is an autopsy by a medical examiner necessary?

Answer. Yes.

Question. If during a routine examination of a 10-year-old boy, loop marks are found that are many years old, what should be done? That is, if there is lasting physical evidence of past child abuse, but there is no suggestion of recent child abuse, how should this be handled?

Answer. The parents and child should be questioned individually as to the source of the marks. If the parents admit to causing the marks in the past and the examiner is convinced that there is no current maltreatment occurring and the child is not suffering any physical or emotional sequellae of the former maltreatment, it may not be useful to report the case at this time. If the child is now living in a nonabusive home, if the parents are honest about the origin of the old marks and the child is not suffering any negative effects of the former abuse, it usually serves no purpose to report the case.

Question. If a young infant has a high fever and meningitis is in the differential diagnosis, what should be done if the parents refuse to have a lumbar puncture performed on their child?

Answer. If it is medically necessary to diagnose or treat an organic condition with a high risk of morbidity or mortality, such as meningitis, the physician is obligated to obtain permission from the appropriate social service agency or family court to overrule the parents' objection. The child's right to life supersedes any objections, religious or otherwise, that the parents may present. (See Chap. 16.)

Question. What should the physician do who suspects that the child whom he is examining is abused, but cannot prove it?

Answer. Report it.

Question. Is a report of possible child maltreatment indicated if a child lives in a home in which the parents are drug abusers?

Answer. If there is a suspicion that the child may be receiving drugs or alcohol from his parents, this should definitely be reported. However, if the child does not appear to be adversely affected in any way by the substance abuse of his parents, a report is not necessarily indicated. In today's society, it is suspected that a large number of people use drugs for recreational purposes, but are still able to carry on productive lives; most likely this includes being able to be effective parents. However, when substance abuse interferes with the parents' ability to care adequately for their child, this should undoubtedly be reported to the child protection agency. (See Chaps. 16 and 17.)

Question. Can a parent sue a physician who reports a case of suspected abuse or neglect if the result of the investigation is that there is no evidence of maltreatment?

Answer. The state laws that mandate physicians to report suspected cases of abuse and neglect protect the physician who is reporting. The laws clearly state that if a physician reports a suspected case in good faith, he is immune from liability whether or not the case is valid. (See Chap. 3.)

All of us in the medical profession must become familiar with the problem of child abuse and neglect. In the chapters that follow, many subject areas about abused and neglected children are explored. I hope that this information will aid the physician in caring for children who may be maltreated.

REFERENCES

1. Sturner WQ: Pediatric deaths, in Curran WJ, McGarry AL, Petty CS (eds): *Modern Legal Medicine Psychiatry and Forensic Science*. Philadelphia, FA Davis Company, 1980, p 236.

2. Solomon T: History and demography of child abuse. *Pediatrics* 51:773, 1973.

3. Radbill SX: A history of child abuse and infanticide, in Helfer RE, Kempe CH (eds): *The Battered Child*, ed 2. Chicago, University of Chicago Press, 1974, p 3.

4. Caffey J: Multiple fractures in the long bones of infants suffering from chronic subdural hematoma. *Am J Roentgenol, Radium Therapy, Nucl Med* 56:163, 1946.

5. Silverman FN: The roentgen manifestations of unrecognized skeletal trauma in infants. *Am J Roentgenol, Rad Ther, Nucl Med* 69:413, 1953.

6. Woolley PV Jr, Evans WA Jr: Significance of skeletal lesions in infants resembling those of traumatic origin. *JAMA* 158:539, 1955.

7. Kempe CH, Silverman FH, Steele BF, et al: The battered child syndrome. *JAMA* 181:105, 1962.

8. Helfer RE: Why most physicians don't get involved in child abuse cases and what to do about it. *Child Today* 4:28, 1975.

9. Schmitt BD, Kempe CH: The pediatrician's role in child abuse and neglect. *Curr Probl Ped* 5:3, 1975.

10. Sanders RW: Resistance to dealing with parents of battered children. *Pediatrics* 50:853, 1972.

2
The Etiology of Child Abuse

Carolyn Moore Newberger
Eli H. Newberger

Child abuse has been noted to have many causes: as a childhood symptom of mental illness in parents, as the culmination of a lifelong experience of violence toward the caregiver, of environmental and social stresses on the family, and of society's acceptance and promotion of physical violence. Contained in each causal explanation is a theory of etiology. And within each theory, researchers extract from the complexity of families' lives those particular factors that are believed to be causal agents for violence against children. Clinicians are frequently frustrated by the limited focus and use of the diverse theories on child abuse. In order to select which factors to study, researchers must exclude other factors. Clinicians, facing a variety of distinctive life events, personal characteristics, and unique circumstances of the families and children they serve, are not always content with the explanations for the origin of child abuse found in the research literature.

Child abuse and *child neglect* are catchall euphemisms for a variety of childhood injuries that are believed to be derived from parental acts of omission or commission. The diagnostic tags focus attention on symptoms and propose entirely too simple formulations of etiology (1). In this chapter, child abuse refers to the many problems suggested by child abuse and child neglect. This is to focus more on the causes than on the manifestations of child maltreatment.

This chapter is devoted to a critical review of the major theories of human function and dysfunction that have been applied to the study of child abuse. The object is not to promote a single view that explains the phenomenon sufficiently, but to offer an analysis of several approaches to etiology that, when considered together, leads to more comprehensive knowledge about child abuse.

We propose a series of *levels of analysis of the process of cause and effect*: individual, familial, community, and society. We hope such a treatment will lead to more sensitive and discriminating understanding of how different factors lead to particular symptoms in individual children in particular families.

THE INDIVIDUAL LEVEL OF ANALYSIS

The Psychoanalytic View

Initial efforts to understand child abuse following its description in the American medical literature in the early 1960s by C. Henry Kempe (2) focused on the psychological problems of the parents of the victims. Steele and Pollock (3), in a highly influential study in the book *The Battered Child*, pointed to abusing parents' distorted expectations of their children, frustrated dependency needs, personal isolation, and histories of having themselves been abused as children. In a review of the abundant literature viewing child abuse from a psychoanalytic perspective, the primary causes were seen to be in the parents' psychological troubles. Kempe (2), for example, described the abuser as "the psychopathological member of the family," while Galdston (4) noted that parents "illustrate their psychopathology" in psychiatric sessions. Psychodynamic characteristics of the parent, the argument follows, must be understood in order for treatment to take place.

In the current psychiatric literature, psychoanalytic interpretations of the abuse phenomenon are diverse. The child may be looked on to give love and comfort to parents who are themselves unsure of being loved (5).

> Kathy made this poignant statement "I never felt really loved all my life. When the baby was born I thought he would love me but when he cried all the time it meant he didn't love me so I hit him." Kenny, age three weeks, was hospitalized with bilateral subdural hematomas. (3)

The child is expected to provide the nurturance and protection his parents never received, despite his helplessness, his limited abilities, and his own needs. The child cannot possibly fulfill such a role and, as a result, is punished, his own needs unperceived.

Another psychoanalytic view suggests that the parent sees the child as a symbolic or delusional figure who represents the psychotic or "bad" portion of the parent that the parent wishes to control or destroy. Thus the parent's difficulties are projected onto the child, and anxiety is relieved by attacking the child (3).

Nurse (6) finds that her data "do not support the proposition that abuse reflects generalized parental harshness in discipline. Indeed, parental discipline of children other than the victim was only haphazardly maintained and infrequently involved physical punishment." The abused child acts as a buffer for other children in the family; if the scapegoat for parental tensions is removed, another child may take his place.

Parents who abuse children have been described as being totally immersed in the action of inflicting deliberate, consistent, and controlled punishment "without regard for its cause and purpose" and as being frustrated, unhappy, and isolated people with poor impulse control who act randomly and apathetically (7,8). Psychoanalytically oriented studies suggest that many abusing parents show severe neurotic or psychotic tendencies, but that abuse may derive from one of several different personality types. A consistent finding was that abusing parents in general have an inability to empathize with their children (9–12).

It must be acknowledged that for many of these parents, there may be a core of individual psychopathology that must be addressed; yet a unitary theory of individual psychopathology does not necessarily explain the presence of a history of child abuse. A particular psychiatric diagnosis does not predict abuse. The theory does not enable a differentation between parents with a given diagnosis who do and do not abuse a child, and because of the relatively small number of cases that are systematically studied from a psychoanalytic perspective, the available data should be regarded skeptically.

The psychoanalytic orientation does, however, guide most modern child welfare work. As with all theories, its action consequences are derived from how the problem is understood. To a great extent, the limits of some current protective service work are set by the collective belief in the curative value of love and talk. By assuming that the cause of the problem lies with the person who inflicts the injury, there is a risk of failing to take into account the complexity of family functioning, the diversity of individual family members, life circumstances, and psychological illness. The psychodynamic approach, as it has been traditionally applied to child abuse research and practice, fails to provide flexible alternative interpretations and interventions should counseling fail to achieve its objective of better parental adaptation. The usual alternative to modification of the perpetrator's behavior has been the removal of the child to a surrogate home, an intervention with effects on children and their families that are too little understood (13). Also, the current foster care system frequently fails to provide the quality and continuity of surrogate home placement necessary for the satisfactory growth and development of the child (14).

A model based on individual psychopathology may overlook the important questions of family strength, of what keeps people and families healthy; of prevention, of how troubled family relationships might be identified before the child is physically and emotionally damaged; and of the complexity of interpersonal family dynamics, of how other family members and circumstances may contribute to a parent's inability to protect and nurture his child adequately. On the other hand, many thoughtful, analytically oriented clinicians are aware of the limitations of individual psychotherapy for complex family problems, as well as its importance in cases where individual psychopathology contributes importantly to family dysfunction. Innovative, psychoanalytically derived treatment modalities such as family and group therapy offer greater flexibility in intervention for complex family problems. The sensitivity of many clinicians to external as well as internal issues also helps correct many of the limitations of the traditional, individual-based model.

The Cognitive View

A new approach to understanding child abuse has been offered by research on parental awareness (15). This research identifies and describes four developmental levels of parental thinking about children and the parental role. These levels progress from concrete and physicalistic conceptions of the child and an understanding of the parental role only in terms of the parent's own needs and desires to an awareness of the child as a complex psychological being and of the parental role as embedded in an ongoing and reciprocal relationship between parent and child. A parent's level of awareness can be determined through an interview that is scored from a manual containing examples of parental reason at each level for each of the subject areas contained in the interview.

In order to examine the relationship between parental awareness and child abuse and neglect, eight families with a recent history of having abused a child were selected from the Family Development Clinic at Children's Hospital, Boston. Each parental respondent was matched individually on the basis of social class, race, age of the oldest child, and whether the parent had a child who was being seen in another clinic for a comparably acute medical condition unrelated to child abuse.

The abusive parents scored significantly lower on the measure of parental awareness than their matched counterparts. These findings are replicated in a second controlled study in rural Maine of eight parents with a history of protective service involvement for child neglect (16). These data suggest that the developmental level at which a parent understands the child and the parental role bears a relationship to child abuse and neglect. There was not, however, a predictive relationship between parental awareness and a parental history of having abused or neglected a child. In the original study, there were many parents with low parental awareness scores who as far as was known did not have a history of child abuse or neglect, and within the child abuse samples a few parents' scores were not at the lowest levels.

A reasonable inference suggested by these studies was that for higher scoring parents from the child abuse samples, other factors in their lives may interact with or overwhelm parental reasoning to weaken the parent-child relationship. Conversely, for low scoring parents without a history of dysfunction in the parental role, there may be factors in their lives that protect their relationships with their children. A more detailed review of the records of parental partici- pants supported this conclusion (17).

Notwithstanding the precise match on social class developed from occupation and education, the average income for the child abuse sample was about one- half that of the control group, as well as of other low scoring parents from the original study who did not have a history of having abused or neglected a child. Low income and the exigencies it imposes may, then, interfere with a parent's ability to nurture a child at any level of parental awareness. On the other hand, many higher scoring parents have been found to be severely impoverished, and in a larger normative sample no association was found between low income and low parental awareness score. But the higher scoring parents within the child abuse samples appeared to be burdened with even more stresses, both economic and personal, than other parents within that group. Social isolation is another familiar distinguishing feature of this child abuse sample, and here in compar- ison with the matched controls and other low scoring parents is found a clue to what may strengthen or protect families in the face of low levels of awareness. Comparing the families on number of adults in the home gave these findings: four of the eight abusive parents lived alone with their children, and within the abuse group, three of the five with the lowest parental awareness scores were alone. But eight of the ten parents in the low scoring nonabusing group were married and living with their spouses. It may be that the additional adult enables a parent with few conceptual resources to cope more adequately, as well as to buffer the stresses of rearing children.

A developmental approach identifies levels of adequacy, so that "normal" and "troubled" parent-child relationships can be compared along the same dimensions, and sources of strength can be identified as well as sources of vulnerability. For example, a high level of parental awareness may contribute to some parents' abilities to rear well-functioning children, despite economic deprivation or psychological vulnerability.

The value of the social cognitive-developmental approach to clinical practice is not to provide an alternative explanation for understanding parental functioning, but rather, to supplement sociological and psychological approaches and insights in order to arrive at a more comprehensive understanding of function and dysfunction in the parent-child relationship.

THE FAMILIAL LEVEL OF ANALYSIS

Just as families exist within a social context and the interaction between character and context must be considered (as is illustrated in the preceding section on the interaction between parental awareness and family stress), so do individual family members exist within the context of family relationships. The interaction between parent and child, the child's contribution to that interaction, and the relationship between spouse and spouse in the etiology of child abuse must be considered.

The Contribution of the Child

A child's own qualities that may stimulate violence in the family may include physical deformities, acute or chronic illness, slow intellectual development, psychiatric problems, and a temperament that is inadequately understood or tolerated by his or her parents (18). An abused child may be the product of an unwanted pregnancy. The child may place an unwanted financial burden on the parents, may have interfered with educational or occupational plans, may have created tensions between the parents or between parents and kin, or may have forced a hasty marriage or welfare dependency.

Children who are born prematurely or with low birth weights are at greater risk for the developmental disabilities that create stress and are associated with child abuse (19). Studies suggest an association between low birth weights and abuse (20–22).

Prematurity also carries with it a greater likelihood of maternal illness, of difficulties with pregnancy and delivery, and of separations between the child and parent during the first 6 months of life. The bond of attachment that develops between parent and child may be compromised by the conditions imposed by and associated with prematurity (23).

The concept of attachment is used to describe the phenomenon by which animals maintain close proximity to their mothers. Its biological function is protection and survival. John Bowlby (24) applied the concept to the human mother-child relationship. The infant is described as genetically programmed to elicit closeness to and protection from his or her caregiver. Maternal behaviors (Bowlby did not consider father-infant attachment, although such a literature is now being generated) also function to elicit attachment of the infant to the mother.

In order for attachment to develop normally, a reasonable amount of proximity must be maintained between the child and its parent. Deviations in attachment can occur for several reasons: insufficient contact between parent and child; difficulty of the mother in responding to the baby's signals, leading to distortions in development; difficulty of the baby in responding to the mother's signals, leading to a diminution of protective responses; and a baby whose signals are difficult to read, as is frequently the case with premature infants who are delayed in establishing predictable rhythms and who may be ill and irritable.

In a small controlled study of abused children, signs of attachment conflict were consistently found in the abused group (25). Although the evidence is preliminary, it suggests that increased attention must be paid to the early parent-child relationship. Hospital routines that oblige the protracted separation of newborns from their parents may contribute to a greater subsequent risk for child abuse or neglect (26).

When violence is the major mode of communication between parent and child, the relationship may take on a quality that maintains the violence. The child may behave provocatively in order to attract attention, even violent attention from a parent, who in turn may express remorse for "having" to beat the child.

The Relationship Between Parents

Recent research suggests that the relationship between a child's parents is importantly implicated in the etiology of child abuse. In homes where husbands and wives reported that they had used violence on each other during the previous year, there was a 129% greater incidence of reports of severe violence toward their children. Respondents who reported that they had observed their parents hit one another also had a much higher rate of violence toward their own children than respondents who said that they had never seen their parents hit each other. A power domination of one parent by the other has also been identified as concomitant in cases of child abuse (27).

THE COMMUNITY LEVEL OF ANALYSIS: A SOCIO-SITUATIONAL VIEW

Because child abuse occurs across classes, some psychoanalytically oriented thinkers suggest that socio-situational factors are not immediately relevant to child abuse (3,4). There is increasing evidence that factors accounting for violence toward children are not confined to psychological characteristics such as individual parental pathology, developmental disability in the child, or personality deviations in parent or child. A recent survey reveals that violence toward children does vary by such social categories as social class, income, occupation, education, employment, number of children, family power, and stress (26). The position of the family in the community must be examined for further evidence of factors implicated in the etiology of child abuse. Gil (28) and Elmer (29) find that abusive homes tend to have larger families than nonabusive homes, lower incomes, lower educational levels of fathers, and contained a higher number of people receiving welfare aid than usual. As these studies were carried out respectively with a hospital population or on the basis of reported cases, the data was skewed by the large number of lower class families who receive services at institutions that report the large majority of cases. From the data available, it cannot be inferred that child abuse is a phenomenon of poverty, as Gil (28) contends, but one must ask whether child abuse could be the result of overwhelming environmental stress, a stress that may indeed be experienced disproportionately, but not exclusively, among the poor.

Child abuse can also be seen in a broad context as symptomatic of distress in a family that compromises the family's ability to protect and nurture its children (1). Causes of breakdown in family functioning may derive from many factors that in a particular family may contribute to family distress, such as unemployment, inadequate housing, loss of a family member, or a recent move to a new environment.

Social isolation has been found to be a principal concomitant of child abuse (1,28). If parents are without friends, have no telephone contact with the outside world, or are detached from contact with other adults, they will have no access to support in times of trouble. Many families feel rejected by their communities, and the variabilities of the employment market keep many families on the move. It is well to keep in mind in clinical work that isolation can be both a characteristic of an individual parent's personality or the given family's style; it may also be imposed by the exigencies of the economic and social setting.

Larger aggregates of people, such as neighborhoods, can be seen as distinctive settings of risk for child abuse. Garbarino and Sherman (30) mapped repeated child abuse cases in 400 neighborhoods, and they found from interviews that families with the greatest needs for social contact and support were "clustered together in settings that must struggle to meet these needs." They suggest that this phenomenon derives from a combination of personal, political, and economic forces. They conclude that "ecological niches can 'make or break' risky families."

The socio-situational view emphasizes identifying those factors in the environmental context of a family that, by being felt as overwhelmingly stressful, interfere with a parent's ability to care for its young. Treatment is directed toward changing or ameliorating environmental sources of family stress.

This view has several important strengths: it addresses the family rather than an individual family member as the unit of practice; its approach is to strengthen family functioning by removing or modifying external sources that impede a family's ability to meet the minimal needs of its members; it lends itself to research aimed at identifying sources of stress that seem predictive of family dysfunction, leading to efforts to *prevent* child abuse by intervening to remove or ameliorate sources of stress to families.

Yet this model has limitations. Spinetta and Rigler (9) argue that while socioeconomic factors might sometimes place added stress on basic personality weakness, these stresses are not of themselves sufficient or necessary causes of abuse.

This model fails to acknowledge adequately internal sources of family strength and stress that render individual families more or less sensitive to external circumstances and events. It does not deal with the qualities of the interaction among family members and their importance to a family's capacity to nurture its young. It does not address the question of how it is that stress in one family might be reflected in an alcoholic father and in another with an abused child (of course, these are not mutually exclusive symptoms of family stress), nor does it adequately account for child abuse in seemingly privileged homes.

THE SOCIETAL LEVEL OF ANALYSIS: A SOCIO-CULTURAL VIEW

At each level of analysis described in this chapter, family stresses are noted as being consistently linked with child abuse. These stresses are frequent accompaniments of poverty. Poverty carries with it a higher risk of low birth weight and prematurity and of developmental disability following perinatal risk. Poor families are more likely to suffer unemployment, chronic illness, inadequate housing, and geographic mobility with its attendant isolation. Gil (28) argues that poverty, and not parental failure, is the principal abuser of children.

From a socio-cultural perspective child abuse can be viewed as a product of several fundamental and interacting elements that have their roots in American values. Gil observed that in our culture, where competition is more valued than cooperation, physical force may be a normal way to resolve conflicts. Where the basic social structure is hierarchical and inegalitarian, the weak and dependent are necessarily near the bottom of the social ladder. Further, corporal punishment may be encouraged to prepare children for adult roles in a competitive social system (31).

There is increasing consensus on the association between the acceptance of violent means of socializing children and the occurrence of child abuse. The use of corporal punishment is widespread, and it could be argued that physical punishment of children reflects societal values expressed in a familial context. Confusion remains on the legal and moral legitimacy of violence toward children. The support of corporal punishment by such institutions as the United States Supreme Court appears to sanction violent practices in the American home, some of which culminate in incidents of serious harm. The depiction and promotion of violence in the movies and on television may also affect how adults and children approach issues of conflict. Whether media violence is associated with childhood aggressive behavior remains a subject for lively debate, but there is a developing consensus that a milieu of violence fosters actions of violence. It could be argued further that the use of violence by media heroes conveys an essential value that violence is manly, smart, and successful.

AN ECOLOGICAL MODEL FOR CHILD ABUSE

With the development of a field from a set of unitary views to a set of integrative hypotheses, investigations shift in focus from trying to find *the cause* to enabling the identification of individual differences in etiology. Basic research into the identification of the many variables that are implicated in child abuse is still needed, but the focus is on elaboration rather than closure.

It is in what has come to be called ecological theory that major strides have been made in understanding and dealing with the interrelationships among attributes of child, parent, family, community, and society. Child abuse is seen in this context as a symptom of disturbance in a complex ecosystem with many interacting variables. David Gil (31) calls for a more holistic notion of child abuse and its prevention, with a conceptualization of cause and effect which operates at different levels and with different modes of etiology for different children and families. A decade or so ago, Julius Richmond coined the notion of a family's ecology of health. This seems now to be an especially relevant concept for the understanding and study of child abuse. The child abuse field needs to move more firmly into an integrative stage of understanding where relationships among endogenous and exogenous variables are recognized. To look at internal parental characteristics without attention to the child, to the social context, or to environmental stresses impinging on a parent does a disservice to troubled individuals. It is too easy to "blame the victim" or overlook critical factors that contribute to child abuse or neglect, by assuming that all parents who harm their children have something inside themselves or have some identifiable way of thinking that "compels" them to abuse or neglect their children.

A sociological approach to child abuse and neglect is also constrained by the limitations of sociological theory to individual functioning. Although it may identify factors in a person's social, physical, and economic environments which seem to contribute to parental dysfunction, it does not allow for an understanding of what personal qualities or characteristics keep parents and families healthy in the face of similar hardships or of what renders families vulnerable in the relative absence of sociologically defined stresses. Internal and external factors must be considered in relation to each other if a more accurate understanding of the etiology is to be achieved.

Practically, all the factors impinging on a family's functioning can never be acknowledged, because at some point and in some way every problem affects every family. On the other hand, attempts should be made to acknowledge and conceptualize broader dimensions of family functioning in order to arrive at a better understanding of the diversity of familial adaptation and dysfunction.

REFERENCES

1. Newberger EH, Reed RB, Daniel JH, et al: Pediatric social illness: Toward an etiologic classification. *Pediatrics* 60:178, 1977.

2. Kemp CH, Silverman FH, Steele BF, et al: The battered child syndrome. *JAMA* 181:17, 1962.

3. Steele BF, Pollock CB: A psychiatric study of parents who abuse infants and small children, in Helfer RE, Kempe CH (eds): *The Battered Child*, ed 2, Chicago, University of Chicago Press, 1974, pp 89–133.

4. Galdston R: Observations on children who have been physically abused and their parents. *Am J Psychiatry* 122:440, 1965.

5. Morris MG, Gould RW: Role reversal: A necessary concept in dealing with the "Battered child syndrome." *Am J Orthopsychiatry* 33:298, 1963.

6. Nurse S: Familial patterns of parents who abuse their children. *Smith College Studies in Social Work* 35;11, 1964.

7. Young LR: *Wednesday's Children: a Study of Child Neglect and Abuse.* New York, McGraw-Hill Book Company, 1964.

8. Gregg GS, Elmer E: Infant injuries: Accident or abuse? *Pediatrics* 44:434, 1969.

9. Spinetta JJ, Rigler D: The child abusing parent: A psychological review. *Psychol Bull* 77:296, 1972.

10. Melnick B, Hurley HB Jr: Distinctive personality attributes of child abusing mothers. *J Consult Clin Psychol* 33:746, 1969.

11. Berg PI: Parental expectations and attitudes in child abusing families. *Dissertation Abstracts International* 37:1889-B, 1976.

12. Smith SM, Hanson R, Noble S: Parents of battered babies: A controlled study. *Br Med J* 17:388, 1973.

13. Kadushin A: *Child Welfare Services.* New York, MacMillan, Inc, 1974.

14. Gruber AR: *Foster Home Care in Massachusetts.* Commonwealth of Massachusetts, Governor's Commission on Adoption and Foster Care, 1973.

15. Newberger CM: Parental conceptions of children and childrearing. Unpublished doctoral dissertation, Harvard University, 1977.

16. Newberger CM, Cook S: Parental awareness and child abuse and neglect: Studies of urban and rural parents, paper presented at the biennial meeting of the Society For Research in Child Development, April, 1981.

17. Newberger C: The cognitive structure of parenthood: Designing a descriptive measure, in Selman R, Yando R (eds): *New Directions for Child Development,* vol 7. San Francisco, Jossey-Bass, Inc, Publishers, 1980, pp 45–67.

18. Friedrich WN, Boriskin JA: The role of the child in abuse: A review of the literature. *Am J Orthopsychiatry* 46;580, 1976.

19. Newberger EH, Newberger CM, Richmond JB: Child health in America: Toward a rational public policy. *Milbank Memorial Fund Quarterly* 54:249, 1976.

20. Klein M, Stern L: Low birth weight and the battered child syndrome. *Am J Dis Child* 72:15, 1971.

21. Martin HP, Beezley P, Conway EG, et al: The development of abused children, in Schulman I (ed): *Advances in Pediatrics,* vol 21. Chicago, Year Book Medical Publishers, Inc, 1974.

22. Fomufod A, Sinkford S, Louy V: Mother-Child separation at birth: A contributing factor in child abuse. *Lancet* 2:549, 1975.

23. Faranoff A, Kennell J, Klaus M: Follow-up of low birth weight infants—The predictive value of maternal visiting patterns. *Pediatrics* 49:287, 1972.

24. Bowlby J: *Attachment and Loss,* vol 1. New York, Basic Books, Inc, Publishers, 1969.

25. George C, Main M: Social interactions of young abused children: Approach, avoidance, and aggression. *Child Dev* 50:306, 1979.

26. Klaus MH, Kennell JH: *Maternal Infant Bonding.* St. Louis, CV Mosby Co, 1976.

27. Straus MA, Gelles RJ, Steinmetz SK: *Behind Closed Doors: Violence in the American Family.* New York, Anchor Press/Doubleday, 1980.

28. Gil D: *Violence Against Children.* Cambridge, Mass, Harvard University Press, 1970.

29. Elmer E: *Children in Jeopardy: a Study of Abused Minors and Their Families.* Pittsburgh, University of Pittsburgh Press, 1967.

30. Garbarino J, Sherman D: High risk neighborhood and high risk families. The human ecology of child maltreatment. *Child Dev* 51:188, 1980.

31. Gil D: Unraveling child abuse. *Am J Orthopsychiatry* 45:345, 1975.

3
What Physicians Should Know About Child Abuse Reporting Laws

Douglas J. Besharov

The concept of mandatory reporting of certain situations of suspected child abuse or maltreatment is a recent one. After the United States Children's Bureau first proposed a model reporting law in 1963, in "the span of four legislative years all 50 states enacted laws seeking reports of injuries on children" (1). Paulsen comments, "In the history of the United States, few legislative proposals have been so widely adopted in so little time" (2).

Throughout this period, under the leadership of Drs. C. Henry Kempe and Vincent J. Fontana, individual physicians as well as the American Academy of Pediatrics played a crucial role in shaping and supporting the expansion of reporting procedures. For example, in 1966, the Academy's Committee on Infant and Preschool Child issued recommended guidelines for the identification and reporting of abused children (3); in 1972, the committee called for the strengthening of protective agencies, the creation of central registers of reports, and the granting of immunity to physicians reporting known or suspected child abuse (4).

At the present time, all states, Washington, D.C., and the three territories have laws that require certain persons to report suspected abuse and maltreatment (5). However, such reporting laws are only one step taken to protect endangered children. By 1970, the inability of existing agencies to protect endangered children was widely admitted. Most child protective systems had grown into patchwork programs of blurred responsibility, often based on vague and superficial considerations. Responsibility was frequently passed from one agency or individual to another; continuous referrals caused frequent loss of information and delays in providing services. Studies found that many children suffered further injury or died after a report was made to the authorities because of administrative breakdowns among "balkanized" agencies (6). In response to growing public and professional awareness that existing child protective procedures needed to be strengthened and upgraded, states began to reform their child protective systems as well as their child abuse reporting laws. As part of this broadening concern, the United States Congress passed the Child Abuse Prevention and Treatment Act in 1974 (Federal Act) (7), which required states to upgrade their child protective programs in order to receive special federal grants.

In part because of the impetus of the Federal Act, but more importantly because of public and professional demands for improved child protective systems, since 1975, over 40 states have amended their laws and procedures: to require the reporting of suspected neglect as well as abuse; to prescribe procedures for investigations and other aspects of case handling—often a specialized child protective agency is designated or established; to provide a guardian *ad litem* for the child; to upgrade central registers of reports; to ensure confidentiality of records; to require independent investigations of institutional child maltreatment; and to mandate professional training and public education efforts. This "second generation" of state child protective laws demonstrates "an increased public concern about child abuse and neglect and a continually rising level of sophistication in the public response to that problem" (8).

For the physician, the significance of reporting laws goes beyond their "casefinding" requirement to identify abused and maltreated children. Information gathered in the reporting process often is invaluable in discovering, through a record of prior reports, a pattern of injuries or medical treatment indicative of abuse or maltreatment. This information may also be essential in proving the abuse or maltreatment in court. Many statutes provide that the reports themselves are admissible in court proceedings relating to alleged abuse or maltreatment (9). This chapter, however, confines itself to the legal issues surrounding the reporting process and does not address these court-related elements of the legal framework for child protection.

PROTECTING INDIVIDUAL RIGHTS

Implicit in most recent child protective legislation is the finding that the balance between children's rights and parents' rights must be weighted in favor of protecting children. Yet, it is important to protect traditional American values of freedom and legality while trying to protect endangered children. A report of known or suspected child abuse or neglect sets in motion an unavoidably stressful investigation that may lead to the removal of a child from his home and the stigmatization of a family within its community. The benign purposes and rehabilitative services of child protective agencies do not prevent them from being unpleasant and sometimes destructive, though well-meaning, coercive intrusions into family life.

If society is to intrude into family life without the free consent of parents, it must do so with due regard to parental rights, as well as to the needs of children. Thus, even though the experience of all states shows that only a handful of reports are not made in good faith, as states seek to improve their child protective systems generally, they should also seek to improve the provisions they make to protect the rights of all involved. Legal safeguards can be provided to protect parental rights without unreasonably endangering children. State law should accord to both the child and the parent the full safeguards of fundamental fairness, confidentiality, and due process of law. Coercive intervention into family life should not be authorized unless there is sufficient reason to believe that child abuse or neglect exist. Moreover, these terms should be carefully defined in state law to minimize their improper application to situations where societal intervention is not justified. All records should be kept confidential to protect both parents and children and should be made available only in clearly defined situations. Furthermore, treatment services should be offered first on a voluntary basis. The child protective agency should resort to court action only if necessary. When the powers of the court must be invoked to protect the child, a civil proceeding in a juvenile or family court should be sought in preference to criminal court action. Although referral to criminal court may be appropriate in certain situations, the criminal court can protect the child only by jailing the abusive parent. The juvenile court, on the other hand, can help mobilize social and psychological services necessary to deal with some of the fundamental problems that led to the abuse. If a case reaches court, both the child and the parents should have independent legal counsel.

PROVISIONS FOR SELF-HELP AND VOLUNTARILY SOUGHT SERVICES

In our society, parents have the prime responsibility of caring for their children. Unless a child's health or welfare is endangered, the family's right to privacy and right to be left alone are well established (10,11).

Encouraging parents to seek help on their own is the most humanitarian, practical, and the least intrusive approach to preventing child abuse and neglect, because helping services are most effective when they are accepted voluntarily. If parents who need help understand their need, they will seek help on their own and will be more willing to accept it when it is offered to them. Moreover, self-help may be the only way to reach large numbers of families who would otherwise not receive help. (Because large numbers of cases are never recognized or reported, many situations of abuse and neglect become known only when family members seek outside assistance.)

The need to encourage parents to seek help on their own is only now being addressed by state child protective laws and procedures. Until recently, states sensitive to the need to encourage or protect parental efforts for self-help have reacted by refusing to extend the reach of reporting laws, usually by restricting mandatory reporting to situations of serious physical abuse or by limiting those who must report to a selected group of professionals. But today, more positive approaches are being used: by staffing the reporting hotline with social workers who can direct parents to the services that seem most appropriate, a number of states are ensuring that their reporting systems can provide an informed and sensitive response to parents who ask for help. There is also a discernible movement to enhance the parents' right to understand the child protective process, by informing them that a report has been made, that the report may be amended or expunged, that the purpose of the investigation is to protect endangered children and provide needed services, that services may be refused, and that the effect of refusing services may be referral to court. Finally, a growing trend in public awareness efforts is to provide a direct message through mass media to parents who may need help in adequately caring for their children. These messages seek to persuade parents that they are not alone in their difficulty and to inform them where they can get help.

A commitment to voluntarily sought helping services should permeate a state's formal and informal child protective system. The years ahead should see greater elaboration of such efforts, as states seek to ensure that families receive the most appropriate services possible with a minimum of state intrusion.

THE PURPOSE OF MANDATORY REPORTING LAWS

Because helping services are most effective when they are voluntarily sought, all communities encourage parents facing an abuse or neglect situation to seek help in meeting their child care responsibilities. But if parents do not seek help on their own, the responsibility to take protective action falls on others. When a child is endangered, American society is unwilling to rely solely on parents seeking help. Adults who are attacked or otherwise wronged can go to the authorities for protection and redress of their grievances. But the victims of child abuse and neglect are usually too young or too frightened to obtain protection for themselves. Protection for these helpless children is often possible only when a third person—a friend, a neighbor, a relative, or a physician—recognizes the child's danger and reports it to the proper authorities. Reporting begins the child protective process. If a case of suspected child abuse or neglect is not reported, neither the police nor a child protective agency can become involved, emergency protective measures cannot be taken, and a treatment plan cannot be developed. Reflecting the preeminence of reporting in an adequately functioning child protective system, the Federal Act, as a prerequisite for special funding, requires that states "provide for the reporting of known and suspected instances of child abuse or neglect".

The purpose of reporting is to foster the protection of children, not to punish those who maltreat them. Hence, child protective laws have no provisions for criminal court prosecution because, in most situations, criminal intent is absent. While criminal prosecutions occur in certain situations, usually when the child has died or has been severely harmed, or when the child has been abused while in an institution, such cases are dealt with in child protective laws only to the extent of recognizing that they should be referred for or coordinated with a criminal prosecution.

Unfortunately, many professionals and private citizens fail to report situations suggestive of child abuse or child neglect, thus subjecting many children to continued suffering and sometimes permanent harm and even death. In 1971, George Wyman, then Commissioner of the New York State Department of Social Services, explained the reasons for underreporting in New York state. They are applicable to all states.

Although many persons will casually accept the possibility that some children may be subjected to abuse, it appears that only the tragedy of death or severe maiming of a child in one's own community with its ensuing publicity and notoriety provides the stimulus for reporting the suspected abuse of other children. Other factors would seem to be: more restrictive definitions being applied [in some areas of the state], i.e., the tendency to report abuse only when injury is severe; diagnostic capabilities not sufficiently well-developed, particularly in areas where medical centers are not involved; reluctance to become involved due to fear of criminal prosecution of parents or automatic removal of children, more personal relationship with one's neighbors in rural communities mitigates against being willing to speak out even though this will protect a child; frustration that reports have not in fact resulted in the desired goals, i.e., rehabilitation treatment for the child and family, or successful adjudication in Family Court; lack of organized, vigorous program of casefinding and interpretation. (6)

The failure of many professionals to report child abuse and neglect has led all 50 states to pass laws requiring certain professionals or all citizens to report known and suspected child abuse and neglect.

Mandatory reporting laws seek to encourage fuller reporting of known and suspected child abuse and neglect: (1) by requiring certain professionals to report their reasonable suspicions of child abuse or neglect; (2) by providing immunity from liability for those reporting in good faith; (3) by providing penalties for failure to report as required by law; (4) by providing a convenient and easily useable reporting system; and (5) by identifying effective investigative and treatment services.

PERSONS REQUIRED TO REPORT

The medical profession was the first, and remains the foremost, target of reporting statutes. Doctors are considered the professionals most likely to see injured children, and they are presumed most qualified to diagnose the signs and symptoms of abuse and neglect.

The early focus on physicians quickly widened to include most other professionals in the "healing arts," such as nurses, osteopaths, podiatrists, chiropractors, dentists, and pharmacists. Some statutes also require coroners, general hospital personnel, optometrists, and even Christian Science practitioners to report. As of 1980, at least 45 states specifically require designated medical professionals to report. The remaining states require medical professionals to report under reporting mandates that cover all citizens.

Recognizing that other professionals having regular contact with children are also in a position to identify abuse and neglect before a child needs medical care for serious injuries, most states now also mandate specific nonmedical professionals to report. Among those commonly required to report are teachers or other school officials, social workers, police officers, child care workers, clergymen, and attorneys.

State laws often contain a limiting phrase requiring professionals to report only situations "known to them in their professional or official capacity" (12). Thus, for example, if a physician suspects that a neighbor's child, who is not his patient, is abused or neglected, he is *not required* to make a report—in recognition of the inability to enforce such a provision and the social and community pressures involved. Nothing, however, prevents physicians from making a voluntary report like any other citizen; and, indeed, they are encouraged to do so.

VOLUNTARY REPORTING

Despite all the attention paid to mandatory reporting laws, and despite the constantly expanding coverage of these laws, the great bulk of abuse and neglect reports continue to be made by individual concerned citizens. Private citizens— friends, neighbors, and relatives—though not subject to a mandatory reporting law in 30 states, make about 50% of the nation's reports. It is only within this broader context of reporting by private citizens as well as mandated professionals that the detection of child abuse and child neglect—and hence, the initiation of child protective services—can be understood.

But because these reports are not "mandated," they are often not "accepted" for investigation by child protective agencies. And even when they are accepted, they often are given the lowest investigative priority, regardless of the danger to the child. Distinctions based on who makes a report have no place in child protective efforts; the danger to the child is no less serious merely because the report is made by a private citizen or a nonmandated professional instead of a legally mandated reporter. Reports from any source should be handled in the same way, with the child protective service establishing investigative priorities based only on the real urgency of the case, not on the basis of who made the report.

Routing all reports through the formal reporting channels established by a reporting law helps ensure that they are duly recorded and promptly investigated. Thus, to combat the tendency to neglect nonmandated reports, at least 20 states have a specific statutory provision requiring and at least 20 states have a provision permitting "anyone" to report. (Voluntary reporting provisions often give the voluntary reporter immunity from liability for a good faith report and abrogate any privileged communication that might otherwise apply.)

These are some special considerations involved with voluntary reports. Nationwide, 50–70% of the reports from mandated professionals are considered "valid" or "founded"—somewhat amorphous and ambiguous terms—after investigation, depending on the specific profession involved. Only 40% of the reports from voluntary reporters, on the other hand, are found to be valid. Many of these invalid reports are made by spouses or relatives seeking to gain custody of a child. Thus, while voluntary reports must be accepted and investigated, continuous vigilance on the part of child protective agencies is necessary to deal with inappropriate or biased reports.

Recognizing the concern some professionals and private citizens have about associating their names with child abuse and neglect reports, most states allow anonymous reports by not prohibiting them. Nationwide, 30% of these anonymous reports are found to be valid. But states do not encourage anonymity because of the obvious dangers in investigating reports for whom no one is willing to take responsibility. Moreover, when professionals and citizens identify themselves, the investigating agency can often learn more about the case by interviewing the person who made the report.

CIRCUMSTANCES REQUIRING A REPORT

Although state laws still vary greatly in specifying what circumstances or conditions must or may be reported, an increasing number of states are going beyond the special attention that was earlier given to the "battered-child syndrome." Early reporting laws, generally based on the United States Children's Bureau guidelines (13), required reporting of "nonaccidental injuries," and sometimes added the broader phrase "other serious abuse or maltreatment." However, placing attention on only one form of abuse or neglect establishes false and dangerously misleading distinctions. Child neglect can be just as damaging and just as deadly as child abuse.

Even before the passage of the Federal Act in 1974, which requires states to provide for the reporting of child neglect as well as child abuse in order to receive special grants, states had begun to deal with other forms of inadequate parental care of children, including physical attack, delinquency, abandonment, emotional maltreatment, failure to provide adequate food, clothing, shelter, and failure to provide proper supervision and care. Either expressly or within broader reporting mandates, all but a handful of states require mandated professionals, including physicians, and allow all others to report child neglect, sexual abuse, and emotional abuse.

While the expansion of reporting requirements has resulted in an increase in the number of abuse and neglect situations coming to the attention of the authorities, many of the reports now handled within the formal process were previously handled outside the mandated reporting process—by the police, welfare agencies, and the courts. Thus, much of the increase in cases being reported merely reflects a shifting of investigative responsibilities from a haphazard and uncoordinated amalgam of independent agencies to one single, specialized child protective agency.

There is some question about whether reports should be "accusatory." It is argued that compelling a potential reporter to state whom he suspects is responsible for the abuse or neglect may discourage reporting because: (1) it is often impossible or too early for a potential reporter to make such a determination; (2) the potential reporter may fear possible retribution for blaming a parent; and (3) an accusatory report is inconsistent with the rehabilitative and nonpunitive philosophy of the child protective process. The major arguments in favor of accusatory reports seem to be that: (1) potential reporters will not report injuries unless they have cause to suspect that the parents are responsible; (2) it is unfair to parents who clearly do not abuse and neglect their children to report them to the child protective agency and enter their names in a central register merely because their children have sustained injuries; and (3) it is unfair to the child protective agency to be burdened with so many additional reports of cases in which the reporter has no reason to suspect the parents of any misbehavior. Balancing these various considerations, 28 states expressly require accusatory reports.

REPORTER'S STATE OF MIND

Almost without exception, state reporting laws do not require people making a report to be certain a child is abused or neglected. Usually the law is couched in terms such as "has cause to suspect," "reasonably suspects," "has cause to believe," or "believes." Except for the last example, these phrases are all meant to describe degrees of conviction in the reporter's mind between an unfounded suspicion and probable cause to believe. Because of the impracticality of making minute distinctions in subtle child maltreatment cases, there seems to be general agreement that these terms are fundamentally equivalent and represent a lesser quantum of evidence than probable cause.

> The effect of this language is that the reporter's diagnosis need not be absolute. He does not have to prove conclusively, even to himself, that the child is a victim of inflicted injury. If the circumstances are such as to cause him to feel doubt about the history given; if he has cause to doubt the truthfulness of the person who tells him about the alleged accidental cause of the injury; or other examinations reveal symptoms and facts inconsistent with the circumstances described, then he has sufficient "reasonable cause to suspect" that the injuries may have been inflicted rather than accidental. This would be enough to satisfy the requirements of the law. (1)

The basis for a report can include the nature of the child's injuries; the history of prior injuries to a child; the condition of a child, his personal hygiene, and his clothing; the statements and demeanor of a child or parent, especially if the injuries to the child are at variance to the parental explanation of them; the condition of the home; and the statements of others. After a report is made, the child protective agency is responsible for determining the child's true condition and if action is necessary for beginning the process of protection and treatment.

IMMUNITY FROM LIABILITY FOR REPORTING

Fear of being sued unjustly for libel, slander, defamation, invasion of privacy, and breach of confidentiality is frequently cited as a deterrent to more complete reporting. This fear exists even though applying existing legal doctrines leads to the conclusion that anyone making a legally mandated or authorized report would be free from liability so long as the report was made in good faith. "[T]he point is that the common law and all of our decisional authority already confers such immunity, and there is no American case that even suggests that there may be liability for a good faith report of the kind required by battered-child statutes" (14).

Nevertheless, in the experience of many states, only an explicit statutory grant of immunity from liability for reporting in good faith erases the hesitancy of potential reporters. Hence, *all* states specifically grant mandated reporters immunity from civil and criminal liability for good faith reports. In addition, at least 40 states now extend immunity from liability to voluntary reporters, as long as the report was made in good faith, partly in response to the requirements of the Federal Act. At least 40 statutes specifically extend the grant of immunity to participation in judicial proceedings and at least eight to the performance of other acts authorized by law, such as taking photographs and x-ray films, although this, too, seems legally superfluous.

To reassure potential reporters further, some states have added a provision to their immunity clause that *presumes the good faith* of those acting under the reporting law.

Because fear of lawsuits is frequently cited as a deterrent to more complete reporting, the immunity provisions of state law should be clearly explained in any public and professional education campaign.

ABROGATION OF CERTAIN PRIVILEGED COMMUNICATIONS

Child abuse and child neglect usually occur behind closed doors without witnesses. In determining whether a child has been abused or neglected, great reliance is placed, necessarily, on medical evidence, on the statements of the child, and the admissions of the parents. However, many physicians and other professionals most likely to see abused and neglected children are subject to statutory privileges making confidential the communications between them and their clients or patients. Depending on the state, statutes establish privileges in relation to the communications between physician and patient, social worker and client, psychologist and client, and priest and penitent. (There is an exception in some states to the confidentiality rule when a crime has been or will be committed. In all states, most forms of child abuse and child neglect, besides being the subject of civil court jurisdiction, are also crimes.) Ordinarily, persons subject to such privileges are prohibited from divulging anything told to them within the scope of the privilege, unless the protected person gives permission.

If the privileged nature of such communications were to remain intact, many cases of known and suspected child abuse and neglect could not be reported. For example, physicians might feel unable to report suspicious injuries without the permission of parents. Investigative efforts would also be hampered if persons having important information about a case were prohibited from revealing it. For example, parents often tell spouses or helping professionals what caused a child's injuries. Unless the spouse or professional can give this information to the protective services worker and can testify about it, a child demonstrably needing protection may not receive it.

Even though a legal mandate to report presumably overrides any other law creating a privileged communication, especially if the reporting law was enacted after the law creating the privilege, in order to allay any residual concerns that potential reporters may have about relating information gained as a result of their confidential relationship with clients, many state reporting laws contain specific clauses abrogating statutorily created privileges. Some statutes abrogate the privileges attached to those professionals required to report. Other statutes abrogate all privileges, even if the professionals involved are not required to report. Many reporting statutes also specifically abrogate these privileges for the purpose of participating in judicial proceedings relating to abuse or neglect. (Such provisions appear to be unnecessary unless either (*1*) the person wishing to testify is not a person required or authorized to report child abuse and neglect, or (*2*) the person wishing to testify has a privilege that does not contain an exemption when a crime has been or will be committed.)

When a parent is already receiving help from a treatment professional, the need to report abuse or neglect is sometimes questioned because reporting to the child protective agency and testifying in court may only reinforce the insecurity and hostility many abusive and neglectful parents feel and may disturb the treatment already in progress. Obviously, such concerns collide head-on with the abrogation of privileged communications. In order to prevent mandated reporting from disrupting ongoing therapeutic relationships, many treatment professionals do not report known or suspected child abuse and neglect except in extreme situations. In fact, a large number of local child protective services and some state child protective offices encourage professionals to disregard the legal requirement to report such cases (15). This procedure is both healthy and dangerous, for, while it engrafts necessary flexibility onto absolute legal strictures, it also weakens the imperative of the law without making provision for monitoring its application. Furthermore, most professionals cannot provide the full range of services that a child protective agency can provide. Even when the professional is of the highest quality, he or she cannot become involved in the total family situation, cannot make regular home visits, and may not view the protection of the child as his or her primary responsibility.

A better approach would seem to be to formalize a procedure through which the local child protective agency can review a situation after a report is made to decide whether a full child protective investigation is necessary. Under the Model Child Protection Act, for example, the local child protective agency, though still responsible for handling cases, is authorized to

> waive a full child protective investigation of reports made by agencies or individuals specified in the local plan if, after an appropriate assessment of the situation, it is satisfied that (i) the protective and service needs of the child and the family can be met by the agency or individual, (ii) the agency or individual agrees to do so, and (iii) suitable safeguards are established and observed. Suitable safeguards shall include a written agreement from the agency or individual to report periodically on the status of the family, a written agreement to report immediately to the local service at any time that the child's safety or well-being is threatened despite the agency's or individual's efforts, and periodic monitoring of the agency's or individual's efforts by the local service for a reasonable period of time. (16)

In summary, although abrogations of privileges are absolute, protective workers, judges, and prosecutors should apply them with discretion, especially in situations involving communications between spouses and with treatment professionals with whom the parents have developed a trusting relationship.

PENALTIES FOR FAILURE TO REPORT

If provisions for immunity from liability, the abrogation of privileged communications, and public education are the carrots to encourage fuller reporting, penalties for failure to report are the stick to enforce it. Although the ultimate success of a child protective reporting system must depend on the willing cooperation of professionals and the public, reporting requirements need enforceable provisions for those who refuse to accept their moral obligation to protect endangered children. Thus, as of 1980, the reporting laws of at least 39 states contain specific penalty clauses for failure to report. Of that number, 30 provide a criminal penalty only, one provides a civil penalty only, and four states and one territory provide both criminal and civil penalties. The criminal penalty is usually of misdemeanor level with the potential fine and/or imprisonment ranging from $100 and/or 5 days up to $1000 and/or 1 year. Some states provide penalties for failure to take other mandated protective actions, such as the taking of photographs and x-ray films of areas of visible trauma.

However, "[w]hile failure to report is criminal in most states, there has never been, nor is there likely to be, a prosecution" (17). But perhaps there should be a criminal prosecution when the failure to report reflects a willful disregard of danger to a child. In fact, police agencies seeking to enforce reporting requirements have brought mandated physicians before magistrates, although only verbal warnings have resulted so far.

A more likely, and, as a consequence, probably a more effective, encouragement to fuller reporting is the prospect of a civil lawsuit for damages arising from failure to report. Although five states and one territory have explicitly legislated civil liability, such liability probably already exists in all states with a mandatory reporting law. Under common law tort doctrines, the violation of a statutory duty—in this instance the required reporting of known and suspected abuse and neglect—is "negligence *per se*" (18). In 1967 Dean Monrad Paulsen predicted:

> [I]t seems likely that reporting statutes which require reporting and which carry criminal penalties create a cause of action in favor of infants who suffer abuse after a physician has failed to make a report respecting earlier abuse brought to his attention. Further, the failure to comply with a mandatory statute which is not supported by criminal penalties may well give rise to civil liability by analogy to the cases upholding recovery based on negligence established by a breach of the criminal law. (19)

The correctness of Dean Paulsen's analysis has since been established in two California cases. In 1972, a lawsuit was brought against the police, a hospital, and individual doctors in California for failure to report a child's suspicious injuries that had come to their attention (20). Because they did not report, the unprotected child was further beaten by his parents and suffered permanent brain damage. The case was settled out of court for over half a million dollars. The case, and especially the settlement, received wide notice within the medical community. The other case, *Landeros v. Flood* (21), was not settled out of court, and the California Supreme Court was called on to decide whether the plaintiff had stated a cause of action against a doctor who failed to diagnose and report a case of the battered-child syndrome. The child had been brought to the hospital with a broken leg, caused by a twisting force for which there was no natural explanation. Furthermore, the child had bruises and abrasions over her entire body and appeared fearful when approached by adults. As a result of the physician's alleged negligence, the child was returned to her parents and severely beaten again, suffering permanent physical injury. The California Supreme Court found that the plaintiff had stated a cause of action on theories of both common law and statutory negligence.

There are also positive treatment reasons for civil and criminal penalties. Penalty clauses tend to assist mandated reporters in working with parents by making it easier to explain to parents why a report must be made. In addition, experience shows that a penalty clause is invaluable to staff members of agencies and institutions who often must persuade their superiors of the necessity of making a report. For example, nurses frequently related how the mention of potential liability for failure to report is the only argument that convinces reluctant hospital administrators to commence protective action.

A common basis of liability in state statutes is "knowing and willful failure" to report. Since negligence *per se* is established by merely proving failure to comply with a statutory mandate, this specific standard of liability may limit the situations in which liability can arise and may narrow the broader common law liability. Most states having adopted this stricter standard of liability seem to do so on the grounds that it is unfair to penalize honest mistakes in interpreting the difficult and ambiguous facts surrounding most child abuse and neglect situations. They conclude that a person must know about his obligations under the reporting law and must intentionally fail to fulfill them before being held criminally or civilly liable. Thus, in those states using the "knowing and willful" test, the mandated reporter must have a conscious suspicion that a child is abused or neglected and know that he must report and still not do so. Among the situations that could lead to the conclusion that a person "knowingly or willfully" failed to report would be: (*1*) when a child complains to such a person that he is being abused or neglected, (*2*) when the parents tell such person about their abusive or neglectful conduct, and (*3*) when a reputable individual warns such a person that a child is being or was abused and neglected, and instead of disputing the accuracy of the warning, the person says, in effect: "So what, it is none of my business."

PHOTOGRAPH AND X-RAY AUTHORIZATIONS

Photographs and x-ray films can be crucial to the identification and management of child abuse and neglect cases. For example, x-ray films often reveal telltale past injuries. Photographs and x-ray films also preserve evidence to support subsequent child protective decision-making and possible court action, particularly when case records lack sufficient detail. Long after memories have faded, photographs and x-ray films can provide graphic and incontestable documentation of the severity of the child's initial condition.

Ordinarily, however, there might be some question about the authority of hospital, child protective, and law enforcement officials to take photographs or x-ray films without parental permission. Hence, at this writing, at least 10 states have enacted statutes authorizing mandated reporters to take, or to arrange to have taken, photographs and x-ray films without parental permission. Sometimes, the head of a medical facility is mandated to take x-ray films or photographs of areas of visible trauma.

To encourage the use of such provisions, at least six states provide for the reimbursement, at public expense, of the costs of photographs and x-ray films.

PROTECTIVE CUSTODY AUTHORIZATIONS

In most child abuse and neglect situations, the child need not be removed from his parents' care in order to protect his well-being and future development. Indeed, in many situations, removal may be harmful to the child. Children identify with their parents at a very early age, seeing them as models for and as part of themselves. Separation from parents can be experienced as a profound rejection, or the child can introject into his own self-image the parental inadequacy that led to the removal (22). As a result, the child may see separation from his parents as a deprivation or as a punishment for his own inadequacy. The psychological wounds that can be caused by removing a child from his parents have been repeatedly described (23). The conditions of foster care are frequently not conducive to a child's emotional well-being (22). Furthermore, removal may hinder treatment efforts with the parents; it may destroy a fragile family fabric and make it more difficult for the parents to cope with the child when he is returned to their care.

But sometimes a child has to be removed from his parents' home for his own safety or as part of an appropriate treatment plan for the parents. When this happens, removing a child with the parents' consent is preferred, because resort to unnecessary legal coercion can be detrimental to later treatment efforts. In recognition of the importance of parental consent, a number of states require that the parents' agreement be sought before protective custody is invoked.

Frequently, however, a child must be removed from his home without parental consent, and indeed against parental wishes, to protect him from further harm. In such situations, the preferred method of removing a child is through a court order. As in all situations in which individual discretion is preeminent, there is always the danger of careless or automatic, though well-meaning, exercise of the power to place a child in protective custody. Prior court review lessens such dangers by ensuring that a judge, an outsider, reviews the administrative decision to place a child in custody. Indeed, a police and child protective agencies having authority to remove a child against the parents' wishes are often hesitant to do so without court authorization and often seek court approval before placing a child in protective custody. When the court is not in session, for example, at night or on weekends, authorization can usually be obtained by telephoning a judge at home.

Nevertheless, sometimes removal must occur before court review is possible because, in the time it would take to obtain a court order, the child might be further harmed or the parents might flee with the child. In all states, the police are authorized to take a child into protective custody, either under specific child protective legislation or through their general law enforcement powers. Moreover, under the common law, anyone has the legal authority to use force in the protection of a third person, although this is usually contingent on the existence of imminent danger (18). In recognition of the prime decision-making responsibility of child protective workers, and presumably in the belief that authority should accompany responsibility, a growing number of states, at least 13 as of 1980, also grant protective custody power to child protective agencies. However, despite the fact that child protective workers make most of the important decisions about the initial handling of child abuse and neglect cases, some observers feel that giving them direct authority to remove children will unduly hamper their efforts to develop trusting treatment relationships with families. As a practical matter, forcible removal of a child ordinarily is not attempted without police or law enforcement assistance, because of the possible danger to the protective worker.

More recently, a number of states have granted hospitals and similar institutions a protective custody power called "24-hour hold." This authority is much broader than standard protective custody authorization because there is usually no need to establish that the child is in "imminent danger." Indeed, the person in charge of such a facility is usually authorized to place a child in protective custody "where he believes the facts so warrant." Such broad language is designed to give hospitals and similar institutions a flexible tool with which to deal with home situations that appear explosive or dangerous. Frequently, for example, hospital staff are concerned about the safety of a child with suspicious injuries, or are unsure of the child's real name or address, or fear that the parent will flee before a protective worker can make a home visit. These situations often arise in the middle of the night when outside guidance and assistance are unavailable. The "24-hour hold" is a stopgap measure to enable other components of a community's child protection system to have enough time to mobilize.

Protective custody is only the beginning of the child protective process. In utilizing protective custody, officials should bear in mind that subsequent treatment efforts may be impaired if the parents are not accorded full due process, are not treated fairly, or are not fully informed about what is going on. (All of these, of course, are important goals in themselves.) Some appropriate person, preferably from the child protective agency, should tell the parents where the child was taken, in order to calm their fears and to enable them to maintain contact with their child. In unusual or severe cases, it may not be prudent to inform the parents of the child's exact whereabouts if it appears that the parents may seek to regain custody of the child forcibly or otherwise interfere with his care. In such cases, contact between the child and parent may have to be limited to highly structured situations.

Protective custody must not be considered a final disposition of the case. If not a child protective worker, the person taking a child into protective custody should immediately notify the appropriate local child protective service so that necessary protective, assessment, and treatment efforts can begin. During all stages of the case, whether or not court action is commenced, the need for protective custody should be continually reviewed, and an attempt should be made to return the child to his home, whenever it seems reasonable and safe to do so. Even after a court proceeding has begun, the child protective agency may still recommend to the court that the child be returned to the parents pending further court action.

REPORTING PROCEDURES

Reporting laws usually specify that reports are to be made orally, often also requiring subsequent written confirmation. The first generation of reporting laws left .the mode of implementing these requirements to administrative decision. Generally, reports were to be made directly to a local child protective or law enforcement agency. But ignorance of the local agency's telephone number and the frequent absence of a specialized phone line at the agency remained major stumbling blocks to more complete reporting. Consequently, in the early 1970s, a number of communities and states established centralized reporting hotlines, at least 10 through legislation. Such hotlines were meant to encourage reporting by simplifying the reporting process, by having an easily publicizable telephone number, and by ensuring that qualified personnel would answer the phone at all hours of the day or night. For statewide hotlines, a toll-free number was used to remove the obstacle caused by the cost of a long distance call. A number of states have begun to use facsimile telecopiers and remote access computer terminals to receive and transmit reports.

Hotlines can perform important, ancillary functions by providing information and assistance to people who call. Qualified, professional staff can refer inappropriate reports and self-reports from parents seeking help, can advise potential reporters about the law and child protective procedures, can assist in diagnosis and evaluation, and can consult about the necessity of photographs, x-ray films, and protective custody. Thus, whether a state or local system is used, staff answering the telephone should have social-work or comparable qualifications, enabling them to offer effective and sensitive assistance to parents and others calling for help.

AGENCIES THAT RECEIVE REPORTS

Without child abuse and neglect reporting laws, reports of child maltreatment would continue to be made, as they were before the passage of such laws, to law enforcement, child welfare or social service agencies, and juvenile courts. When a law requires reports to be made, it also must designate an agency to receive them. The issue of which agency should be designated to receive reports has been described as "one of the most critical elements of the reporting law. The nature and orientation of the agency first receiving the report will often determine the community's response to child abuse" (1).

Designating the police as recipients of reports, while helping to ensure thorough investigations, has the disadvantage of stressing the punitive tenor of the process and tends to discourage reporting by physicians and other professionals. Designating social service agencies emphasizes the rehabilitative and treatment aspects of the process, but is sometimes seen as a "soft" response to brutal crimes. The first model legislation proposed by the United States Children's Bureau (13) recommended that mandated reports be made to law enforcement agencies, not because criminal prosecution is needed, but because police agencies are available 24 hours a day, an essential capability in emergency child abuse cases. The present recognition that only social service agencies have access to the treatment resources needed to handle maltreatment cases has led most experts to advocate improving the investigative capability of child protective and social service agencies. Thus, even though child abuse and neglect are crimes in all states, at least 35 states now require reports to be made to social services agencies, usually specially designated child protective agencies. Only a few states still require that reports be made solely to law enforcement agencies.

Often, however, no single agency is designated as the sole agency to receive reports. Sixteen state statutes allow mandated reporters to choose between the police or a child protective agency, seven states allow mandated reporters to choose between three or more specified agencies, and six provide for a joint police and child protective investigation. Four states attempt to cover all contingencies by requiring reports to be made to two or more agencies. To determine the reporting requirements in a particular state, the reader should contact a local police or public social service agency.

The legislative ambivalence concerning the designation of the agency to receive reports mirrors and magnifies the fragmentation of basic child protective responsibility in most communities. This diversity of overlapping reporting avenues increases the likelihood of lost reports and administrative breakdowns. As cases are misdirected, misplaced, or seriously delayed between agencies, the lives of children who need immediate and sustained protection are endangered.

A recent statutory development of some note is the specific requirement in at least 12 states that suspected child abuse and neglect fatalities be reported to medical examiners or coroners and district attorneys. Theoretically, these provisions should not be necessary, since all suspicious fatalities of adults as well as children are required to be investigated by such officials. However, child fatalities are often not reported to them because of confusion, administrative breakdown, or the assumption that someone else has already reported the case to them. In some respects, this is an example of how the wise decision not to require criminal court action in most child abuse cases has been carried beyond reasonableness; even cases of criminal homicide are not being brought to the attention of law enforcement agencies. It could be said that the advocates of the decriminalization of child abuse cases have been too successful. Some cases, especially brutal homicides, must be referred for potential criminal prosecution.

LOCAL CHILD PROTECTIVE AGENCIES

After early emphasis on the "rescue" of children and the prosecution of "offending" parents, there has been an accelerating movement toward the provision of noncriminal and nonjudicial social and rehabilitative services. In the decades after 1875, one sees a slow but steadily increasing acceptance of the proposition that criminal intent is usually not present in child abuse and neglect cases and that treatment and ameliorative services, rather than punishment and retribution, are the best means of protecting endangered children. The handling of child maltreatment now has been almost completely decriminalized.

In nearly all communities, most reports are referred ultimately to a child protective agency, regardless of which agency the reporting law specifies initially to receive reports. The reasons for this reliance on child protective agencies include: (1) the necessity and benefits of providing treatment services that are most readily available through a social service agency like a child protective agency; (2) the inadequacy of criminal court remedies and the unlikelihood of successful prosecution; (3) the advantage of using social casework skills in the investigation itself; (4) the fact that the family benefits if therapeutic treatment begins during the investigation; and (5) the very existence of child protective agencies, on which the police can "dump" messy family matters that they are unprepared to handle. But whatever the motive, when child protective agencies investigate reports and begin the process of helping parents, the underlying causes of the abuse or neglect are most likely to be addressed and a family's ability to nurture and protect its children is most likely to be strengthened (24).

The local child protective agency is the heart of any community's child protective system. The local agency focuses state and community efforts to prevent and treat child abuse and neglect. Designating one, single agency in each community to receive and investigate all reports eliminates the confusion and lack of accountability that result when reports are handled by a number of different agencies. It is important to emphasize that a new agency need not be established if an existing agency, or part of one, can provide child protective services.

Specifically, the child protective agency is assigned the crucial first steps of:

1. Providing immediate protection to children, through temporary stabilization of the home environment or, where necessary, protective custody.
2. Verifying the validity of the report and determining the danger to the children.
3. Assessing the service needs of children and families.
4. Providing or arranging for protective, ameliorative, and treatment services.
5. Initiating civil court action when necessary, to remove a child from a dangerous environment or to impose treatment on his family.

The local child protective agency offers the family whatever available services can help the parents or the family. Many of these services, such as financial assistance, day care, or homemaker care, are concrete efforts to relieve the pressures and frustrations of parenthood. Individual and family counseling services are also used to ease the tensions of personal problems and marital strife. Referrals are made to family service agencies, mental health clinics, self-help organizations, hospitals, and other social and child welfare services. If the parent is an alcoholic or a drug addict, he may be referred for detoxification and rehabilitation. Only when such services are refused or are inadequate is court action sought, usually in juvenile or family court.

After the initial child protective intervention, efforts to preserve and improve family stability are, and must remain, the domain of community resources and agencies that have broader and more long-range responsibilities toward children and families than do child protective agencies. Reporting should not be used as an excuse to divest these agencies of their traditional responsibilities. The purpose of child protective intervention is to protect the health and enhance the welfare of children and families by beginning the process of helping parents meet their child care responsibilities. Except for certain extremely specialized services, treatment is best provided by community human service agencies. It would be imprudent to shift this fundamental social welfare responsibility away from community resources that are already successfully helping children and families, or to discourage the development of additional community-based treatment and prevention programs. To do so would be a costly duplication of existing services not likely to receive the support of budgetary authorities. Instead, every effort must be made to encourage existing agencies to assume greater prevention and treatment responsibility and to expand their capacity to do so.

Until recently, however, insufficient attention has been paid to the need to establish strong and viable child protective systems. In almost all states, child protective responsibility has been blurred. Responsibility to ensure that reports are promptly and effectively investigated and that treatment efforts are initiated is often dispersed among a number of public and private agencies that have many other, often conflicting, duties competing for scarce resources and attention. The result has been breakdowns in communication, delays in the implementation of case plans, and an absence of accountability for the ultimate handling of cases.

Many child protective agencies have been unable to fulfill the life-saving responsibilities assigned to them. After receiving a report of suspected abuse or neglect, the protective agency's investigation must determine whether the child is in danger and what services should be offered to the family. But because abuse or neglect usually happen in the privacy of the home, without any witnesses, gathering information about what happened can be exceedingly difficult. If the parents are looking for help, they may tell the worker what happened, but often they deny any wrongdoing. The worker must then seek whatever information is available from schools, neighbors, relatives, as well as the source of the report. As a result, caseworkers have great difficulty in getting genuine information about families. The staggering responsibilities placed on protective workers and the unique skills demanded by protective work require protective agencies to have a specialized, highly qualified staff with sufficient resources to handle the complexities of child maltreatment cases. Yet, many agencies are too understaffed to handle the reports they receive, the number of which increases each year. Furthermore, many agencies are plagued with staff turnovers as high as 100% every year, making it all but impossible to develop and maintain qualified staffs.

The strengthening of reporting requirements during the last decade has had detrimental effects on the functioning of some child protective agencies and on the welfare of families enmeshed in the system. Some reporting laws were enacted without ensuring that a system existed to respond to the reports generated by the law. The purpose of reporting known and suspected child abuse and neglect is to bring endangered children, who might otherwise go unprotected, quickly to the attention of agencies who are able to help them and their families. Increased reporting is meaningless and often harmful to the children and families involved, if sufficient services are not available to deal with the problems revealed.

Hence, the most important aspects of recent child protective legislation is its emphasis on the development of expanded and strengthened helping services to respond to increased reporting. A number of states have sought to upgrade the child protective services offered by public child welfare agencies by statutorily designating a single agency to be responsible for all aspects of initial child protective work, including receipt of reports, investigations, and case disposition. This is a marked departure from earlier statutes that, basically, only provided for reporting. Perhaps the most significant aspect of recent legislation has been the degree to which it has detailed the specific responsibilities and functions of child protective agencies. For example, the New York statute provides:

Each child protective service shall:

1. receive on a twenty-four hour, seven day a week basis all reports of suspected child abuse or maltreatment . . . ;

2. maintain and keep up-to-date a local child abuse and maltreatment register of all cases reported under this title together with any additional information obtained and a record of the final disposition of the report including services offered and accepted;

3. upon the receipt of each written report made pursuant to this title, transmit, forthwith, a copy thereof to the state central register of child abuse and maltreatment. In addition, not later than seven days after receipt of the initial report, the child protective service shall send a preliminary written report of the initial investigation, including evaluation and actions taken or contemplated, to the state central register. Follow-up reports shall be made at regular intervals thereafter . . . to the end that the state central register is kept fully informed and up-to-date concerning the handling of reports;

4. give telephone notice and forward immediately a copy of reports made pursuant to this title which involve the death of a child to the appropriate district attorney . . . ;

5. forward an additional copy of each report to the appropriate duly incorporated society for the prevention of cruelty to children or other duly authorized child protective agency if a prior request for such copies has been made to the service in writing by the society or agency;

6. upon receipt of such report, commence or cause the appropriate society for the prevention of cruelty to children to commence, within twenty-four hours, an appropriate investigation which shall include an evaluation of the the environment of the child named in the report and any other children in the same home and a determination of the risk to such children if they continue to remain in the existing home environment, as well as a determination of the nature, extent, and cause of any condition enumerated in such report, the name, age and condition of other children in the home, and, after seeing to the safety of the child or children, forthwith notify the subjects of the report in writing, of the existence of the report and their rights pursuant to this title in regard to amendment or expungement;

7. determine, within ninety days, whether the report is "indicated" or "unfounded";

8. take a child into protective custody to protect him from further abuse or maltreatment when appropriate and in accordance with the provisions of the family court act;

9. based on the investigation and evaluation conducted pursuant to this title, offer to the family of any child believed to be suffering from abuse or maltreatment such services for its acceptance or refusal, as appear appropriate for either the child or the family or both; provided, however, that prior to offering such services to a family, explain that it has no legal authority to compel such family to receive said services, but may inform the family of the obligations and authority of the child protective service to petition the family court for a determination that a child is in need of care and protection;

10. in those cases in which an appropriate offer of services is refused and the child protective service determines or if the service for any other appropriate reason determines that the best interests of the child require family court or criminal court action, initiate the appropriate family court proceeding or make a referral to the appropriate district attorney, or both;

11. assist the family court or criminal court during all stages of the court proceeding in accordance with the purposes of this title and the family court act;

12. coordinate, provide or arrange for and monitor, . . . rehabilitative services for children and their families on a voluntary basis or under a final or intermediate order of the family court. (25)

In the past, the enactment of expanded reporting laws was assumed to be the cure for a state's child abuse and neglect problems. But sharply increased case loads, which inexorably flow from strengthened reporting, come as a rude shock to social service systems and state and local administrators. By fully and honestly describing the investigative and treatment services necessary to support a strengthened reporting law, contemporary child protective legislation seeks to ensure that everyone considering the enactment of such laws also appreciates the need for expanded services and the need for increased funding. All elements of the community should be clearly and unambiguously prepared for the full costs of an effective child abuse and neglect prevention and treatment program. Only if the real issues of prevention and treatment are faced openly can sufficient community and professional support be developed for the needed long-term effort. To do less would be irresponsible and indefensible.

CHILD PROTECTION TEAMS

Child abuse and neglect derive from a wide range of social and psychological problems that cannot be managed by one discipline or one profession alone. Social workers, physicians, nurses, lawyers, judges, psychiatrists, teachers, and many others must all work together if the cycle of abuse and neglect is to be broken. But helping efforts remain fragmented among various disciplines; communication and coordination are high-sounding catchwords that are difficult to implement. Fear and hostility among competing social agencies and approaches are constant obstacles impeding service delivery.

Although the weight of the literature and developing statutory law agree in assigning prime child protective responsibility to designated social service agencies—"child protective agencies"—optimal diagnostic and treatment efforts require the contributions of a broad range of professional and community agencies. In many parts of the country, the creation of interdisciplinary teams, based on the original Denver model, has succeeded in bringing the collective expertise of relevant professionals to bear on identification and treatment. Depending on the community and circumstances of individual cases, such teams include representatives of relevant medical, mental health, law enforcement, and social service agencies. Five states specifically mandate and three others permit the creation of such interdisciplinary child protection teams.

CENTRAL REGISTERS OF CHILD PROTECTION CASES

Forty-seven states and the District of Columbia have established some kind of central register of child protection cases in order to improve case diagnosis and monitoring or statistical systems, or both.

Verifying to a certitude reports of suspected child abuse or neglect is almost always difficult; often it is impossible. Even the most thorough investigation may not reveal clear evidence of what happened; a medical report describing severe physical injuries that suggest child abuse may not establish a connection between the parents and the condition of the child. In most cases, then, the protective worker must form an opinion about whether or not the report appears to be valid. The opinion will be based on certain signs or indicators including (1) the child's or sibling's physical condition, (2) the child's or sibling's behavior or demeanor, (3) the parent's behavior or demeanor, (4) the family's home situation, and (5) the history of the family, including previous suspicious injuries to the child or siblings.

Often, the most crucial factor in the diagnosis and evaluation of child abuse and neglect situations is the circumstantial evidence showing a pattern of previous suspicious injuries. Since child abuse and neglect are usually part of a repetitive or continuing pattern (26) information concerning the existence of prior injuries can assist physicians and protective workers in determining whether an injury is an isolated accident or one of a series of injuries suggesting abuse or neglect. Knowledge of a previous incident, similar in kind, can turn doubt into relative certainty. Unfortunately, because health and social service agencies in most communities are fragmented and because abusing parents often take their children to different doctors or hospitals to treat the injuries they inflict, a cumulative record of prior suspicious injuries and social service treatment efforts is not ordinarily available. By maintaining a community-wide or statewide record of prior reports and treatment efforts and their outcomes, a central register can provide immediate, concrete assistance to child protective workers and others who need such information to assess the danger to a child whom they suspect is being abused or neglected.

Furthermore, even after protective workers, physicians, and law enforcement officials determine that a child is or seems to be abused and neglected, they often cannot assess the immediate danger to the child or the treatment needs of the family. Knowledge of previous reports and their outcome can help in evaluating the seriousness of the family's situation and can be an important factor in determining whether the child is in such danger that he should be removed immediately from his home.

Perhaps equally as important, if a central register monitors how reports are handled, it has the potential to help ensure that investigations are properly performed and that services are provided. If a register can receive and process reports immediately, and if it can review them for their timeliness, it can monitor and measure the system's overall performance while at the same time presenting at least a partial picture of the problems with which the system must deal. And, as a research tool, a register can help determine the incidence of abuse and neglect in a state or community and the impact of different types of treatment. Once information from a properly functioning register is available, the rational evaluation of agency and human needs can begin.

However, nothing is so striking as the failure of almost all existing central register systems to fulfill their stated diagnostic, case monitoring, and statistical functions. Nothing is more disappointing than to visit a much heralded central register, only to find it hopelessly overwhelmed by a flood of cases.

Central registers are easy to criticize because they raise genuine concerns over unwarranted record keeping and potential "Big Brotherism" and because, in the past, most have not proven useful. But those who say central registers are dangerous or do not work make a serious miscalculation based on a misunderstanding of their nature and functions. A central register is fundamentally nothing more than an index of cases handled by an agency or a number of agencies. Those who advocate the abolition of central registers do not realize that all agencies, as bureaucratic institutions, must have an index of cases if they are to function in any organized fashion. Without an index, or register, there would be no way of knowing if a case is currently being handled by an agency, unless every member of the agency's staff were polled individually each time a letter or referral arrived at the agency. Each worker would then have to consult his own individual index of cases or rely on his memory. Such a chaotic arrangement would cause far greater harm to children and families needing help. So there can be no question about the need for a register; no agency could do without a master index.

The failings in the establishment and operation of most central registers have made them legitimate targets for criticism. Nevertheless, a central register, properly designed and adequately operated, can be a prime tool for the immediate and long-term improvement of a child protection system. Central registers take on their character—either good or bad—either successful or unsuccessful—according to the data they contain, how the data is maintained, who has access to the data, and how those who have access to the data use it.

A properly operated central register can:

1. Assist in diagnosis and evaluation by providing or locating information on suspicious occurrences and prior treatment efforts.
2. Improve the handling of child abuse and neglect cases by providing convenient consultation on case handling to workers and potential reporters.
3. Measure the performance of the child protective service by monitoring follow-up reports.

4. Coordinate community-wide treatment efforts by monitoring follow-up reports.

5. Facilitate research, planning, and program development by providing statistical data on the nature and handling of reports.

6. Encourage the reporting of suspected child abuse and neglect by providing a focus for public and professional educational campaigns. (27)

PROVISIONS FOR CONFIDENTIALITY OF RECORDS

The rights and sensibilities of families named in child protective records must be protected, for these records contain information about the most private aspects of personal and family life. Whether or not the information is true, improper disclosure could stigmatize the future of all those mentioned in the report.

In order to qualify for funding under the Federal Child Abuse Prevention and Treatment Act, a state must "provide for methods to preserve the confidentiality of all records in order to protect the rights of the child, his parents or guardians" (7). Under the regulations that implement this section, a state must have a law "which makes such records confidential and which makes any person who permits or encourages the unauthorized dissemination of their contents guilty of a crime" (28). Largely under this impetus, states have moved rapidly in recent years to provide specific legislative blankets of confidentiality; at least 40 states now make unauthorized disclosure a misdemeanor.

Nevertheless, the information in child abuse and neglect records must be available to those who need to make critical child protective decisions. The question is: Who should have access to those records? Limiting access necessarily limits use, while broadening access increases the possibility of misuse.

In general, states take three approaches to access to records. Some statutes prohibit access to anyone outside the child protective agency; others make the records confidential, but authorize the responsible state agency to issue regulations allowing some persons access, and others enumerate who has access in the statute itself. As a general rule, states that allow exceptions follow the longstanding approach taken in the regulations (29) implementing Title IV of the Social Security Act (30). These permit access for purposes directly connected with the administration of the program. The regulations implementing the Federal Act enumerate the specific persons, officials, and agencies and the specific situations under which the access is deemed directly connected with the administration of the child protective program (28).

Theoretically, any person who must decide whether a child is abused or neglected would find information about prior suspicious occurrences and prior treatment efforts helpful in reaching a decision. For this reason, a number of states give access to the central register and other child protective records to all persons who are required to report cases of child abuse and neglect. However, when such a large number of strangers have access to records, guarding against unauthorized disclosure of information is all but impossible. More importantly, such enormous and widespread access to personal and family data unreasonably compromises the right of privacy of the children and families involved. Some professionals also see a danger that many of those who would be given such information might not know how to evaluate it intelligently; a potential reporter, for example, might allow the presence or absence of a prior record to influence his actions inordinately.

Although the sharing of information between professionals, as will be discussed below, is often a suitable alternative to direct access to records, it is impractical when the protective worker, police officer, or physician needs the information immediately or in the middle of the night. For instance, a physician seeing a bruised or emaciated child in a hospital emergency room must not only decide whether there is sufficient cause to report but must also decide whether the child should be placed in protective custody. One aspect of such a doctor's dilemma is the need to evaluate the risk that may be incurred if a child is taken home before a protective worker can visit the family. An equally serious problem, particularly for urban hospitals, is posed by the knowledge that, once returned to the parents' custody, the child and family might disappear into the anonymity of the city. In both situations, it can be crucial for the physician to know about prior treatment efforts and the prior history of the family.

Therefore, carefully designated professionals who have responsibility for making decisions about protective custody are often given direct access to information at the time they need it most—when they may be making a life or death decision. Depending on the state, these professionals include child protective workers, law enforcement officials, physicians in at least 20 states, and other persons authorized to place a child in protective custody.

Direct access to the records for all other professionals coming in contact with abused and neglected children is not necessary. Protective workers can share relevant information with other appropriate agencies and professionals as a cooperative treatment plan is being developed. Professionals who know and trust each other should be able to discuss a case in their professional capacities. Treatment agencies, such as foster care agencies, also need a clear picture of family history in order to develop and implement successful treatment strategies. For this reason, many states specifically authorize their access to the information in these records.

As a matter of fundamental fairness, if not constitutional right, persons alleged to abuse or neglect their children ought to know what information a government agency is keeping about them. Subjects of a report should have access to it because (1) they have a right to know what allegations against them have been recorded by a public agency, even though the record is confidential, and (2) only if they know what is in the record can they pursue their legal rights to have the record amended, expunged, or removed from the register and other agency files.

Perhaps the greatest controversy surrounds the opening of child abuse and neglect records to program administrators, legislators, and researchers in pursuit of their official or professional responsibilities to plan, monitor, audit, and evaluate services or to conduct other research. Some observers have suggested that if those outside of designated investigatory and service agencies are given access to records, the identifying information in the records should be expunged. But numerous types of important research, including longitudinal studies and cross-agency studies, require charting the movement of cases as they travel through time or among agencies. Such studies are crucial in gauging the effectiveness of different treatment techniques, and they cannot be performed without information that identifies the case and the people in it.

Confidentiality can be exploited to shield the malfunctioning of an agency as well as to protect the privacy of the people. Various advocate organizations have been denied access to their client's records on the false ground of confidentiality—even when they need the records to protect their client's rights by showing a pattern of bias or discrimination. A few years ago, lawyers in New York City were denied access to the records of their clients which, they claimed, would prove a pattern of religious and racial discrimination by foster care agencies. A court order was necessary to obtain the information sought. Legitimate concerns for privacy can be met with adequate provisions to ensure that disclosure of information to outsiders is strictly limited to situations in which the need for personal identifiers is essential to the research purpose and the information will not be improperly shared with others.

LEGAL REPRESENTATION

The involuntary intrusion into family life by courts and child protective agencies can have profoundly important consequences for the children and parents involved. The process itself can be a frightening experience that may ultimately result in the children being removed from their parents and placed in foster care or institutions for months or years. In a few cases, children are permanently removed from their parents and placed for adoption. For these reasons, both children and parents should have their own legal representation.

Counsel for the Child or Guardian Ad Litem

Since the interests of parents and children often conflict in child protective cases, it is important that the child's interest in a safe home environment be represented before the court. Partly as the result of the work and writings of Brian Fraser (31), Congress required that states provide a "guardian ad litem to represent the interests of abused and neglected children in judicial proceedings" (7). Unfortunately, there has been some question about whether a child should be represented by a guardian ad litem or by an attorney. There is some imprecision in using the term "guardian ad litem," since it does not require that the guardian be a lawyer, and indeed under traditional practice the guardian ad litem would not be an attorney (32). Hence, the regulations implementing the Federal Act do not require that the guardian be an attorney (28). Nevertheless, although a lay guardian ad litem can perform important functions, it is unlikely that courts would give to the guardian the right to settle or concede a judicial proceeding alleging abuse or neglect. But if the guardian ad litem does not have this power, it is difficult to distinguish his role from that of the child protective worker, unless he is a lawyer who can represent the child's legal rights and interests. Therefore, section 25 (a) of the Model Child Protection

Act recommends that the guardian ad litem should be an attorney assigned to protect the legal rights and to express the wishes of children in child protective court proceedings (16).

As of 1980, at least 24 states provide for the mandatory appointment of a lawyer to represent a child. And at least 10 states provide for the mandatory appointment of a guardian ad litem who need not be a lawyer and is often a child protective worker or probation officer. Seven more states appoint a guardian ad litem in all cases as a matter of administrative policy.

Counsel for the Parents

In criminal proceedings, the right to counsel for parents alleged to have abused or neglected their children is well established. But the parent's right to counsel in juvenile or family court proceedings is not as widely accepted. Noting the "civil" nature of child protective proceedings, courts are divided on whether parents have a consitutional right to counsel in such proceedings. Yet, even in civil proceedings, parents or guardians, in effect, also stand "accused." A finding of abuse or neglect may encourage a criminal prosecution, may result in the removal of a child from parental custody, and, ultimately, may result in the termination of parental rights. Even if these more extreme events do not take place, the intrusion on family rights through the proceeding itself and the possibility of probation or other agency supervision of the home situation are reasons enough to conclude that the liberty of parents in child protective proceedings is at stake. For these reasons, 22 states provide counsel as a statutory right, even in the absence of an apparent consitutional mandate.

Counsel for the Child Protective Agency

The child protective agency also needs legal assistance when appearing in court. Historically, prosecutors played a minor role in child protective proceedings. If evidence had to be collected or witnesses called to testify, the protective worker did so. As long as juvenile courts were informal with relaxed rules of evidence, the petitioning protective worker did not need legal assistance. But the expanded participation of counsel for the parents has increased the formality of juvenile court proceedings, and protective workers unassisted by legal counsel are at a severe disadvantage. Without counsel to assist the worker in pretrial investigation, case preparation, petition drafting, courtroom presentation, and legal argument, otherwise provable cases are often dismissed when the parent has the one-sided advantage of vigorous defense counsel.

It might seem to the parents' advantage if the protective worker's case preparation and presentation suffer from a lack of legal assistance. But this is not always so. Fearing that an abused child might be returned unsafely to his parents, judges may feel the "uncomfortable pull toward a prosecutive stance when zealous defense counsel have elicited a one-sided development of case facts with no one to intervene but the judge (33). Yet, if a judge becomes the advocate of the petitioner's case and performs the functions of the absent prosecutor, he cannot maintain an unbiased view of the case and he cannot assess the evidence impartially—or at least that would be the appearance to those involved in the proceeding.

A few states require the presence of an attorney to assist the petitioner in child protective proceedings. In other states, however, the law merely provides that the judge may request that a local public law official assist the petitioner. In many communities, this function is served by the district attorney or similar criminal court prosecutor. But even though many prosecutors understand and strive to achieve the juvenile court's social purpose in child protective cases, a number of communities use the civil law officer to represent the child protective agency in order to minimize the punitive nature of juvenile court proceedings. Sometimes, the local agency hires its own counsel or uses internal legal staff.

All attorneys representing the child protective agency must understand the child protective system's emphasis on treatment and ameliorative services and must appreciate that their preeminent professional, ethnical (34), and constitutional (35) obligation is to see justice done. In child protective proceedings, this means they must seek to protect, fairly and honestly, the physical and legal rights of the child. If the child's interests seem to conflict with the position of the child protective agency, the attorney must be prepared to disagree and to take appropriate action. For example, if the agency decides that court action is required, but the attorney concludes that there is insufficient evidence or that the child's interests indicate court action to be inappropriate, he must be free to prevent the commencement of the proceeding, or, if it already has been commenced, to move for its dismissal.

CONCLUSION: IMPLEMENTING ISSUES

After being ignored for so long, the plight of abused and neglected children has become the subject of widespread professional and public concern. As a result, there has been major progress in our ability to protect the abused and neglected child and to assist his family. But we still face enormous gaps between what we want to do to protect children and what we can do.

Although all 50 states have child abuse reporting laws, the legal framework for child protective work is incomplete and unnecessarily complex in most states, thus making it difficult to implement effective programs successfully. Moreover, the financial and institutional support necessary to sustain adequate treatment and preventive services continues to be widely lacking. In almost every community in the nation, there are major inadequacies, breakdowns, and gaps in the child protective process. Preventive efforts are uneven or absent; detection and reporting are haphazard and incomplete; protective investigations are often backlogged or poorly performed; and suitable treatment programs are almost nonexistent for the majority of families needing them. Child protective workers are generally not given the training, skills, and ancillary services necessary to meet the important responsibilities assigned to them; they have unmanageably large case loads and show rapid "worker burnout" and consequent high job turnover. Too often, the only treatment alternatives available to them are infrequent and largely meaningless home visits, overused foster care, and unthinking reliance on court action. Lacking suitable long-term treatment services, most American communities are faced with a grim choice in cases of serious abuse or neglect—either break up families or leave the children at home without help, where they might be seriously injured or even killed. For far too many endangered children, the existing child protection system is inadequate to the life-saving tasks assigned to it; too many children and families are processed through the system with a paper promise of help.

Yet, despite all the problems facing existing child protective systems, their promise is great. Children can be protected and their well-being can be fostered by helping parents to "parent." There are programs in all parts of the nation helping parents to cope with the stresses of family life in our modern society. Social casework, psychological and psychiatric services, child abuse teams, lay therapists, parent surrogates, day care, parents anonymous groups, homemaker service, education for parenthood, and a wide range of other concrete services and programs can and do make a difference in the level of family functioning.

The challenge we face is not so much to discover what works; to a great extent we know that. We must now discover how to develop the cooperative community structures necessary to provide needed services efficiently, effectively, and compassionately.

As a society, we have provided a combination of laws and procedures through which physicians and other citizens who come in contact with endangered children can, and in some situations must, take protective action. Laws have established reporting procedures, authorized the taking of children into protective custody, and assigned child protective responsibilities to social agencies and the police. Laws have also created juvenile and criminal court jurisdiction and foster treatment programs—all to protect vulnerable children and assist families in need.

But no law is the ultimate answer to child abuse and neglect. No law can eradicate child abuse and neglect. No law can remedy its underlying causes. The causes of child abuse and neglect are too complex. Some stem from individual psychological problems; others have roots deep in our social structure. A law may mandate the treatment of parents, but it cannot rehabilitate them. Thus, no law can wipe out child abuse and neglect. Though an improved law is a necessary step, it is merely one of many steps that must be taken to provide sufficient and suitable helping services for vulnerable children and parents in need. A renewed sense of respect for the humane growth of all people within the context of the family will do more to lower violence and aggression against the young than any number of social agencies, which usually become involved only after the process of family breakdown has progressed almost past the point of irremediable damage. Ultimately, the prevention and treatment of child abuse and child neglect depend less on laws and more on healthy family and community life.

REFERENCES

1. DeFrancis V, Lucht C: *Child Abuse Legislation in the 1970's*, Revised ed. Denver, American Humane Assoc, 1974.

2. Paulsen M: The Legal Framework for Child Protection. *Colum L Rev* 66:679, 1966.
3. Kamerman S, Harte A: Child Abuse and Neglect: Problems, Policies, and Provision. Unpublished manuscript, 1975.
4. Committee on Infant and Preschool Child: Committee Statement of February 1, 1972, in *Newsletter Supplement*. Chicago, American Academy of Pediatrics, 1972.
5. Besharov DJ: The Legal Aspects of Reporting Known and Suspected Child Abuse and Neglect. *Vill L Rev* 23:458, 1978.
6. Besharov DJ, Duryea PB: *Report of the New York State Assembly Select Committee on Child Abuse*, 1972.
7. 42 USC. §§ 5101–5106 (Supp V 1975).
8. Dahl G: *Trends in Child Abuse and Neglect Reporting Statutes 2, Report No 95*. Denver, Educ Comm for the States, 1977.
9. NY Fam Ct Act § 1046 (a) (v) (McKinney) 1973.
10. *Griswold vs Connecticut*, 381 US 479, 485, 1965.
11. *Pierce vs Society of Sisters*, 268 US 510, 534, 1925.
12. NY Soc Serv Law § 413 (McKinney) 1976.
13. US Children's Bureau, US Department of Health, Education and Welfare: *The Abused Child— Principles and Suggested Language for Legislation on Reporting of the Physically Abused Child*. 1963.
14. Foster H, Freed D: Battered Child Legislation and Professional Immunity. *ABAJ* 52:1071, 1966.
15. Maine Revised Stat tit 22 § 3853(1) (Supp 1977).
16. The National Center on Child Abuse and Neglect, US Department of Health, Education and Welfare: *Model Child Protection Act (Draft)*, 1977.
17. Dembitz N: Child Abuse and the Law—Fact and Fiction. *Rec NY City BA* 24:613, 1969.
18. Prosser W: *Law of Torts*, ed 4. St. Paul, West Publishing Company, 1971.
19. Paulsen M: Child Abuse Reporting Laws: The Shape of the Legislation, *Colum L Rev* 67:1, 31–34, 1967.
20. *Time* 100(21):74, 1972.
21. 17 Cal 3d 399, 551 p 2d 389, 131 Cal Rptr 69 (1976).
22. Goldstein J, Freud A, Solnit A: *Beyond the Best Interests of the Child*. New York, Free Press, 1973, p 19, 20, 33, 40–42.
23. Weinstein EA: *The Self Image of the Foster Child*. New York, Russel Sage Foundation, 1962.
24. Helfer RE, Kempe CH: *The Battered Child*, ed 2. Chicago, University of Chicago Press, 1974.
25. NY Soc Serv Law § 424 (McKinney) 1977.
26. Fontana V: The Maltreated Children of our Times. *Vill L Rev* 23:451, 1978.
27. Besharov DJ: Putting Central Registers to Work: Using Modern Management Information Systems to Improve Child Protective Services. *Chic-Kent L Rev* 54:687, 1978.
28. 45 CFR § 1430.3-3(d) (1976).
29. 45 CFR § 205.50(a) (1976).
30. 42 USC § 601–44 (Supp V 1975).
31. Fraser B: Independent Representation for the Abused and Neglected Child: The Guardian Ad Litem. *Calif Western L Rev* 13:16, 1976–77.
32. Redeker J: The Right of an Abused Child to Independent Counsel and the Role of the Child Advocate in Child Abuse Cases. *Vill L Rev* 23:521, 1978.
33. Skoler DL: Counsel in Juvenile Court Proceedings—A Total Criminal Justice Perspective *J Fam L* 8:243, 1968.
34. ABA Code of Professional Responsibilities, EC 7-13, 1978.
35. *Brady vs Maryland*, 373 US 83, 1963.

4
Prevention of Child Abuse and Neglect

Jane D. Gray

Over the last 25 years, child abuse and neglect have become recognized as one of our society's most complex and devastating problems. No exact statistics are available, but some experts estimate that there are a million cases of child abuse and neglect in the United States per year (1). In addition to the physical injuries, many of these cases result in emotional and psychological problems that affect the child's future including his or her potential ability to parent.

In this country child abuse and neglect was first reported under the statutes of prevention of cruelty to animals (2). The case of Mary Ellen was reported in New York in the late 1800s as cruelty to an animal, but it was not until much later that laws were passed that directly applied to the maltreatment of children. In 1946 John Caffey (3) radiologically identified children with subdural hematomas often associated with fractures of long bones in various stages of healing. The full significance of these findings did not become evident until Dr. C. Henry Kempe and colleagues (4) described "the battered-child syndrome" in 1962. In this publication it was made clear that the injuries had been inflicted by the child's caretaker.

The "serious disease model" for investigation of newly identified medical diseases was also applied to child abuse and neglect (5). Many articles appeared on the physical findings associated with child abuse. These articles classified the pediatric, radiologic, neurologic, dermatologic, and ophthalmologic manifestations of the maltreatment syndrome. Other professionals became interested in the diagnosis of neglect as another example of maltreatment. From this came the descriptions of children who failed to thrive (6) and those with deprivational dwarfism (7). More recently, there has been an increased interest in emotional and sexual abuse. Currently, the physical findings, the psychological aspects, and the family dynamics involved in these areas of maltreatment are being assessed. Concomitantly, psychiatrists, psychologists, and social workers began investigating the behavioral and psychological characteristics that appeared in children who had suffered nonaccidental physical injuries. As more maltreated children and their families were evaluated, it became evident that these children were exhibiting a complex mixture of physical, behavioral, emotional, and developmental deficits. In keeping with the medical model of the study of diseases, once the physical problems, developmental deficits, and emotional characteristics of the children were identified, and the prevalent psychological characteristics of the parents were evaluated, treatment programs began to be instituted. Finally, as with other disease entities, the ultimate goal becomes prevention. Child abuse and neglect is no different; currently experts in the field of child maltreatment are beginning to wrestle with both the philosophic and practical aspects in the final step of this medical format, the prevention of child abuse and neglect.

DEFINITION

Prevention of the complex problem of child abuse and neglect will take many and varied approaches, depending not only on the needs of the family but also on the facilities, talents, and interests of those providing services. Even though the definitions of prevention are as yet tentative, the scope of prevention can be placed within the framework of primary, secondary, and tertiary prevention. Basically, primary prevention is aimed at the entire population and takes place before any abuse or neglect has occurred. This encompasses such ideas as classes for junior high and high school students on parenting, classes for prospective and new parents, and various techniques for promotion of bonding and attachment to newborns. Not only must future families be educated, but support systems for young families must also be built into any prevention program. Through public awareness the value and availability of this type of help must be made known and acceptable to society. Some experts would argue that primary prevention must also be aimed at a reduction in poverty, alleviation of environmental stresses, and better and more self-satisfying job opportunities for both men and women. These ideas focus in part on governmental roles, but they would also mandate a change in society's attitudes toward parenting.

Secondary prevention is aimed at people who are thought to be most likely to have difficulty parenting, those who are "at risk" or in need of "extra services." This value judgment of risk is based on psychosocial, interpersonal, and intrapsychic dynamics that have been shown to be related to child abuse and neglect (8). Included are parents who were abused children themselves, who now have low self-esteem, who live in isolation with few effective support systems, and often, but not always, those living in poverty, stressed by poor environment, alcohol or drug abuse.

The medical profession can provide significant secondary prevention to these families. Physicians need to schedule more frequent visits, more time per appointment (prenatal through pediatric follow-up care), and be willing to listen to the families' psychosocial problems, as well as to their medical symptoms. The physician needs to feel comfortable referring the family to a public health nurse or a lay health visitor and then offering consultation and support to those who are providing direct services in the home environment.

The least controversial definition is that of tertiary prevention, which may also be called treatment. At this level of intervention child abuse and/or neglect has already occurred. Treatment is initially directed to the parents in an effort to prevent reinjury, to keep the family together, to reunite a broken family, or when necessary to help other families relinquish a child. Each family has different needs and treatment must, therefore, be individualized to fit the varied circumstances. Equally important, treatment must also be given to the children in an effort to break the generational cycle of abuse and neglect. Treatment has taken many forms: individual psychotherapy, group therapy for the parents, play therapy for the children, self-help groups (Parents Anonymous), homemakers, lay therapists, health visitors, foster care, crisis nurseries, residential facilities, etc.

Very few experts in the field have difficulty relating to the concept of tertiary prevention. The need for treatment is now routinely recognized for abusive and neglectful parents. Currently there is an increasing thrust to treat all the children involved in an abusive home, in an effort to free the next generation from child maltreatment.

Many intervention efforts may overlap the three levels of prevention. But, at the same time, these definitions give a framework to guide ideas and discussion. Ideally the goal is for primary prevention to reach all strata of society. If primary prevention could ever be successfully implemented, there would be a decreased need for secondary and tertiary prevention and a hope of eradicating child abuse and neglect.

MULTIDISCIPLINARY APPROACH

Since there are varying expressions of the maltreatment syndrome in children, in their parents, and in total family dynamics; the family assessments, treatment programs, and evolving prevention models must encompass a multidisciplinary approach. Physicians (pediatricians, psychiatrists, family practitioners), nurses, psychologists, developmentalists, nutritionists, as well as social workers, attorneys, judges, and educators need to be involved. No one person or discipline has all the expertise needed to deal with this multifaceted problem nor with its prevention.

Therefore, one of the initial problems in approaches to prevention will be that professionals must be able to communicate and work well together. This involves the establishment of trust and of the mutual sharing of ideas and professional roles. The model of the multidisciplinary approach built on mutual trust and respect has occurred in some sections of the country, particularly on hospital and community child protection teams (9). This concept of multidisciplinary effort currently needs to be extended to implementing prevention. This may mean that there is a greater need for involvement of other professionals and nonprofessionals. Roles will exist for trained lay persons. In some areas of the country, experienced lay persons are managing the local hotlines, serving as babysitters in crisis nurseries, or functioning as health visitors to families of newborns.

RESEARCH FOCUS

There are many areas of prevention that must still be researched. This research must address issues of feasibility and implementation of services. Since child abuse and neglect are such complex problems, it is probable that not all preventive programs will be applicable to all persons or all communities. It is also quite likely that prevention may take different approaches depending on the needs and assets of the various communities in which prevention programs are established. It is also suspected that not only will a variety of disciplines and a variety of programs be involved in the provision of preventive services but also that many community and hospital facilities that have not previously been used may prove to be ideal, nonthreatening prevention resources. In other words, since previous research has shown that there is no single cause of child abuse and neglect, there will be no single resource or simple answer to prevention.

THEORETICAL AND PRACTICAL APPLICATION

Prevention of child abuse and neglect brings up both theoretical and practical considerations. There are those in this country who feel that enforced programs of preventive intervention will invade their God-given individuality and the families' constitutionally assured privacy. They fear "big" government taking over the individual's and family's right to rear children as they please. It is suggested that preventive programs not be forced or offered selectively; rather they must start for the newborn, be offered to all families, and be viewed as attractive and desirable.

Also, the American cultural stigma of reaching out for help must be dissolved. However, if this is ever to be accomplished, it will probably evolve over a long period of time. America is a society of people who have been taught that they must be able to resolve their own troubles. To many people there is still a stigma attached to confiding in their physician, to consulting a psychiatrist, to attending a self-help group (Alcoholics Anonymous, Parents Anonymous), or even reaching out to a neighbor or friend. There is an even greater societal stigma attached to a child abuser, making reaching out even more difficult for him or her. Society's misperceptions are that children are conceived to be loved and nurtured; therefore, feelings of anger and frustration toward a child are not well understood or accepted either by the parents or by society as a whole. Many professionals also have difficulty empathizing with battering parents, dealing with their own feelings, and subsequently in establishing a helping relationship with these parents.

After abuse has occurred, families and society are faced with the realities of the problem. Receiving help before a child has suffered maltreatment is unfortunately rare in our society. The parents are reluctant to admit to the fact that they are having child-rearing problems, and society has not yet established treatment programs for families who are having difficulty parenting but in which no abuse or neglect has actually taken place.

In some locales once a family is labeled as "high risk" for abuse or neglect, minimal services can be provided. However, this brings up the ethical issue of labeling people as being "high risk" for abnormal parenting practices. It makes us wonder if by labeling parents we are perpetrating a self-fulfilling prophecy. If these parents are categorized as probable abusers/neglectors, will they then carry out the prophecy and be the ones who abuse their children? As yet there is no answer to this question. Thus a "Catch-22" situation arises: if these families are not labeled, they are also not eligible for services, but if no services are provided, the family that is barely able to cope, may resort to physical violence when a crisis occurs. At our present level of knowledge about predicting and preventing child abuse, we do not yet know what happens to families who are incorrectly labeled, either as "high risk" or as "low risk." There is some evidence that families correctly labeled as "high risk" who are offered services do benefit. Their children have been shown to have fewer serious injuries requiring hospitalization (10).

One possibility is to offer all services to all families. This would negate the issue of labeling, and would allow families who were functioning marginally to receive supportive services and, hopefully, enhance their family's strengths. Voluntary, creative, community-based preventive programs for the families may be more successful, because they would be better accepted by society. However, on the practical side of the question, providing services to all families would be extremely expensive.

There is yet another factor that has not been fully evaluated. What are the characteristics of the families who identify their own problems and engage themselves in available services? These, of course, are few in number and are the easier families to treat. If the strengths allowing these people to become involved in preventive programs can be identified, the lack of such characteristics should alert us to the fact that a certain family may need intervention. Once the need for intervention with a certain family has been clearly identified, professionals can confidently institute an outreach prevention program and persist in their preventive efforts.

PRELIMINARY RESEARCH

Early studies on prediction and prevention of child abuse and neglect showed that a high risk population can be identified and that even modest intervention with risk parents prevents serious injuries requiring hospitalization. At the University of Colorado Health Sciences Center in Denver, a predictive and preventive study was begun in 1971 and identified families with the potential for parenting difficulties by the use of (1) a prenatal interview, (2) a questionnaire, (3) labor and delivery room observations, and (4) a postpartum interview and observations (See Table 1). Both warning signs (sections A, B, C) and positive family circumstances (section D) are included in Table 1.

Every family has a complex interplay of positive and negative attributes, and any assessment must include both. Risk is not just the presence or absence of a single factor, but a number of factors (both positive and negative), the family's emphasis on them, and their rigidity to change that will influence the total assessment.

One hundred families that were felt to be "at risk" for parenting difficulties were randomized, and one-half of these received intervention in the form of "extra services." This intervention involved close office and telephone contact with a single pediatrician, a public health nurse visiting in the home, and a lay

Table 1. Warning Signs (Negative Factors) (A,B,C) for High Risk Families and Signs of Positive Family Circumstances (D)

A. Information to be gathered during the prenatal period
   1. Does the mother seem overly concerned with the baby's sex or performance?
   2. Does the mother exhibit denial of the pregnancy (not willing to gain weight, no plans for the baby, refusal to talk about the situation)?
   3. Is this child likely to be "one too many?"
   4. Is the mother extremely depressed over the pregnancy?
   5. Is the mother very frightened and alone, especially in anticipation of delivery, while careful explanations do not seem to dissipate the fears?
   6. Is there a lack of support from husband and/or family?
   7. Did the mother and/or father formerly want an abortion or seriously consider relinquishment and have changed their minds?
   8. Do the parents come from an abusive/neglectful background?
   9. Is the parents' living situation overcrowded, isolated, unstable, or intolerable to them?
   10. Do they lack a telephone?
   11. Is there an absence of supportive relatives and/or friends?
B. Information to be recorded during delivery
   1. Record the following regarding the parent's reaction at birth:
       a. How does the mother *look*?
       b. What does the mother *say*?
       c. What does the mother *do*?
   2. When the father attends delivery, record his reactions as well.
   3. Record passive reaction, either verbal or nonverbal; does the mother refuse to touch, hold, or examine the baby?
   4. Record hostile reaction, either verbal or nonverbal; does the mother make inappropriate verbalizations, glances, or disparaging remarks about the physical characteristics of the child?
   5. Do the parents express disappointment over sex of the baby?
   6. Do the parents avoid eye contact with the baby?
   7. Are there nonsupportive interactions between the parents?
C. Information to be gathered during the postpartum period
   1. Is the mother not having any fun with the baby?
   2. Does the mother avoid eye contact with the baby?
   3. Are verbalizations to the infant negative, demanding, harsh, etc.?
   4. Are most of the mother's verbalizations to others about the child negative?
   5. Do the parents remain disappointed over the sex of the child?
   6. Do the parents make negative identification of the child: significance of name, who he/she looks like and/or acts like?
   7. Do parents have expectations far beyond the child's capabilities?
   8. Is the mother very bothered by baby's crying; does it make her feel hopeless, helpless, or like crying herself?
   9. In feeding, does the mother see the baby as too demanding; is she repulsed by his or her messiness; does she ignore his or her demands?
   10. Does she see changing diapers as a very negative, repulsive task?
   11. Does the mother not comfort the baby when he or she cries?
   12. Are the husband's and/or family's reactions to the baby negative or nonsupportive?
   13. Is the mother not receiving meaningful support from anyone?
   14. Are there sibling rivalry problems; or is there a complete lack of understanding of this possibility?

Table 1 (Continued)

15. Is the husband very jealous of the baby's drain on mother's time, energy, and affection?
16. Does the mother lack control over the situation; is she not involved; does she relinquish control to the doctors or nurses?
17. When attention is focused on the child in her presence, does the mother see this as something negative for herself?
18. Does the mother make complaints about the baby that cannot be verified?

D. Information about related family circumstances
    1. Do the parents see likeable attributes in the baby, do they see baby as separate person?
    2. Is the baby healthy and not too disruptive to parents' life-style?
    3. Can either parent rescue the child or relieve the other in a crisis?
    4. Is the marriage stable?
    5. Do the parents have a good friend or relative to turn to, a sound "need-meeting" system?
    6. Do the parents exhibit coping abilities; i.e., capacity to plan and understand need for adjustments because of a new baby?
    7. Are the mother's intelligence and health good?
    8. Did the parents have helpful role models growing up.
    9. Can the parents have fun together and enjoy personal interests or hobbies?
    10. Was this baby planned or wanted?
    11. Is birth control planned for in the future?
    12. Does the father have a stable job?
    13. Do the parents have their own home and stable living conditions?
    14. Is the father supportive to mother and involved in care of baby?

health visitor to help relieve family stresses and to serve as a supportive friend. The other risk group of 50 received whatever services the hospital and community routinely provided. A third group of 50 families who were assessed by the four groups of criteria to be clearly low risk for parenting difficulties served as a control.

In the "at risk" group of 50 families who received routine follow-up care, there were five children who suffered injuries that were thought to be secondary to abnormal parenting practices and which were serious enough to require hospitalization. Two of these children have medical and intellectual handicaps from these injuries. There were also two cases of failure-to-thrive in this group that were thought to be secondary to nutritional neglect. Six children who were in the "at risk" intervention group received minor (bruises and soft tissue) injuries, but the "extra services" provided immediate and more comprehensive intervention whenever there was cause to believe maltreatment was occurring and thus prevented more serious injury. Increased intervention was accomplished by notifying child protection teams, county departments of social services, law enforcement officials and/or courts at the earliest indication of parental dysfunction.

None of the 50 children in the at risk group who had received "extra services" and no child in the "low risk" control group suffered an inflicted injury that was serious enough to require hospitalization or to leave physical sequelae. There were no reported cases of abuse or neglect in the central registry in the control group of 50 families who were thought to be at low risk for abnormal parenting practices (10).

In 1971 Drs. Klein and Stern (11) reported a higher incidence of abuse and neglect in premature babies. These early reports were retrospective in nature. More recently Hunter et al. (12) prospectively studied the incidence of maltreatment in 255 infants admitted to a neonatal intensive care unit. The incidence (3.9%) of maltreatment among these infants substantiates the retrospective studies, which have also shown a greater incidence of abuse in children with special needs. In this study the information gathered on the parents had the same focus as that elicited in the Denver predictive study (10), Table 1. This information covered maternal personality characteristics, a background history of abuse and neglect, isolation, mental problems, etc. In Hunter's study, the intensive care nursery had open visiting policies and parents were encouraged to take advantage of these and to become involved with their sick newborns. The families were also offered (1) counseling around the crisis of having a baby in the intensive care nursery, (2) the support of a public health nurse, and (3) follow-up multidisciplinary medical care. Reevaluation of the children took place at the mean age of 12 months, and the specific outcome measure used was abuse and neglect reports to the department of social services. Ten of these children had confirmed reports in the central registry. Two of these were for serious physical injuries and the other eight were primarily reports of neglect. All of the children who were reported had been classified as "at risk" by the interview criteria before they were discharged. No abuse or neglect occurred in the children thought to be at low risk. The infants who were subsequently abused also had demonstrated more medical problems in the nursery. They were of smaller birth weight, gestationally less mature, had experienced longer hospital stays, and had an increased incidence of congenital defects (6/10 reported for maltreatment). Parents of these infants visited the nursery less frequently, even though visiting was encouraged and parents were given help with this.

Other researchers have also recognized the importance of parental visitation to a newborn in the neonatal intensive care unit and have thought that the separation of mother and infant during the period when parents are ordinarily claiming their infant and beginning to attach to him or her has special significance in terms of future abuse, neglect, and relinquishment (13).

These studies have given hope as well as insight into some medical aspects of prevention of child abuse and neglect. One thing that is clear is the great importance of the perinatal period. In a practical sense, most American women do deliver their babies in hospitals. This gives the medical profession a chance to reach young parents just as they are becoming a family. During the postpartum period, parents are a captive audience and are available for teaching. They also are openly honest and very vulnerable at this time, and because of this, many are willing to accept extra services. This, of course, is of great advantage in beginning intervention even before the newborn is discharged from the hospital.

PRENATAL PERIOD

The first contact between a pregnant woman and her physician ordinarily begins with the first prenatal visit. During the prenatal period the physician (obstetrician or family practitioner) is collecting medical data on the mother in an effort to anticipate physical problems in either the mother or baby. The gathering of psychosocial data should also be done during the prenatal visits. Actually, the prenatal period may be a time that is less stressful than the perinatal period, more relaxed, and, therefore, more conducive to the collection of this type of data. Information as to the parents' feelings about pregnancy, their expectations for the birthing process, as well as their expectations for the baby, their support systems, and any undue stresses on the family should be assessed and recorded. In addition to the interview data, observational and interactional data are important. Noting who brings the mother in for her medical visits and the mother's interaction with that person can give valuable clues to the family's support system. Observing the mother with her older children in the crowded office waiting room will give valuable insight into how she parents the present children and her ability to cope with one more child. The office or clinic staff's subjective reactions to the expectant mother is also important; if the mother is having difficulty relating to and communicating with the staff, this is another clue that further assessment is necessary. The most important of these observations are those interactions between the expectant mother and her spouse, her own mother, and her older children.

In many cases these interviews, observations and assessments of psychosocial data are time consuming and difficult for the busy practitioner to fit into his or her schedule. However, nurses and physicians' assistants have been successfully used in this role. Each expectant mother needs a primary caretaker with whom to relate. This builds trust and confidence and provides a continuity of information that will lead to the most appropriate methods for intervention.

The necessity for gathering psychosocial data on all expectant mothers in order to provide more comprehensive prenatal care is obvious. This data collection must be done on all families, but the information will generate more concern about some families than others. Experts interested in the area of prediction and prevention have investigated the possibilities of screening prenatal patients for their parenting potential.

Brody and Gaiss (14) have suggested the use of the phrase "degree of parenting potential" rather than the more emotionally charged label of "high" or "low risk" for child abuse or neglect. If those families at greatest risk for abnormal parenting practices could be identified early, they could receive the thrust of preventive services. Drs. Schneider and Helfer (15) have formulated a questionnaire that is presently undergoing field trials to assess the feasibility of using it in a prenatal setting. Certainly, there are specific advantages to administering a questionnaire to determine parenting potential. First of all, it can be done in the prenatal period before a baby would be exposed to abnormal parenting practices. Second, if the questionnaire is valid, intervention programs could then be concentrated on the people who need the most help. Third, it could be self-administered and therefore would probably require less staff time.

However, to be of value, screening procedures must adhere to specific guidelines. These concepts are set forth by Dr. William Frankenburg (16) who states that any screening test must have both sensitivity and specificity. He defines sensitivity as the degree of accuracy of the test in identifying high risk parents. Specificity is defined as the degree of accuracy of the test in identifying low risk parents. If it is to be useful, any screening instrument must adhere to these definitions. Ethically, screening instruments must be administered to all prenatal patients, not just those attending public prenatal care programs. Even though evidence is currently minimal, there is some indication that mothers seeing private physicians also have difficulties parenting. If screening instruments for parenting potential prove to be feasible, there must be a network of medical and community resources available to provide services for these parents. Identification without adequate intervention resources is of more harm than good.

In addition to evaluating medical and psychosocial information, physicians can encourage parents to participate in educational and social groups concerned with the birthing and nurturing of newborns. These would include any prenatal classes offered by the clinic or hospital itself, as well as more community-based groups such as La Maze classes for both parents and La Leche League groups for mothers who plan to nurse their newborns. La Maze classes are extremely valuable in promoting paternal (and family) involvement, providing education, teaching usual anesthesia, labor, delivery, and postpartum policies. They also explore feelings in a supportive group, which will soon undergo a "shared crisis experience"—the birth of a new baby. In addition, La Maze classes provide a social outlet for young peers who are in similar circumstances. These classes also afford an element of self-help and sharing, since primagravid parents can learn from the experiences of those who have older children. The supportive bonds formed between parents in the same La Maze classes are evidenced by the fact that many group members continue to see each other after the birth of their babies. Some of this contact is on an individual, informal basis, and some contacts continue in a more formal mode, with organized reunions, picnics, and social events that the entire family attends.

Obstetricians and family practitioners can also provide referrals to La Leche League for any mother who is considering breast-feeding. This self-help group of nursing mothers provides much the same function as La Maze classes. The La Leche League also provides didactic teaching, learning from more experienced mothers, and a chance to share fears and frustrations in a supportive social setting. La Leche encourages paternal involvement and helps the mother to recognize her partner's feelings about breast-feeding. La Leche League meetings involve both mother and baby and in this way also promote positive mother-infant interaction.

Another appropriate prenatal function of the obstetrician or family practitioner is to ask the mother who will be providing ongoing well child care for the baby. The physician can then initiate a referral to the pediatrician or family practitioner or clinic of the family's choice. With the mother's permission, medical as well as psychosocial data can then be shared with the physician who will be giving well child care. Communication of all data to the subsequent caretaker will facilitate optimal follow-up. The parents should also be encouraged to make an appointment with their pediatric caretaker 2 to 3 weeks before the expected date of delivery. This affords the pediatric caregiver the opportunity to begin to build a relationship with the parents before the birth of the baby. He or she can explain his or her policies and, hopefully, through open-ended questions begin to explore the parents' needs and expectations. Information from this beginning relationship coupled with the prenatal assessments will give valuable insight into how to make labor, delivery, and the early postpartum period as positive an experience as possible for the new family.

Finally, the prenatal physician should spend time explaining his or her policies in regard to labor and delivery and how these relate to hospital protocol. The parents may have to be encouraged to ask questions, investigate their feelings in regard to the policies, and explore their options. The birthing experience is so important to the attachment process that parents need to have input, express their wishes, and have their desires considered important by the physician caring for them.

On occasion a patient will present to the prenatal clinic seeking advice and information about termination of pregnancy. Some families who are cognizant of their difficulties with parenting and who are honestly trying to create a warm, stimulating environment for their present children realize that another child will only complicate their endeavors. The physician must explore their feelings with a nonjudgmental attitude in order to help the family make a decision that will be most appropriate for them. If a family elects a therapeutic abortion, they will need understanding and sensitive care, not only during the decision period but after the abortion has been accomplished, for a therapeutic abortion is certainly a crisis experience. If they elect to continue the pregnancy, extra services should be provided immediately.

Certainly all families need information on family planning, whether it is given after an abortion or after the birth of a baby. This family planning discussion is best done by the mother's health care provider and needs to be presented in a practical manner that both parents can understand. Future family planning should be an integral part of every obstetrician/family practitioner's discussion with each family he sees for pregnancy.

PERINATAL PERIOD

Physician's philosophies and hospital policies are in a state of flux. This is partially a result of the greater assertiveness and consumerism of new parents. Some families will want to use a birthing room, and they should know clearly what to expect, know of the need to compromise, or know how to explore an alternative. It is becoming commonplace for fathers to be in the labor and delivery rooms, for the baby to nurse in the delivery room, for the parents and new baby to be alone together in the recovery room, and for grandparents as well as siblings to visit the postpartum ward. Families must know their options, for many have strong feelings on how they want to be involved in their infant's birth. If the physicians and hospital policies are not made clear, it will only lead to dissatisfaction, disappointment, and even hostility in the parents. These emotions strongly affect bonding with the new baby and can be avoided if foresight and concern are shown.

The importance of positive experiences during the perinatal period must be realized by all personnel working in this area. Medical personnel cannot influence certain factors that contribute to attachment, that is, the parents' own childhood, their cultural values, and their previous experiences with children. However, their verbal and nonverbal interactions with parents can have a powerful influence, either positively or negatively, on attachment. The entire staff needs to recognize the importance of positive verbalizations about the new baby, as all parents are very vulnerable in the delivery room. Staff's comments about how the baby is sticking out his tongue at the mother or about his irritating cry can only have a negative effect on the parents' earliest impressions of the infant. The staff must be sensitive to the needs and wants of each individual family and attempt to make the family comfortable while implementing their requests during the birth of the baby without jeopardizing the medical safety of either the mother or baby.

Ideally, the parents must feel comfortable and free enough to make their wishes known, and the hospital staff must be sensitive and caring enough to implement what can be done expediently. Fathers (or significant other supportive persons) should be offered the opportunity to be in the labor and delivery rooms. Many fathers do not realize that being in the delivery room can be one of their options. They must be informed of the lasting significance this may have for them in regard to their feelings for the new baby. Most fathers state that they feel closer to their children whom they have seen delivered. Having the father present is also of significance to the mother. By his presence, the father can show his support, love, and concern for the mother. He also can show his involvement in the start of their new life together as a family. On the other hand, no father should be forced to be involved during labor and delivery, for this may place unrealistic expectations on a person already stressed by the responsibilities of a new baby. This added stress may have an effect that is opposite to the desired one and thus be a negative influence on the bonding.

After the baby has stabilized, Apgars done, and the baby is warm, he/she should be offered to the parents (again, not forced on them). At this time parents usually begin the physical claiming of the baby. They explore the child, count fingers and toes, and finally establish eye contact in the en facé position. En facé is defined as the position in which the mother keeps her face aligned so that her eyes are in the same vertical plane of rotation as those of her infant. This is the ideal position for mother and infant to establish eye contact (Fig. 1). Many mothers may want to breast feed while they are still on the delivery table. This sucking provides the additional advantage of causing the uterus to contract. Afterward, the father can carry the baby from the delivery room to the nursery. When the nursery has completed their admission procedures, the baby and parents can be reunited in the recovery room. This period of time is especially important, because from the work of Desmond et al. (17) we know that this is a time when the infant has his eyes wide open and is very alert. This is an ideal time for parents to establish the en facé position and then the important eye-to-eye contact. However, after about one hour in this alert, wakeful state, the baby

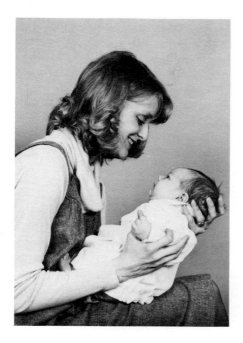

Figure 1. The en facé position. Note that the mother has aligned her face with the baby's and that in this position she has been able to establish eye contact with the infant.

will fall into a deep sleep lasting several hours and the opportune time for early reciprocal interaction is lost.

Promoting a strong attachment to the new baby may be an important factor in preventing child abuse and neglect, as there is some evidence that parents with strong and positive attachments to their infants may be less likely to maltreat them. Logically, the enhancement of attachment during the late prenatal, perinatal, and early postpartum periods is a variable that the medical profession can influence. Listening, communicating, offering support, referring to appropriate resources and preparation for delivery room protocol and hospital policies can reinforce positive attitudes and parental strengths. Anxiety and fear about birthing can contribute negatively to the parents' experience and thus make early interaction and bonding with the infant more difficult.

POSTPARTUM PERIOD

Drs. Klaus and Kennell (18) have interpreted the early postpartum period as a critically sensitive time for the mother-infant dyad to begin to form an affectional bond. They studied two groups of mother-infant pairs, those who were given "early and extended contact" and those who had routine contact with their infants. When the babies were approximately 1 month old, the mother-infant interaction was assessed and it was found that those who had been in the "early and extended" contact group tended to pick up their babies when they cried and had stayed home with the baby during the first month. If these mothers (from the "early and extended" group) had gone out and left the child, they had tended to think about their babies more often during their absence and returned earlier than expected. During the physical examination, the "extended contact" mothers stood closer to their babies and soothed them more; they fondled and spent more time en facé with their babies. At subsequent evaluations when the babies were a year old, the extended contact mothers spent more time assisting the physician with the physical examination and soothing the babies when they cried. Later, linguistic characteristics were studied in a small subsample of the original groups. The extended contact mothers asked twice as many questions; they used more words per preposition, fewer content words, more adjectives, and fewer commands than did the control mothers (19).

In preliminary studies of fathers, John Lind (20) noted that fathers were more involved in their infants' care during the first 3 months of life if they had established eye contact with their babies for 1 hour during the first 3 days of life and had undressed their infants twice. This data again supports that there is a sensitive period of time for both parents in the establishment of affectional bonds.

This period might be sensitive but may not be as critical as was originally thought. Some parents who are separated from their infants because of excessive maternal anesthesia, caesarean sections, or illness in either the mother or infant will be able to establish strong bonds with their children. It is certainly realized that many adoptive parents are firmly attached to their children, even though they may have had no contact with them during the neonatal period. However, for some families (because of their background, lack of social supports, isolation), the perinatal period is a critical time. Even though attachment can and does occur, in spite of separations, the longer the separation the more chance there is for problems to occur.

The importance of rooming-in on the postpartum ward must be emphasized. Mothers having this time of contact with their newborns not only begin to feel affectional bonds more quickly, but also gain confidence in the mothercrafting skills of feeding, burping, changing, and dressing their babies. A rooming-in unit can also provide an informal atmosphere for teaching. Interaction with sensitive physicians and nurses can increase the mother's awareness of her baby's cues, his or her needs and abilities, and thus increase not only her self-confidence but also her self-esteem. In addition to the teaching of mothercrafting skills in a rooming-in unit, an experienced, sensitive staff can begin to teach mothers their newborns' capabilities. Brazelton's Neonatal Assessment Scale (21) has a number of items that can be used appropriately to promote attachment. With the mother comfortable and the baby alert and responsive, a knowledgeable medical professional can demonstrate the newborn's capabilities and interactional responses to the mother. Mothers are excited to learn that the baby can focus his/her eyes on her, follow her with his/her eyes, and be alert to verbal and auditory stimuli. All of these are powerful responses to the mother's interaction and form a basis for a beginning reciprocal relationship.

Parents whose babies are either premature or have medical problems can also interact with their infants, albeit not in the more idealistic way described. These parents often need to be encouraged and even helped to touch, hold, and when appropriate, begin to feed their babies. Medical personnel must remember that these parents are frightened and often overwhelmed by feelings of guilt, uncertainty, and anxiety. They need to be supported and nurtured through the crisis experience of having a sick newborn. All staff need to be mindful that the baby belongs to the parents and not the doctors or nurses. Even though the medical personnel are working diligently to alleviate medical problems, the parents' feelings, interactions, and fears need to be recognized and addressed on a basis that is the most helpful and appropriate for each individual family.

DISCHARGE PLANS

With this focus on teaching and support during the prenatal, perinatal, and postpartum periods, it makes little sense to abandon a family at the time of hospital discharge. Again, referrals need to be made to sensitive, supportive medical staff, who have had the benefits of receiving information from earlier health providers. This relay of information is needed to ensure continuity of care. Certainly, pediatric follow-up care must be arranged and appointments made before discharge. The pediatric follow-up care provider should be the one who began a relationship with the parents during the late prenatal contact. He/she should interview the parents on the postpartum ward, examine the baby in their presence, demonstrate their child's unique abilities, and be available to answer questions. An appointment should be scheduled during the first two weeks after hospital discharge and the health care provider's telephone number should be given to the parents. Most parents will need to be encouraged to call if questions or problems arise. Dealing with a relatively minor problem in its early stages can prevent it from becoming a crisis situation to the family. Families who have exhibited difficulties or caused concerns as to their potential for parenting will need a more persistent and sensitive outreach approach (Table 2). If the health care provider exhibits genuine concern and interest, parents who find themselves experiencing difficulties are more likely to use health resources as a lifeline in a time of crisis.

Many families can also benefit from the outreach services offered by a public health nurse. Public health departments are a well-established community-based medical outreach program. Therefore, these nurses are usually well accepted

Table 2. Special Well Child Care for High Risk Families

1. Promote maternal attachment to the newborn.
2. Contact the mother by telephone on the second day after discharge.
3. Provide more frequent office visits.
4. Give more attention to the mother.
5. Emphasize nutrition.
6. Counsel discipline only around accident prevention.
7. Emphasize accident prevention.
8. Use compliments rather than criticism.
9. Accept phone calls at home.
10. Provide regular home visits by public health nurse or lay health visitor.

in the home. When referring a family to the public health nurse, the physician should supply background information and be very specific as to the reasons for the referral. Some young mothers will need help with mothercrafting skills: mixing formula, diapering, and other such skills. Others will need knowledge of normal growth and development (in order to normalize their own expectations); others will need to be encouraged to keep medical appointments; others will need to deal with physical problems in the baby; and many may need a friend and supportive person on whom to rely.

A concept newer to the United States is that of the lay health visitor. Health visitors have been used in Great Britain for many years. The philosophies of establishing such a program in the United States have been stated by Dr. C. Henry Kempe (22). Several programs based on this concept have been started in the United States. Among these are those located in Hawaii and Denver.

The health visitor program in Denver began in 1977. A lay health visitor is offered to all mothers who deliver at the University Hospital and who also live in Denver County. All families are interviewed on the postpartum ward by a pediatrician and/or a registered nurse. This is to gather background information, to evaluate support systems, and to determine extent of isolation. Observations of the parents' interaction with the baby are assessed. In addition, all charts are reviewed, nursing observations noted, and any psychosocial assessments taken into consideration. This is done in an effort to obtain a complete data base, so that discharge plans can be as comprehensive as possible. After the information is gathered, all families are offered the services of a lay health visitor. The parents may then voluntarily accept (in our experience 80% do accept) or refuse these services. If they accept, the lay health visitor meets the mother and newborn while they are still on the postpartum ward. At this time the lay health visitors begin to establish a relationship, make plans to visit the family at home during the first week after discharge, and give their home telephone number to the mother.

From the data collected on the postpartum ward, a tentative plan that benefits the entire family is formulated. Health visitors and the families work together to enhance family strengths and to decrease stresses on the family. However the discharge plan and its implementation are flexible and may change as the family or the lay health visitor deem necessary. The primary function of the lay health visitor is to serve as a liaison between the family, the medical facilities, and the resources of the community agencies. Another focus of lay health visitor intervention is to reduce the stresses on the family in an effort to give the family more time and energy to devote to the children. Reducing stress takes many forms depending on the individual needs of the family. At times, the lay health visitor may work with community agencies to provide a better environment (housing, food, clothing) for the family; she may drive the parents to meet with housing authorities, or help them fill out forms for food stamps or food supplements. Some families need help in understanding the necessity for well child care and will need encouragement to schedule and keep medical appointments. They may also require help with transportation or babysitting in order to keep those doctors' appointments. In other families, the lay health visitor may fill the families' needs for a supportive friend. Even though there may not be an immediate problem to solve, the family often views the lay health visitor as a lifeline in time of crisis.

The data from the Denver lay health visitor program has not yet been fully analyzed, but in the over 800 families who voluntarily accepted the health visitation services, there have been only two very minor injuries that were thought to be nonaccidental. The 20% of families who refused the services of a lay health visitor was a mixed population. Many of them were experienced mothers who exhibited early evidence of attachment to the baby and who had strong support systems. They had not generated any concern as to parenting potential during the prenatal, perinatal, or postnatal period. Pediatric follow-up care for the babies was confirmed, and they were discharged with confidence. However, others in the refusal group had generated great concern in many of the staff. When these families refused lay health visitor intervention, referrals were made for follow-up care for both mother and baby, for a public health nurse to visit in the home, and on occasion for the child protective unit of the department of social services to assess the safety of discharging this infant to his or her home. This refusal population will serve as a control group in the final analysis of data.

This type of voluntary home visitation program, offered to all new mothers, needs further investigation, but seems to hold valid hope for abuse prevention. Further research needs to address whether this type of program merely prevents child abuse and neglect, or whether it improves total family functioning or both. How such a program can be efficiently implemented (through geographic districts, e.g., counties, public health jurisdictions, or school districts) and who should administer it (hospitals, community agencies) are also important issues that need to be addressed.

EDUCATION

In addition to the medical aspects of sensitive and caring prenatal, perinatal, and postpartum intervention, comprehensive and appropriate referrals, and close follow-up care, physicians must be involved in the broad scope of education. Education encompasses primary, secondary, and tertiary prevention and has the potential of reaching the greatest number of people. Physicians, nurses, and paramedical professionals can contribute to education on all levels of prevention and with all age groups. Primary prevention can start in the public schools as early as junior high school. Health, sex education, and family living classes are now being offered in most schools. In addition, preparation for parenting classes needs to be made part of the curriculum. Physicians can be curriculum consultants, help guide school administrators, and provide counsel and support to those who do the actual teaching. The courses on parenting need guidelines of factual information that can be presented in a didactic manner by either educators or medical personnel. In addition, they need to offer group discussions around the feelings that parents might have toward their children. It must be stressed that parents have ambivalent feelings toward their children and that this is a normal reaction. The students also need to receive the message that if in the future they become uncomfortable about their feelings toward a child, there are resources available that can be helpful.

The concept of practical experience in a learning situation offers new possibilities. Certainly adolescents need to be taught about parenting, to learn about growth and development, and to explore their feelings with their peer group under the guidance of an experienced discussion leader. It is equally important that all students be exposed to groups of babies, toddlers, and preschoolers. They need first-hand experience in dealing with young children while they begin to use their new knowledge and to test their feelings of both joy and frustration. This can be done by having "field experience" in day-care centers or in preschools. Some high schools now have day-care facilities on their own premises, and students work and learn in the day-care center much as classroom and laboratory experience is combined in some science classes. Currently in our society of nuclear and smaller families, adolescents, especially boys, have little experience in caring for younger children. Reaching teenagers is one of the most productive means of prevention, because it can influence young adolescents before they begin to make decisions regarding marriage and family life. Adolescents have not had time to experience themselves yet, and they are unclear as to their own needs and wants. Therefore, teaching must start before they begin their own families and are prematurely forced to deal with others' needs and wants. Boys need the freedom to experience child care and, at the same time, girls need to get the message that marriage and childrearing are not the only options open to them. In today's society with birth control measures, girls also have career opportunities. Both sexes need to know themselves well enough to set priorities and make intelligent decisions about their own lives. Parenting is a learned art for which our society ill prepares its children. These junior and senior high school programs would afford the opportunity for better parenting by enabling young adults to make more appropriate decisions about their desires and motivations for parenting.

The medical profession must also educate the present medical, nursing, law, and education students. These students need to know the physical manifestations of abuse and neglect as well as the concomitant behavioral, emotional, and developmental lags and how these relate to the total picture of a child's well-being. They also need to be taught to assess mother-child interactions in a sensitive and meaningful way. This is probably most important for those in the medical profession, but needs to be extended to all who deal with children and their parents.

Physicians also need to teach educators, administrators, school nurses, and teachers' aides the warning signals of family dysfunction. This would include the physical, emotional, behavioral, developmental, and interactional signs that might indicate that a child is in trouble. This information can first be presented in structured college-level courses by multidisciplinary personnel including medicine, psychology, and social work. Eventually this knowledge must be integrated into the policies of individual school systems. This needs to be done by the school administrators under the guidance of interested physicians.

It is not enough for physicians to alert educators to the signs of abuse and neglect, but they must also accept responsibility for consulting with the school system about problem situations, accept referrals from teachers, evaluate children, and be prepared to share their conclusions with social services, a child protection team, or other multidisciplinary group. Educators cannot work in a vacuum, and they particularly need medical backup, either to confirm their suspicions or allay their fears.

THE COMMUNITY

Community centers, schools, and churches can also serve in the broader community approach to prevention. The use of school and church facilities offers the advantages of being located in neighborhoods, and they are thus more accessible. They already have classrooms that can be used for teaching and for group-discussions as well as areas for children to play. When some neighborhood resources are used, not only is there greater accessibility but it also may make splitting the family for therapy unnecessary. Various family members can have their individual needs met in different areas of the same building. Currently, many families are separated for individual treatment, which means driving to different parts of town, geographically splitting the family. Individual therapy is important, but so is family therapy, especially if treatment is to enhance family interaction and build on strengths.

Many communities offer parent effectiveness training classes, transactional analysis, structured groups, and self-help groups such as Parents Anonymous. These classes and groups can meet in local community centers, churches, or schools. All neighborhoods have these types of facilities already in existence, and parents usually think of them as safe places.

Preschools, including Head Start, are ideal places for parent education. They teach growth and development, explore parental feelings within a peer group, provide relief for the parents from the constant care of the child, and also provide a social outlet for both parents and children. In addition, preschools generally encourage parental involvement and, if this parental motivation for involvement can then be transferred from the preschools into the homes, there should be increased stimulation of the child. The physician can be a consultant to preschools, helping them to teach normal growth, development, adequate nutrition, and effective stimulation.

Many communities have begun programs for families in crisis. These include hotlines where parents can call when they feel they can no longer cope and may injure their children. Hotlines are just the initial step; communities must have the backup resources to offer services to any family who calls for help. Some communities, usually through the auspicies of the county department of social services, have resources such as crisis nurseries, homes for battered wives, and shelters for families in crisis. Frequently these facilities need consultation from physicians. Such consultations may be in regard to the general technicalities of maintaining health standards in a large facility or may be around the illness or injuries of one of the clients in the nursery or shelter. Physicians can accomplish a valuable community service by their consultation and support of these crisis facilities.

Some areas have established citywide or metropolitan councils for child protection. These councils are multidisciplinary and may function to review both verified and potential cases of abuse and neglect. Physicians are needed to serve on the advisory and review boards. Their suggestions for prevention and their willingness to provide direct services to children are sorely needed.

SUMMARY

In summary, child abuse and neglect are complex problems. Therefore, prevention will not be simple. Prevention will take many and varied forms, depending on the level of prevention needed, the clients' stresses, the medical and community resources available, and the expertise of the personnel in these agencies. Prevention will require that professionals of many disciplines learn to trust, communicate, and serve the clients with a comprehensive and sensitive approach. Physicians need to be involved in these varied aspects, for it will take persistent effort by all involved professionals to prevent the many problems of abusive and neglectful families. The physican can function at many levels of prevention. This role may involve direct client services, education to various disciplines, consultation to educators and community agencies, or participation on child protection teams and metropolitan councils on child abuse and neglect.

REFERENCES

1. *A Community Plan for Preventing Child Abuse*, Report of a Wingspread Conference, The Johnson Foundation, Racine, Wisconsin, 1979, p 1.
2. Radbill SX: History of child abuse and infanticide, in Kempe CH, Helfer RE (eds): *The Battered Child*, ed 2. Chicago, University of Chicago Press, 1974, p 13.
3. Caffey J: Multiple fractures in long bones of infants suffering from subdural hematomas. *AJR* 56:163–173, 1946.
4. Kempe CH, Silverman FH, Steele BF, et al: The battered child syndrome. *JAMA* 181:17–24, 1962.
5. Helfer RE: Basic issues concerning prediction, in Helfer RE, Kempe CH (eds): *Child Abuse and Neglect: The Family and the Community*. Cambridge, Mass, Ballinger Publishing Co, 1976, p 363–372.
6. Schmitt BD, Kempe CH: The pediatrician's role in child abuse and neglect. *Curr Probl Pediatr*, a monograph. Chicago, Yearbook Medical Publishers, 1975.
7. Silver HK, Finkelstein M: Deprivation dwarfism. *J Pediatr* 70:317, 1967.
8. Steele BF, Pollock CB: A psychiatric study of parents who abuse infants and small children, in Helfer RE, Kempe CH (eds): *The Battered Child*, ed 2. Chicago, University of Chicago Press, 1974, p 89–131.
9. Schmitt BD: Team purpose and structure, in Schmitt BD (ed): *The Child Protection Team Handbook: A Multidisciplinary Approach to Managing Child Abuse and Neglect*. New York, Garland STPM Press, 1978, p 7.
10. Gray JD, Cutler C, Dean J, et al: Prediction and prevention of child abuse and neglect. *Child Abuse and Neglect: The International Journal* 1:45, 1977.
11. Klein M, Stern L: Low birth weight and the battered child syndrome. *Am J Dis Child* 122:15, 1971.
12. Hunter R, Kelstrom N, Kraybill E, et al: Antecedents of child abuse and neglect in premature infants: A prospective study in a newborn intensive care unit. *Pediatrics* 61:629, 1978.

13. Kennell J, Voos D, Klaus M: Parent-infant bonding, in Helfer RE, Kempe CH (eds): *Child Abuse and Neglect: The Family and the Community*. Cambridge, Mass, Ballinger Publishing Co, 1976, p 50.

14. Brody H, Gaiss B: Ethical issues in early identification and prevention of unusual child rearing practices, in Helfer RE, Kempe CH (eds): *Child Abuse and Neglect: The Family and the Community*. Cambridge, Mass, Ballinger Publishing Co, 1976, p 375.

15. Schneider C, Hoffmeister J, Helfer R: A predictive screening questionnaire for potential problems in mother-child interaction, in Helfer RE, Kempe CH (eds): *Child Abuse and Neglect: The Family and the Community*. Cambridge, Mass, Ballinger Publishing Co, 1976, p 393–407.

16. Frankenburg W: Pediatric screening, in Schulman I (ed): *Advances in Pediatrics*, Vol 20. Chicago, Year Book Medical Publishers, Inc, 1973, p 149–175.

17. Desmond MM, Rudolph AJ, Phitaksphraiwan P: The transitional care nursery: A mechanism of preventive medicine. *Pediatr Clin North Am* 13:651, 1966.

18. Kennell JH, Jerould R, Wolfe H, et al: Maternal behavior one year after early and extended postpartum contact. *Dev Med Child Neurol* 16:172, 1974.

19. Ringler NM, Kennell JH, Jarvella R, et al: Mother-to-child speech at two years: Effect of early postnatal contact. *Behav Pediatr* 86:141, 1975.

20. Kennell J, Voos D, Klaus M: Parent-infant bonding, in Helfer RE, Kempe CH (eds): *Child Abuse and Neglect: The Family and the Community*. Cambridge, Mass, Ballinger Publishing Co, 1976, p 32.

21. Brazelton TB: Neonatal behavioral assessment scale. *Clinics in Developmental Medicine, No. 50*, a monograph. Philadelphia, JB Lippincott Co, 1974.

22. Kempe CH: Approaches to preventing child abuse: The health visitor concept. *Am J Dis Child* 130:941, 1976.

5
Central Nervous System Injuries

David M. Klein

Trauma to the central nervous system (CNS) accounts for a majority of the disability and death associated with physical child abuse. Although incidence will vary according to patient selection, 40 to 70% of battered children will show some external evidence of trauma to the face and head, with higher incidence noted among those generally more gravely injured (1–3). In roentgenograms of 95 consecutive battered children, Kogutt et al. (4) found 22% to show skull fractures and an additional 18% showed suture separation, indicating increased intracranial pressure. Among 187 abused or neglected children, Ryan and associates (5) reported eight deaths, with craniocerebral injury responsible for five deaths where details are given. In a 5-year experience at Vanderbilt University (6), 32 of 110 abused children had some form of CNS injury. Of eight deaths in this series, six resulted from intracranial injury. Serious cerebral injury is frequently the result of a single violent act in a child who has been battered previously (2,5,6).

A complete discussion of all CNS trauma is beyond the scope of this chapter. Most forms of CNS injury can be seen as a result of abuse, but there are certain anatomical qualities of infancy and childhood that warrant special emphasis here.

INCREASED INTRACRANIAL PRESSURE

The skull may be looked on as a closed bony box in the older child or adult. Because the cranial volume is fixed, abnormal expansion of any mass increases intracranial pressure. Manifestations of *increased intracranial pressure* can vary according to the speed with which a problem develops, but they are not otherwise specific to the underlying disease or its location. Signs of acutely increased intracranial pressure, such as diminished response, bradycardia, and hypertension, will be the same whether the origin lies in an expanding tumor, a clot, a swollen brain, or fluid accumulation. Ultimately any type of mass can also produce a shift of structures and *brain stem compression*, with signs such as pupillary fixation, respiratory irregularity or apnea, and decerebrate posturing.

73

In infancy, patent *sutures* and an *open fontanelle* may provide volumetric release over days and weeks, dampening other signs of increased intracranial pressure while producing accelerated head growth, protruding fontanelle, and separated sutures. Even here, however, conditions producing rapidly rising intracranial pressure may act more swiftly than sutures can accommodate, and the picture of acute decompensation supervenes. This is particularly common with acute *intracranial hemorrhage* and traumatic cerebral swelling.

TRAUMATIC CRANIAL DISTORTION AND DIFFERENTIAL MOTION

The *dura*, a thick tough membrane that acts as the internal periosteum of the skull, is firmly adherent to that bony surface (Fig. 1). The *arachnoid*, on the contrary, is attached to the surface of the brain by its weblike projections, and the thin subarachnoid space between this membrane and the brain surface is filled with circulating *cerebrospinal fluid*. Under normal circumstances, with brain and fluid filling the cranial vault, arachnoid and dural surfaces are approximated but free from each other in most areas; the "subdural space" between these two surfaces is thus a potential space and is expanded only in disease states. However, since the brain and its attached arachnoid can move differentially within the skull and dura, blood vessels crossing this space may be broken by shearing or stretching forces, creating *subdural hemorrhages*. A large proportion of blood leaves the brain through veins bridging arachnoid and dura to enter venous sinuses that lie within folds of the dura. These *bridging veins* are particularly vulnerable to injury during craniocerebral acceleration

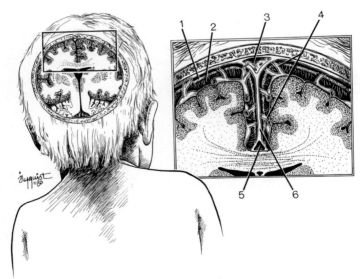

Figure 1. The relationship of the cerebrum and its coverings. (1) Arachnoid; (2) subarachnoid space; (3) superior sagittal sinus; (4) bridging veins; (5) inferior sagittal sinus; (6) falx cerebri. The membranous falx lies between the cerebral hemispheres and is a continuation of convexity dura. Dura and arachnoid are separated by the potential subdural space, which is crossed by bridging veins.

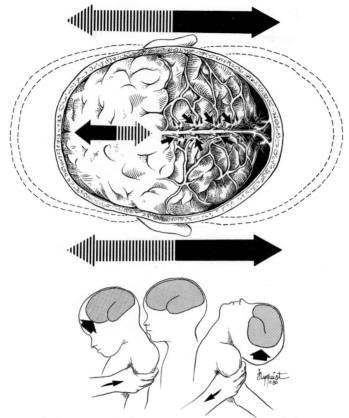

Figure 2. Rapid acceleration/deceleration of the head, as exemplified by shaking injuries, produces differential motion between the skull and its contents. Bridging vessels may be torn and brain may be contused by shearing or compression.

and deceleration (Fig. 2). Since venous bleeding may be under low pressure and collect only slowly, hemorrhage from such veins may initially be silent, with no signs or symptoms until a significant volumetric effect is gradually developed.

Along with stretching and shearing of bridging veins, the brain may be contused or lacerated as it moves across the irregular skull surface, and there may be shearing within the brain itself, resulting in internal hemorrhage and disruption. A direct blow produces momentary skull deformity, with compression in the direction of the blow and elongation at right angles to this. Elastic recoil results in contrary oscillations, until the system dampens itself and the skull returns to normal shape or cracks along lines of stress (Fig. 3). This type of distortion is transmitted to the brain and can produce serious damage even without any linear motion of the head as a whole.

INJURY TO THE SKULL

Thin, pliable bone, open fontanelle, and patent suture lines make the infant's skull particularly vulnerable to distortion with blunt trauma. A sudden wave of

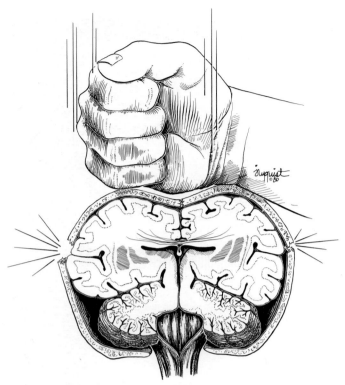

Figure 3. With impact, craniocerebral distortion can result in brain damage or skull fracture along stress lines. Fractures may be linear, as on the right, or "bursting" may occur, with diastasis and meningocerebral tears, as on the left (see also Fig. 4). Bone may remain depressed at the point of impact.

increased intracranial pressure may be produced by the blow, and severe distortion can also result in the sort of *diastatic, "bursting" fracture* that occasionally evolves into an enlarging defect over subsequent weeks (Fig. 4).

At the same time, pointed objects can produce localized areas of bony depression or perforation more easily, often with relatively little force required and less disturbance to surrounding skull or brain than when bone is thicker and harder. As a consequence, there may be little or no change in state of consciousness or neurologic function to warn the examiner that significant depression of bone has occurred. Routine skull x-rays thus have greater importance in the evaluation of head injuries at this age than for older people.

Unexplained fluctuant swelling beneath infant scalp, frequently without an alteration in the child's behavior, is often of traumatic origin and may overlie skull fracture. Similar swelling in an older child can result from violent hair-pulling. Blood loss into such extravasations can be significant to the infant, and the hematoma can expand slowly over a period of days, so that serial observation is required. Typically these collections take many days or even several weeks to reabsorb. The development of pulsation in such a mass suggests underlying diastatic ("bursting") fracture with dural disruption.

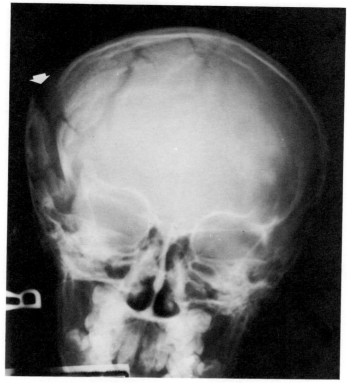

Figure 4. Anteroposterior skull film shows "bursting" fracture (arrowhead) as well as multiple linear fracture lines, the result of a 15-foot fall in a 7-year-old girl.

Basal skull fracture may be suggested by ecchymosis about the orbit or in the mastoid area ("battle sign") (Fig. 5), but such ecchymoses may also develop after bleeding into deep scalp layers, as a result of downward dissection of blood into these points of scalp attachment. Such dissection may be asymptomatic and can occur several days after injury. Discharge of blood or fluid from the nose or ears should also suggest communicating basal skull fracture.

CEREBRAL CONTUSION

Brain contusion is common and is responsible for most of the morbidity and mortality associated with severe head injury. Areas of architectural disruption, hemorrhage, and edema may be localized or may be scattered throughout the brain; the distribution of damage is only rarely characteristic of a specific type of impact, since the craniocerebral distortion producing the contusion is often generalized, as has been described above.

Coalescent areas of intracerebral hematoma can occasionally be evacuated, but the more common scattered, infiltrative hemorrhages unfortunately cannot be helped by surgery. Severe brain swelling associated with contusion remains the single most difficult and life-threatening consequence of head trauma.

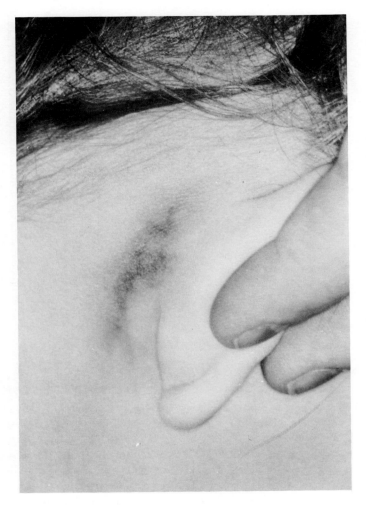

Figure 5. Ecchymosis over the mastoid area ("battle sign") associated with basal (petrous temporal) skull fracture in a physically abused 5-year-old boy.

Osmotic diuretics may be effective in intermittent intravenous doses, and hyperventilation is helpful. The place of steroids and barbiturate coma in treatment of traumatic edema remains to be determined.

Signs and symptoms of direct damage to the brain can generally be distinguished from those of increased intracranial pressure, even if these problems coexist. Injury to significant areas results in focal neurologic deficit, such as weakness, loss of general or special sensibility, incoordination, or dementia. Functional loss may be recovered or may be permanent, depending on the nature and extent of tissue damage and its location. Acute irritation or chronic scarring can give rise to seizures.

The infant brain is particularly soft, gelatinous, and vulnerable to anoxia and mechanical stress. Large areas of infarction or atrophy may follow a trauma that seems initially to be limited and localized (Fig. 6). Diffuse cellular loss can

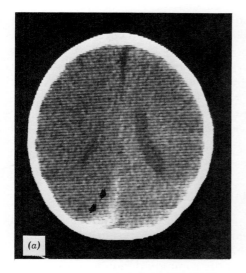
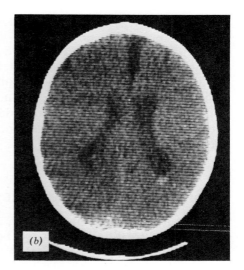
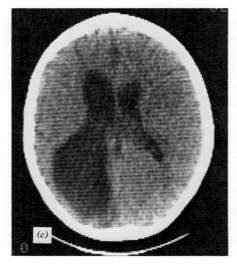

Figure 6. Sequential CT scans demonstrate the true extent of posttraumatic damage that may initially appear limited. (*a*) Horizontal scan on the day of injury shows fresh hemorrhage along the left posterior falx and occipital pole, typical for acceleration/deceleration injury (arrowheads). (*b*) Ten days later blood is absorbing, ventricles are slightly larger, and there is lower density in the left occipital white matter. (*c*) Scan 22 months later reveals large porencephalic defect in this area and generalized ventricular enlargement, left greater than right, consistent with corresponding atrophy.

ultimately result in a generalized thinning of the entire cerebral mantle, with enlargement of CSF pathways (*hydrocephalus ex vacuo*). There may be additional hydrocephalus of a progressive type; the fluid retention results from obstruction of cerebrospinal fluid pathways by bleeding, tissue breakdown, and scarring. A single act of violence can thus produce profound impairment to both existing function and future development.

RETINAL HEMORRHAGE

Retinal hemorrhages are so often seen with abusive head injury that they are considered by some authors to be characteristic of battering (7). In fact, however, they can follow any sudden increase in intracranial pressure, such as that produced by spontaneous intracranial hemorrhage, sudden chest compression, difficult delivery (8), or with compressive head injury of any sort. A tight grip on the chest or neck may account for retinal hemorrhages in the "shaken infant" (9). A blow to the pliable skull of an infant or toddler is more likely to result in massive cranial distortion and a wave of sudden intracranial hypertension than is a similar blow to an older person. Age selectivity rather than the nature of the injury could, therefore, account for the frequency of retinal hemorrhage in battering.

SUBDURAL HEMATOMA AND "THE SHAKEN CHILD"

Physical abuse is recognized today as a leading cause of infant subdural hematoma, a relationship that has become clear only in recent years. Caffey (10) first observed the association of multiple long-bone fractures with chronic subdural hematoma of infancy in 1946, but the common denominator of abuse was not appreciated because other signs of trauma were not present. Ommaya and associates (11) investigated the results of experimental whiplash injury in monkeys, reproducing "the violent flinging of the head" by simulated rear-end collision. They noted damage to both brain and upper cervical spinal cord, with contusion and subdural hemorrhage particularly prominent along the medial aspects of the parieto-occipital cortex, as well as on the undersurfaces of frontal and temporal lobes. In 1971 Guthkelch (12) related these findings and other prior case reports to his own experience with battered children. Noting that the infant spine is supple and cervical musculature is inadequate to control a relatively large head at this age, he suggested that violent shaking or other wrenching forces applied to the trunk could cause the subdural hematoma frequently seen in child abuse by producing whiplash motion of the head, without external signs of scalp trauma or evidence of skull fracture. Caffey (13,14) has since emphasized the frequency of this mechanism in child abuse by describing "the whiplash shaken infant syndrome," including subdural hematoma, cerebral injury, retinal hemorrhages, and avulsion fractures and periosteal reactions in long bones, all the result of acceleration/deceleration injury. There may be telltale petechiae or bruising in a pattern to fit the offender's hands about the victim's chest or other part that has been gripped or wrenched.

Craniocerebral computed tomography (CT) findings support these concepts. Zimmerman et al. (15) found acute subdural hematoma by CT to be located in the posterior parieto-occipital portion of the interhemispheric fissure, along the falx, in 15 of 17 such cases in abused infants (Fig. 6). This localization for acute hematoma and contusion is striking, for it is less common in direct, nonabusive head injury and corresponds to the localization in experimental whiplash trauma noted by Ommaya and associates (11). Moreover, parenchyma and bridging veins in this area lie close to the midsagittal plane and near the poles of the brain where they might suffer the greatest stresses of acceleration and deceleration during rapid flexion and extension of the neck, as in shaking.

The clinical presentation of subdural hematoma can vary widely, depending on the speed with which the hematoma collects and the nature and extent of associated cerebral injury. Since there may be no external evidence of trauma or skull fracture on x-ray film, the diagnosis may not come to mind if there is no obvious intracranial hypertension or neurologic deficit. Slowly progressive cases of this sort can be manifested by failure-to-thrive, sporadic vomiting, unexplained anemia and fever, and late onset of seizures or accelerated head growth.

The diagnosis is most easily made by CT scan, on which extracerebral collections of fluid or blood can be identified, and at the same time the dynamic relationship to any brain injuries can be appreciated (Figs. 6, 7). Where sutures or fontanelle are open, direct subdural taps immediately identify traumatic subdural collections, and drainage of this fluid also provides some initial volumetric relief. This immediate improvement in a situation of acute intracranial hypertension can be deceptive, however. The more solid components of an acute hematoma cannot be evacuated by needle drainage, there may be a more significant intracerebral hematoma compartmentalized away from the needle tip, and cerebral edema may be present. Finally, while subdural collections are reduced by repeated taps, this same treatment may encourage the expansion of underlying hydrocephalus (16). A diagnosis of subdural or other intracranial hemorrhage should therefore inspire as prompt and complete an evaluation as is possible, so that all contingencies may be considered in planning neurosurgical treatment. Cerebral angiography may be useful where CT scanning is not available, or in those rare instances when the CT scan and subdural taps are insufficient to settle diagnostic questions.

As with other forms of intracranial trauma, infant subdural hematoma may vary in its treatment requirements. Emergency craniotomy, subdural shunting, and intermittent subdural taps, or a combination of these maneuvers may be indicated in individual cases.

The possibility of child abuse should be seriously considered whenever

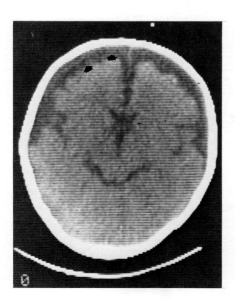

Figure 7. Horizontal CT scan shows bilateral chronic subdural hematomas in a 5-month-old boy. Arrowheads indicate the cortical margin. The subdural collection extends between the cerebral hemispheres along the anterior falx.

subdural hematomas are found in the infant or toddler without adequate explanation, such as documented accident, infectious meningitis, blood dyscrasia, or shunted hydrocephalus. Survey skeletal films for battering should include a full skull and spine series.

It should be reemphasized, however, that while subdural hematoma has special implications in infancy, direct contusion of brain is more often responsible for the neurologic symptoms and chronic sequelae of abusive CNS injury.

FOLK PRACTICES

Certain societal practices can result in cerebral damage that could be inadvertent, but are still dangerous. "Fallen fontanelle" (*caida de molera*) is believed by some Hispanic people to require forceful physical replacement in an infant. The sunken fontanelle, observed in an infant who is perhaps otherwise ill and dehydrated, is thought to represent a mechanical displacement of normal structures, such as might result from a fall or, according to folklore, from sudden withdrawal of a nipple from the infant's mouth. A series of maneuvers may be undertaken to physically "replace" the fontanelle, including upward finger pressure on the hard palate, suction applied to the fontanelle, and bodily inversion with emersion of the fontanelle in boiling water accompanied by vigorous shaking. Subdural hemorrhage and cerebral damage may result (17).

Sewing needles have been found within the cranial cavities of people becoming symptomatic in later years. These have apparently been inserted through open fontanelle and suture lines in infancy, according to case reports from the Middle East. This method for covert infanticide, known in the folklore of that region, might well escape detection unless x-ray films are taken (18,19).

Shaking and vigorous slapping may be used by a panic-stricken parent to correct acute airway obstruction or apnea. Serious cerebral injury can result with mechanics as discussed above.

SPINAL INJURY

Spinal injury is relatively infrequent in early life, a phenomenon attributed to flexibility of the spinal column at this age. When such injury does occur, there is often a wide disparity between the damage sustained by the vertebral column and that suffered by the spinal cord within, suggesting that these elements, although each perhaps tolerant of considerable distortion, are not flexible in identical ways. The infant vertebral column is largely cartilagenous and it can withstand considerable elongation or angulation and still make a good elastic recovery with no evidence of permanent anatomical change. Considerable force is apparently necessary to produce fracture or permanent dislocation in the first two years of life. In contrast, the spinal cord is fixed in position by outgoing roots and radicular blood vessels and by its continuity to brain stem above and tethered filum below. Its blood supply, delivered by segmental radicular vessels, is easily compromised.

From the above it is seen that transient distortion of the vertebral column may result in severe cord damage with no abnormality to be found in the bony spinal column itself. Even total dural and spinal cord disruption can occur without evidence of bony injury (20,21). Ischemic infarction of spinal cord may be a factor in producing severe neurologic deficit, even after minor trauma, with negative myelogram as well as normal plain x-ray films (22,23).

On the contrary, vertebral column injury is often present without neurologic damage evident. Swischuk (24) described the x-ray findings in seven cases of spinal injury as a result of child abuse. In six of these there were x-ray abnormalities noted in the vertebral column, and none of these six children had neurologic deficit; the seventh child had serious neurologic abnormality and an abnormal myelogram, but no fracture or dislocation was found on plain films. Swischuk found intervertebral disc narrowing, notching of the anterior vertebral borders, compression fracture, and dislocation to be characteristic in battering. Severe shaking and hyperflexion were postulated as likely mechanisms. Cullen (25) reports similar findings and conclusions in five children, two of whom probably had neurologic deficit.

Spinal injuries are easily overlooked in the infant and toddler. Partial neurologic deficit in the lower extremities may be difficult to appreciate in the infant, and even complete cord transection may occur at this age with some preservation of reflexes. The development of a kyphosis, without other adequate explanation for anterior compression fracture or disc narrowing, is highly suspicious at this age. Pain on motion of extremities, localized spine tenderness, reluctance to stand, or regression in walking are also suggestive and should inspire x-ray study (24–26). The sudden development of paraplegia, quadriplegia, a transverse sensory level, urinary retention, or progressive neurologic deficit suggesting spinal localization can require study and treatment on an emergency basis.

ASPHYXIA

Mechanical obstruction to respiratory effort, if not immediately fatal, can produce cerebral anoxia and swelling. Coma, seizures, neurologic deficit, and increased intracranial pressure may follow. This type of problem is not rare in childhood, either as a result of accident or abuse.

External and internal occlusion of major airways, termed *suffocation* and *choking* respectively, are frequently accidental. "Overlaying" of the infant by a larger sleeping bedmate, aspiration of a foreign body, or occlusion of nose and mouth by plastic bag or wrapper are allegedly common mechanisms. When the mouth and nose have been forcibly occluded by hand, there may be a telltale pattern of bruises and fingernail scratches. On the contrary, malicious suffocation with a soft object, such as a pillow, may leave no external marks.

It should be emphasized that any healthy fullterm infant over 2 months of age can turn his head away from bed clothes and will cough to clear his airway. Older infants and toddlers do not "smother" accidentally. Similarly, vomiting and aspiration commonly follow profound asphyxia and should not automatically be construed as the cause of the obstructive episode.

The term *strangulation* is usually applied to encircling neck compression, but more specifically indicates airway obstruction accompanied by vascular occlusion. Venous return from the head is more often obstructed than arterial supply. Accidental strangulation and hanging are seen in the first year of life as a result of entanglement in clothing or in strings attached to toys and pacifiers. An infant may become strangulated or his chest may be compressed by wedging between the slats of a crib or, when placed in an undefended adult bed, between bed and wall (27,28). Chest compression can obstruct respiratory effort and venous return in the upper half of the body. Coalescent petechiae beneath the skin and mucous membranes of the upper body and venous hemorrhages in retina and brain are particularly prominent where this type of venous obstruction occurs; such changes are less constant and milder in other types of mechanical asphyxia. In intentional strangulation or chest compression, bruises corresponding to the encircling fingers or ligature may be found. Asphyxial changes may be associated with other injuries produced in the same impulsive act, such as by shaking or striking.

Near-drowning can also leave little or no clear-cut evidence of the event. Reflex laryngospasm may prohibit the direct entry of any fluid into the lungs or aspirated fluid volume may be so small that it has no significant osmotic effect. Pulmonary effusion is, therefore, not invariably present (29,30).

The outlook for children suffering severe asphyxial injury remains poor, despite early resuscitative efforts and vigorous intensive care. Of 22 childhood strangulation victims who lived to be hospitalized, Feldman and Simms (28) report that seven died and three survived with severe neurologic residuals. Need for resuscitation and mechanical ventilation carried the poorest prognosis. In Fandel and Bancalari's series (29) of 34 near-drowning victims, 12 (35%) required mechanical ventilation; six of these (50%) died and four others had severe neurologic sequelae.

Whenever there is a question of asphyxiation, the victim should be admitted to the hospital for observation even if initial examination is negative, since the consequences of pulmonary effusion, cerebral swelling, or upper airway edema and obstruction can be delayed in onset (28,31).

CHRONIC DISABILITY

It is difficult to assess how often physical abuse ends in mental retardation in our society: the definition of "abuse" varies in existing reports; the nature of individual head injury is often unspecified; and the mental status of victims before injury is usually poorly documented. Furthermore, the tutorial, nutritional, and emotional conditions produced by "the abusive environment" may themselves limit intellectual and social performance (2,32,33). There is no question, however, that cerebral injury in early life can result in profound psychomotor deficit, and it is probable that battering contributes significantly to the sector of children requiring chronic institutional care. Buchanan and Oliver (34) estimated that between 3% and 11% of children residing in hospitals for the retarded are handicapped as a result of violent abuse. Of 42 abused children, Martin (32) found 33% to be intellectually impaired and 43% to have other neurologic sequelae. Other studies suggest a somewhat lower (5–20%) incidence of permanent neurologic handicap, but those dying or untestable as a result of battering are excluded from these calculations (2,6,35).

There are some permanent sequelae of CNS injury that are well known to neurologists and neurosurgeons, but are less often appreciated as possible consequences of battering. Post-traumatic hydrocephalus and seizure disorders are fairly common. Visual loss may as often result from damage to optic tracts and cortex as from retinal injury (36). Massive cerebral infarction and atrophy can result in microcephaly, and this has been reported as a consequence of abuse (37). Post-traumatic pituitary insufficiency can result in true growth retardation that is not reversible by correction of environmental factors (38).

Physical or mental disability may be a contributing cause of child abuse as well as its consequence. The frustration of unrealistic expectations of the child, family burdens enhanced by disability, and the weight on the parent of continuous responsibility for personal care can produce altered family dynamics that may predispose to abuse. These problems have been eloquently summarized by Solomons (39). It may be difficult to distinguish the disability that precedes abuse from that which is produced by it.

THE IDENTIFICATION OF ABUSIVE CNS INJURY

The identification of battering requires two separate diagnostic considerations. First, has there been trauma to the body part in question? Second, is this injury accidental or intentional?

Injury or Disease?

Signs and symptoms of CNS involvement may arise as well from intrinsic disease as from injury, and this differentiation must be carefully made. The opinion of a neurologist or neurosurgeon is best obtained as soon as the CNS is implicated by any development, such as seizure, retinal hemorrhage, neurologic deficit, signs of increased intracranial pressure, or coma. Similar care must be taken in evaluating traumatic marks about the head or back, or with spine tenderness, deformity, or immobility. Intrinsic illness and external bruises can be coincidental; a stroke or seizure may be the cause rather than the result of a fall.

As a rule, x-ray films of the skull and spine and a CT scan of the brain are indicated whenever serious CNS trauma is among the diagnostic possibilities in an infant or toddler. Lumbar puncture, EEG, or other special studies may be necessary depending on the neurologist's or neurosurgeon's evaluation. Similar screening for covert CNS damage should be made in every case where other abuse is identified.

In early childhood, *meningitis* and *encephalitis* are important nontraumatic causes of rapidly developing unconsciousness, seizure, or increased intracranial pressure. External evidences of trauma will be absent, CT scan will not show hemorrhage or mass, and lumbar puncture will produce either clear or purulent fluid with elevated protein.

Nontraumatic intracranial hemorrhage may be more difficult to differentiate, since signs and symptoms can be similar to those of trauma without external marks. Retinal hemorrhages, bloody CSF, and extravasation on CT scan can occur in both conditions. Frequently, however, the location and pattern of intracranial bleeding can be recognized on CT scan as more typical for intrinsic disease than for trauma, and CT with contrast enhancement or subsequent arteriography will show the responsible vascular abnormality. Where spontaneous hemorrhage is suspected, studies should be made for blood dyscrasia, tumor with hemorrhage, and possible cardiopulmonary source of *embolus* as well as for *cerebral arteriovenous malformation* or *aneurysm*.

Other conditions deserve special mention in the differential diagnosis of early childhood head injury. Where physical and radiographic findings of trauma are inadequate to account for a child's diminished state of responsiveness, drug intoxication should be considered and appropriate screening studies performed. *Serial seizures* unrelated to trauma can produce unconsciousness, transient focal weakness, and pupillary and reflex changes. With any associated airway obstruction, there may be increased intracranial pressure. At an ambulatory age, an uncontrolled seizure disorder can result in falls, so that the findings of acute or chronic multiple traumas may be superimposed on those of the underlying convulsive state. The neglected infant may be sluggish or unresponsive as a result of *hypothermia*; the malnourished infant under corrective treatment can show transient separation of cranial sutures as a result of "catch-up" cerebral growth rather than any pathologic increase in intracranial pressure (40).

As noted above, distant past trauma should be suspected where there is neurologic deficit, seizure disorder, hydrocephalus, or mental retardation that is not otherwise explained.

Trauma: Accident or Abuse?

Since infants are essentially immobile and dependent, CNS trauma in infancy can be viewed as invariably resulting from either custodial negligence or abuse, excepting for unpreventable accidents. With proper supervision and restriction, even the young walker should not be able to propel himself into serious injury. When a toddler falls to a level surface from standing height, this self-limited drop generally produces minor injury, if any. It is fair to conclude that any significant trauma to a child at these ages is suspect and should be carefully investigated. However, the shape or location of any individual CNS lesion is rarely typical of either accident or abuse, and it may be difficult to identify intentional injury from medical evidence alone. Classically, two sorts of less direct clinical findings are highly suggestive of battering: multiple injuries and injury presenting with inadequate explanation. These concepts are valid for CNS trauma and are helpful.

The presence of multiple injuries, by location or in time, is strong evidence for abuse. Multiple areas of impact can be identified in scalp injury, and this is particularly significant when a repeated pattern is imprinted on or through the scalp, indicating the use of the same object for repeated blows. Similarly, since depressed fractures result from localized impact with a protruding or pointed object, multiple areas of punched-in depression strongly indicate the delivery of multiple blows. Conversely, deformation of the skull by a single, broadly delivered blow can produce several fractures along lines of stress, and even bilateral linear fractures do not necessarily mean multiple injury. Old, healing fractures may be differentiated on x-ray film from fresh fracture lines, or a fracture of one age may be associated with scalp trauma of another. Similarly, the age of an intracranial or intracerebral hematoma may be clearly different from another cranial injury or from injuries elsewhere in the body. Evidence of chronic residuals, such as an unexplained seizure disorder or cerebral atrophy, should raise a suspicion of abuse when the evidence of new trauma is added; but proof is obviously less strong, since the traumatic origin of the residuals usually cannot be established with certainty.

Inadequate or inappropriate explanation for a single injury should immediately raise questions, but the matter may be more difficult to clarify. The extent of craniocerebral injury produced by a given traumatizing event can vary widely, and there are few clinical reports and no experimental studies that enable the examiner to specify the minimum force required to produce each injury. Every case becomes a matter of judgment, based upon clinical experience. As a result, firm conclusion can be reached only within rather gross limitations. For example, the infant slipping from a parent's arms or falling from the height of a bed or lap to the floor may sustain a linear skull fracture or scalp hematoma, but more serious intracranial injury is very unlikely, in the author's experience. Furthermore, this common type of household fall to a flat surface will not account for depressed fracture, penetrating cranial injury, or retinal hemorrhages. This experience is substantiated by the report of Helfer et al. (41). These authors studied the injuries sustained by infants and children under 5 years of age falling from a height of less than 90 cm (35 in) where history was believed reliable and abuse was not a factor. In more than 200 falls sustained at home, 80% resulted in no observable injury, 17% resulted in minor bumps and bruises, and only 3% were somewhat more severe: there were three fractured clavicles, two fractures of the skull, and one fracture of the humerus. None had a serious intracranial injury. In 85 similar hospital incidents, these authors found only one child with a fracture of the skull, and there was no other significant intracranial injury. It may be impossible to state with certainty, however, that serious damage cannot be produced by a fall from just slightly greater height. In the author's experience, there seems to be a critical difference for an infant, for example, in falling 5 to 6 ft as compared to a 3-ft drop, but there is no experimental or statistical evidence to conclusively support this. Again, a discrepancy of mechanism may be more easily appreciated than a disparity in the estimated force required. For example, depressed bone and penetrating skull lesions cannot be produced by impact on a flat surface, and flexion fractures of the vertebral bodies cannot be produced by a blow to the forehead. Even then, care must be taken not to jump to conclusions regarding intent from evidence regarding mechanism, as the following case illustrates:

CASE 1

The baby-sitter reported that he found this 2½-year-old boy lying on his bed with back arched and body stiff, gagging and unresponsive. When he attempted to clear the child's throat and applied mouth-to-mouth resuscitation, the patient vomited and became limp.

The baby-sitter went out of the room momentarily to find a towel with which to wipe off the child's mouth, and when he returned the boy was found lying on the floor at the bedside, still unresponsive. He was brought immediately to the hospital where he was observed to have a focal seizure involving the left body-half. Further examination showed moderate nuchal rigidity, multiple retinal hemorrhages, and little response other than withdrawal to painful stimuli. As the child became slightly more responsive, a right hemiparesis could be identified. There were no other stigmata of trauma found. Lumbar puncture produced grossly blood fluid which was ultimately sterile on culture. A CT scan showed subarachnoid blood with a wedge-shaped area of extravasation along the left occipital falx in a pattern consistent with acceleration injury. Contrast enhancement showed no other abnormality.

The sudden onset and evidence of subarachnoid hemorrhage initially suggested spontaneous intracranial bleeding, but the characteristic CT finding, with no physical evidence of trauma, raised the question of injury as a result of shaking. On further questioning of the family and the baby-sitter, and without revealing what specific maneuver was suspected, the baby-sitter volunteered that, after several attempts at mouth-to-mouth resuscitation, he picked up the child, held him upright, and tried to "shake some life into him." He then resumed resuscitative efforts and also attempted to stimulate him with cold water. After thorough investigation, the home situation was judged reliable and nonabusive, and it was concluded that the child was the unfortunate victim of both a seizure disorder and a well-intentioned but misguided attempt to resuscitate.

Where there is no explanation at all for an injury, careful search must be made for possible causes before presuming that the lack of explanation is suspect. A wide range of disorders can result in injuries that seem disproportionate to cause. Difficult labor and delivery, for example, can result in retinal hemorrhages or serious craniospinal damage that may not be obvious initially. Although the retinal hemorrhages may clear in a matter of several days, scalp hematomas, depressed fracture, manifestations of cerebral contusion, or the signs of cervical fracture-dislocation can all endure to be discovered even after many weeks of life. Subdural hematoma is a well-known complication of hydrocephalus, both after shunting and with minor trauma in the unshunted patient (16). Fractures are more easily produced in the handicapped, bedridden child who is osteoporotic and has imbalances of muscle tone. For example, fractures of the femur may occur spontaneously in the infant with myelodysplasia. Seizure disorders may result in repeated minor injuries as a result of falls in the ambulatory child. Other types of underlying disease should also be considered where injuries present without apparent explanation. In the following case, a congenital deformity of the craniospinal junction exemplifies the sort of problem that may be revealed only when a major neurologic deficit is produced by trivial injury:

CASE 2

This 5-year-old girl was brought to the hospital emergency room because of pain and immobility in the neck, which the mother reported had developed immediately after the child fell from bed to floor, striking her left shoulder and head. Examination showed an alert, frightened child with severe, diffuse posterior cervical tenderness and reluctance to move her head in any direction. There were no external marks. There was weakness in upper extremities and hyperreflexia in lower extremities in a pattern consistent with high cervical cord injury. Initial cervical spine films showed dislocation of C_1 on C_2

(Fig. 8a). Because the injury seemed inconsistent with the reported mechanism, abuse was initially considered. Suspicions were dispelled with further x-ray evaluation, however. Tomograms of the cervical spine (Fig. 8b) showed a congenital defect in ossification of the odontoid process with inherent C_{1-2} instability resulting, a situation wherein dislocation and serious neurologic deficit can be precipitated by relatively minor trauma. Spinal fusion was successfully performed.

The physician's opinion regarding mechanism of injury is often weighed heavily in determinations of child abuse. Legal agencies may press the physician for an unequivocal statement, since there is often no other tangible evidence available. Careful consideration must be given before any firm position is taken, and the physician should also clearly indicate if no absolute conclusions can be drawn from the data available. Unfortunately, conscientious consideration is not always enough. Since the medical opinion may be pivotal, the witness must be solidly prepared for attack in court by whichever side is displeased with his conclusions. Whatever tactic or humbug an attorney may employ in behalf of his client should not be surprising, as the author discovered in the following case:

CASE 3

This 7-month-old male was brought to the hospital emergency room for treatment of a frontal scalp laceration, which the parents said he sustained by rolling off a bed approximately 2 feet above floor level, striking his head on a radio, which was on the

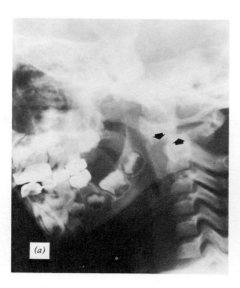 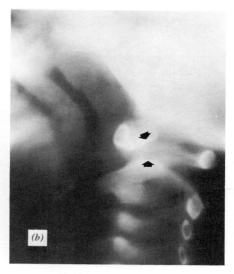

Figure 8. Cervical spine x-ray films of a 5-year-old girl with serious spinal cord damage following minor trauma (Case 2). (a) Initial plain lateral film suggests fracture of the odontoid with considerable dislocation (arrowheads). (b) Subsequent tomograms show the margins of separate odontoid segments to be smooth and intact (arrowheads), indicating a developmental origin for the segregated odontoid tip, accounting for the patient's susceptibility to dislocation.

floor at the bedside. The height of the infant's drop from bed to radio was an estimated 18 inches. There had been no reported loss of consciousness. The scalp laceration was initially sutured by an emergency room physician who noted no underlying abnormality, but neurosurgical consultation was sought when subsequent films suggested depressed skull fracture (Fig. 9). Recognition of the problem and a recommendation for surgical exploration evoked agitation and anger in the father, who heatedly denied that the injury could be anything but trivial. At surgery a triangular area of bony depression was found, with its apex of impaction extended through torn dura and into cerebral substance. The bone could be removed only piecemeal, using instruments and considerable force. Postoperative recovery was uneventful. A mild right hemiparesis gradually cleared, and no other evidence of trauma was found.

Because of the discrepancy between history and findings, abuse investigation was made. When the circumstances of the case were provided in court by the author, who was the attending neurosurgeon, with the opinion that the accident described was inadequate to explain the injury, the father's attorney sought to defend the parents against a charge of abuse by attacking the credibility of the witness and the hospital. How, the attorney asked, could such a depressed fracture be missed by the physician intitially suturing the laceration, yet be found so readily on x-ray and by the neurosurgical consultant? Considering this and the family's description of a fall, which was obviously minor, was it not even more likely that the child had sustained a second, subsequent injury? Specifically, how could the neurosurgeon on the witness stand prove that he himself or some other staff member had not dropped the child in the course of hospital evaluation? The judge actually seemed interested in pursuing this question, until it was pointed out by the witness that it would be almost impossible to drop the baby so as to produce a depressed fracture which would be perfectly congruent with the scalp laceration already present. The child was ultimately removed by the court to a foster home.

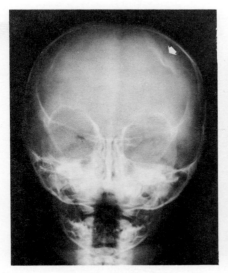
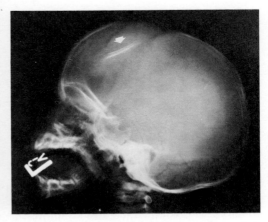

Figure 9. Anteroposterior and lateral skull films show the double density characteristic of depressed skull fracture (arrowheads) in a 7-month-old boy reported to have fallen only 18 inches (Case 3).

MANAGEMENT IN THE INTENSIVE CARE UNIT

All too often, acute CNS injury brings an abuse victim to the hospital intensive care unit (ICU) in mortal jeopardy. Those experienced in this situation will recognize its special needs.

The physical care of a critically injured child can be burden enough for any physician or ICU, yet the element of abuse adds day-to-day demands that cannot be ignored. The charged emotional and legal atmosphere surrounding this type of injury requires that continuous special attention be given to protect the interests of every individual and agency involved. Pending investigation, a court order frequently has lifted the child from parental custody and prohibited hospital discharge to their care. The parents, often affected by resentment and guilt and perhaps also fearing the legal consequences of a poor medical outcome, can become demanding and belligerent. Polarization is enhanced when medical personnel express their own anger or indignation on behalf of the child, and they must be reminded to maintain objectivity and sympathy for the family's interest.

The burden of continuous patient management is greatly eased when all concerned understand that the nursing unit and the child's medical care are to be thought of separately from any social and legal consideration surrounding the alleged abuse, and every effort should be made to maintain this sense of immunity for the patient, family, and staff while on the intensive care unit. Full information regarding a patient's progress should be freely given to appropriate family members, but on-going discussion between medical personnel and family regarding causality and responsibility is best avoided once the matter is placed in the hands of proper authorities. Investigational interviews should not be allowed in public areas, such as nursing units or parents' waiting rooms; personnel should scrupulously avoid discussing the case with those who are not directly involved, and inquiries from the press should be referred to hospital or legal authorities.

At the same time, however, responsible staff members must remain mindful of their legal responsibilities, to protect themselves and their institution and to avoid any action that might become a significant factor in subsequent investigation or trial. For example, child protection authorities are usually prompt in providing a written court order to remove a child from parental custody and prohibit hospital discharge when battering is suspected; they are often much more casual, offering only telephone release, when their investigation subsequently suggests the parents to be innocent. This should not be accepted, nor should the original restraining order be removed from the chart. Both the initiating order and a written release should remain as permanent parts of the hospital record as the instiution's receipts for the enforced hospitalization and for the release of a child to acceptable custodians. Permission for surgical procedures must be obtained from appropriate legal guardians, if other than the family, but it is always best to discuss any major treatment plan with the parents, so that they do not feel thrust aside. It is even helpful to have their signed permission as well as that of the guardian so that consonance in management is clearly demonstrated. The author does not recommend organ donation or discontinuance of life support efforts in any case where legal action may be pending, even when these things are desired by the legally responsible parent or guardian.

SUMMARY

Injuries to the central nervous system (CNS) account for a majority of the deaths and chronic organic disability resulting from child abuse. Any type of CNS injury can occur as a result of abuse, but there is a predisposition to certain injury patterns because of the special structural qualities of infancy and early childhood. These include a soft, pliable skull, open fontanelle and suture lines, a supple spine, poor muscular control of a relatively large head, and the extreme sensitivity of a developing brain to mechanical stress or ischemia. Although infant subdural hematoma is often associated with abuse, cerebral contusion is much more frequently responsible for the resulting neurologic disability and deaths. Trauma to the CNS must be carefully differentiated from intrinsic disease, and intentional injury may be difficult to segregate from that which is accidental, excepting for a few characteristic lesions. Multiple injuries and inadequacy of explanation are the most helpful factors in identifying most abusive CNS injuries.

Every effort should be made to remove moral and legal considerations from the intensive care environment, and medical communication with the victim's family should be dignified, impartial, and compassionate. This segregation of functions facilitates patient management and is in the best tradition of the health care professions.

REFERENCES

1. Tate RJ: Facial injuries associated with the battered child syndrome. *Br J Oral Surg* 9:41, 1971.
2. Smith SM, Hanson R: 134 Battered children: a medical and psychological study. *Br Med J* 3:666, 1974.
3. Sills JA, Thomas LJ, Rosenbloom L: Non-accidental injury: a two-year study in Central Liverpool. *Dev Med Child Neurol* 19:26, 1977.
4. Kogutt MS, Swischuk LE, Fagan CJ: Patterns of injury and significance of uncommon fractures in the battered child syndrome. *Am J Roentgenol Rad Ther Nucl Med* 121:143, 1974.
5. Ryan MG, Davis AA, Oates RK: One hundred and eighty-seven cases of child abuse and neglect. *Med J Aust* 2:623, 1977.
6. O'Neill JA, Meacham WF, Griffin PP, et al: Patterns of injury in the battered child syndrome. *J Trauma* 13:332, 1973.
7. Eisenbrey AB: Retinal hemorrhage in the battered child. *Child's Brain* 5:40, 1979.
8. Schenker JG, Gombos GM: Retinal hemorrhage in the newborn. *Obstet Gynecol* 27:521, 1966.
9. Tomasi LG, Rosman NP: Purtscher retinopathy in the battered child syndrome. *Am J Dis Child* 129:1335, 1975.
10. Caffey J: Multiple fractures in the long bones of infants suffering from chronic subdural hematoma. *Am J Roentgenol Rad Ther Nucl Med* 56:163, 1946.
11. Ommaya AK, Faas F, Yarnell P: Whiplash injury and brain damage. *JAMA* 204:285, 1968.

12. Guthkelch AN: Infantile subdural hematoma and its relationship to whiplash injuries. *Br Med J* 2:430, 1971.

13. Caffey J: On the theory and practice of shaking infants. *Am J Dis Child* 124:161, 1972.

14. Caffey J: The whiplash shaken infant syndrome: manual shaking by the extremities with whiplash-induced intracranial and intraocular bleedings, linked with residual permanent brain damage and mental retardation. *Pediatrics* 54:396, 1974.

15. Zimmerman RA, Bilaniuk LT, Bruce D, et al: Computed tomography of craniocerebral injury in the abused child. *Radiology* 130:687, 1979.

16. Klein DM: Simultaneous subdural effusion and hydrocephalus in infancy. *Surg Neurol* 6:363, 1976.

17. Guarnaschelli J, Lee J, Pitts FW: "Fallen fontanelle" (Caida de Mollera). *JAMA* 222:1545, 1972.

18. Ameli NO, Alimohammadi A: Attempted infanticide by insertion of sewing needles through fontanels. *J Neurosurg* 33:721, 1970.

19. Askenasy HM, Kosary IZ, Braham J: Sewing needle in the brain with delayed neurological manifestations. *J Neurosurg* 18:554, 1961.

20. LeBlanc HJ, Nadell J: Spinal cord injuries in children. *Surg Neurol* 2:411, 1974.

21. Leventhal HR: Birth injuries of the spinal cord. *J Pediatr* 56:447, 1960.

22. Ahmann PA, Smith SA, Schwartz JF, et al: Spinal cord infarction due to minor trauma in children. *Neurology* 25:301, 1975.

23. Glasauer FE, Cares HL: Traumatic paraplegia in infancy. *JAMA* 219:38, 1972.

24. Swischuk LE: Spine and spinal cord trauma in the battered child syndrome. *Radiology* 92:733, 1969.

25. Cullen JC: Spinal lesions in battered babies. *J Bone Joint Surg* 57B:364, 1975.

26. Dickson RA, Leatherman KD: Spinal injuries in child abuse: case report. *J Trauma* 18:811, 1978.

27. Bass M: Asphyxial crib death. *N Engl J Med* 296:555, 1977.

28. Feldman KW, Simms RJ: Strangulation in childhood: epidemiology and clinical course. *Pediatrics* 65:1079, 1980.

29. Fandel I, Bancalari E: Near-drowing in children: clinical aspects. *Pediatrics* 58:573, 1976.

30. Hoff BH: Multisystem failure: a review with special reference to drowning. *Crit Care Med* 7:310, 1979.

31. Conn AW, Edmonds JF, Barker GA: Cerebral resuscitation in near-drowning. *Pediatr Clin North Am* 26:691, 1979.

32. Martin H: The child and his development, in Kempe CH, and Helfer RE (eds): *Helping the Battered Child and His Family*. Philadelphia, JB Lippincott, 1972, p 93.

33. Elmer E, Gregg GS: Developmental characteristics of abused children. *Pediatrics* 40:596, 1967.

34. Buchanan A, Oliver JE: Abuse and neglect as a cause of mental retardation: a study of 140 children admitted to subnormality hospitals in Wiltshire. *Br J Psychiatry* 131:458, 1977.

35. James HE, Schut L: The neurosurgeon and the battered child. *Surg Neurol* 2:415, 1974.

36. Harcourt B, Hopkins D: Ophthalmic manifestations of the battered-baby syndrome. *Br Med J* 3:398, 1971.

37. Oliver JE: Microcephaly following baby battering and shaking. *Br Med J* 2:262, 1975.

38. Miller WL, Kaplan SL, Grumbach MM: Child abuse as a cause of post-traumatic hypopituitarism. *N Engl J Med* 302:724, 1980.

39. Solomons G: Child abuse and developmental disabilities. *Dev Med Child Neurol* 21:101, 1979.

40. Capitanio MA, Kirkpatrick JA: Widening of the cranial sutures. A roentgen observation during periods of accelerated growth in patients treated for deprivation dwarfism. *Radiology* 92:53, 1969.

41. Helfer RE, Slovis TL, Black M: Injuries resulting when small children fall out of bed. *Pediatrics* 60:533, 1977.

6
The Neuro-psycho-developmental Aspects of Child Abuse and Neglect

Harold P. Martin

To understand the neuro-psycho-developmental consequences of abuse and neglect on children, abuse needs to be viewed as a syndrome, wherein physical mistreatment is the most prominent sign, indeed, the sine qua non of the syndrome. But physical trauma must be appreciated as a marker of a more extensive picture of family dysfunction. It is an indication that there is an aberrant parent-child interaction that is pervasive and many faceted. Physical mistreatment should prompt the professional to look for other signs of harmful parenting practices. For, it may well be that neurologic damage, developmental deviation, and personality abnormality are rooted in other facets of the syndrome and not etiologically based in the physical trauma per se.

Physical trauma to a child is inherently harmful; it can result in a spectrum of sequelae from death, through brain damage, to no discernible permanent consequence. Physical trauma, like fever or a seizure, can result in physiological and psychological consequence to a child; and they each may require treatment. But perhaps more importantly, they alert the physician to some larger process that requires investigation; for example, what has caused a seizure, an elevated body temperature or the infliction of trauma. Other potentially harmful processes at work need to be explored.

In essence, physical abuse of a child may lead us to discover that there are other dangers to the child such as physical neglect, emotional abuse, psycho-pathologic parents, sexual abuse, or undernutrition; any one of which, or in combination, can harm the child. Further clarification of the components of the syndrome in each child is essential, for neuro-psycho-developmental consequences to the child may result from various aspects of the abusive home.

In this chapter, the neurologic, psychological, and developmental consequences of child maltreatment are presented. The etiology, pathogenesis, and treatment implications are discussed.

MORBIDITY OF CHILD ABUSE

Neuro-developmental Morbidity

Studies of abused children report impaired cognitive, motor, language, or learning abilities (1–15). The morbidity rates are usually so impressive that there seems to be no question that there is a correlation between abuse and later neuro-developmental disability, even without control groups with which to compare. For example, one of the very first reports of abused children described an 88% morbidity using mental retardation, speech and language delay, emotional disturbance, and physical defects as criteria (16). Over one-half of the abused children (all of whom had had fractures) were later functionally retarded. Almost one-third had independent signs of brain damage. Martin found in two early studies of abused children that at follow-up over 30% of the children had low intelligence quotients (7,8). Of the abused children in one study 31% had significant and handicapping neurologic findings, ranging from paresis, sensory loss, and focal signs, to less severe but handicapping neurologic abnormalities. Less than one-half of the children had fractures or head injuries, suggesting that the morbidity may not have been exclusively due to structural brain damage.

There are now appearing more studies with control populations, all of which continue to warn the clinician of the high risk of neurologic and developmental sequelae. Sangrund et al., reporting on abused and neglected children, showed that there was seven to eight times greater chance of IQs below 70 than in a nonabused control group (14). Oates and his colleagues, in a series of papers from Australia (5,13,17), show significantly higher risk of impaired neuro-developmental function as compared with control groups. A master's thesis recently showed lower mental abilities on the Bayley test in infancy as compared with a control group (18).

There are data concerning cerebral palsy as well as other forms of brain damage. MacKeith noted that in about one-half of the 1,600 new cases of cerebral palsy and 600 cases of severe mental handicap in England there was no adequate cause found (19,20). He estimated that approximately 400 of these cases per year are a result of child abuse. Solomons, in the Presidential Address to the American Academy of Cerebral Palsy in 1978, highlighted the risk of cerebral palsy in the abused child (21). He points out that head injury and intracranial hemorrhage are the two most common causes of acquired motor handicap, suggesting that physical abuse may be a prominent cause of cerebral palsy.

Retardation remains the neuro-developmental problem of most concern in surviving abused children. Buchanan and Oliver reviewed 140 children sequentially admitted to two residential schools for retardation in 1972 and 1973 (2,22). Of these children 22% had evidence of physical assaults before admission to the hospital. At least 3% of the children had "definitely" suffered assaults that caused brain damage and 11% of the children had physical abuse that "could have been" the cause of the mental handicap. Even more shocking was the evidence that 41% had suffered a habitual pattern of child neglect, with 24% of the total population having neglect as a contributory factor in reducing intellectual potential. They emphasize the importance of abuse and neglect as a cause of mental retardation, which may equal or exceed metabolic disorders or even Down's syndrome. These data also emphasize what Kent showed in a study of children in custody in Los Angeles County (6). Kent wrote that neglected children are at greater risk of retardation than physically abused children, although it is important to note that the two frequently coexist.

Appelbaum studied 30 abused children with a control group and found the Mental Index of the abused to be 75 compared to 106 in the nonabused matched controls. Motor abilities were also affected in the abused infants as they had a Motor Index of 85 compared with 125 in the controls (23).

Most of these studies and reports are descriptions of certain subsets of abused children. They may be children who come to a specific hospital or children who had fractures. In some studies, abused children who are retarded or brain damaged are deliberately excluded from investigation. This makes the true incidence of neuro-developmental disability impossible to document precisely.

Some reports of abused children point out that even when the abused children are not clinically low in mental function, they are lower than nonabused siblings or control children. Cohn's review of federally-funded treatment programs for abused children (3) indicated that the children scored at or slightly below one standard deviation below the mean, so that these children were functioning poorly but not evidencing grossly serious delays. A recently completed study of 5- to 8-year-old abused children (where retarded children were deliberately excluded from study) showed that the children had clinically normal IQs (24). However, the IQs were 11 points lower than a very carefully matched control group. In addition to neurologic abnormality, cerebral palsy, and mentally retarded function, two other neuro-developmental problems require brief mention—language dysfunction and learning disability.

Language seems especially vulnerable to all types of insults, including child abuse (3,25,26). In Martin's study of abused children, it was noted that 43% of the abused children with normal intelligence test scores had language delays of significance (7). A more recent study found that at follow-up 36% of abused children had language delays as compared with only 8% of the controls (27).

Even when the abused child has normal mental abilities, learning disabilities are frequent. Kline first alerted us to the high frequency of learning disabilities in the abused population (28). In a follow-up study of 58 abused children, 27% of the school-aged children were having significant learning problems that could not be accounted for by mental deficiency (10). A more recent 6-year study of neglected children reported that 66% had reading disabilities (5). A recent study in Boulder, Colorado's public schools revealed that there were over four times the proportion of abused/neglected children in special education than in the regular classrooms. This increase was found in every type of special education program, including those for the learning disabled (29). There can be no doubt but that the abused/neglected child is at heightened risk of neuro-developmental damage and disability.

Psychological Morbidity

There is much less documentation and description of the psychological morbidity of child abuse. Yet, the caseworker, physician, or teacher who works with abused children regularly finds that they have disturbing personality traits. A great deal more work needs to be done to clarify the various psychological scars in abused children.

The clinician must realize from the outset that there is no pathognomonic personality of abused children. There is no specific set of traits and characteristics that are diagnostic of, nor even necessarily typical of, abused children. But almost every abused child pays some psychological price for being reared in an abusive family. The exact typology of the abused child's personality will vary according to factors such as the type of parents, age of abuse, type of treatment given the family, and innate factors within the child.

In Cohn's review of three treatment programs for abused children, she notes that 70% of the children did not relate well with peers and 57% had deviant interrelationships with adults (3). Over one-half of the children had a poor self-concept and had difficulty giving or receiving affection. They were described as generally unhappy children with over 40% exhibiting aggression or apathy and having difficulty in reacting to changes in their environment.

Martin and Beezley's description of 50 abused children (10) points out the extremes of behavior, noting that the child may be quite oppositional, or conversely, quite obsequious and unduly concerned about pleasing others. They were most impressed with the children's general unhappiness and poor self-concept.

Aggressive behavior of abused children has been noted by many. Green, in a series of papers (30–32), emphasizes aggression that is turned inward in forms of self-abuse. In one report, 8.3% of abused children, whose mean age was 8.5 years, had attempted suicide; in addition, 20% had self-mutilative behavior. Kent (6) and Reidy (33) have also documented the aggressiveness of abused children. In a more recent study of toddlers and matched controls, George and Main (34) described abused children as frequently physically assaulting their peers and harrassing their caregivers verbally and nonverbally. This seems especially significant given the young age (1–3 years of age) of the children. The reader must understand that all abused children are not overtly aggressive, and even more importantly, may only act out their aggression in specific settings while inhibiting their aggressivity in other settings.

There is a body of data that suggests that the abused child is at higher risk of aggressive behavior with passing years (35–38). Records and interviews with adults in prison for assaultive crimes show high percentages of inmates who reported being from abusive homes. Further, the intergenerational "transmission" of abusive behavior makes us consider abused children at high risk of growing up to perpetuate a family pattern of abusive behavior, if there is no effective treatment for the child.

Lewis et al.'s research (39) with juvenile delinquents also correlates aggressive assaultive behavior in juvenile delinquents with a history of being abused, as well as having witnessed interpersonal violence in the home. Earlier epidemiologic studies by Lewis et al. (40,41) correlated injuries about the face and head and other forms of child abuse to more violent offenses in two groups of incarcerated and nonincarcerated delinquent adolescents. Bradley (42) correlated borderline personality disorder with early maternal deprivation, without clarifying whether physical abuse was part of the emotionally neglectful environment or not.

After general unhappiness, poor self-concept, and aggressivity, the most striking psychological problem of abused children is impaired interpersonal relationships. Not unexpectedly, emotional attachments to adults are frequently deviant. This often manifests in children by indiscriminately friendly and even affectionate behavior to virtual strangers. Perhaps just as frequently, the child reacts opposite, with unduly prolonged anxiety and fear of new acquaintances. A recent study of 12- to 19-month-old children with nonorganic failure-to-thrive, when compared with a control group, showed more problems with firm attachment of infant to mother (43). Gaensbauer's study of abused infants and toddlers (44) demonstrates early signs of interpersonal deviation; the infants showed poor ability to communicate emotion and demonstrated withdrawal and shallowness of emotional communication.

The clinician must consider the adaptations that the child has had to make to growing up in an abusive environment. While the child may have no overt symptoms of emotional disturbance, this same child may have traits and personality characteristics that impede normal childhood activities of work, play, learning, and peer relations. Some symptoms, such as aggression, may not surface until adolescence. The child may behave in an adaptive way so as not to signal others of his emotional distress and thereby exhibit inhibition and shy withdrawn behavior. The overly compliant, shy, or inhibited child is of special concern, inasmuch as he does not openly signal adults of his distress. Just as it may be only the squeaky wheel that gets attention, it is all too often only the acting-out child who is noticed and given services.

It is clear that abused children are at high risk of emotional disturbance. It is uncommon for an abused child to escape paying some psychological price for growing up in an abusive home. The question for the clinician is how deep and pervasive the emotional problems of the child are and to what degree they are impeding normal growth and development.

NEURO-DEVELOPMENTAL DYSFUNCTION PRECEDING ABUSE

When a clinician sees an abused child and also notes retarded function or other signs of neurologic abnormality, the question arises as to whether this dysfunction preceded the abusive incident or was secondary to abuse. Indeed, the question has been raised as to whether retarded, anomalous, or dysfunctional children are at greater risk of abuse than their more fortunate peers.

Cohorts of abused children are overrepresented by premature births and/or low birth weights. Most investigators have noted this, recording that from 20% to over 30% of abused children had low birth weights. Lynch, from England, reported on a group of 25 abused children and their supposedly nonabused siblings (45,46). She found that the abused children came from pregnancies and deliveries that were more fraught with medical complications than their nonabused siblings. Further, she stresses a higher frequency of separation of newborn and mother, secondary to medical illness in the newly born baby. The question is posed, then, as to whether children who are different from birth are at greater risk of being abused.

The answer is a tentative but complex yes. It is clear that the overwhelming majority of premature or small-for-dates infants are not abused; indeed, they are parented quite nicely. Similarly, most children born to mothers who had difficult pregnancies are loved and well parented. However, each of these factors increases the chances of abusive behavior by some parents.

There are some adults who are at higher risk of abusive behavior than the average parent. It may be that some special and specific conditions have to be met for that parent, otherwise adequate, to cross over the line and become abusive. It may be social stress or psychological stress that triggers the maltreatment. It might also be a particularly unrewarding baby, an infant for whom it is more difficult to care or a baby who is less capable of eliciting and reinforcing good parenting. The newborn whose nervous system is less mature or capable than average may be just such a baby. These children are typically more difficult to feed, less easy to soothe, and may be more irritable or lethargic. When the expectations of parents and clinicians are for the child to be normal, this child may elicit anger and frustration in any parent. When that parent, confronted with such a minimally rewarding baby, is an adult with a greater than usual propensity to mistreat a child, the child's condition may ignite the abusive behavior. Clinicians who work in high-risk follow-up baby clinics are aware of the difficulties in parenting many neurologically immature babies. When child abuse is seen as an etiologically multifactorial syndrome, then the temperament and responsivitiy of the child can be viewed as additive factors leading to the maltreatment.

If, then, there are a subset of abused children who start life with an imperfect nervous system, it might well be that these children will manifest, as a group, more neurologic abnormalities and less competent mental functioning in later life, even if the parenting had been normal. It is known that prematures and small-for-dates newborns are at some increased risk for later developmental deviations (47). The morbidity of child abuse may be partially based, in some children, in a preexisting immature or slightly dysfunctional nervous system, related to prematurity, intrauterine growth retardation, or illness in the neonatal period.

The question still remains as to whether the overtly abnormal newborn is at increased risk of inflicted parental trauma. The literature is not precise on this point. There are a few investigators who have found increased prevalences of congenitally retarded children in their cohorts of abused children. However, more frequently, this has not been the case. Some feel that the child who is diagnosed as mentally retarded or otherwise abnormal is not at increased risk of abuse, but may be at increased risk of parental neglect. Unquestionably, there are some adults who will physically abuse a retarded child or a child with a variety of congenital anomalies. However, this is felt to be uncommon in the experience of mental retardation center professionals. A recent paper corroborates this view (48) by pointing out the greater risk of neglect than abuse in retarded children.

It is the child who is slightly or subtly different from his peers and for whom there are normal expectations who seems at increased risk for abuse. This child may fail to meet those normal expectations. The identified abnormal newborn does not usually precipitate normal expectations in professionals and parents. In the child presumed to be normal but who is subtly different, there are not the support systems supplied to parents that are usually established for parents of a new baby with Down's syndrome or some anatomical anomaly. And so, the slightly slow or immature baby is presented to the parents and is presumed to be as easy to care for as any other baby.

The overtly "different" baby may be at increased risk of parental neglect. The equivalent of total parental neglect is the immediate relinquishment and institutionalization of the infant, which used to be so common in this country. Even though that practice is less common now, neglect in the home is still a not uncommon adaptation for some parents to make to a handicapped child.

In addition to considering the baby who is subtly different or imperfect being at increased risk of deviant parenting, another paradigm to consider is the transactional model of Sameroff (49,50). Both the parent and the child contribute to the interaction in such a way as to change the other's behavior. Perhaps the temperament research of Chess, Thomas, and Birch (51–53) points this out most clearly by noting that it is the match between a baby's personality and the adult personality that is critical, rather than the presence of any particular trait in the child or in the adult per se. It is not the exact temperament or neuro-developmental profile of a baby that might make prediction of later adaptation as possible as the match between that baby and the caregiver. Zeskind and Ramey have shown this in another type of research (54). In a control group of small for gestational age (SGA) babies who did not have special infant stimulation, lagging developmental abilities were accompanied by less and less attentive and appropriate parenting, which could then in turn negatively affect the child's subsequent development. It is within the rubric of a bidirectional transaction where we can appreciate the complex and subtle early basis of developmental and psychological delay in abused children.

In summary, it may well be that some of the developmental delay seen in abused and neglected children could be related to biological high-risk factors that preceded the mistreatment. The possibility is much more likely that a transactional paradigm should be looked for to tease out the preabuse factors. The imperfect or slightly different baby may affect the parent-child interaction in such a way as to then deleteriously affect the child's development. Werner's classic Island of Kauai studies suggest just such an interplay between high-risk events, parenting, and subsequent outcome (55,56). There is unconvincing data that obviously and seriously impaired or anomalous children are at increased risk of abuse, although parental neglect may be the outcome of such deviancy in children.

ETIOLOGY AND PATHOGENESIS OF THE MORBIDITY OF CHILD ABUSE AND NEGLECT

Given the previous section, the question remains as to why and how mistreated children are at such high risk of neuro-psycho-developmental deviancy. Neurologic damage, developmental delay, and psychological problems may each be the result of at least three basic causes: biological damage from physical assault or physical neglect, a pervasive pattern of aberrant parent-child relationship, or iatrogenic complications of intervention.

Biological Damage

Biological damage to the central nervous system from inflicted trauma is the most obvious cause of neuro-developmental abnormality in the abused child. Trauma to the head can result in hemorrhage, edema, atrophy, death of neurons, or hydrocephalus. Even shaking of infants has been shown to cause bleeding within the skull (57) so that biological damage to the brain can occur without a history or without signs on physical examination of assault to the head of the young child. The entire panorama of neurologic sequelae may follow these pathologic processes, with the most commonly noted being mental retardation, cerebral palsy, neuromotor dysfunction, seizure disorder, learning disabilities, and sensory impairment. In infants, retinal hemorrhage and other pathologic processes in the eye may result in impaired vision. Damage to the eight cranial nerve or middle ear are less common but are not rare.

The neglect of children may also result in neuro-psycho-developmental deviations. Up to 30% of abused children are nutritionally deprived or have other signs of physical neglect (7,58–60). There is adequate evidence that calorie and protein malnutrition during periods of rapid brain growth can cause structural and biochemical changes in the brains of animals (61–65). There is also rather good evidence that this type of undernutrition correlates with poor head growth and neurologic damage, including retardation, in the human (66–70). Even after 2 years of age, poor nutrition affects learning, attention span, activity level, and perhaps through these mechanisms, mental functioning (71–72).

There are other forms of physical neglect that may play some role in delayed development of the abused child. Investigations have noted that abused children are less healthy than other children, with more lapses in physical health care. This raises the question of a relationship between inadequately treated middle ear infections and long-term delays in language and speech function (73–75). The increased frequency of illness in abused children raises the possibility that parental neglect may play a role in the unhealthy child having less opportunity for learning.

The effects of physical neglect and emotional deprivation on the personality of the abused child, via a biological model, might be considered. One model of viewing this would be to consider biological changes in the brain from emotional neglect. Kandel has discussed the potential for changes in central nervous system structure and function due to life experiences (76).

Perhaps it is easier to consider the behavior of children with biological damage to their brains. Modulation of sensory input, inhibition of impulses, social perception, and adaptation to changes in the environment are all clearly regulated by the brain and can be altered by biological changes in the central nervous system. Empirically, it is known that the incidence of emotional disturbance in children with brain damage or dysfunction (even excluding those with mental retardation) is six times greater than the incidence in the general population of children (77). And so while the exact pathogenesis is unclear, a provocative consideration is that some of the personality sequellae in abused children may be secondary to aberrations in brain structure and function from inflicted trauma or from their distorted life experiences.

The Abusive Milieu

It is the whole fabric of the abusive home that is the basis of most neuro-developmental delays in abused children. After eliminating the abused children with neurologic findings and those with a history of head trauma, the remainder of the children's intelligence scores vary according to the stability of the home, whether it be biological, foster, or adoptive (8). Further, the mental functioning of the child years after abuse is related to the number of moves the child experiences and the sense of permanence or impermanence the child perceives in his present family placement. This section will detail some of the dynamics by which abusive parenting styles can stultify learning and competence and affect personality development.

Abusive families might be artifically divided into those who do and those who do not emotionally neglect the child. The neglectful parents are basically not invested in the child's welfare and supply inadequate nurturance and understanding. In layman's terms, there is insufficient love for the child, an ingredient that is needed for normal psychological growth and development. A substantial minority of abused children come from such homes. The emotional deprivation the child suffers is usually more potent than the physical assaults in leading to psychic trauma and distortions of personality.

In other abusive families there is considerable investment and interest in the child but it is a distorted and pathological investment. In many abusive families, compliance, obedience, and meeting of parental expectations (which are un-realistically high) are the major investment the parents have in the child. While these parents are attached to their child and invested in his welfare, the method of parenting is a coercive, threatening attempt to get the child to comply with expectations. This goes beyond a reasonable authoritarian style of parenting, as it includes severe physical assaults when the child is not responding in martinet fashion to the parents' admonitions and expectations.

Another common type of abusive home deserves mention as a cause of psychological deviation in the child. This is the family wherein there is a dynamic of role-reversal between parent and child. Here again, this is a parent who is attached to and invested in the child. In this situation, the parent, usually quite lonely, with a long history of feeling unloved, has expectations that the new baby will make life better and supply love and caring to the parent and restore or instill a positive sense of self in the adult.

This expectation is, of course, almost always doomed to failure. This child is expected to adapt to this home by forfeiting his childhood and becoming, quite prematurely, the "parent" to the mother or father. Occasionally this is acted out by the child taking physical care of the parent. More often, it is a subtle interaction wherein the child is required to take psychological care of the adult, supplying love, understanding, and empathy to the parent, rather than the reverse. The child is abused when he does not meet this assignment. This mistreated child often presents as an obsequious and cooperative child and may not exhibit, in early childhood, symptoms or signs that alert us to his psychological dilemmas. The emotional consequences more often show up in poor peer relations, delays in developmental progress, and a poor sense of self.

These three types of parents—the non-invested neglectful; the lonely, unloved adult who reverses roles; the parent who is highly invested in compliance and obedience—are but three of several types of abusive families. Regardless of the primary type, there are common dynamics that not only affect personality but also affect development and neurologic function. Some of these dynamics are noted below.

The abused child is usually in a family wherein he is a constant or frequent disappointment to the parents. He angers the parent easily, is unable to meet unrealistic expectations, and is a recurrent source of irritation. His self-concept cannot help but be shaped by an atmosphere of disappointment and denigration.

The abused child is usually in a family that is socially isolated from friends, family, and support systems. There is little modeling of trusting relationships. Interpersonal relationships, even between the parents, are deviant, shallow, or basically nonexistent. The child has little opportunity to learn to socialize with peers or nonfamily adults.

The abused child who is also neglected and rejected has minimal opportunities for learning; language stimulation, play opportunities, and loving interchanges are not available to him. The voluminous literature on social deprivation explains how these deprivations lead to cognitive delays as well as social incompetence.

The abused child is usually in a family where there are erratic responses to his stimulae. For example, the infant who cries soon learns that his behavior has some predictable consequences; he may be picked up, fed, stroked, talked to, rocked, or occasionally ignored. But, what of the infant whose cries are just as apt to be responded to by loving behavior, by verbal or physical assault, or by being completely ignored? This type of erratic responsiveness undercuts the infant's earliest opportunities to learn. This infant has limited ability to appreciate cause and effect. This infant has no reason to begin to feel an internal locus of control, as events seem to be completely independent of his behavior or wishes. This infant loses the opportunity to appreciate his ability to control, manipulate, or gain mastery over a world of people and events.

Competence and mastery are difficult to attain in the abusive home. When the child attempts to learn new facts, skills, or abilities, there must be partial successes, bungled first-attempts, and incomplete approximations to successful mastery. In the abusive home these burgeoning attempts at success will likely be met with derision, punishment, anger, or other extinguishing responses. How can the infant and child learn when his attempts at mastery and competence are unacceptable because they are not complete, perfect, or successful? When this dynamic is coupled with the child's own poor sense of himself, the developmental line of mastery and competence is barricaded.

The abused child's cognitive abilities and learning strategies may be warped and derailed from early infancy. He may develop poor self-concept, external locus of control, depression, warped sense of trust, shallow capacity for intimate interpersonal relationships, and a deep sense of anger and hostility. It is not so much the broken femur or fractured ribs that impede the child's development, but parenting behaviors and attitudes that coincidentally include physical assault on children for real or imagined transgressions.

It is this author's experience that the parent-child interaction accounts for the majority of sequelae in the abused child. Neurologic function, developmental progress, and personality structure are all affected by emotional abuse and seriously deviant parenting, with or without biological damage to the central nervous system. All too often intervention may succeed in decreasing, minimizing, or eliminating physically abusive behavior in the home, and yet, rejection, neglect, deprivation, and emotional abuse continue to take their toll on the child's development. It is for this reason that there has been a need to boldly underline this as part of the etiology of deviance in abused children.

Iatrogenic Aspects

Some of the morbidity in abused children must be laid at the doorstep of the clinician. The clinician's culpability is not born out of malice, and indeed, interventive strategies that can impede the child's development and add new additional psychological stress on the child may be necessary and required. Nonetheless, some consideration of our own culpability will lead to treatment and preventive strategies.

Interventive strategies that may be required include: hospitalization; removal of the child from parents to whom the child may be very attached; placement in a substitute home of strangers who will act as parent surrogates (foster placement); and limited contact of child and parents in artificial "visiting" situations. Less acceptable and more harmful is the pattern of frequent foster home changes, which is all too often the standard modus operandi in protective services agencies.

Although hospitalization may be necessary, we can still not ignore the regressive reaction that most children have to hospitalization. Hospital settings are not optimal, or even adequate, environments to foster and encourage normal cognitive or emotional development. Surely, the effects of hospitalization can be minimized and muted through appropriate preventive procedures that will be discussed below. This issue must be raised to serve as a springboard for encouraging such measures and to emphasize the wisdom of avoiding hospitalization when medical indications are absent. Social admission to the hospital should be avoided when alternate care in a more natural home setting can be arranged.

Most mistreated children are attached to their parents, usually as closely as nonabused children. Loss of parents and significant others with the attendant weakening of the bonds of attachment between abused child and parent are the primary destructive consequence of treatment. It may be important, even essential, that the child is separated from abusive parents, but, nonetheless, the child has suffered an important loss of people to whom he was affectively attached. The younger the child the more this is true, as even short separations (by adult standards) may be experienced by the child as extended or even permanent losses. The grieving and mourning behaviors of the child interfere with learning and socialization. The protest and later apathy do not leave him available to learn, to play, or to enjoy interpersonal relationships.

The child must then deal with the stress of adapting to a new and strange environment, the foster home. However, this is greatly compounded by the frequent changes in foster care that most children experience. This, in essence, amounts to exposing the child to repeated losses of parenting figures. At some point this may weaken the child's ability to form special, meaningful relationships and to trust his world—to the degree that there may be permanent obstacles to meaningful intimate interpersonal relationships throughout life.

Indeed, the abused child is often exposed to other losses of important adult figures. Changes in social service caseworkers represent another experience in losing an important adult figure, and all too often the child's response to this loss is ignored. In a similar vein, an abrupt discharge from the hospital gives the child little or no opportunity to say goodbye, to deal with the loss of an important place filled with important caregivers.

Finally, we must consider the infrequent visiting and contact between the mistreated child and his biological parents, which continues to weaken and dilute the bonding and attachment between child and parent. The clinician must keep in mind the considerably different perspective of time that children of different ages have. A few days, a week, or a month may be experienced as a virtual eternity to the infant, toddler, or preschooler. Visiting between parents and child is too often used as a reward or reinforcement for compliant behavior of the abusive parent rather than as a planned event that is based on the psychological needs of the child. When the plans and hopes of the social service agency are for the eventual reunion of the child and biological parent(s), the contact should be as frequent as possible to maintain the investment and attachment of the child to his parent.

An outcome of these stresses is seen in the concerning frequency with which both foster placement and adoptive placement of abused children fail. The child's limited capacity to develop a deep, trusting, loving, and exclusive relationship with a set of new parents is thought to be the basis for such frequent placement failures. Lifelong consequences are more conjectural, but may be the basis of the impaired relationships, marital and other, of abusive adults who, themselves, had a childhood of physical abuse.

In brief, the help we offer mistreated children has side-effects and can lead to iatrogenic damage. The clinician need not feel unduly guilty about this. For, indeed, most treatment strategies in medicine carry with them a predictable amount of pain, suffering, and morbidity. Medications, surgery, and diagnostic procedures easily come to mind as examples. The important point is to be aware of these side-effects; to care about the side-effects; to avoid the stressful intervention unless it is clearly indicated; and most importantly, to devise ways to minimize the side-effects of the necessary intervention we implement.

SCREENING AND TREATMENT

Medical Issues

Abused children are at higher risk of malnutrition, anemia (usually iron deficiency), poor hygiene, inadequate immunizations, poor dental health, and hearing deficits. Medical treatment for these associated problems is frequently overlooked in the flurry of activity surrounding the acute trauma. The abused child needs more than the ministrations of the emergency room physician or the immediate skills of the surgeon. During recuperation from trauma these other medical problems and deficits need evaluation and treatment.

Related to this is the need for the physician caring for the acutely traumatized child to arrange for continuity of medical care after discharge from hospital or emergency room. All too often the abused child has had erratic and inconsistent medical attention from various clinics and physicians. A plan for continuity of medical care should be arranged when the child is being seen and treated for abuse. When protective services are involved, the plan should be presented to them as a strong recommendation without which the child's subsequent development could suffer.

Neurodevelopmental Screening and Treatment

Given a morbidity of over 50%, it seems clear that all abused children should be screened for neurologic deficit and developmental delays.

An extended neurologic examination, going beyond the traditional exam, which includes assessment of cranial nerves, reflexes, cerebellar function, and focal damage, is in order. The quality of neurologic functions, including gross and fine motor ability, articulation, sensory-motor skills, activity level, and attention span should also be assessed. It will depend on the confidence and expertise of the examining physician as to when to seek consultation from a developmental pediatrician or a pediatric neurologist.

Screening for developmental status is, in actuality, part of a neurologic examination of children. The usual separation of development and neurology is an artificial and administrative distinction. Motor abilities, cognitive skills, language use, learning, and personal-social abilities are, after all, reflections of the integrity of the central nervous system. Developmental screening has typically been carried out in one of four ways:

History
An interview of a responsible caretaker may give a rather accurate profile of developmental status as well as an estimate of past developmental progression. This requires a caretaker who has spent adequate time with and attention to the child. It also requires a caretaker who has a degree of objectivity so as to give responsibly valid answers. History of past developmental milestones are notoriously suspect but current developmental abilities can usually be accurately given by the parent or surrogate parent (including a preschool teacher, baby-sitter, or child staff worker at a day-care center). The physician must make an assessment as to the reliability of the parent's history of development.

Observation of the Child
During the physical examination and while the history is being taken, casual observation of the child may reassure the physician of developmental status—but *only* if the physician is a good observer of development and is knowledgeable as to what is normal at different ages. Spontaneous play activity, use of language, and the understanding of directions of the physician are the primary arenas for assessment. Obviously, many children react to the physical examination or medical setting in such a way as to preclude observation of typical behavior.

Developmental Checklists

Any screening procedure requires a knowledge of when children can perform various skills or know different facts. With a checklist available to the physician, she/he is in a position to focus on asking about age-appropriate abilities and knowledge. Table 1 includes a checklist of developmental abilities through 6 years of age. There are many such lists and tables available to the physician.

Formal Developmental Screening

Formal developmental screening is the preferred manner for making screening decisions about a child's development. Developmental screening tests are more reliable and dependable than any of the above mechanisms. They offer a quick way to compare the specific child to the hundreds of children on which the screening test was standardized.

Probably the developmental screening test used most commonly by medical personnel in this country is the Denver Developmental Screening Test (DDST) (78). This screening tool has several advantages over many others. The score sheets show the clinician when 25%, 50%, 75%, and 90% of children are able to pass each item on the test. This is significantly more helpful than a checklist that puts a developmental skill only at the age when at least 50% of children can do it.

Screening tests, like the DDST, should be administered, observed, scored, and interpreted by a clinician, not by a technician. The DDST, like most screening tests, offers the clinician the opportunity to learn a great deal about the child's neurologic status, developmental abilities, and personality other than what is learned by whether a child passes or fails specific test items.

If and when a child "fails" a developmental screening test, the clinician is then faced with the need for consultation for more detailed developmental assessment. This may come from a developmental pediatrician, a developmental clinic, or a clinical psychologist who is trained in infant and child development. Screening tests are just what they purport to be, screening tests. Some children who are quite normal may fail them, although most who do poorly have developmental problems that require more specific diagnosis for appropriate treatment to be planned.

Treatment for developmental delays may take a variety of forms. Sometimes only a specific area of development requires intervention, such as a language delay requiring speech and language therapy or a motor problem requiring physical therapy. More often the developmental disabilities will be more general and pervasive. In such an instance, the clinician will more likely be considering a generalized developmental stimulation program. Most communities have infant stimulation programs that include work in the areas of language, cognition, social skills, and perceptual-motor abilities. Therapeutic day-care centers may also be a treatment source for the infant or young child. At older ages, regular and specialized preschool programs are to be considered. As more and more communities extend education below age 6, public schools are offering specialized treatment services for developmentally delayed children. Certainly, by age 6, almost all communities have specialized services for children with a variety of developmental disabilities.

The resources for treatment of developmentally delayed children may be unknown to the primary physician. Consultation as to resources may come from the local health department, the state education department, or the closest university, which may have a child development center. Other organizations, such as the Association for Retarded Citizens (ARC) and Association for Children with Learning Disorders (ACLD), have chapters in all states and most cities and towns and are a repository for local resources for treatment of children with specific types of developmental problems.

Developmental treatment programs will, in general, be superior when there is a home or parent component. Many programs, including Head Start, learned that the stimulation and treatment they provided needed reinforcement from the parents. This is true even if the child is in foster care. A few hours per day or week can be greatly augmented in efficacy when the goals and the approach to improved function are shared by parenting figures and treatment staff.

Psychological Screening and Treatment

There are less formal mechanisms available to screen children for psychological problems. There are three approaches that might be used to evaluate the psychological status of the child.

Psychological Milestones

Clinicians are aware that there are psychological milestones in child development. We expect children at specific ages to develop smiling, social responsiveness, stranger anxiety, separation anxiety, temper tantrums, use of a transitional object, night terrors, parallel and then cooperative peer play, and other behaviors. When the specific child is not demonstrating age-appropriate behaviors or when the child is still demonstrating behavior long after other children have given up or passed through that stage, then the clinician should consider the existence of emotional problems.

Developmental Stages

A theoretical conceptual framework for considering personality may help in making screening judgments about the child. Although any theoretical paradigm may do, the clinician may find Ericson (79) as helpful as any. In such a framework we expect children to go through specific stages such as trust, autonomy, initiative, industry, and identity. Using these stages we can make some judgment as to whether the child has adequately negotiated the development of trust in others during his first year and whether the 1 to 3-year-old is displaying appropriate autonomous strivings with the independence that is part of the hackneyed "terrible twos" stage. The 3- to 5-year-old should be a child with imagination, creative play, questioning behaviors, and play-acting. The 6- to 12-year-old should be able to successfully negotiate the academic and social skills of a public school setting. When the child is not struggling successfully with the age-appropriate stage or has not dealt with earlier stages of development, then there is cause for concern.

Symptoms

This is the most time-honored method that medical clinicians have used to alert themselves to possible psychological problems. The most obvious symptoms are those that irritate adults—aggression, noncompliance, antisocial behavior—or

Table 1. Developmental Milestones[a]

Age	Motor	Mental	Language	Social
3–6 months	Will bear weight on legs	Looks at objects in hand	Coos	Has a social smile
	Can roll over stomach to back	Looks after a toy which is dropped	Gurgles	Will pat a bottle with both hands
	Engages hands in midline	Uses a 2-hand approach to grasp toys	Chuckles	Anticipates food on sight
	When pulled to sit, head is steady, does not fall back	Looks at objects as small as a raisin	Laughs aloud	
	When on abdomen, can lift shoulders off mat	Turns head to voice, follows with eyes	Squeals	
	When on abdomen, can lift head and look about		Has expressive noises	
	Will begin to reach for and grasp objects			
	Sits with support			
6–9 months	Rolls from back to stomach	Bangs toys in play	Responds to name	Expects repetition of stimulus
	Gets feet to mouth	Transfers objects from hand to hand	Vocalizes to social stimulus, i.e.,	Likes frolicky play
	Sits alone, unsupported, for extended period (over 1 minute)	Reaches for a toy with one hand	Has single consonants, i.e., ba, ka, ma	Discriminates strangers
	Stands with hands held	Picks up a toy he/she drops	Combines syllables, i.e., da-da, ba-ba	Smiles to mirror image
	On back, can lift head up	Is persistent in obtaining toys	Likes to make sounds with toys	Takes some solid food to mouth
	Beginning attempts to crawl or creep	Would pull a toy to self by attached string	Imitates sounds	Bites and chews toys
	When sitting, reaches forward to grasp without falling			Beginning to enjoy peekaboo

110

Age	Motor	Adaptive	Language	Social
9–12 months	Crawls well Can sit steadily for more than 10 minutes Stands holding on to furniture Can pull to sitting position Walks, holding on to a hand or to furniture	Will uncover a toy he/she sees covered up Can grasp object small as raisin with thumb and one finger Beginning to put things in and out of containers Goes for an object with index finger outstretched Likes to drop objects deliberately	Understands no, or inflection of "no!" Uses mama, or dada, first inappropriately, then with meaning By 12 months has at least one other word Knows meaning of 1–3 words	Cooperates in games Will try to roll ball to another person Plays patacake and peekaboo Waves goodbye Will offer toy without releasing it Likes to interact in play with adult
12–18 months	By 18 months, walks well alone Creeps up stairs Can get to standing position alone Can stoop and recover an object Walking, pulls a pull-toy Seats self on chair	Shows interest in pictures Looks at pictures in a book Will scribble spontaneously with pencil or crayon Uses spoon Drinks from cup Will follow one or two directions, i.e., take a ball to . . .	Has 3–5 words Will point to one body part Will point to at least one picture Uses jargon, i.e., unintelligible "foreign" language with inflection Imitates some words	Cooperates in dressing Holds own bottle or cup Finger feeds Points or vocalizes to make desires known Shows or offers a toy
18–24 months	Can run, albeit stiffly Walks up and down stairs with one hand held Hurls a ball Can kick a ball or object Jumps with both feet Stands on one foot with one hand held	Can tower 2 or more 1 inch blocks Turns pages of a book, even if 2–3 at a time Will try to imitate what an adult draws with pencil Can point to 2–3 body parts	By two years, has at least 20 words By two years, is combining two words in a phrase Jargon, which was elaborate by 18 months, is gone by 24 months Verbalizes desires with words	Uses spoon, spilling very little Removes one piece of clothing Imitates housework more and more Handles a cup quite well

Table 1. (Continued)

Age	Motor	Mental	Language	Social
2–3 years	Can walk up stairs without hand held Can balance on one foot for one second Can jump in place Can walk on tiptoe Can jump from the bottom step Kicks ball forward Can throw a ball	Can tower 6 one inch blocks Can dump a raisin from a bottle to attain without hints Can imitate a vertical line, possibly a horizontal line, with pencil Can anticipate the need to urinate or deficate If worked with, can toilet self	Uses 2–4 word phrases Uses plurals Names at least one picture Talks incessantly Vocabulary 100–300 words by 3 years Uses some personal pronouns, i.e., I, me, mine Points to several parts of a doll on request Identifies over 5 parts of own body	Puts on some clothing Washes and dries hands Has parallel play with peers Can pour from a pitcher
3–4 years	Rides a tricyle Alternates feet when going up stairs Can stand on one foot for 2–5 seconds Can broad jump Uses scissors Swings and climbs	Can tower 8–10 one-inch blocks Says full name Can match colors Has sense of round, square, and triangular shaped figures and can match them Copies a circle, line, cross with pencil Can repeat 3 digits	Can answer some questions Knows rhymes and songs Asks questions Has understanding of on, under, and behind	Knows own sex Beginning to play *with* other children Unbuttons Dresses with supervision

112

Age				
4–5 years	Runs well and turns Can hop on one foot 1–2 times Beginning to skip Stands on one leg for 10 seconds Throws ball well overhand Walks down stairs one foot to each step	Can copy a cross with a pencil Can pick the longer of two lines Can copy a square with pencil	Vocabulary over 1000 words Can match colors, and by 5 years, name 3–4 colors Counts 3 objects with pointing Ninety percent of speech intelligible Can define words in terms of use Can answer questions like what do you do when you are cold . . . hungry . . . tired. . . . ?	Can separate from mother easily Dresses with little supervision Buttons Likes to play "dramatic" play, make-believe Imaginative play with a doll
5–6 years	Skips on both feet alternately Can catch a bounced ball Can walk heel to toe on a line Can hop on one foot for 10 feet	Can copy a square or triangle from looking at a copy Gives age Knows morning from afternoon Draws a person with a body, with 3–6 parts Prints simple words	Can repeat 4 digits Asks questions about meaning of words Counts 10 objects Names coins Can tell what some things are made of Can define some words	No supervision necessary for dressing Plays "dress-up" Elaborate dramatic play Does simple chores unattended at home

SOURCE: Martin, H.P.: *Treatment for Abused and Neglected Children: A Users Manual.* DHEW Publication No. (OHDS) 79-30199, August, 1979, pp. 32–33.

[a] If child is not accomplishing two or three of these milestones, consider developmental consultation.

symptoms that strike adults as bizarre—cruelty to animals or fecal smearing. The clinician must also consider those symptoms that are not so perverse or irritating, such as excessive shyness or fearfulness, unhappiness, or apathy.

The clinician might well inquire as to peer relations and make some judgment as to the general affective state of the child. Is the child generally happy, sad, frustrated, afraid, etc.? And just as importantly, how does the child deal with those feelings? Another area to be considered is how the child deals with stress, through over-reaction or through inappropriate nonchalance.

In the final analysis, the clinician will use his clinical judgment as to whether the child seems to be troubled, disturbed, or unhappy. The methods of data gathering noted above may augment those clinical intuitions and help reinforce the need or lack of need for more intensive psychological evaluation.

A small percentage of abused children, approximately 10%, will require individual psychotherapy or group therapy. Most abused children's psychological problems can be dealt with in a less formal way. The clinician must keep in mind the differentiation between therapy and what is therapeutic. There are many people and settings that can be therapeutic to a child without offering formal therapy. A foster parent, a day-care worker, a preschool teacher, a nurse, a physician, or the protective service caseworker can play a critically important therapeutic role—a role that may be sufficiently therapeutic to help the child deal with his emotional turmoil.

One time for therapeutic intervention is when the child is first identified as abused or neglected. It is at this time that the child needs an adult to engage in crisis intervention. The adult needs to talk to the child, explain what is happening, and clarify distorted fantasies the child has as to what is happening and why. There is a need to elicit from the child his feelings and fears, his fantasies and concerns to help him deal with these in a realistic manner. The child is at a point of crisis when recently injured, when hospitalized, when removed from parents, and when entering foster care. The child often assumes culpability for these events and fears the worst. The general principles of preventive crisis intervention, which physicians have learned to apply when a child has lost a parent or is critically ill, are applicable here as preventive psychological therapy.

Later, the therapeutic role of the physician or others takes on different forms and goals. Apart from dealing with the child's specific psychological problems, the therapeutic milieu should include the following:

· A healthy adult model to whom the child can relate
· An adult who tries to understand the child's behavior and feelings
· An atmosphere where the child is valued apart from his accomplishments or his compliance
· Assistance in verbalizing feelings
· Assistance in helping the child develop a positive self-image
· Reinforcement of the child enjoying age-appropriate play and activities
· Ways to help the child deal with anger and aggression in age-appropriate means

Much of the above translates into a child being able to learn to trust an adult as a fairly predictable person who will supply adequate nurturance, understanding, limit setting, and affection. A psychologically attuned child worker, school teacher, nurse, caseworker, or physician can provide these if the child is in their care or seen by them on a regular and frequent basis.

Foster parents can be therapeutic agents but will often need psychological consultation to understand and manage the abused child. The failure rate of foster care for abused children is extremely high. Part of that frequent turnover in foster care is related to abused children being more difficult children to understand and to care for than other children. Foster parents should have regular meetings with a child psychologist or psychiatrist to discuss the abused children in their care. This can be done most efficiently in group meetings of foster parents. This can decrease the frequency of foster care changes and help the foster parents become more effective psychotherapeutic change agents— becoming professional therapeutic foster parents rather than only playing the role of temporary caregivers.

Therapeutic day-care centers or preschools are especially good modalities of treatment for abused children. Staff of such centers and schools are often trained in identifying and working with character traits and personality problems of children that interfere with learning, socialization, and developmental progression. They have the added benefit of being able to supply cognitive, motor, and language stimulation. Further, the availability of other children with whom the abused child can learn to relate makes them an especially valuable treatment resource.

Hospitalization should be avoided when medical indications are lacking. Emergency foster care placement should be supplied rather than hospitalization when there is no need for in-patient medical care. Avoidance of unnecessary hospitalization can minimize some of the negative forces to which the child is exposed.

When the child and biological parents are likely to be reunited in the future, it is imperative to arrange frequent contact between them. The younger the child or infant, the more frequent the contacts should be. Visiting between parents and child can be arranged in settings more conducive to normal adult-child interaction than the common practice of one-hour visits in a caseworker's office. Indeed, it is possible for the biological parents to visit the child in the foster home but the caseworker must prepare the foster parents to avoid the frequent antipathy foster parents build toward the abusive parents. When physical visits are not possible, phone contact or letters to the child should be encouraged. In summary, ways must be found to maintain the attachment and bond between the child and biological parent when the plan is to attempt reunion of parents and child.

Parenting

Treatment must include specific plans for changing parenting beyond a cessation of physical abuse. If the morbidity of child abuse is embedded in deviant or pathologic parent-child interaction, then the treatment plan must address this interaction. Cessation of physical abuse is a primary and essential goal. However, more than that is needed. There is a need to change the parents' feelings, attitudes, and behaviors toward the child so that neglect, emotional abuse, and other forms of pathologic parenting do not persist when the child returns to the abusive adults (80–82). The child's physician should be willing to speak to this need at the child protection team meeting or in whatever format is available to him. There may be no other child advocate who takes this need into account. Too often the plans of a treatment team may only include a safe placement for the child and therapy for the parents. There needs to be someone who speaks up forcefully for the needs of the child. This child advocate can point out the medical, neurologic, psychological, and developmental treatment needs of the child—as well as addressing the critical need for a plan to alter and improve the parenting that the child can receive from foster or biological parents.

SUMMARY

It is a conservative estimate that 3% to 4% of children in this country are significantly mistreated. Given a neurologic and developmental morbidity of at least 50%, it can be appreciated that child abuse represents a major basis for handicapping conditions in our child population. The psychological consequences are of equal concern, especially when we consider the long-term effects of increased risk of antisocial behavior and the generational transmission of abusive behavior (83). While the etiologies of these consequences are many and varied, the whole fabric of aberrant parenting attitudes and practices represent the most ominous and pervasive basis for the common neuro-psycho-developmental sequellae. Pathogenesis and treatment procedures to mute and modify these consequences have been presented. The importance of a child advocate cannot be overestimated. Health professionals are in unique positions to identify these problems and to agitate for treatment procedures for the child. This requires an awareness of the multiple problems for which the abused child is at risk, in addition to the acute injuries for which he is seen. It requires screening and diagnostic procedures to identify clearly the many needs of the child. The child's physician must be constantly aware of the neurologic, psychological, and developmental causal and consequential aspects of maltreatment.

REFERENCES

1. Birrell RG, Birrell JHW: The maltreatment syndrome in children: A hospital survey. *Med J Aust* 2:1023, 1968.
2. Buchanan A, Oliver JF: Abuse and neglect as a cause of mental retardation. *Br J Psychiatry* 131:458, 1977.
3. Cohn AH: An evaluation of three demonstration child abuse and neglect treatment programs. *J Am Acad Child Psychiatry* 18(2):283, 1979.
4. Elmer E, Gregg GS: Developmental characteristics of abused children. *Pediatrics* 40:596, 1967.
5. Hufton IW, Oates RK: Non-organic failure to thrive: A long-term follow-up. *Pediatrics* 59:73, 1977.
6. Kent JT: A follow-up study of abused children. *J Pediatr Psychol* 1(2):25, 1976.
7. Martin HP: The child and his development, in Kempe CH, Helfer RE (eds): *Helping the Battered Child and His Family*. Philadelphia, JB Lippincott Company, 1972, p 93.

8. Martin HP, Beezley P, Conway EF, et al: The development of abused children - Part I: A review of the literature - Part II: Physical, neurologic, and intellectual outcome. *Ad Pediatr* 21:25, 1974.

9. Martin HP: *The Abused Child: An Interdisciplinary Approach to Developmental Issues and Treatment.* Cambridge, Ballinger Publishing Company, 1976.

10. Martin HP, Beezley P: Behavioral observations of abused children. *Dev Med Child Neurol* 19:373, 1977.

11. Martin HP: *Treatment for Abused and Neglected Children: A Users Manual* DHEW Publication No (OHDS) 79-30199, 1979.

12. Martin, HP: The consequences of being abused and neglected: How the child does fare, in Helfer RE, Kempe CH (eds): *The Battered Child*, ed 3. Chicago, University of Chicago Press, 1980.

13. Ryan MG, Davis AA, Oates RK: 187 Cases of child abuse and neglect. *Med J Aust* 2(19):623, 1977.

14. Sandgrund A, Gaines RW, Green AH: Child abuse and mental retardation: A problem of cause and effect. *J Ment Defic* 19:327, 1975.

15. Smith SM, Hanson R: 134 Battered children: A medical and psychological study. *Br Med J* 3(5732):666, 1974.

16. Elmer E: *Children in Jeopardy.* Pittsburgh, University of Pittsburgh Press, 1967.

17. Oates RK, Davis AA, Ryan MG, et al: Risk factors associated with child abuse. *Child Abuse and Neglect: The International Journal* 3(2):547, 1979.

18. Dietrich KM: *The Abused Infant: Developmental Characteristics and Maternal Handling.* Masters Thesis, Wayne State University, Detroit, 1977.

19. MacKeith R: Speculations on non-accidental injury as a cause of chronic brain disorder. *Dev Med Child Neurol* 16:216, 1974.

20. MacKeith R: Speculations on some possible long-term effects, in Franklin AW (ed): *Concerning Child Abuse.* London, Churchill-Livingstone, 1975.

21. Solomons G: Child abuse and developmental disabilities. *Dev Med Child Neurol* 21(1):101, 1979.

22. Buchanan A, Oliver JE: Abuse and neglect as a cause of mental retardation: A study of 140 children admitted to subnormality hospitals in Wiltshire. *Child Abuse and Neglect: The International Journal* 3(2):467, 1979.

23. Appelbaum AS: Developmental retardation in infants as a concomitant of physical child abuse. *J Abnormal Child Psychol* 5(4):417, 1977.

24. Barahal R, Waterman J, Martin HP: Social-cognitive functioning in abused latency-aged children. Accepted for publication, *J. Consulting Clin Psychol*, 1981.

25. Blager F, Martin HP: Speech and language of abused children, in Martin HP (ed): *The Abused Child: A Multidisciplinary Approach to Developmental Issues and Treatment.* Cambridge, Ballinger Publishing Company, 1976, p 83.

26. Blager F: Effect of intervention on speech and language of abused children, in *Abstracts: Second International Congress on Child Abuse and Neglect.* London, Permagon Press, 1978, p 21.

27. Oates RK, Davis AA, Ryan MG, et al: Risk factors associated with child abuse, in *Abstracts: Second International Congress on Child Abuse and Neglect.* London, Permagon Press, 1978, p 171.

28. Kline DF: Educational and psychological problems of abused children. *Child Abuse and Neglect: The International Journal* 1:301, 1977.

29. Wilkinson J, Donaruma P: Incidence of abuse and neglect among children in special education versus regular education. Unpublished report, Family Resource Center, Boulder, Colorado.

30. Green AH: Self-destruction in physically abused schizophrenic children: Report of cases. *Arch Gen Psychiatry* 19:171, 1968.

31. Green AH: Self-destructive behavior in battered children. *Am J Psychiatry* 135(5):579, 1978.

32. Green AH: Psychopathology of abused children. *J Am Acad Child Psychiatry* 17(1):92, 1978.

33. Reidy TJ: The aggressive characteristics of abused and neglected children. *J Clin Psychol* 33(4):1140, 1977.

34. George C, Main M: Social interactions of young abused children: Approach, avoidance, and aggression. *Child Dev* 50:306, 1979.

35. Curtis GC: Violence breeds violence—perhaps? *Am J Psychiatry* 120:386, 1963.

36. Duncan GM, Frazier SH, Litin EM, et al: Etiological factors in first-degree murder. *JAMA* 168:1755, 1958.

37. Easson WM, Steinhilber RM: Murderous aggression by children and adolescents. *Arch Gen Psychiatry* 4:27, 1961.

38. Steele BF: Violence in our society. *Pharos* 33:42, 1970.

39. Lewis DO, Shanok SS, Pincus JH, et al: Violent juvenile delinquents: Psychiatric, neurological, psychological, and abuse factors. *J Am Acad Child Psychiatry* 18(2):307, 1979.

40. Lewis DO, Shanok SS: Medical histories of delinquent and non-delinquent children: An epidemiological study. *Am J Psychiatry* 134:1020, 1977.

41. Lewis DO, Shanok SS, Balla DA: Perinatal difficulties, head and face trauma, and child abuse in the medical histories of seriously delinquent children. *Am J Psychiatry* 136:419, 1979.

42. Bradley S: Relationship of early maternal deprivation to borderline personality in adolescence and children. *Am J Psychiatry* 136:424, 1979.

43. Gordon AH, Jameson JC: Infant-mother attachment in patients with non-organic failure to thrive syndrome. *J Am Acad Child Psychiatry* 18(2):251, 1979.

44. Gaensbauer TJ, Sands K: Distorted affective communications in abused and neglected infants and their potential impact on caretakers. *J Am Acad Child Psychiatry* 18(2):236, 1979.

45. Lynch M: Ill health and child abuse. *Lancet* 2:317, 1975.

46. Lynch M: Risk factors in the child: A study of abused children and their siblings, in Martin HP (ed): *The Abused Child: A Multidisciplinary Approach to Developmental Issues and Treatment.* Cambridge, Ballinger Publishing Company, 1976, p 43.

47. Hack M, Fanaroff A, Merkatz I: The low-birth-weight infant: Evaluation of a changing outlook. *N Engl J Med* 301(21):1162, 1979.

48. Glaser D, Bentovim A: Abuse, neglect, and risk of handicapped, chronically or severely ill children, in *Abstracts: Second International Congress on Child Abuse and Neglect.* London, Permagon Press, 1978, p 172.

49. Sameroff AJ, Chandler MJ: Reproductive risk and the continuum of caretaking casualty, in Horowitz FD, Hetherington EM, Scarr, Salapatek S, Siegel IF (eds): *Review of Child Development Research Vol IV.* Chicago, University of Chicago Press, 1975, p 187.

50. Sameroff AJ: Early influences on development: Fact or fancy?, in Chess S, Thomas A (eds): *Annual Progress in Child Psychiatry and Child Development.* New York, Brunner/Mazel, Inc, 1976, p 3.

51. Chess S, Thomas A, Birch HG: *Temperament and Behavior Disorders in Children.* New York, New York University Press, 1968.

52. Chess S, Thomas A: *Temperament and Development.* New York, Brunner/Mazel, Inc, 1977.

53. Chess S, Thomas A: Temperamental individuality from childhood to adolescence. *J Am Acad Child Psychiatry* 16:218, 1977.

54. Zeskind PS, Ramey CT: Fetal malnourishment: Evidence for a transactional model of infant development, in *Abstracts: Society for Research of Child Development,* 1979, p. 214.

55. Werner E, Bierman JM, French F, et al: Reproductive and environmental casualties: A report on the 10-year follow-up of the children of the Kauai pregnancy study. *Pediatrics* 42:112, 1968.

56. Werner E, Smith RS: *Kauai's Children Come of Age.* Honolulu, University Press of Hawaii, 1977.

57. Caffey J: On the theory and practice of shaking infants: Its potential residual affects of permanent brain damage and mental retardation. *Am J Dis Child* 24:161, 1972.

58. Ebbin AJ, Gollub MH, Stein AM, et al: Battered child syndrome at the Los Angeles County General Hospital. *Am J Dis Child* 118:660, 1969.

59. Gregg, GS, Elmer E: Infant injuries: Accident or abuse. *Pediatrics* 44: 434, 1969.

60. Morse CW, Sahler OJZ, Friedman SB: A three-year follow-up study of abused and neglected children. *Am J Dis Child* 120:439, 1970.

61. Birch HG: Malnutrition: Learning and intelligence. *Am J Public Health* 62:773, 1972.

62. Manocha SL: *Malnutrition and Retarded Human Development.* Springfield, Ill, Charles C Thomas, publisher, 1972.

63. Martin HP: Nutrition: Its relationship to children's physical, mental, and emotional development. *Am J Clin Nutr* 26:766, 1973.

64. Scrimshaw NS: Early malnutrition and central nervous system function, in Chess S, Thomas A (eds): *Annual Progress in Child Psychiatry and Child Development.* New York, Brunner/Mazel, Inc, 1970, p 246.

65. Scrimshaw NS: Gordon JE: *Malnutrition, Learning, and Behavior.* Cambridge, Mass, The MIT Press, 1968.

66. Cabak V, Naj danvic R: The effect of undernutrition in early life on physical and mental development. *Arch Dis Child* 40:532, 1965.

67. Chase HP, Martin HP: Undernutrition and child development. *N Engl J Med* 282:933, 1970.

68. Graham CG: Effect of infantile malnutrition on growth. *Fed Proc* 26:139, 1967.

69. Monekeberg F: The effect of early marasmic malnutrition on subsequent physical and psychological development, in Scrimshaw NS, Gordon JE (eds): *Malnutrition, Learning, and Behavior.* Cambridge, Mass, The MIT Press, 1968, p 269.

70. Stock MG, Smythe PM: Does undernutrition during infancy inhibit brain growth and subsequent intellectual development? *Arch Dis Child* 38:546, 1963.

71. Cravioto J, DeLicardie ER, Birch HG: Nutrition, growth, and neurointegrative development. *Pediatrics* 38(supp):319, 1966.

72. *Iron Nutrition in Infancy.* 62nd Ross Conference in Pediatric Research, Columbus, Ohio, Ross Laboratories, 1970.

73. Holm VA, Kunze LH: Effect of chronic otitis media on language and speech development. *Pediatrics* 43(5):833, 1969.

74. Needleman H: Effects of hearing loss from early recurrent otitis media on speech and language development, in Jaffe BF (ed): *Hearing Loss in Children.* Baltimore, Md, University Park Press, 1977, p 640.

75. Zinkus PW, Gottlieb ML, Schapiro M: Developmental and Psychoeducational sequelae of chronic otitis media. *Am J Dis Child* 132:1100, 1978.

76. Kandel ER: Psychotherapy and the single synapse: The impact of psychiatric thought on neurobiologic research. *N Engl J Med* 301(19):1028, 1979.

77. Graham P, Rutter M: Psychiatric aspects of physical disorder, in Rutter M, Tizard J, Whitmore K (eds): *Education, Health, and Behavior.* New York, John Wiley & Sons, 1970, p 309.

78. *Denver Developmental Screening Test (DDST):* Manual, Test Kit, and Teaching Materials. LADOCA Project & Publications, Denver, Colorado.

79. Erickson EH: *Childhood and Society.* New York, WW Norton & Co, Inc, 1963.

80. Burgess RS, Conger RD: Project interact: Patterns of interaction in abuse, neglect, and control families, in *Abstracts: Second International Congress on Child Abuse and Neglect.* London, Permagon Press, 1978, p 85.

81. Kempe CH: Approaches to preventing child abuse: The health visitors concept. *Am J Dis Child* 130:941, 1976.

82. Robison E, Solomon F: Some further findings on the treatment of the mother-child dyad in child abuse. *Child Abuse and Neglect: An International Journal* 3(3):247, 1979.

83. Martin HP: A child-oriented approach to prevention of abuse, in Franklin AW (ed): *Child Abuse: Prediction, Prevention, and Follow-up.* New York, Churchill-Livingstone, 1978 p 9.

7
Ophthalmic Manifestations of Child Abuse

J. Allen Gammon

HISTORICAL REVIEW

The eyes have long served as signposts of child abuse. Gouged eyes were listed by Annaeus Seneca among the deformities inflicted on children for begging about the time of Caesar (1). Ocular abnormalities were present in five of the six children reported by Caffey in 1946 associating long-bone fractures and subdural hematomas (2). Silverman (3) further defined the radiologic characteristics of physically abused children. However, visual function and ocular findings were not described. Most subsequent authors have failed to emphasize the importance of a thorough eye examination in victims of nonaccidental trauma. Interest in physically abused children began in the ophthalmologic literature after Kiffney (4) reported a battered child with bilateral cataracts and retinal detachments in 1964. Later, Gilkes and Mann (5) suggested that retinal and vitreous hemorrhages in young children should trigger suspicion of physical child abuse. Characteristic peripheral retinal lesions in abused children were described by Maroteaux et al. (6,7) and later confirmed by Harcourt and Hopkins (8) who also found these lesions in more posterior parts of the eye. Friendly (9) reported ocular manifestations in 22 of 54 battered children studied retrospectively. At least six (11%) of these patients died from their injuries. Like Caffey's early series, Friendly found retinal hemorrhages associated with intracranial bleeding was the most common ocular abnormality in abused children. Direct trauma to the eye was documented in only 11 (20%) of Friendly's cases. Retinal hemorrhages similar to the retinopathy described after sudden compression of the thorax, called Purtscher's retinopathy, were reported in two physically abused children by Tomasi and Rosman (10). Permanent visual impairment in 8 of 11 children with ocular manifestations of nonaccidental trauma was reported by Harcourt and Hopkins (11). These authors described macular scarring, optic atrophy, and cortical blindness. The poor visual prognosis for physically abused children was further documented by Mushin (12) who reported permanently impaired vision in 12 of 19 battered babies.

Recurrent attacks of hemorrhagic conjunctivitis in two siblings eventually proven to be chemical injuries intentionally inflicted by the father were reported by Taylor and Bentovim (13). The 6-year-old child in this family was blinded by corneal scarring secondary to the recurrent injuries to her corneas (Fig. 1). Another atypical case simulating congenital glaucoma was investigated by Tseng and Keys (14). This 9-week-old infant presented with hazy, enlarged corneas, elevated intraocular pressures, and a hyphema.

SPECTRUM OF OCULAR TRAUMA

The visual system represents a rich repository for various manifestations of physical child abuse (Fig. 2 *a*, *b*). Ocular lesions described in abused children are summarized in Table 1. These same lesions may also be seen following accidental trauma and are thus not pathognomonic for physical child abuse. However, like the characteristic bone fractures of abused children, these ocular abnormalities imply substantial antecedent trauma or recurrent injury. Mushin and Morgan (15) also warn that childhood ocular injuries from physical child abuse are easily confused with pseudoglioma, Coats disease, spontaneous lens dislocation, and intraocular bleeding from causes other than *non*accidental injury. The history is often decisive.

Children with amblyopia from crossed eyes or refraction errors suffer permanently decreased vision unless appropriate therapy of the amblyopia is instituted at an early age. Willfull neglect by parents of amblyopia treatment or other medically necessary ocular measures represents child neglect of yet undefined scope.

Acute injury of the visual system results when violent forces strike fragile visual structures. Equally important are chronic secondary sequelae of trauma, such as glaucoma from angle recession or intraocular scar formation. Blunt forces striking the front of the eye often inflict damage to both the front and the back of the eye.

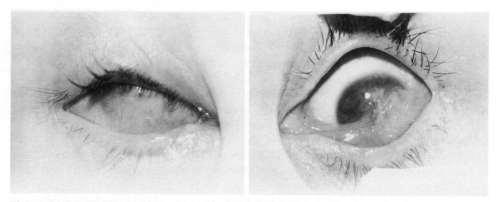

Figure 1. Scarred corneas after unusual child abuse. Recurrent chemical injuries inflicted by the father resulted in corneal scarring and vascularization that blinded this 6-year-old girl. (Taylor, D., Bentovim, A.: Recurrent Nonaccidentally Inflicted Chemical Eye Injuries to Siblings. *J. Ped. Ophthalmol.* 12:238, 1976.)

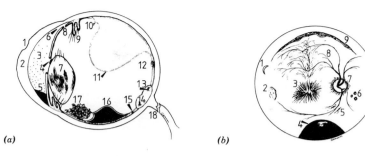

Figure 2. (*a*) The traumatized eye. Injury to the surface of the cornea (2) results in corneal abrasions and lacerations (1). Pigment or blood cells may float (3) or layer (5) in the anterior chamber after ocular trauma. Impaction of the posterior pigmented surface of the iris against the lens can leave a ring of pigment (Vossius ring) on the anterior lens capsule (4). Recession of the angle (6) is visible only with special instruments. Iridodialysis, tearing of the iris at its base (8), is easily seen, while rupture of the zonules (9) with subluxation of the lens (7) is best seen with the slit-lamp after dilating the pupil. Trauma may cause a cataract (7). Posterior lesions include retinal holes or dialysis (10) with associated retinal detachment (11). Intraocular hemorrhages include flame-shaped hemorrhages (13) in the nerve fiber; small "dot" hemorrhages deep in the retinal layers (15); large, bulging, or crescent-shaped sublaminar hemorrhages (16); and vitreous hemorrhages (17). Macular scarring (12) can result from intraocular injury or bleeding. Swelling of the optic nerve (14) is seen with increased intracranial pressure, and traumatic injury can occur at various locations along the optic nerve (18). (*b*) Traumatic lesions in the posterior pole. Ocular trauma with traction along the vitreous base may cause a retinal hole (1) or dialysis (9) with resulting retinal detachment (8). Characteristic lacunar-shaped chorioretinal lesions with pigmented borders are seen after ocular trauma (2). Increased intracranial pressure results in papilledema or swelling of the optic disc (7). Fibrosis and scarring of the macula (3) is a complication of retinal edema or periretinal fibrosis. Three types of intraretinal hemorrhages are illustrated: the large sublaminar hemorrhage (4) is separated from the vitreous only by the thin internal limiting membrane, flame hemorrhages lie along the nerve fibers (5), and circular "dot" hemorrhages (6) are seen deep within the retina.

Contusion or direct bruising with mashing and disorganization of tissue structures is one mechanism of damage to the visual system in physically abused children. Indirect injury from concussive forces occurs during shaking, jolting, and jerking of the child. Blows to the front of the head may result in contrecoup injury to the visual cortex at the brain-skull interface opposite the striking force (16). Wolter (17) has applied these findings to explain traumatic ocular injuries. A column of force (energy) directed across the ocular structures may successively injure the tissues along this path (Fig. 3).

Hydraulic forces may also damage fluid-filled chambers of the eye. Sudden compression or indentation of the front of the eye presses aqueous and vitreous posteriorly and peripherally with consequent distortion and eventual rupture of the intervening partitions. Structural damage occurs at the weakest anatomical points, for example, at the narrow iris root, at the delicate lens zonules, or at the thinnest section of the sclera (Fig. 4).

Injuries that distort, scar, or opacify the cornea, lens, or retina often decrease

Table 1. Ophthalmic Lesions Reported in Physical Child Abuse

	Anterior Lesions	
Periorbital ecchymosis	Recurrent conjunctivitis	Shallow anterior chamber
Eyelid lacerations	Conjunctival hemorrhage	Iris sphincter rupture
Periorbital edema	Subconjunctival hemorrhage	Angle recession
Strabismus	Endophthalmitis	Iris synechiae
Proptosis		Iridodialysis
	Corneal scarring	
	Enlarged cornea	
	Descemet's tears	
	Corneal edema	
	Hyphema	
	Posterior Lesions	
Dislocated lens	Retinal hemorrhage	Optic atrophy
Subluxated lens	Retinal detachment	Cortical blindness
Cataract	Chorioretinal scars	Papilledema
	Retinal dialysis	Glaucoma
	Macular scars	Hemianopia
Vitreoretinal detachment		
Vitreous hemorrhage		
Ruptured globe		

124

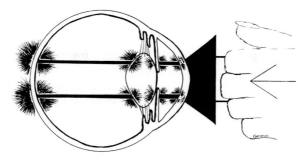

Figure 3. Force vectors. Trauma to the eye results in the propagation of force vectors across the ocular structures causing damage at the intervening tissue interfaces. The blunt blow shown here impacts the cornea, transmitting forces against the iris and lens, through the vitreous to the retina, the choroid, and the sclera. (Adapted from Wolter, J.R.: *Am. J. Ophthalmol.* 56:785, 1963.)

vision. Likewise, blood, tissue debris, or scar tissue formation within the normally transparent ocular spaces will prevent light rays from reaching the retina, thereby decreasing visual acuity (Fig. 5).

Blood cells and other debris released inside the eye after trauma may impede aqueous outflow resulting in increased intraocular pressure called glaucoma. Glaucoma can also be a complication of recession and scarring of the anterior chamber angle where the aqueous drains from the eye.

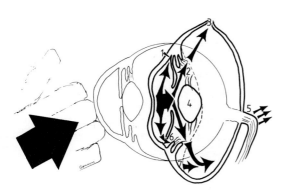

Figure 4. Hydraulic forces. Sudden trauma to the eye deforms and compresses the ocular structures with distortion and disruption of the underlying tissue partitions. Blows to the front of the eye force fluid filling the chambers of the eye peripherally and backward (arrows). These hydraulic forces stretch and may tear the intraocular tissues. Peripheral dissection of aqueous tears the angle with resulting angle recession (1). Posterior displacement of the lens-iris diaphragm can rupture the zonules (2) that support the lens. Complete loss of zonular support results in luxation of the lens (4). Severe trauma may tear through the iris base leaving an iridodialysis (6), rupture the sclera (3), or damage the optic nerve (5). Sudden displacement of the vitreous (dotted lines) away from the underlying retina may cause retinal tears or retinal dialysis, especially at the vitreous base (7).

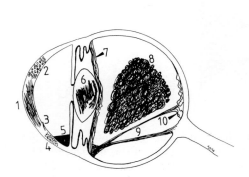

Figure 5. Obstacles in the visual axis. Ocular trauma may disrupt the structures that focus light rays on the retina. Corneal scars (1), corneal edema (2), tears in Descemet's membrane (3), and corneal blood staining (4) secondary to hyphemas (5) interrupt the path of light rays and decrease the vision. Lens opacities (6) block light passage through the lens, and scar tissue, such as a cyclitic membrane (7), or blood in the vitreous (8) prevents focused rays from reaching the retina. Fibrous bands (9) and periretinal scar tissues (10) may distort or detach the retina with resulting decreased vision.

Strabismus, or misalignment, of the eye during early childhood leads to "suppression" of the vision in the deviated eye. If disuse of this eye continues, decreased vision called amblyopia will result from asymmetrical maturation of the visual pathways. Amblyopia therapy must begin at an early age.

Subdural hematomas and retinal hemorrhages frequently occur in the absence of external signs of head trauma. Caffey (18) explains this fact by citing infantile whiplash and child shaking sufficient to produce subdural and retinal hemorrhages. Shaking and whiplash head movements may tear bridging cerebral veins that then fill the subdural space with blood. Therefore, subdural hematomas should never be excluded from consideration because of the absence of known trauma or external signs of injury to the head or eyes.

Swelling of the optic disc, papilledema, is an important sign of increased intracranial pressure resulting from obstruction to the flow of axoplasm along the optic nerve. Elevated intracranial pressure in abused children may be due to subdural fluid collections, intracranial bleeding, brain edema, or hydrocephalus.

Physicians should be aware that minor bumps and common childhood falls are seldom sufficient explanation in otherwise healthy children for a dislocated or cataractous lens, retinal detachment, intraocular hemorrhage, rapid loss of vision, or sudden onset of paralytic strabismus.

OCULAR ANATOMY AND SPECIFIC INJURIES

The eye consists of three functionally distinct layers (Fig. 6). The outer protective layer is formed by the tough cornea and sclera. The middle layer is a vascular, nutrient layer called the uvea and includes the iris, ciliary body, and choroid. The delicate, innermost layer is the retina, which is itself composed of multiple distinctive tissue layers. Rods and cones embedded in the retina convert light energy into electrical impulses that travel from the eye through the optic nerve, across the optic chiasm, to the visual areas of the brain. The occipital cortex is the visual center of the brain, and loss of this area results in cortical blindness. The anatomy of the back of the eye is visualized with the ophthalmoscope (Figs. 7 and 8).

The conjunctiva is a mucous membrane covering the white sclera of the eye. Injury to the conjunctiva results in hyperemia, chemosis, hemorrhage, or

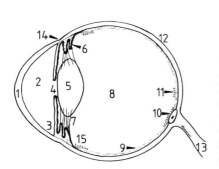

Figure 6. Normal ocular anatomy. The three layers of the eye are the outer, protective wall consisting of the cornea (1) and the sclera (12); the nutrient, vascular middle layer is represented by the iris (4), ciliary body (6), and the choroid (the dotted line under the retina); the inner layer is the retina (9) with its sensitive macula and fovea (11). Light rays are focused by the cornea (1) and the lens (5) whose power varies with the traction of the zonules (7). The anterior chamber (2) contains the angle of the eye (3) where the aqueous leaves the eye. The vitreous space (8) is filled with a transparent gel with adhesions (xxx) along the vitreous base (15), around the optic disc (10), and over the macular area (11). The optic nerve (13) is attached posteriorly to the globe. The junction of the cornea and sclera forms the limbus (14).

laceration. Isolated conjunctival injuries heal rapidly without sequelae. The importance of conjunctival injuries is their frequent association with underlying serious ocular damage, such as scleral lacerations or ruptures. Signs of a ruptured globe include prolapse of intraocular contents, a shallow anterior chamber, or low intraocular pressure called hypotony. Radiologic studies to rule out retained intraocular foreign bodies and careful surgical inspection of the wound are indicated after penetrating ocular injury.

The cornea is the transparent front window of the eye composed of five distinct layers. The outermost layer consists of rapidly regenerating squamous epithelial cells that are easily abraded by foreign bodies, chemicals, or trauma to the corneal surface. Corneal abrasions heal quickly without scarring when the basement membrane of the surface epithelial cells, known as Bowman's membrane, remains unharmed. Deeper, more extensive injuries that penetrate Bowman's membrane to involve the corneal stroma result in permanent scarring. Descemet's membrane is located between the thick stromal layer and the endothelium. Linear tears or splits in Descemet's membrane result from birth trauma and stretching of the eyeball by increased intraocular pressure. Traumatic damage to the corneal endothelium, as well as greatly elevated intraocular pressure, weakens the endothelial barrier, with resulting overhydration and opacification of the cornea called corneal edema. Corneal blood staining occurs

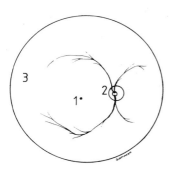

Figure 7. The normal ocular fundus. The anatomy inside the eye can be studied with the ophthalmoscope. The fovea (1) is the depressed, pigmented spot at the center of the macula. The optic disc (2) is a light-colored circular structure nasal to the fovea. The retinal blood vessels enter the eye through the optic nerve and fan out over the retina in branching patterns. The peripheral retina (3) is most easily examined with the indirect ophthalmoscope.

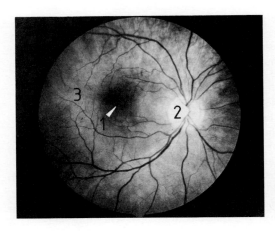

Figure 8. Actual ophthalmoscopic view of normal posterior ocular anatomy. (1) Fovea, (2) optic disc, (3) peripheral retina.

when blood breakdown products are forced into the stroma by elevated intraocular pressure complicating a hyphema, a term meaning blood in the anterior chamber of the eye.

The sclera is a strong elastic connective tissue that forms the outer wall of the posterior five-sixths of the eye. Lacerations of the sclera are usually caused by sharp objects or missiles and are associated with lacerations of the overlying eyelids and conjunctiva. Scleral ruptures occur most frequently between the equator of the globe and the insertion of the eye muscles where the sclera is the thinnest.

The iris is a tissue diaphragm that forms the pupil and separates the anterior and posterior chambers. The pupillary margin rests on the lens capsule whereas the iris base is continuous with the ciliary body.

Trauma to the eye often causes spasm of the iris sphincter with resulting miosis, which is constriction of the pupil. This spastic miosis may be followed by a traumatic mydriasis, dilation of the pupil. Iridoplegia, a fixed unreactive pupil, and cycloplegia, which is the loss of accommodation or the ability to sharply focus close objects, also result from ocular trauma. The pupil may assume irregular shapes; traumatic tears of the iris sphincter can leave triangular defects along the pupillary margin. A pupillary occlusion exists when an inflammatory membrane extends across the entire pupil. A cyclitic membrane is a fibrovascular structure arising from the ciliary body and extending across the anterior vitreous behind the lens (Fig. 5). This grave end result of ocular trauma and intraocular inflammation leads to cessation of aqueous production by the ciliary body with resulting hypotony and phthisis bulbi, an irreversible shrinking and atrophy of the eye. Heterochromia is a difference in color of the irises of the two eyes and can be caused by traumatic atrophy of the iris stroma, which exposes the underlying iris pigment. Absorption of blood pigments by the iris after bleeding into the anterior chamber may also darken areas of the iris. Iridodialysis is a separation of the iris root from the ciliary body where the iris is thinnest.

The ciliary body is a vascular structure encircling the periphery of the lens. The ciliary muscles are responsible for the accommodation of the eye. Aqueous humor, produced by the ciliary body by secretion and diffusion, is a clear fluid that passes from the ciliary body into the posterior chamber, across the lens, and through the pupil to fill the anterior chamber. The aqueous leaves the eye by filtering through the trabecular meshwork, a connective tissue sieve in the angle. Concussion or contusion of the eye may result in inflammation of the iris and the ciliary body called iridocyclitis. Decreased intraocular pressure from injury to the ciliary body is caused by cessation of aqueous production. Traumatic cyclodialysis is a detachment of the ciliary body from its scleral foundation. The fine suspensory ligaments of the lens are called zonules. Severe trauma may tear or rupture these zonules with subluxation or dislocation of the lens.

The anterior chamber, bounded anteriorly by the corneal endothelium and posteriorly by the iris and pupillary portion of the lens, contains the angle of the eye that can be visualized only with specialized instruments. Separation and scarring of this angle is called angle recession and is permanent evidence of past ocular trauma. Small, uncomplicated hyphemas filling less than one-third of the anterior chamber usually resolve without sequelae, but total hyphemas are often complicated by glaucoma, irreversible corneal blood staining, or severe intraocular injury. Timely surgical intervention can often prevent complications.

The vitreous is a transparent, viscous gel that fills the space between the lens and the retina. Vitreoretinal attachments surround the optic disc, cover the macular area, and extend across the vitreous base for several millimeters along the peripheral anterior margin of the retina (Fig. 6). Ocular trauma may avulse the vitreous base from the peripheral retina causing tears, dialysis, and detachments at these vitreoretinal traction sites (Figs. 2 and 4). Hemorrhage into the vitreous may complicate tears of the retina or other intraocular injury. Absorption of vitreous hemorrhage is slow and often complicated by formation of fibrotic bands and intraocular membranes. These scar tissues can produce traction retinal detachments when the fibrotic tissues contract and shorten (Fig. 5).

The lens is a transparent optical structure suspended by the zonules that, together with the ciliary body, regulate lens power by altering its thickness. Injury of the ciliary body or traumatic displacement of the lens disturbs normal focusing of the eye. The pupillary margin of the iris slides across the anterior lens capsule and is easily impacted against the lens capsule by blunt trauma. This leaves a characteristic ring of pigment known as Vossius ring. The lens is frequently damaged by ocular trauma causing sudden or gradual opacification called a cataract. A luxated lens is a lens that is completely detached from its zonular support. A subluxated lens, however, is only partially torn from its zonular attachments (Fig. 2a).

Increased tremulousness of the iris called iridodonesis is a sign of lens dislocation.

The retina is the delicate innermost layer of the eye and consists of 11 microscopic layers (Fig. 9). Retinal hemorrhages are the most frequent ocular manifestations of physical child abuse; but they cannot be differentiated morphologically from retinal hemorrhages due to other causes, for example, retinal hemorrhages of the newborn. These hemorrhages of the newborn, which apparently result from head trauma associated with the birth process, occur in 8% to 50% of healthy babies examined on the day of birth (19).

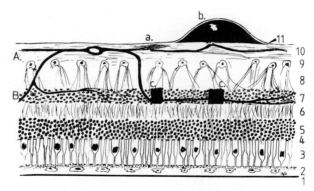

Figure 9. Traumatic intraretinal hemorrhages. The 11 layers of the retina are: Bruch's membrane (1), pigment epithelium (2), rods and cones (3), external limiting membrane (4), outer nuclear layer (5), outer plexiform layer (6), inner nuclear layer (7), inner plexiform layer (8), ganglion cell layer (9), nerve fiber layer (10), and the internal limiting membrane (11). Two capillary networks (A and B) nourish the inner layers of the retina and supply the blood which causes intraretinal hemorrhages. Nerve fiber layer hemorrhages (a) and sublaminar hemorrhages (b) result from bleeding from the superficial capillary network (A). Bleeding from the deep capillary network of the retina (B) results in small, circular hemorrhages deep within the retina (c).

The majority of these hemorrhages resolve spontaneously during the first few days of life. Giles (20) found retinal hemorrhages in 40 of 100 newborns examined on the first day of life. Only 20 (20%) of these infants still had retinal hemorrhages on the third day of life. The sublaminar type of retinal hemorrhages in the newborn may be visible for several weeks. Barsewisch (19) described distinctive types of retinal hemorrhages in newborns (Table 2); these same hemorrhages are seen in physically abused children (Fig. 10). Sublaminar hemorrhages often incorrectly called "preretinal," are extravasations of blood beneath the internal limiting membrane of the retina and appear dome-shaped, bulging into the vitreous. If the internal limiting membrane ruptures, blood enters the vitreous. Nerve fiber layer hemorrhages, "flame" hemorrhages, are flat with feathered edges. When hemorrhage occurs from the deep capillaries of the retina, the blood is tightly compartmentalized within the inner retinal layers. These hemorrhages are, therefore, small and circular in shape with sharp margins (Fig. 2b). Retinal hemorrhages in physically abused children probably occur secondary to brain trauma, which suddenly elevates intracranial pressure causing compression of the central retinal vein and increased pressure at the choroidal anastomosis at the optic disc. This blockage of intraretinal blood flow ruptures weak intraretinal capillaries, which leak blood into the nearby tissues. Most retinal hemorrhages resolve spontaneously in days to weeks depending on hemorrhage type. Edema of the macula or retinal scarring may complicate intraretinal hemorrhages. Forces transmitted to the back of the eye can also cause retinal edema and scarring. Permanent damage of the macular area results in irreversible loss of visual acuity.

Authorities agree that trauma is the most frequent cause of retinal detachments in children. Deforming and concussive forces pull at the peripheral

Table 2. Retinal and Vitreous Hemorrhages

Location	Common Name	Description
Intraretinal		
Sublaminar (Submembranar)	"Preretinal hemorrhage" Boat hemorrhage	Large, dome-shaped hemorrhage bulging into the vitreous Blood may layer in crescent, boat shape Vitreous hemorrhage results with rupture of internal limiting membrane Slow resolution of hemorrhage (weeks)
Nerve fiber layer	Flame hemorrhage	Flat, linear hemorrhage with feathered margins Peripapillary location in papilledema
Inner retinal layers	Dot hemorrhage	Deep, circinate hemorrhage with sharp margins Light colored fibrin centers may be present May resolve quickly (days)
Vitreal		
Localized vitreal	Vitreous hemorrhage	Pooling of blood into dependent areas of the vitreous Often associated with vitreous haze Slow resolution (weeks to months)
Generalized vitreal	Vitreal hemorrhage	Diffuse hemorrhage that blocks vision and view of intraocular structures Associated intraocular fibrosis and scarring possible Slow resolution (months)

131

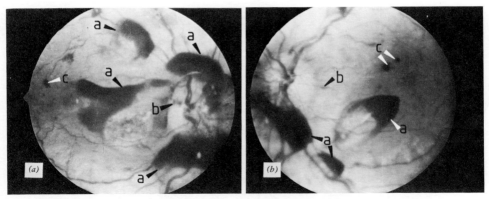

Figure 10. Retinal hemorrhages in abused children. Retinal hemorrhages are present in both fundi of a 6-month-old infant who died with skull fractures and subdural hematomas. At 3 months of age, this same infant was treated for a fractured femur after "falling out of bed." (*a*) Multiple intraretinal hemorrhages are present in the right eye with involvement of the macula. Large sublaminar hemorrhages (a) obscure underlying retinal structures. Flame hemorrhages (b) are seen oriented along the nerve fiber layer. Small, round hemorrhages (c) are present in the inner retinal layers. (*b*) The left fundus also shows the three types of retinal hemorrhages: sublaminar hemorrhages (a) predominate, but flame hemorrhages (b) are seen along the margin of the optic disc and round hemorrhages (c) in the inner retinal layers are also present. (Harcourt, B., Hopkins, D.: *Trans Ophthalmol. Soc. of the United Kingdom* 93:199, 1973.)

vitreoretinal adhesions causing retinal holes or dialysis if the traction at the retinal surface is abrupt or severe (Figure 2*a,b*). When the retina is torn, intraocular fluid can dissect the retina away from its nourishing pigment epithelial foundation. Early recognition of a detachment may allow surgical repositioning of the retina back onto the pigment epithelium.

The choroid consists of a rich capillary bed called the choriocapillaris, which nourishes the outer layers of the retina. Ocular trauma can produce intrachoroidal hemorrhages that may bleed subretinally or may dissect between the choroid and sclera resulting in a choroidal detachment. Severe trauma to the eye may break the choroid with resulting light-colored, crescentic fundus lesions concentric to the optic disc. When choroidal breaks involve the macula, visual loss is severe. The lacunar-shaped chorioretinal lesions described in physically abused children are localized areas of chorioretinal injury.

The optic nerve relays visual information from the retina to the brain. Injuries to the optic nerve following head trauma are not rare (21,22) and normally result from contusion or tearing of the nerve fibers. Pressure on the optic nerve from surrounding fractures, hematomas, or edema has also been described (23,24). However, the usual site of optic nerve damage following trauma is intracranial where the nerve leaves the optic canal. The nerve is firmly fixed at this point and subject to shearing forces from neighboring cranial structures (25). Injuries to the anterior optic nerve involve the central retinal artery, which enters the optic nerve several millimeters posterior to the globe (Fig. 11). Because of this anatomy, anterior optic nerve injuries present clinically like a central retinal artery occlusion with sudden loss of vision and a

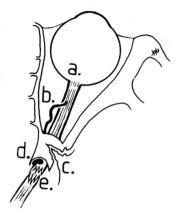

Figure 11. Traumatic optic nerve injuries. Injury of the optic nerve anterior to the entry of the central retinal artery (b) results in disruption of both the optic nerve fibers (a) and the central retinal artery blood supply to the retina. Trauma and fractures of the optic canal may result in direct laceration by bony fragments (c) or pressure on the nerve within the optic canal by edema and hemorrhage (d). Avulsion of the optic nerve fibers occurs most frequently at the point where the optic nerve leaves the canal as it enters the cranial fossa (e). (Adapted from Runyan, T.E.: Concussive and Penetrating Injuries of the Globe and Optic Nerve. C.V. Mosby, St. Louis, 1975, p. 158.)

white, edematous retina with a central red spot. Park (26) reported sudden visual loss without external evidence of trauma in a young basketball player who was jabbed in his eye. Some cases of visual loss with optic atrophy in abused children may occur by similar mechanisms. Visual loss remaining more than 4 days following injury of the optic nerve is usually permanent and optic atrophy appears 2 to 6 weeks later (Fig. 12).

OPHTHALMOLOGIC EXAMINATION OF THE CHILD ABUSE SUSPECT

The child's visual behavior and eye movements are observed while the history is reviewed with the parent(s). Unexplained nystagmus, or jerky eye movements, purposeless roving of the eyes, and poking or rubbing of the eyes signal

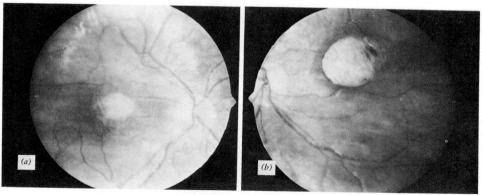

Figure 12. Masular scars and optic atrophy. This 6-year-old retarded child was known to have had a subdural hematoma at 3 months of age when he "fell out of bed." This child is legally blind (20/400) from loss of central vision due to optic atrophy. (a) The right fundus shows scarring of the macula with a white, atrophied optic disc. (b) Chorioretinal scarring of the left macula with pigmentary changes along the border of the lesion is associated with optic atrophy. (Harcourt, B., Hopkins, D.: *Trans. Ophthalmol. Soc. of the United Kingdom* 93:199, 1973).

underlying visual problems. Periorbital swelling, bruising around the eyes, or bulging of the eyes, called proptosis, may be associated with ocular damage. Injury to both eyes should arouse suspicion because accidental injuries normally involve only one side of the face (Fig. 13). Restraint of the child and the use of lid retractors or a lid speculum, made comfortable by topical anesthesia, are often required to examine the eyes in children with periorbital swelling, photophobia, and blepharospasm. Pressure on the eyes is avoided until penetrating injuries are ruled out.

Nutritional neglect and inadequate hygiene have often been described in child maltreatment cases. However, ocular findings secondary to nutritional neglect have not been described in these children.

Measurements of visual acuity and determination of the field of vision in each eye are the first tasks of the ophthalmologic examination. If the child normally wears glasses, these should be used during vision testing. Simple qualitative testing based on observation of visual behavior yields adequate information in younger children. Before touching the patient, ocular fixation and following responses of the eyes are observed by holding an interesting toy first on one side and then on the other side of the child. Normal children look to the side where the toy is held and follow it with the eyes from one side to the other. When visual responses cannot be demonstrated using toys, a light in a room darkened to eliminate other competing visual stimuli is often useful.

Peripheral vision is difficult to examine in young children but extensive visual field loss can often be demonstrated, if present. After patching or covering one eye, the visual field in the uncovered eye is determined by slowly bringing a toy into the child's peripheral view. A child with normal side vision turns his eyes and head toward the approaching toy well before it reaches the midline in front of the tested eye. Hemianopia, the loss of vision to one side, is suspected when the toy remains unnoticed by the child until it crosses the midline.

Disorders of ocular alignment are called strabismus, which means crooked. Ocular alignment is estimated by observing the corneal reflections of a light centered exactly between the two eyes with the patient looking directly at this

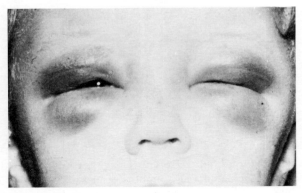

Figure 13. Bilateral eye injuries. This 2-year-old child was the victim of nonaccidental injury. Obvious trauma involving both eyes should always raise suspicions of child abuse. (Photograph courtesy of Medical Illustration Department, Great Ormond Street Hospital for Sick Children, London.)

Figure 14. The Hirschberg corneal light reflex. The esotropia or inturning of the right eye is emphasized by the asymmetry of the corneal light reflexes shown here with the patient looking at the light with her left eye.

light. Normally, the corneal light reflexes are symmetrically located nasal to the center of each pupil. Asymmetry of the corneal reflexes indicates strabismus, which is confirmed by a cover test (Fig. 14). The cover test is used to determine if each eye is simultaneously viewing the object of regard with its fovea. The child's attention is focused on an interesting object in the distance, and each eye is covered while observing the uncovered eye. A consistent movement of the uncovered eye, when covering the contralateral eye, proves that the uncovered eye is misaligned. Ocular rotations are evaluated in gaze right, gaze left, gaze up, and gaze down. When one or both eyes do not fully rotate during these versions, an ocular motility disorder exists and a complete study is required (Fig. 15). Ocular rotations can be stimulated in babies by rotating the patient around the examiner at eye level. The resulting vestibulo-ocular eye movements are observed and deficiencies of abduction to the side as seen with sixth nerve palsy can be detected. Blind babies may continue their nystagmus for some time after the spinning because they lack the visual input needed to quickly dampen their vestibularly produced eye movements. Abnormal ocular alignment, rotations, and other details of the external eye examination are best recorded on a pictorogram of the eyes (Fig. 16).

If the eyes appear normal, the globes are gently palpated through the closed eyelids. Glaucoma is suspected if the eyeball is hard, while a very soft globe may indicate hidden rupture, and the eye is covered with a protective shield pending ophthalmologic consultation. The cornea, anterior chamber, and iris are satisfactorily examined with a penlight or ophthalmoscope with simultaneous evaluation of the pupillary reflexes. Traumatic iritis with flare, an abnormal turbidity of the anterior chamber aqueous fluid, is common after ocular trauma. Blood in the anterior chamber is easily seen, but flare, as well as cells and fine pigment particles, are seen only with the magnification of a slit-lamp.

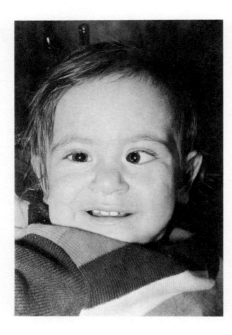

Figure 15. Ocular versions to the right. Deficiency of abduction or lateral rotation of the right eye is apparent when the child looks to her right as shown. The right eye does not rotate to the right side because of paresis of the sixth nerve, which innervates the right lateral rectus muscle.

The iris is inspected for tears, damage to the pupillary sphincter, and color changes. Damage to the optic nerve may leave an amaurotic or blind eye with loss of the direct pupillary constriction to light. Consensual pupillary constriction to light is usually preserved in the damaged eye because this reflex reaches the iris by the third cranial nerve rather than the optic nerve.

Unless there is neurologic contraindication, the pupils are dilated. The lens, the optic disc, the macula, and the peripheral retina are examined. If necessary, the patient is restrained to allow adequate evaluation of the intraocular anatomy. Peripheral retinal scars, tears or detachments of the retina, and optic disc elevation are best detected with the indirect ophthalmoscope. Of course, the intraocular examination in young children is greatly facilitated during sedation or general anesthesia indicated for other procedures.

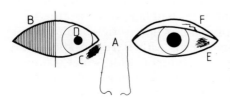

Figure 16. Ocular diagrams document the findings. The eyes are sketched, and the injuries and abnormalities are recorded. Large amounts of data can be quickly and clearly displayed. Abnormalities shown in this example include strabismus (crossed eyes) (A), limitation of gaze to the right as seen in paralysis of the sixth nerve (B), bruising of the right lower eyelid (C), unequal pupils called anisocoria (D), conjunctival hemorrhage of the left eye (E), and a laceration with ptosis, or droop, of the left eyelid (F). (Adapted from Jampolsky, A: A Simplified Approach to Strabismus Diagnosis, in Symposium on Strabismus. *New Orleans Acad. Ophthalmol.* C.V. Mosby, 1967, p. 49.)

A ONE-MINUTE VISUAL SYSTEM SCREENING TECHNIQUE

Often the busy clinician is unable to complete a comprehensive evaluation of every organ system in each of his patients. The following simplified visual screening procedure has proven useful for efficient identification of abnormal visual states in young children. The only requirements for this test are a bright ophthalmoscope and an examining room that can be darkened. All lights except the light of the direct ophthalmoscope are extinguished. Given no other visual stimuli, normal children readily fix their attention and their eyes on the ophthalmoscope light, which is moved about to stimulate eye movements. Unexplained photophobia, nystagmus, and apparent blindness demand complete investigation. Ocular rotations are assessed by placing the ophthalmoscope light to the child's right and left while observing the quality and extent of the eye movements. Using the largest aperature of the ophthalmoscope and with the light shining at maximum brightness, the examiner backs away from the patient while looking through the ophthalmoscope. Both red reflexes from the retinas are seen side by side within the large circle of light falling on the child's face; that is, the two red reflexes are simultaneously visualized. These two fundus reflexes are easily compared and studied in the darkness of the examining room. The quality, intensity, and color of the two red reflexes should be equal (27). Abnormalities of the ocular media, such as corneal opacities, cataracts, vitreous hemorrhages, intraocular foreign bodies, tumors, and large retinal detachments, are readily apparent and evidenced by asymmetry or abnormality of the red reflexes. Ocular alignment is surveyed by noting the position of the corneal light reflexes (Hirschberg), which can be seen against the red retinal reflexes. A cover test is completed by placing the examiner's hand between the ophthalmoscope and the patient's eye while observing the uncovered eye. If the patient's uncovered eye moves to take up fixation of the light, this confirms that this eye was not previously aligned on the light. Any eye movement that occurs when covering one eye proves the presence of strabismus. Leaving the room dark, the pupillary reflexes are tested next. The ophthalmoscope is used to stimulate each eye separately, observing the pupil's constriction to direct light stimulation. The ophthalmoscope light is then swung from one pupil to the other while watching for paradoxical pupillary dilation, which would indicate a defect in the afferent visual pathway. The external parts of the eye are examined using the light, and finally the optic discs and retina are surveyed through the undilated pupil with the smallest light aperature of the ophthalmoscope. When ocular abnormalities are found or suspected, a complete ophthalmologic evaluation with dilation of the pupils is scheduled. Patients with known ocular trauma should always have a complete dilated examination.

LABORATORY TESTING OF THE VISUAL SYSTEM

Increasingly sophisticated radiologic examinations are available for studying the visual system. Computed tomography (CT) of the orbit and head graphically dissects the visual system to reveal intraorbital and intracranial anatomy.

Structures important to visual function that can be selectively viewed with CT scans include the globe and its chambers, the lens, the extraocular muscles, the optic nerve, and areas of the brain associated with vision. Standard skull radiographs with special views of the optic foramen are useful when optic nerve damage is suspected.

Ultrasound scanning of the eye and orbit is indicated when the internal ocular structures cannot be visualized; for example, when blood or cataracts block the view of the inside of the eye.

Neuro-physiological testing, available in major centers, can be useful in the evaluation of children with visual loss. The electroretinogram (ERG), visual evoked potential (VEP), and the electroencephalogram (EEG) are three tests helpful in certain cases of child abuse.

The circulatory system of the eye can be studied by injecting fluorescein dye into the circulation and photographing the dye as it travels through the ocular vessels. Subtle macular lesions, abnormal vessels, and leakage of dye from the optic disc in papilledema are a few of the abnormalities that can be studied with fluorescein angiography.

MULTIDISCIPLINARY TEAMWORK

Modern management of child abuse cases requires multidisciplinary teamwork. The medical charts in these cases are especially important and should be clearly recorded avoiding medical and specialty jargon so that the patient and various members of the child abuse team can profit maximally from all evaluations and consultations. Cooperation and explicit exchange of information between primary care physicians and ophthalmologists increases the probability of comprehending the messages sequestered in the eyes of many of these children who are too young or too frightened to tell about their injuries.

REFERENCES

1. Radbill SX: A history of child abuse and infanticide, in Hefler RE, Kempe CH (eds): *The Battered Child.* Chicago, University of Chicago Press, 1968, p 6.
2. Caffey J: Multiple fractures in the long bones of infants suffering from chronic subdural hematoma. *AJR* 56:163, 1946.
3. Silverman RN: The roentgen manifestations of unrecognized skeletal trauma in infants. *AJR* 69:413, 1953.
4. Kiffney GT Jr: The eye of the "battered child." *Arch Ophthalmol* 72:231, 1964.
5. Gilkes MJ, Mann TP: Letters to the editor. *Lancet* 2:468, 1967.
6. Maroteaux P, Lamy M: Fundi of battered babies. *Lancet* 2:829, 1967.
7. Maroteaux P, Fessard C, Aron J, et al: The sequelae of Silverman's syndrome—A study of 16 cases. *Presse Med* 75:711, 1967.
8. Harcourt B, Hopkins D: Permanent chorio-retinal lesions in childhood of suspected traumatic origin. *Trans of the Ophthalmol Soc of the United Kingdom* 93:199, 1973.
9. Friendly DS: Ocular manifestations of physical child abuse. *Trans Amer Acad Ophthalmol & Otolaryn* 75:318, 1971.

10. Tomasi LG, Rosman NP: Purtscher retinopathy in the battered child syndrome. *Am J Dis Child* 129:133, 1975.

11. Harcourt B, Hopkins D: Ophthalmic manifestations of the battered baby syndrome. *Br Med J* 3:398, 1971.

12. Mushin AS: Ocular damage in the battered baby syndrome. *Br Med J* 3:402, 1971.

13. Taylor D, Bentovim A: Recurrent nonaccidentally inflicted chemical eye injuries to siblings. *J Pediatr Ophthalmol* 13:238, 1976.

14. Tseng SS, Keys MP: Battered child syndrome simulating congenital glaucoma. *Arch Ophthalmol* 94:839, 1976.

15. Mushin A, Morgan G: Ocular injury in the battered baby syndrome. *Br J Ophthalmol* 55:343, 1971.

16. Courville CB: Coup-contre-coup mechanism of craniocerebral injuries. *Arch Surg* 45:19, 1942.

17. Wolter JR: Coup-contre-coup mechanism of ocular injuries. *Am J Ophthalmol* 56:785, 1963.

18. Caffey J: The whiplash shaken infant syndrome: Manual shaking by the extremities with whiplash induced intracranial and intraocular bleedings, linked with residual permanent brain damage and mental retardation. *Pediatrics* 54:396, 1974.

19. Barsewisch von B: *Perinatal retinal hemorrhages.* Berlin, Springer Verlag, 1979.

20. Giles CL: Retinal Hemorrhages in the Newborn. *Am J Ophthalmol* 49:1005, 1960.

21. Russell WR: Injury to cranial nerves and optic chiasm, in Brock S (ed): *Injuries of the Brain and Spinal Cord and their Coverings,* 4th ed. New York, Springer Publishing Company, Inc, 1960, 5:118.

22. Turner JWA: Indirect injuries of the optic nerve. *Brain* 66:140, 1943.

23. Hammer G, Ambos E: Traumatic hematoma of the optic nerve and the possibility of surgical treatment. *Klin Monatsbl Augenheilkd* 159:818, 1971.

24. Hughes B: Indirect injury of the optic nerves and chiasma. *Bull Johns Hopkins Hosp* 111:98, 1962.

25. Seitz R: Etiology and genesis of acute blindness as a consequence of blunt skull traumas. *Klin Monatsbl Augenheilkd* 143:414, 1963.

26. Park JH, Frenkel M, Dobbie JG: Evulsion of the optic nerve. *Am J Ophthalmol* 72:969, 1971.

27. Bruckner R: Exakte strabismusdiagnostik bei ½–3 Jährigen Kindern mit einem einfachen verfahren, dem "Durchleuch tungstest." *Ophthalmologica* 144:184, 1962.

8
Bite Marks and Oral Manifestations of Child Abuse and Neglect

Joseph E. Bernat

Oral lacerations, jaw and teeth injuries, dental neglect, and epidermal bite marks are among the manifestations of child maltreatment. The head is a common area of injury (1,2). Cameron et al. (3) reported that out of 29 cases of physical child abuse, 79% suffered head trauma. They also reported that 48% of the cases demonstrated face, cheek, and lower jaw trauma and that 45% of the cases showed upper lip injuries. Skinner and Castle (4) reported 78 cases and found that facial trauma was present in 43.5% of them. O'Neill et al. (2) examined 110 abused children and found that 65% presented with head trauma. Head injuries are even more frequent in fatal cases, where it has been reported to occur in up to 80% of the cases (3). A possible reason that head injuries occur so frequently is that this part of the body best represents the "self" of the attacked child (5,6). The implications for the practitioner who is examining young children are apparent. Oral and facial injuries should alert the examiner to the possibility of maltreatment when there are injuries to other parts of the body and the history does not adequately explain the injuries.

In this chapter, recognition and initial management of the numerous oral and facial manifestations of child abuse will be presented. Many of them, when taken by themselves, would not necessarily arouse the suspicion of the examiner as to the true cause of the injury. These injuries include any traumatic injury of the lips, teeth and surrounding alveolar structures, and the jaws. Fractured, luxated or avulsed teeth, contusions and lacerations on the lips and tongue, and acute jaw fractures are all specific examples of the injuries seen in the maltreatment cases. In addition, the torn labial frenum in specific age groups is felt by many authorities to be pathognomonic of child abuse (3,7). Since child abuse is not limited to preschoolers, many older children who visit a dentist routinely may be the victims of maltreatment. Also, sequelae of oral trauma can be seen in the older child; these include the presence of discolored and devitalized teeth, old root and jaw fractures, and scarring in and around the mouth.

Neglect of a child's dentition is another aspect of the maltreatment of children. Dental caries is man's most prevalent disease with epidemiologic studies showing that 50% of 2-year-old children have at least one carious lesion (8,9,10). By the time a child has reached school age, this number has increased to eight lesions (8–10). Clearly this can be an area of severe neglect; this is especially true considering the high sucrose diet of today's children. Every physician should become familiar with the many clinical signs and symptoms of dental caries. This would include discolored, fractured, and grossly carious teeth. If the examining physician has any doubts about the condition of the teeth, a dental consultation is in order. Not having teeth repaired, whether they be permanent or deciduous, can be very painful and debilitating for the child.

A separate but related topic, bite marks, will also be discussed in this chapter. Bite marks have been defined by MacDonald (11) as "a mark made by the teeth either alone or in combination with other mouth parts." As incriminating evidence, they have been found in foodstuff, human flesh, and other objects (12–15). Like fingerprints, teeth marks can be used for identification, and their use historically predates that of fingerprints. The first paper on bite marks was published over 100 years ago (16). Since that time there has been a steady stream of papers on the subject. Within the last few years, there has been an increasing incidence of reported lesions, particularly in sexual assault, murder, and child abuse. Some authors now feel that they figure predominately in child abuse cases (7). The main reason more and more cases have been reported is better recognition and reporting techniques. This section of the chapter is devoted to the recognition of bite marks in human flesh in suspected child maltreatment cases.

ORAL INJURIES

THE NORMAL DENTITION

The first teeth appear in the mouth at approximately 6 months of age, and from this point until around 3 years of age the normal child will be completing his deciduous dentition. From 3 years until 6, the dentition remains relatively stable with only minor growth changes being evident. At approximately 6 years of age the permanent dentition begins to appear and is complete around 12 except for the third molars. For the sake of simplicity, only the normal complete deciduous dentition will be discussed. However, except for tooth size and configuration, the two normal dentitions will look the same.

Figure 1 shows the normal complete deciduous dentition and surrounding oral structures. First note that the lips are symmetrical and of normal size. The vermillion border is intact and without scars. Upon opening, the commissures are symmetrical. If the lips are reflected back, they reveal the maxillary and

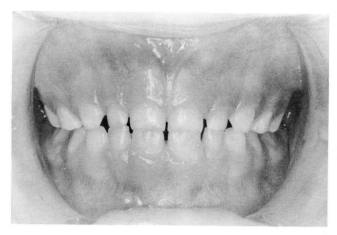

Figure 1. The normal dentition of a 5-year-old child. Note that there are no broken or carious teeth; all teeth meet evenly and at the same time. There are bilateral spaces (diastema) between the teeth. The maxillary labial frenum is intact.

mandibular labial frena. In their normal state they are V-shaped and attach the lips to the alveolar ridges. The apex of the V attaches from 1 to 5 mm above or below the midline between the two central incisors. The mucosa of the lips, cheeks, and alveolar processes is smooth, pink, keratinized to varying degrees, and intact. The tongue basically fills in the space between the lower teeth. It should be mobile enough to protrude from the mouth, touch the posterior portion of the palate, and have enough lateral movement to protrude each cheek. When the tongue is lifted up, it reveals the lingual frenum. Like its counterparts the labial frena, the lingual frenum is a V-shaped muscle attachment in the midline of the mouth.

The teeth are 20 in number. Both arches should be parabolic in shape without any displaced teeth. The plane of occlusion demonstrates a gentle curve (Fig. 2). A space or diastema between the teeth is either at the midline or bilateral in nature. As the child approaches the age of 6, the upper and lower anterior teeth will begin to show some mobility. Before this age, the teeth should be firm. All teeth should have a uniform white color, show no fractures (Fig. 3), and should not be carious (Fig. 4). When the mandible is closed, all parts should meet simultaneously, painlessly, and without any noise.

When examining the normal dentition, the practitioner must keep in mind that the mouth, like other parts of the body, is subject to a wide range of normal variability.

ORAL INJURIES

As mentioned previously, many different injuries can be seen in the abused and neglected child. Although many of these injuries are best treated by a dentist, a discussion of recognition and initial management is appropriate for the physician. The injuries discussed are organized into the following categories:

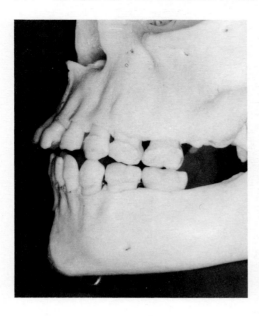

Figure 2. The plane of occlusion is demonstrated on this skull. It is usually a gentle curve from the anterior to the posterior.

frenum tears, lip injuries, tooth and alveolar injuries, jaw fractures, and tongue lacerations.

Frenum Tears

As stated earlier, in abuse cases that demonstrate head injuries, the frenum tear occurs in nearly half of them and is considered by many to be pathognomonic of child abuse (3,7). The tear can occur through two mechanisms. One is a direct blow to the mouth, possibly to silence a screaming or crying child. Besides the split frenum, there may be associated contusions, broken teeth, and fractures of the facial bones. A second mode of injury occurs at feeding time.

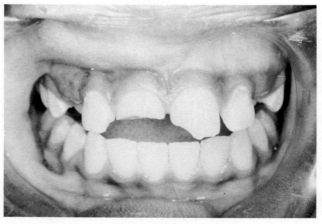

Figure 3. Three incisors are fractured in this patient. Immediate treatment of these injuries may prevent the loss of a tooth at a later date.

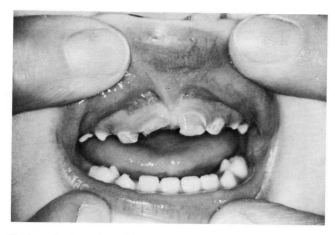

Figure 4. Carious incisors in a 22-month-old child. Note the range of destruction.

An angry parent, frustrated at a slow eater, may force a spoon or bottle into the baby's mouth, ripping the frenum. There are usually no other injuries associated with this injury (Fig. 5). However, the circumstances surrounding the tear will arouse suspicion. The age of the child is significant. A frenum tear can happen accidentally to the young toddler who falls on a coffee table while learning to walk. Generally, children less than 6 months of age do not have the opportunity to traumatize themselves; and 2- to 5-year-old children are usually too stable. Therefore, the frenum tear in a nonambulatory infant must evoke a careful history on the part of the examining physician since it is unlikely to have been caused accidentally.

The treatment of frenum tears is similar to that of any laceration with one exception; the healing time in a healthy child's mouth is very short, thus in

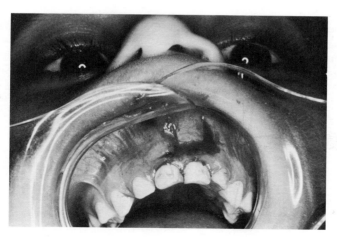

Figure 5. This torn frenum in a 4-year-old child demonstrates the typical "three corner tear." The lip has been retracted upward and, since there is no separation of the wound, no sutures are needed.

small and medium tears, suturing may not be necessary. In some instances the sutures may even retard healing. When determining the treatment of these lacerations, several factors must be considered. These include the patient's age, medical history, the need for other medical treatment, the size of the tear, and the mobility of the lip.

The age of the patient may dictate the treatment of a small frenum tear. If a child is very young and the emergency room personnel cannot control the patient, the physician must evaluate his suturing ability under these circumstances. Certainly, if the tear is large as outlined below, all attempts must be made to restrain the child and suture the wound.

As is true with all intraoral injuries, a history of rheumatic fever or cardiac defects must elicit special consideration. It has long been recognized that an event that may cause a bacteremia from oral organisms can be the primary factor in subacute bacterial endocarditis. With this in mind, the child with a cardiac problem must be treated with penicillin (17,18).

When evaluating the local factors for suturing a torn frenum, the examining physician first must assess the size of the wound. This is best done by firmly grasping the lip and reflecting it upward. The wound is then visualized and it is determined if the underlying alveolar bone is exposed. Continue to stretch the lip upward, and notice whether the wound separates. If the bone is exposed or the tear separates and moves with lip movement, the wound should be sutured. However, if the gingival tissue has rolled up on itself or is very friable, it is virtually impossible to place sutures, and healing must occur by secondary intention. As with all wounds, debride thoroughly before placing any sutures. It is also advisable but not necessary to use a resorbable material. Antibiotic therapy is usually not necessary, but if the wound is dirty or has exposed large areas of bone, it should be considered. In addition, the status of the patient's tetanus immunizations should be updated if necessary (19).

Lip Injuries

The lip may be injured at the same time that the frenum is torn, but in most cases, they appear as separate injuries. Lip injuries are most frequently seen as contusions, lacerations, and abrasions. Occasionally they may present as burns. Most of the injuries to the lips that result from child abuse are not very serious. In most cases they look much worse than they actually are, and the treatment is conservative. Treatment consists mostly of observation; this is especially true of contusions. The mechanism of lip wounds is that of a blunt force trapping the lip between it and the teeth. This produces a wound where the skin or mucosa is not broken. Contamination and infection of the wound are seldom seen. Wounds may be extremely painful due to the abraded epithelial tissue. Treatment of these wounds is no different from that of any other abrasion.

Since the lip may also be lacerated, this wound should be treated first. As with all lacerations, superficial and deep closure may be necessary. Suturing the lip requires that close detail must be paid to the alignment of the vermillion border. This is the red margin of the upper and lower lip that begins at the exterior edge of the intraoral mucosa and extends outward to the extraoral labial cutaneous junction (20). If this is not properly aligned, a cosmetic defect will result. If there is any question about the proper positioning of the flaps of the wound, an oral or plastic surgeon should be consulted.

Burns of the lips can be seen in child abuse cases and are caused by hot utensils or cigarettes. The management of these wounds is the same as that for other burns unless the angle, or commissure, is involved. If the commissure is involved it is possible that the opposing lips may adhere to one another during healing. This will cause scarring and contractions of one side of the mouth, with the results being an asymmetrical mouth (21,22). A plastic or oral surgeon should be involved in the treatment and follow-up of these injuries.

Tooth and Alveolar Injuries

Traumatic injuries to the deciduous teeth of preschool children are very common. Some authorities report the incidence to be as high as 50%; that is, half of all children under the age of 5 will exhibit evidence of oral trauma (23–25). Obviously, only some of these injuries can be attributed to abuse. However, child abuse cannot be ruled out in any of the injuries unless the examiner is sure that the reported history is true. Certainly, if the injury is accompanied by other physical injuries consistent with abuse, suspicions must be aroused.

Injuries to the teeth can fall into the following categories: luxation, intrusion, avulsion, and fractures.

Luxation

Luxated teeth are those that are loosened in the mouth but have not left the socket. Both deciduous and permanent teeth are easily luxated by a blow to the mouth. With the luxation, the tooth may be displaced in any direction. The severity of the blow need not be intense, as a well-directed hit may cause the teeth to become loosened. It is very difficult to hit only one tooth; so although only one is apparently luxated, all teeth must be examined for their degree of mobility. A tooth is considered to be mobile if it moves more than 1 mm in any direction when force is placed on it. Notations as to which teeth are mobile and their specific degree of mobility should be made in the chart.

Treatment of luxations will depend on the age of the patient, the degree of mobility, the bite (occlusion) of the patient, and other injuries to the surrounding tissue. A child who is 5 or 6 years old usually has some loose teeth due to normal exfoliation and eruption patterns. Therefore, any severe luxations in the deciduous dentition of this group should be considered for removal. Those that occur in the younger age group should be retained for functional, esthetic, and orthodontic considerations. They can be left alone without any treatment if there is no danger of the teeth being aspirated, they do not interfere with the occlusion, and there are no other intraoral injuries. The patient should be referred to a dentist as soon as possible in all luxation injuries.

Intrusions

Intruded teeth are those that have been forced into the alveolar bone. Clinically they will appear to be shorter than the rest of the teeth in the arch. They have been forced deeper into the supporting (alveolar) bone than the socket will allow (Fig. 6). Intrusions are caused by a severe blow to the incisal edge of the tooth. Deciduous teeth are more prone to being intruded than permanent teeth due to their short crown/root ratio. Many times the teeth will be hit hard enough to drive them completely out of sight and give the clinical appearance of avulsed teeth (Fig. 7). A complete exam including radiographs will reveal the true extent of the injury.

The child should be seen by a dentist as soon as possible following the injury. A dental radiograph can best ascertain that there are no fractures of any kind. Treatment of intruded teeth is usually that of observing the teeth until they reerupt, which they will usually do in 3 to 12 months (26).

Avulsions

Avulsions are those injuries where the teeth are totally removed from the socket. A sharp blow to the facial side of a tooth can cause the tooth to be removed from the socket. This injury happens more commonly with permanent teeth. The examiner must make an attempt to locate the missing tooth, as it may have been swallowed or aspirated. A dental radiograph is necessary to determine the location of the tooth, since many times it will have been intruded. It may be necessary to take abdominal films to rule out aspiration. Once the tooth has been located, determine whether it is deciduous or permanent, evaluate the wound for the need of a tetanus booster, and begin immediate treatment.

The treatment of avulsed teeth is immediate replantation. Studies have shown that the most important factor in whether the replantation is successful is the amount of time the tooth is out of the mouth (27,28). Deciduous teeth cannot be replanted; those that are avulsed should be treated as if the tooth had been extracted, if there are no other injuries. This includes control of the hemorrhage with pressure and instructions to the parents that the child cannot drink any carbonated beverages or through a straw and cannot rinse for 24 hours. For

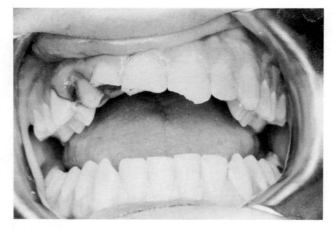

Figure 6. The upper right canine in this patient has been intruded while the incisors have been fractured. The amount of intrusion can best be gauged by comparing it to the canine on the opposite side.

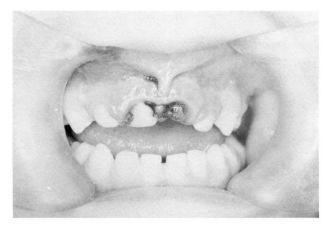

Figure 7. Both central incisors have been intruded, but the left one has been pushed out of sight. Only a radiograph can properly diagnose this.

permanent teeth, the tooth must be put back into the socket. If replaced within the first 15 minutes after avulsion, the success rate approaches 90% (28). However, after 1 hour, the success rate falls to less than 15% (28). To replant the tooth, hold it by the crown only (touching the root may cause later rejection) and gently remove any foreign bodies and debris. This is best done with sterile water and a syringe. Next, gently return the tooth root first to the socket and carefully push it in as far as it will go. Have the patient hold his finger on the tooth so that it will not come out again, and obtain an immediate dental consultation. Do not wait for the dentist to replant the tooth. Replant the tooth even if it has been out longer than an hour, as it is more desirable to have a tooth in place for even a short period of time than to have a prosthetic device. If it is impossible to put the tooth back into its socket, clean off the tooth and have the patient place the tooth under his tongue or in the cheeks. The success rate seems to be higher in those cases where the teeth are immersed in the patient's saliva and the warmth of the mouth (28). If the patient is unable to place the tooth in his mouth, the next best thing is to place it in the mouth of one of the parents. If all this is impossible, place it in a container of sterile water and call a dentist. Evaluate the need for a tetanus booster and begin antibiotic coverage.

Fractures of Teeth

Fractured anterior teeth in children are a common finding. Only a small percentage of these are the result of intentional trauma. Most fractures are the result of a severe blow to the teeth with a fairly hard object. These most likely occur during falling or other accidents, but can also be the result of being struck. A fracture can occur along any part of the tooth from the incisal edge to the tooth apex (Fig. 8). All fractures should be examined with a dental radiograph. As with avulsion, time is the most important factor in the treatment of fractures. Injuries first seen in an emergency room and dismissed by the examiner as "only a chip" have resulted in the loss of the tooth because of the

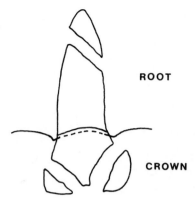

ROOT

CROWN

Figure 8. The most common sites of fractures in anterior teeth. The crown will usually lose one or both corners and the root fractures near its apex. Some accidents may cause damage to all three areas or more.

long time lapse between the accident and the treatment. Treatment of these injuries can be done only by a dentist, and they should be referred to one immediately.

FRACTURES OF THE JAWS

Fractures of the jaws occur most commonly following automobile accidents and assault cases (29). Maxillary fractures are relatively rare in children; when they do occur, it is usually the result of severe trauma and is accompanied by extensive and complicated damage to soft tissue and bones (30,31). The mandible, on the other hand, is very susceptible to fractures. Structurally, the mandible is a hoop of bone suspended at either end by ligamentous joints. The chin remains the most prominent feature of the face, thus making the mandible more prone to receiving trauma. The strongest part of the structure is the middle of the hoop or the chin, and the weakest parts are the two ends or the condyles (29). The severity of a jaw fracture coupled with other body injuries of a suspicious nature should certainly arouse timely questions on the part of the examiner.

As stated above, many of the cases of fractures of the face will be accompanied by other injuries. Some of these injuries may make it difficult to properly examine a small child. Younger patients routinely lack the ability to cooperate for examination and it may be necessary to examine and take x-ray films of the child under heavy sedation or a general anesthetic. A complete examination for facial fractures will include extra-oral and intraoral components along with the standard radiographs. Each of these will be discussed.

A complete radiographic survey is a must in all suspected fracture cases. This survey includes a minimum of right and left lateral oblique views, posterior-anterior views, and a panoramic film of the midface. In reading the films, pay close attention to the bony borders on all films (29,32).

Bilateral fractures of the mandible occur with such frequency that it is assumed that all fractures are bilateral until proven otherwise (33). A condylar fracture on one side is many times accompanied by a body or ramus fracture on the other side; bilateral condylar fractures happen as a result of a blow to the chin. If these fractures are suspected, a lateral oblique jaw film on the side of the suspected fracture will show the injury best. In addition, the improvements made in the techniques involved in taking the panoramic dental x-ray film have made this an ideal film for showing fractures of the mandible. Many of the newer machines can be adjusted to take special views of the condyles and ramus (34). It would be advantageous to obtain a panoramic x-ray film on all suspected mandibular fractures (Fig. 9).

Diagnosing maxillary fractures on routine radiographs can be very difficult. If a fractured maxilla is suspected, the film of choice is a Waters view. Other special views are available for the various fractures of the face. These would include films of the zygomatic arches, the orbits, and the maxillary sinuses. Some authorities believe that if standard x-ray films fail to demonstrate a fracture but clinically one is still suspected, a lateral skull film should be taken (29). If on this radiograph the frontonasal suture line is open, a fracture of the maxilla is very likely. If the suture line is not open, the maxilla still may be fractured and the clinician must rely on the facial and intraoral examinations for further information. In cases where jaw fractures have been demonstrated and in those where extraoral radiographs are unable to demonstrate the break, a series of intraoral films of the suspected area should be taken. These x-ray films (called periapical x-rays) will show not only the routine jaw fractures, but also the alveolar fractures, breaks through tooth buds, and symphyseal fractures. If a dental department is unavailable to take these specialty films, many standard medical x-ray units can be properly columated for this purpose.

In any facial trauma case, jaw fractures must be suspected. The first step in diagnosing these fractures is an extraoral exam. It should begin with the noting of any contusions around the jaws. Many fractures will result in a contusion directly above the fracture site. Next, judge the symmetry of the face. To do this, place two rigid objects, such as tongue blades (Fig. 10), against the face. The normal patient will show the blades slightly divergent toward the top of the head. Deviations from this will strongly indicate a fracture of the mandible, maxilla, or zygomatic processes. Next, palpate the mandibular condyles and the temporomandibular joint. This is done while standing directly in front of the patient, both forefingers placed in the external auditory meatuses with the balls

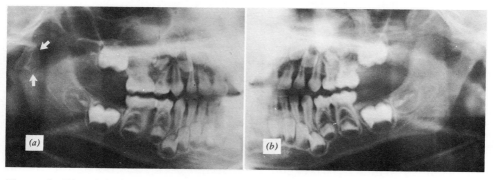

Figure 9. The right and left halves of a panoramic dental x-ray film. The right condyle is fractured (arrow) and displaced. This type of x-ray film best demonstrates the structures of the lower and middle thirds of the face.

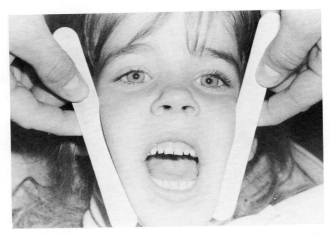

Figure 10. To determine facial symmetry, place two rigid objects such as these tongue blades along the bony facial structures. If unsymmetrical, a fracture should be suspected.

of the fingers turned forward, and the other fingers are rested along the posterior border of the mandible. When the mandible opens, the unfractured condyle will move out of the glenoid fossa. A condylar fracture is suspected if the condyle does not move out of the fossa or if the mandible deviates to one side on opening. The shift of the midline (as determined by the teeth) will be toward the affected side. Using the remaining fingers, palpate the posterior border of the ramus for any discontinuities. This entire examination should be done with extreme care as the patient with a fractured jaw will experience pain and difficulty on opening. The next area of examination is the zygomatic arch. Fractures of the posterior portion are common even when there are no other facial fractures. A dimple over the arch area is considered pathognomonic of a fracture (29). Palpate the entire length of the arch and continue to the infraorbital ridge and lateral rim of the orbit. A notch or moving fragment will indicate a fracture site. If both the posterior segment of the zygoma and the lateral rim of the orbit are fractured, the zygoma will be completely separated from the maxilla. If bilateral zygomatic arch fractures are found, a transverse facial fracture must be suspected. Pay close attention to any bleeding from the ears, cerebrospinal rhinitis, and general neurologic abnormalities. Any of these signs can indicate serious fractures involving the base of the skull and require immediate consultation from the neurosurgery department (29).

Begin the intraoral examination by determining whether or not the arch form is intact. An abrupt change in the occlusal plane of the teeth, diastemata, and gingival tears should all arouse suspicion. When the patient closes his mouth, all teeth should meet at the same time. The maxillary arch overlaps the entire mandibular arch in the normal occlusion and deviations from this will suggest a fracture. If there are no obvious displacements of the teeth, the jaws should be examined manually (see examination section). The anterior border of the mandibular ramus is palpated bilaterally by running a forefinger up and down its length. The coronoid process can best be palpated intraorally at this time.

As with most fractures, facial fractures should be treated as soon as possible. The type of treatment necessary will depend on the age of the child, the location of the fracture, and the severity of the fracture. It must be remembered that bone heals rapidly in children and therefore treatment must begin immediately. It is best to consult with an oral or plastic surgeon for treatment of these injuries as the skills required for reduction and especially fixation are sometimes complicated and are best handled by these specialists.

TONGUE INJURIES

Tongues can be injured during a blow to the mandible forcing the teeth shut and trapping the tongue between them. Most injuries occur on the lateral border. These suggest trauma to the chin and it is essential that the examination include the mandible and the surrounding structures. Injuries caused by the teeth will have jagged edges and will exhibit a crushed appearance. When examining the tongue, it is best to ask the patient to extend it as far as possible while holding a gauze just outside the mouth. As the tip of the tongue enters the gauze, grasp the tongue with the gauze and retract it as far as possible. Rotate it right and left and then lift it up as far as possible. This will allow you to see all parts of the tongue.

Treatment of tongue lacerations can be difficult because of the problems of holding the tongue still. This problem can be overcome with adequate local anesthesia and rapid suturing techniques. The best way to obtain profound anesthesia of the tongue is through a lingual block rather than infiltration around the wound. Many of these wounds will not need suturing. If on movement of the tongue the edges of the laceration do not open, do not suture. However, if the wound travels through the entire thickness, it must be sutured.

NEGLECT

As mentioned earlier, neglect of dental needs can certainly cause a child pain and discomfort. However, there are certain problems in determining whether a child's poor dentition is a result of malicious neglect or nothing more than the normal neglect caused by ignorance, fear, or lack of money. It is virtually impossible for an examining physician or dentist to tell by physical examination alone whether or not the oral conditions seen are due to unjustifiable neglect. Only through an adequate history and repeated attempts to secure treatment for the child, can neglect be proven. Even then, the degree of severity certainly does not compare with that of withholding care from truly ill children. Keeping this in mind, neglected dental care can be used as an additional piece of evidence in the context of other medical neglect.

On seeing a mouth full of carious lesions, an examining physician must refer this child to a dentist for treatment. If neglect is suspected, a follow-up call to the dentist is recommended. If the parents have been adequately counseled as to the importance of the treatment and can afford it, repeated attempts to secure treatment must be made. If the parents still do not conscientiously seek treatment, neglect must be assumed and the proper authorities notified (35).

A QUICK OROFACIAL EXAMINATION FOR SUSPECTED ABUSE VICTIMS

Patients are continually coming to emergency rooms in need of a good oral examination. Traditionally, the medical examination skips lightly over oral structures but a thorough examination will only take slightly longer than a cursory one. Keeping this and the previous sections in mind, the following paragraphs describe a fast thorough orofacial examination for suspected child abuse victims.

Standing directly in front of the patient, look at the face for obvious lacerations, bruises, edema, scars (especially on the lips), and overall facial symmetry. Have the patient open and close his mouth several times while you are in front of him. Check for deviations, listen for noises, and ask if there is any pain. Place your forefingers in the external auditory meatuses and examine the temporomandibular joint and external borders of the mandible (as explained in the above on jaw fractures). Using your forefinger, palpate the infraorbital and supraorbital ridges, the entire length of the zygoma, and the lateral nasal areas.

Proceed to the intraoral examination by placing the patient in a reclining position on an examining table with a good overhead light source. It would be ideal to have a small mouth mirror but if unavailable, a moistened tongue blade will do. Resist the temptation to look directly into the throat, and first reflect the lips back. This is best done one at a time. Check for frenum tears, lacerations, abrasions, scars, and burns. It may be easier to have the child's teeth together at this time. With the mouth closed, the anterior teeth can be inspected for caries, fractures, luxations, avulsions, and intrusions. Remember that intruded teeth may appear to be missing teeth. Ask the child to bite his teeth together and check to see that all parts meet evenly. Ask if there is any pain on clenching.

Have the child open his mouth as wide as possible. Check again for deviations, noises, and pain. Note any discrepancies in the occlusal plane or arch form. Manually examine the jaws by first placing the forefingers of each hand on the occlusal surfaces of the teeth and the thumbs along the lower border of the mandible. The left forefinger is placed as far distal as possible on the right side of the mandible and the right forefinger is placed approximately 3 to 4 cm mesial. An up-and-down motion is made while moving the fingers around the arch (Fig. 11). If there is a fracture present, the pieces should move apart with pain and crepitus. The maxilla is examined by placing the forefinger on the palatal surface of the teeth and the thumb on the facial surface. The segments are rocked back and forth to test for mobility. The normal child will not exhibit any mobility. The examination is first done in the posterior segments and then the anterior segment. Any fracture will demonstrate movement of the segments or of the entire maxilla. Next check for any carious posterior teeth and check the buccal mucosa for scarring. Using two rigid instruments, check for mobile teeth. Have the patient protrude the tongue as far as possible, wrap it in a

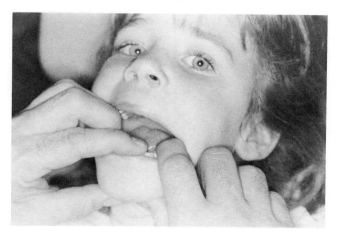

Figure 11. This hand and finger position is used to check for mandibular fractures. An up-and-down motion is applied to the various segments of the mandible.

gauze and examine all surfaces for lacerations or scars. Ask the patient to protrude the tongue as far as possible and note any deviations. Then have the patient touch the posterior portion of the hard palate and examine the floor of the mouth. Finally, visually inspect the hard and soft palates for any lesions.

Done in the above systematic way, an examiner will be able to detect any significant orofacial lesion.

ACCIDENT VS. ABUSE

Obviously many of the above injuries can and do happen accidentally to children every day. It is the examiner's responsibility to provide a detailed account of the history of the lesions to the dentist to whom the patient is referred so that he may help determine the true cause. The primary question to be answered when seeing these lesions is whether the age, ability, and opportunity are consistent with the history offered by the parents. The frenum tear is a prime example of this. A child who is not walking has absolutely no opportunity to injure himself. When a tear is seen in the pretoddler, abuse or neglect must be assumed. This is especially true if it is accompanied by other injuries of the head or body. However, this same injury in a 14-month-old toddler should not arouse as much suspicion since this is the typical age at which a child falls and hits his mouth. As the child gets older, he becomes more stable on his feet, and the opportunity to injure himself lessens. Therefore, any child who has been walking well for several months and demonstrates a frenum tear should arouse suspicion unless the history definitely indicates otherwise.

Injuries to the rest of the orofacial structures fall into the same line of reasoning. Lip injuries must be caused by a forceful blow. These injuries can be from an accidental injury or from an assault weapon such as a hand or even a broomstick (Fig. 12). The clinician must judge whether the child has had the

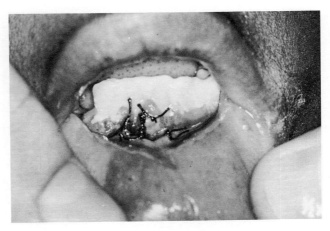

Figure 12. Abraded mucosal surface of the lower lip and lacerated gingival tissue in a 9-year-old boy struck by his mother in the mouth with a broomstick. Laceration is sutured; avulsed lower teeth were replanted, and secured with an acrylic splint. (Courtesy of Dr. Stuart Fischman, Buffalo, New York.)

ability or opportunity to fracture his jaw, tooth, or lacerate his tongue. If the history obtained sounds questionable, the examiner or child protection worker must further explore the case to ascertain the likelihood of risk to the child.

BITE MARKS

Bite marks are important in child abuse cases because they can aid in identifying the perpetrator. They are not an infrequent finding in abuse cases and the literature contains numerous reports (7,36–40). All bites should be considered intentional until proven otherwise but care must be taken in the evaluation of the marks, without immediately assuming that they were inflicted by an attacker. There have been reports of self-inflicted wounds, done by the victim to stifle cries during an attack (40). There is also a report where bite marks left on the body of a young abuse victim led to the identification of his 4½-year-old sibling as the killer (38). Sims, Grant, and Cameron (7) reported three cases of bite marks in child abuse. In each of these cases, the marks were used to identify the perpetrator. Trube-Becker (37) demonstrated 11 out of 48 child abuse cases showing bite marks. Each case resulted in death (not from the bites), and the most common areas where bites were found were the limbs, abdomen, and cheeks. In a fatal child abuse case reported by Sognnaes (41), the mother was identified as the attacker by creating test marks of her teeth with an epoxy model and then comparing them to the marks found on the child's body. To be certain, dental evidence, and in particular bite mark dental evidence, has been recognized as an important tool in the solving of many types of assault and murder cases (42–50). Bite mark evidence must not be overlooked in abuse cases as a means of identifying the attacker. In this section the recognition of bite marks, their differentiation from animal wounds, the basic differences between an adult and a child bite, what procedures must be taken to properly record the mark, and how to identify the suspected attacker are presented.

BITE MARK RECOGNITION

To best understand the scientific basis of the recognition of human bite marks, it is essential to have a knowledge of the mechanisms of the mark. These mechanisms have been studied extensively and are widely reported in the literature (11,51–58). As explained earlier, a bite mark is the mark or registration of the tooth's cutting edges on a substance either alone or in combination with other mouth parts. In many instances, two other marks are inflicted at the same time. These are a suck mark and a thrust mark. The suck mark, "hickey," is caused by a pulling of the skin into the mouth by negative pressure or suction. The thrust mark is caused by the tongue pushing against the skin trapped behind and between the maxillary and mandibular teeth (51). This action results in marks similar to the ones shown in Figure 13. All marks resemble these marks in that they are ovoid to circular areas of tooth imprints. The inner aspect of the mark will either be clear or contain the hickey or thrust mark. These two marks are similar in appearance in that they both resemble a contusion in the central portion of the mark. Their difference, if any, is that a thrust mark occasionally will demonstrate the impression of the rugae or anatomical landmarks of the lingual portion of the teeth on the victim's skin. Although it seems that this may be a relatively simple act, bite marks are frequently complex and need to be studied closely.

To recognize a bite mark, the individual components must be recognized. The marks caused by tooth pressure alone are from the incisal edges of the anterior teeth or the occlusal surfaces of the posterior teeth. The exact nature of the marks made will depend on the force applied, the duration of the application, the degree of movement of the tissues between the teeth during the force, and the position of the tissues between the teeth during the bite. The most clearly defined bites are caused by slow, deliberate, and forceful pressure by the anterior teeth, whereas the poorly defined marks are those caused by rapid, ripping, slight pressure acts by either the anterior or posterior teeth. In the well-defined marks, the incisal edges leave pale areas that represent these edges. Immediately adjacent are areas of bruising caused by damage to the vessels at the area of maximum stretching next to the relatively fixed tissue in contact with the incisal edges (11). It is the action of the teeth that give the bite mark its identification. The mark will have the parabolic shape of the human dental arch, no one tooth will be prominent (as the canines are in animal bites), and most importantly, the marks can give a clear indication of irregularities of size, shape, or position of individual teeth. These are the essentials of identification of a mark as a human bite and also form the basis of suspect identification through a bite mark.

Marks caused by thrusting of the tongue or sucking only occur when enough

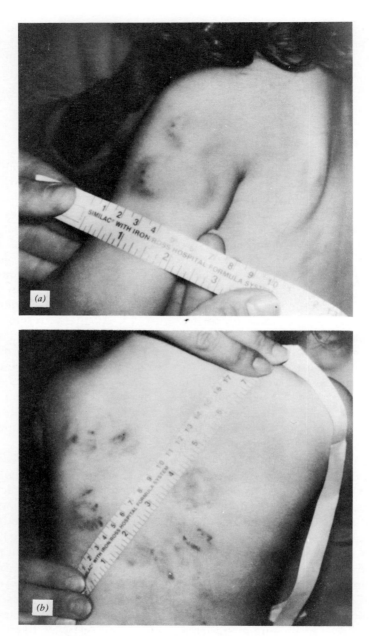

Figure 13. Bite marks show an extremely varied clinical picture. (*a* and *b*) Marks on an 18-month-old child brought to the hospital for "bruises" on her body. The marks were positively identified as bite marks, but it was impossible to identify the perpetrator because poor data collection techniques were used. These photographs were taken with an "instant" camera and are of poor diagnostic quality (Courtesy of Dr. Alan Drinnan, Buffalo, New York.) (*c*) A single bite on the back. This is an older mark with many of its features obscured by healing. (*d*) This mark demonstrates a thrust or suck mark in its central portion. (*e*) Multiple wounds on an abuse victim. In its fresh state, this type of mark can help identify the attacker.

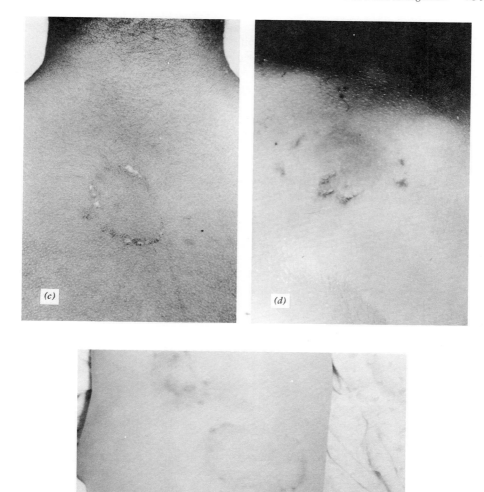

Figure 13. (Continued)

tissue is taken into the mouth. This tissue is pressed by the tongue against the teeth or rugae and can leave distinctive marks. However, most marks caused by the tongue tend to be diffuse in nature and show as a bruise in the central portion of the mark. In a study done by Barbanel and Evans (52) it was found that the pressure generated by the sucking and thrusting was considerably less than that of the biting forces and thus play a smaller role in the appearance of the mark.

The appearance of the mark will also be modified by the mechanical properties of the skin at the site of the bite. For example, skin and subcutaneous tissue on the back is firmer than that of a breast. The binding between the skin and subcutaneous tissue varies from site to site. For example, directional variations, those governed by the movements and extensibility of an area, will produce distortions of bite marks that are dependent on the position of the subject during biting. Distortions and changes can also occur after the bite with movements and changes of body position. These changes are affected by the elapsed time following the bite. Soon after being inflicted, the area will be highly edematous and stiff and will not change as much with movement. However, as the edema subsides, movement of the body, resolution of the ecchymosis, and fading of the bite will cause extensive changes. Finally, whether biting took place first and sucking second or vice versa will produce quite different marks (52).

Knowing the mechanisms of the mark, the examiner must now ask the critical question of whether or not he can positively identify the lesion as a bite mark. All suspected marks should be placed in one of three categories; definite bite marks, possible bite marks, and those marks that show a specific feature that would definitely preclude it from being a bite mark (11). For a mark to be placed in the definite category it must show clearly identifiable tooth marks and an arch form consistent with that of a human. Those that are placed in the possible category will always present a factor that does not appear to be consistent with the above. Those that fall in the nonbite category include marks made by toothed objects such as saws and knives.

Bite marks frequently go undetected by police officers, physicians, and pathologists. If a mark is seen that has any possibility of being a bite mark, a forensic dentist should be notified immediately. The collection of data should begin immediately. Do not wash the body or begin an autopsy before the marks have at least been photographed. Even disturbing the tissues may distort the mark to the point where it will be impossible to be used for suspect identification. The collection of the data will be discussed in a following section.

DISTINGUISHING BITE MARKS

Animal vs. Human

There are three areas where human bites will differ from those of an animal. They are the size of the mark, the form of the dental arch, and the mechanisms of the bite. Most domestic animal bite marks are smaller than that of a human. The common animal bites are those of dogs, cats, and rodents. In general, the incisal edges of an animal are smaller and sharper than that of a human; therefore, the marks are deeper and narrower. The arch form of most animals will be narrower than a human. Animal bites tend to be ripping in nature, whereas human ones are crushing. In addition, the longer, sharper canines of an animal will cause deep wounds at the corners. Very often severe animal bites will resemble surgical wounds (Fig. 14), (12–15).

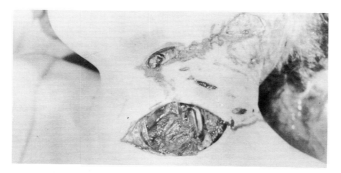

Figure 14. The wounds from animal bites can resemble surgical incisions as this figure illustrates. This wound was caused by a single bite from a dog.

Adult vs. Child

The obvious difference between a child's bite and an adult's is one of size. However, size can be measured in two places; the size of the arch width and the width of the individual teeth. Studies done by Moorees (60) found that the difference between a 5-year-old child's arch width and an adult's is approximately 4.4 mm in the maxilla and 2.5 mm for the mandible. The differences in the widths of individual teeth are even more striking. This same study showed that cumulative widths of the six upper deciduous teeth were 10 mm smaller than those in the permanent dentition. In the lower arch, the differences were approximately 7 mm. Using these basic measurements as a guideline, it is usually possible to distinguish a child's bite from that of an adult.

COLLECTING BITE MARK DATA

Once a mark has been assumed to be from a bite, identification procedures must begin immediately. Even the slightest delay may cause the loss of valuable data. The first step in collecting the data is to take saliva washings of the area. The amount of saliva deposited at a bite mark is approximately 0.3 ml and is distributed over about 6.5 cm^2 (61). ABO blood groupings can be determined from saliva washings. It is very difficult to obtain enough saliva from many of the bites seen, but an attempt should always be made. The most common technique used is swabbing the area with a thin piece of "Rizla" type cigarette paper held by forceps (the hand can contaminate the technique) after the paper has been dampened with distilled water (61). The paper is then dried and examined for ABO groupings. This examination is best done by a pathologist or forensic dentist.

The second step is to take photographs of the wound. These photographs should be in color, taken with a millimeter rule in the visual field alongside, and shot with photographic equipment that is capable of a 1:1 magnification. "Instant" photographs are not acceptable. The photos should be taken immediately and then repeated at 24-hour intervals for at least 7 days. This is very important due to the histologic changes that take place in the skin (thereby changing the definition of the bite) of both the living and the dead. One of these pictures will show the best definition of the mark.

Depending on the definition of the mark, three measurements must be taken. These are the intercanine width, the length of incisal edges, and the widths of the gaps between the teeth. Any or all of these measurements should be taken as soon as possible.

The final step is to obtain dental casts of all possible suspects. A limited number of people have the opportunity to bite the child. These are typically limited to the parents, siblings, or baby-sitters who have close access to the victim. It is usually necessary to obtain permission of the suspects before taking impressions of their teeth; however, in some cases a court order can be obtained.

SUSPECT IDENTIFICATION

It can be possible to include or exclude suspects by noting whether the bites are consistent with their teeth. This is not as difficult as it seems since only a limited number of people have access to a child. On the basis of the size of the arch, all adults or all children can be excluded. Individual characteristics like wear, missing teeth, rotations, arch form, diastemata, dental restorations, fractured teeth, carious teeth, and malposed teeth are seen with enough frequency and certainty to either include or exclude all but the perpetrator of the assault in most cases (38). The bites in child abuse are usually inflicted in a random manner and are, therefore, most commonly distorted and diffused with areas of abrasion. However, many authors feel that a person's dentition, like his fingerprints, is his and his alone (51,62). Therefore, not only the dentition, but the configuration of each mouth is unique, and the bite that it creates is just as unique. Keeping this in mind, even poorly defined marks may give a clue as to the identity of the assailant.

REFERENCES

1. Tate RJ: Facial injuries associated with the battered child syndrome. *Br J Oral Surg* 9:41, 1971.
2. O'Neill JA, Meachum WF, Griffin PP, et al: Patterns of injury in the battered child syndrome. *J of Trauma* 14:332, 1973.
3. Cameron JM, Johnson HP, Camps FE: The battered child syndrome. *Medicine, Science and the Law* 6:2, 1966.
4. Skinner AE, Castle RL: A Retrospective Study. National Society for the Prevention of Cruelty to Children. London, 1969.
5. Sopher IM: The dentist and the battered child syndrome. *Dent Clin N Amer* 21:113, 1977.
6. Schwartz S, Woolridge E, Stege D: Oral manifestations and legal aspects of child abuse. *J Am Dent Assoc* 95:586, 1977.
7. Sims BG, Grant JH, Cameron JM: Bite-marks in the "battered baby syndrome." *Medicine Sci Law* 13:207, 1973.
8. Hennon DK, Stookey GK, Muhler JC: A survey of the prevalence and distribution of dental caries in pre-school children. *J Am Dent Assoc* 79:1405, 1969.

9. Infante PF, Owen GM: Dental caries and levels of treatment for school children by geographical region, socioeconomic status, race, and size of community. *J Public Health Dent* 35:19, 1975.

10. Wisan JM, Lavell M, Colwell FH: Dental survey of Philadelphia pre-school children by income, age and treatment status. *J Am Dent Assoc* 55:1, 1957.

11. MacDonald DG: Bite mark recognition and interpretation. *J Forens Sci Soc* 14:229, 1974.

12. Cameron JM, Sims BG: *Forensic Dentistry*, Edinburgh and London, Churchill Livingstone, 1974, pp 129–45.

13. Gustafson G: *Forensic Odontology*, New York, American Elsevier Publishing Company, Inc, 1966, pp 144–65.

14. Harvey W: *Dental Identification and Forensic Odontology*. London, Henry Kimpton Publishers, 1976, pp 88–123.

15. Luntz LL, Luntz P: *Handbook for Dental Identification*. Philadelphia and London, JB Lippincott Company, 1973, pp 148–162.

16. Skrzeckas: Supararbitrium, betr. dic Verletzung z weier Finger usw. *Vjschr Gerichtl Med Band* 21, 1874.

17. Everett ED, Hirschman JV: Transient bacteremia and endocarditis prophylaxis. A Review. *Medicine* 56:61, 1977.

18. Prevention of bacterial endocarditis: A committee report of the American Heart Association. *J Am Dent Assoc* 95:600, 1977.

19. A guide to prophylaxis against tetanus in wound management. *Bulletin of the American College of Surgeons.* July, 1979.

20. *Stedman's Medical Dictionary*, ed 21. Baltimore, Williams & Wilkins Co, 1966, p 222.

21. Savara BS, Takeuchi Y: A longitudinal study of electrical burns on growth of the orofacial structures. *J Dent Child* 44:369, 1977.

22. Wright GZ, Colcleugh RG, Davidge LK: Electrical burns to the commissure of the lips. *J Dent Child* 44:377, 1977.

23. Ellis RG, Davey KW: *The Classification and Treatment of Injuries to the Teeth of Children*, ed 5. Chicago, Year Book Medical Publisher, Inc, 1970.

24. Carter AP, Zoller G, Harlen VK, et al: Dental injuries in Seattle's public school children: School year 1969–70. *J Public Health Dent* 32:251, 1972.

25. Korns RD: The incidence of accidental injury to primary teeth. *J Dent Child* 27:244, 1960.

26. Finn SB: *Clinical Pedodontics*, ed 4. Philadelphia, WB Saunders Company, 1973, p 224.

27. Andreasen JO: Treatment of fractured and avulsed teeth. *J Dent Child* 38:29, 1971.

28. Andreasen JO: Proceedings of the annual meeting of the American Academy of Pedodontics. Bal Harbour, Florida, 1977.

29. Kruger GO: *Textbook of Oral Surgery*. Saint Louis, CV Mosby Company, 1974, pp 314–386.

30. Rowe NL: Fractures of the facial skeleton in children. *J Oral Surg* 26:505, 1968.

31. Waite DE: Pediatric fractures of jaw and facial bones. *Pediatrics* 51:551, 1973.

32. Stafne EC: *Oral Roentgenographic Diagnosis*, ed 3. Philadelphia, WB Saunders Company, 1969.

33. McDonald RE, Avery DR: *Dentistry for the Child and Adolescent*. Saint Louis, CV Mosby Company, 1978.

34. Panelipse Panoramic X-Ray System. General Electric Company, Dental Systems Operation, PO Box 414, Milwaukee, Wisconsin 53201.

35. Blain SM, Winegarden T, Barber TK, et al: Child abuse and neglect. Proceeding of the IADR, New Orleans, LA, 1979.

36. Sognnaes RD: Forensic stomatology, Part III. *N Engl J Med* 296:197, 1977.

37. Trube-Becker E: Bite marks on battered children. *Z Rechtsmedizin* 79:73, 1977.

38. Levine LJ: The solution of a battered child homicide by dental evidence: Report of a case. *J Am Dent Assoc* 87:1234, 1973.

39. Furness J: Bite marks in non-accidental injuries of children. *Police Surg* 6:75, 1974.

40. Anderson WR, Hudson RP: Self-inflected bite marks in battered child syndrome. *Forensic Sci* 7:71, 1976.

41. Sognnaes RF: Forensic bite-mark measurements. *Dent Survey* April, 1979, pp 34–47.

42. Gladfelter IA: No fingerprints? Try BiteMarks. *J Acad Gen Dent* Jan–Feb 1976, p 9.

43. Luntz LL, Luntz P: A case in forensic odontology: A bite-mark in a multiple homicide. *Oral Surg* 36:72, 1973.

44. MacDonald DG, Laird WRE: Bitemarks in a murder case. *Int J Forens Dent* 3:26, 1976.

45. Simon A, Jordan H, Pforte K: Successful identification of a bite mark in a sandwich. *Int J Forens Dent* 2:17, 1974.

46. Weinstein RA, Stephen RJ, Morof A, et al: Human bites: review of the literature and report of case. *J Oral Surg* 31:792, 1973.

47. Sognnaes RF, Therrell R: In human skin caused by an. *Cal Dent Assoc J* 3:21, 1975.

48. Vale GL, Sognnaes RF, Felando GN, et al: Unusual three-dimensional bite mark evidence in a homicide case. *J Forensic Sci* 21:642, 1976.

49. Stoddard TJ: Bite marks in perishable substances. *Br Dent J*, September 1973, p 285.

50. Rohrer R: The telltale apple. *Chronicle* 41:69, 1978.

51. Beckstead JW, Rawson RD, Giles WS: Review of bite mark evidence, *J Am Dent Assoc* 99:69, 1979.

52. Barbanel JC, Evans JH: Bite marks in skin—Mechanical factors. *J Forens Sci Soc* 14:235, 1974.

53. Solheim T, Leidal TI: Scanning electron microscopy in the investigation of bite marks in foodstuffs. *Forens Sci* 6:205, 1975.

54. Jonason C, Frykholm KO, Frykholm A: Three dimensional measurement of tooth impression of criminological investigation. *Int J Forens Dent* 2:70, 1974.

55. MacFarlane TW, MacDonald DG, Sutherland DA: Statistical problems in dental identification. *J Forens Sci Soc* 14:247, 1974.

56. Whittaker DK: Some laboratory studies on the accuracy of bite mark comparison. *Int Dent J* 25:166, 1975.

57. Yano M: Experimental studies on bite marks. *Int J Forens Dent* 1:13, 1973.

58. Rawson RD: Solarisation as an aid to bite mark analysis. *Int J Forens Dent* 3:31, 1976.

59. Goodbody RA, Turner CH, Turner JL: The differentiation of toothed marks: Report of a case of special forensic interest. *Med Sci Law* 16:44, 1976.

60. Moorees CFA: *The Dentition of the Growing Child*. Massachusetts, Harvard University Press, 1959, pp 79–110.

61. Clift A, Lamont CM: Saliva in forensic odontology. *J Forens Sci Soc* 14:241, 1974.

62. Cowlin W: Current legal status of bite mark evidence. *Transactions of the Annual American Academy of Forensic Science*, 1979.

9
Chest and Abdominal Injuries

Theodore C. Jewett, Jr.

The problem of child abuse was first suggested in 1946 by Caffey (1) in his report on the association of subdural hematoma and skeletal fractures in infants. In 1953 Silverman (2) elaborated on the characteristic bony lesions seen in the physically abused child, which facilitated recognition of the battered child by radiographic studies. However, it was not until 1962 when Kempe (3) described the "battered child syndrome" that physicians began to be aware of the seriousness of this problem. Following this, numerous reports have appeared in the literature, particularly by Fontana (4), describing the multiplicity of symptoms and signs associated with child abuse and the importance of early recognition to prevent permanent disabilities or death.

Child abuse encompasses the spectrum from mental or physical deprivation to sexual maltreatment or physical abuse. The latter form most commonly involves the cutaneous, skeletal, or central nervous systems. These manifestations have been well described in the literature and are familiar to all physicians who care for children. However, there has been little attention paid to the potential hazards of thoracic and particularly abdominal injuries from child abuse (Table 1). The importance of these injuries is underlined by O'Neill (5) who described nine major abdominal injuries due to child abuse. McCort (6) has reported a 40% mortality in 10 cases of abdominal trauma from child battering.

The importance of recognizing abdominal and thoracic injuries as part of the myriad complex of child abuse is twofold: first, to alert the physician that abdominal trauma may be due to child abuse in order to protect the child from the danger of subsequent battering, and second, that abdominal or thoracic injury may be overlooked in the presence of the more obvious cutaneous or central nervous system manifestations. Lack of early recognition of abdominal trauma may account partially for the high mortality reported by Touloukian (7), O'Neill (5) and McCort (6). Careful abdominal examination is always mandatory in suspected child abuse since this part of the syndrome is often the most lethal even though not the most conspicuous.

The abused child with thoracoabdominal injuries has a history that is, in most cases, vague and misleading as related to the manner of injury. Since most

Table 1. Spectrum of Thoracic and Abdominal Injuries

Thoracic Trauma	Abdominal Trauma
Rib fractures	Retroperitoneal
Pneumothorax	Renal trauma
Hemothorax	Arterial or venous laceration
Pulmonary contusion	Intraperitoneal
Bronchial rupture	Stomach
	Duodenum
	Small bowel
	Colon
	Mesentery
	Pancreas
	Liver
	Spleen

victims are infants, direct patient history is not available. The explanation of the cause of injury may be inappropriate for the severity of the injury. Thoracic disease should be suspected if a history of chest pain or respiratory distress is volunteered. The most common complaint found in abdominal injury is that of vomiting. The emesis may be bilious or bloody.

The physical examination is most important in evaluating these children. Isolated thoracic or abdominal injuries are generally not encountered in the abused child. Consequently, if the infant presents with abdominal symptoms and signs, careful examination of the child, with particular attention to the soft tissues, skeletal, and central nervous systems should be performed. Bruises and wounds at different stages of healing are highly suggestive of battering. If the clinical picture is that of involvement of other organ systems, examination of the chest and abdomen should not be overlooked. Since most of these children will be less than 3 years of age, they may well be uncooperative, making the abdominal examination difficult or imposible to perform and interpret. Sedation is often helpful in this situation once head injuries have been excluded. Important physical findings of trauma are abdominal distention, muscle rigidity, and absent bowel sounds.

If the clinical picture is suggestive that there is a life-threatening process occurring that involves thoracic or abdominal viscera, immediate resuscitative and diagnostic measures should be undertaken. Serious respiratory distress demands immediate airway control, usually best accomplished with endotracheal intubation. Evidence of abdominal pathology with hypovolemic shock is managed by fluid replacement through a cutdown catheter. Response to replacement therapy is best monitored by measuring arterial pressure via the radial artery, central venous pressure by percutaneous subclavian vein catheter, and urine output with an indwelling Foley catheter. Nasogastric tubes are mandatory with either suspected thoracic or abdominal injury to prevent aspiration. Children with respiratory distress tend to swallow large quantities of air resulting in gastric dilitation, which impairs their respiratory ability and increases the danger of aspiration. Once resuscitative efforts are underway, diagnostic studies should be started to determine the extent and precise nature of the injuries incurred.

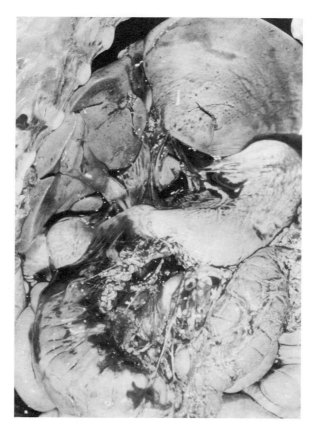

Figure 1. Autopsy findings in a 9-month-old infant with numerous signs of child abuse, including CNS, cutaneous and abdominal lesions. The infant could not be resuscitated on admission and the autopsy disclosed a laceration of the liver, acute pancreatitis, and retroperitoneal hemorrhage as well as severe CNS trauma.

THORACIC INJURIES

Major intrathoracic injuries are rare following child abuse. However, rib fractures are relatively common (5). Costochondral disarticulations also occur frequently and result in nodular firm masses along the anterior rib ends that may be mistaken for neoplasm. Thomas (8) in a study of rib fractures during infancy noted that fractures due to child abuse were rare in children under 6 months of age, but common after this age. He also comments that fractures located in the posterior aspect of rib ends and the lower ribs favor child abuse as the cause. Rib fractures that are undisplaced may be difficult or impossible to diagnose radiographically at the time of injury. Consequently, children with suspected fractures, particularly if there is a question of battering, should have repeat radiograms in several weeks when the pathology will become obvious.

The ribs of the young child are much more elastic than the adult, which allows greater compression force to occur without fracture. Consequently, when fractured ribs do occur, there is less tendency for displacement of the fracture ends and laceration of the lung with resultant hemothorax.

However, when rib fractures do occur it suggests a blow of excessive force with a greater possibility of underlying visceral injury. This is of particular importance in lower thoracic cage fractures as serious injuries to the liver, kidney, or spleen are seen more frequently in this situation.

Once the diagnosis is suspected by the physical signs of respiratory distress, decreased breath sounds, and mediastinal shift and confirmed by radiography, treatment should consist of placement of an intercostal tube with underwater seal drainage. If the situation is critical, immediate needle aspiration should be done to confirm the diagnosis without the delay of radiographic confirmation followed by placement of a drainage tube.

Pulmonary contusion may occur without rib fracture as the direct result of compression of the rib cage. This seldom involves enough lung parenchyma to cause serious respiratory distress. Treatment is expectant except for antibiotics to prevent secondary pneumonitis in the damaged lung tissue.

Major bronchial tears with tension pneumothorax have not been reported secondary to child abuse. However, if the trauma is forceful enough, this entity could occur. Suspicion of a bronchial rupture should be entertained in the child with massive uncontrolled pneumothorax and lobar atelectasis.

ABDOMINAL INJURIES

Once resuscitation of the patient has been instituted and serious abdominal trauma is suspected, definitive diagnostic studies should be undertaken. The two major abdominal catastrophies that must be suspected are hemorrhage or gastrointestinal tract perforation. Abdominal roentgenograms and, in particular, an upright or lateral decubitus film will show the presence of free air and confirm the suspicion of gastrointestinal perforation (Fig. 2). If hemorrhage is suspected, abdominal paracentesis with saline lavage is a fairly reliable indicator of free blood in the peritoneal cavity. It should be stressed, however, that a negative result should not be considered to exclude completely bleeding within the abdominal cavity.

The definitive diagnosis and management of abdominal pathology from child abuse differs little from that seen in other forms of trauma. Once routine diagnostic tests have been obtained, specific studies are often necessary to delineate the particular organs involved and how best to manage the catastrophe. The clinical approach to these lesions will be discussed in the following text.

Following blunt abdominal trauma there is the possibility of single or multiple organ system involvement. There are no specific statistics available relative to the frequency of specific organ involvement in the battered child. However, by interpolating existing data on accidental blunt abdominal trauma, an indication of the risk to specific organs following battering may be obtained. In accidental trauma to the abdomen the kidney is the organ damaged most frequently. The spleen is the next most susceptible structure followed by the intestine, liver, and then pancreas (9). However, other authors (10,11) have found the spleen to be involved more frequently than the kidney. Lacerations of major or minor blood vessels in the mesentery or retroperitoneum may also be seen.

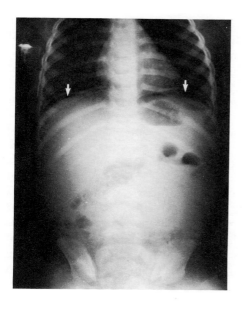

Figure 2. Upright roentgenogram of 3-year-old infant struck in the abdomen. Note distended fluid-filled stomach and dilated loops of jejenum in left upper quadrant. Arrows indicate free air under the diaphragm. At surgery, a laceration of the jejunum was found and repaired.

Multiple organ involvement may occur; the most common injury involves the spleen and left kidney. Liver and right renal combined injury also occurs at times. When duodenal or pancreatic injury occurs to one of these organs, the other organ should be suspected of having concomitant involvement.

The mechanisms that cause abdominal injury in blunt trauma have been described clearly by Haller (12). He delineates three different etiological factors, namely compressing, crushing, and accelerating types of forces. Compression injuries, caused by a punch or kick to the abdomen, affect the intestinal tract, particularly the stomach and colon. When these organs are distended with gas and fluid, they may not be able to withstand the increased pressure transmitted by the rapid increase in intra-abdominal pressure from the compressing force, which then results in rupture. A crushing injury occurs when an organ is compressed against a solid immoveable structure such as the lower rib cage or vertebral column from a blow to the anterior abdominal wall. This type of injury usually occurs to the kidney, pancreas, spleen, or liver. Sudden acceleration occurs when the child is propelled through the air upon being struck or thrown. This effects intra-abdominal organs at the site of their posterior abdominal attachments due to the shearing effect from the rapid change in velocity. The common injury that occurs is a laceration of the small intestinal mesentery with hemorrhage or small bowel perforation in the area of the ligament of Treitz or terminal ileum.

RENAL INJURY

Even though the kidneys lie retroperitoneally and are well protected by the bony thorax and overlying viscera, they are one of the most common organs damaged as the result of abdominal trauma. Associated injuries are commonly found in other organs such as the brain, spleen, liver, intestine, and ribs. Cass (13) reported over two-thirds of his cases of renal injuries to have associated organ damage. Damage to these structures should always arouse suspicion of possible concomitant renal trauma. Death seldom occurs due to isolated renal injury, but is usually related to associated major damage to other organ systems. Morbidity may be grave if proper management is not instituted. Retroperitoneal infection with abscess can occur following pelvic rupture with extravasation of urine. Persistent hypertension may occur if devascularized renal tissue is not excised.

In the conscious patient, damage to the kidney presents in a classic clinical syndrome of flank pain, often accompanied by overlying contusion of the skin. A flank mass may be palpable, and either gross or microscopic hematuria is invariably found in all but the rare case. The degree of blood in the urine is in no way an indicator of the severity of the renal injury. In the unconscious patient with concomitant head injury, all of the above findings may be absent except for the presence of hematuria. Consequently, a urinary catheter is mandatory early in the management of children with suspected abdominal trauma not only to monitor their response to treatment, but also to obtain urine early so as to determine the possibility of urinary tract damage. Those children in shock from renal trauma will generally become normovolemic following replacement of 25% of their blood volume, as once renal hemorrhage has occurred further bleeding is tamponaded due to the closed retroperitoneal space. Any child who remains hypovolemic following appropriate blood volume replacement should be suspected of having other major associated organ injury.

Morse (9,14) described the pathologic characteristics of the different types of renal trauma and how this effects the management. He divides the kidney into four basic parts, namely the parenchyma, the capsule, the collecting system, and the renal vessels. Treatment is then based on an accurate assessment of which of the foregoing components have been injured. Determination is obtained by roentgen studies.

The most benign form of renal injury is contusion of the kidney parenchyma. In this situation the other three basic components (capsule, collecting system, and major blood vessels) are intact. Edema occurs in the parenchyma with swelling. Because of the intact capsule the parenchymal vessels are compressed reducing the urinary output. As a result of this injury, the infusion pyelogram reveals decreased visualization of the contrast medium as compared to the opposite normal kidney. The calyces can be seen to be intact but often thinned out due to compression from the parenchymal edema. A contused kidney will recover spontaneously as the edema subsides leaving little if any permanent damage. Surgery is never indicated in this form of injury.

Renal laceration occurs when both the parenchyma and capsule are damaged. With disruption of the capsule, blood is no longer confined within the kidney but extravasates into the retroperitoneal space forming a perirenal hematoma. Shock may occur but responds to replacement therapy as the retroperitoneal space confines the hemorrhage and prevents exsanguination. The infusion pyelogram is similar to that seen in a contused kidney with decreased concentration of dye, thinning of the calyces, and an intact collecting system. The diagnosis of laceration of the kidney is differentiated from simple contusion by the suggestion of a flank mass both on physical examination and plain roentgenograms as well as the clinical evidence of significant blood loss. Again surgery is seldom necessary in this form of renal trauma as the hematoma spontaneously absorbs leaving minimal residual scarring. On rare occasions the expanding hematoma may rupture through the posterior peritoneum allowing free extravasation of blood into the peritoneal cavity and require operative intervention to control the hemorrhage.

Rupture of a kidney is a more serious form of renal trauma. When this occurs the parenchyma, capsule, and collecting system are all injured allowing urine to extravasate into the perirenal tissues. Unlike blood alone, urine mixed with blood causes an intense tissue reaction that resolves in marked fibrosis. This scarring often results in hydronephrosis from renal fibrosis. Perinephric abscess is also a common sequella of the extravasation of urine and blood and not only adds to the morbidity of recovery but also may result in loss of the kidney. The diagnosis of renal rupture is made by noting the extravasation of contrast media on infusion intravenous pyelogram (IVP) outside the collecting system. If the radiographic diagnosis of renal rupture is questionable on the initial examination, a repeat study should be performed one or two days later. Surgery is mandatory in the presence of rupture of the kidney because of the previously mentioned complications that occur from this injury. Morse (9) believes that surgery should be delayed for 48 to 72 hours in order to prepare properly the child for operation as well as to allow the areas of necrotic tissue to demarcate better. He does not feel that there is a great risk of perirenal infection materializing this early in the course of the disease.

The most devastating kidney injury occurs when the main renal vessels are damaged. Arterial injury may vary from complete severance of the vessel to intimal damage. The diagnosis should be strongly suspected if the infusion intravenous pyelogram shows complete absence of contrast media in the involved kidney. If this finding occurs, immediate corroberative studies are necessary. Three diagnostic tests are available: retrograde pyelography, renal scan, or renal arteriogram. The retrograde pyelogram will reveal a normal appearing kidney, the renal scan will show no radioactive uptake, and the arteriogram will delineate the actual arterial occlusion. The choice of which study to use depends on the availability at the individual institution. In the presence of renal vascular injury, immediate surgery is necessary if the damaged kidney is to be salvaged. Operation consists of arterial reconstruction if possible or otherwise nephrectomy.

Computerized axial tomography (CT) scans are being used more frequently to delineate renal trauma. The initial experience has been most rewarding, and it appears that this study may give more exact information than the infusion intravenous pyelogram.

The majority of renal injuries are either contusions or lacerations and because of their nature may be treated conservatively with surgical intervention seldom being necessary. The remaining cases, which amount to approximately 20% of renal injuries, require surgery. The majority of these cases are rupture with urinary extravasation, which if properly managed results in salvage of the injured kidney. Nephrectomy is rarely necessary and is usually reserved for vascular pedicle injuries. Prompt evaluation of suspected renal injuries as outlined by Morse (9) has resulted in the salvage of the majority of injured kidneys and the prevention of long-term complications.

GASTROINTESTINAL TRACT INJURY

The gastrointestinal tract is frequently damaged following blows to the abdomen. Philippart (15) has stated that central upper abdominal lesions, namely damage to the duodenum, pancreas, and jejunum, were the most common organs involved in abdominal trauma from child abuse. Several mechanisms come into play to cause these injuries (12). Compressing forces results in perforation of hollow viscera; the stomach and colon are particularly susceptible to this type of injury because of their inability to withstand sudden compression when filled with contents. The small intestine is more susceptible to accelerating or whipping forces that cause shearing at the attachments of the bowel. This may result in disruption of the intestine with perforation at its mesenteric border with concomitant hemorrhage from the mesenteric vessels. The areas most susceptible to the shearing forces, however, are at the points of ligamentous attachment of the intestine, namely the duodenojejunal and ileocecal areas.

Injuries to the intestinal tract are diagnosed by the presence of pneumoperitoneum if free perforation has occurred. However, many of the intestinal injuries are more subtle and are not as readily diagnosed. Impairment of the blood supply to the bowel may result in necrosis of the intestinal wall without free perforation. This patient will have a prolonged ileus or may progress to late perforation with intra-abdominal abscesses. Hemorrhage with hypovolemic shock may be the presenting clinical picture if major mesenteric vessels are damaged.

Rupture of the stomach following a blunt blow is rare. The mechanism of rupture is a sudden compressing force on a stomach distended with contents that cannot readily decompress itself because of the valvular effects of the pyloric and cardioesophageal sphincters. Siemens (16) in a review of gastric rupture described a 2-year-old girl with this entity following battering by her mother.

Perforations of the stomach commonly cause prompt and profound shock because of the massive contamination of the peritoneal cavity with stomach contents and in particular the highly irritating effects of hydrochloric acid. Once the shock has been corrected, these patients should have immediate surgery with closure of the gastric rent and careful cleansing of the peritoneal cavity of all contaminating stomach contents. Postoperative subphrenic and intra-abdominal abscesses with sepsis are common complicating problems and should be treated expectantly with antibiotics and drainage of the abscesses when they occur.

Intramural hematoma of the duodenum is the most common intestinal lesion resulting from blunt abdominal trauma (Fig. 3). The duodenum, because of its fixed position between the relatively weak abdominal wall musculature of the young child and the vertebral column, is most susceptible to crushing forces. When the duodenum with its rich blood supply is injured, extravasation of blood occurs between the mucosal and serosal layers of the bowel. The resulting hematoma expands as further fluid accumulates because of the osmotic effect of the entrapped blood with narrowing of the duodenal lumen and varying degrees of obstruction. An occasional case of duodenal trauma may result in perforation of the bowel wall with local abscess formation.

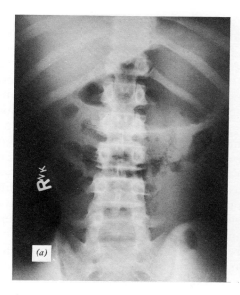
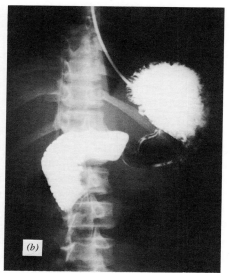
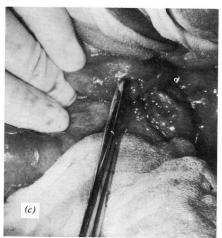

Figure 3. (*a*) Abdominal roentgenogram of patient with four days of green emesis and upper abdominal pain. Abdominal wall ecchymosis noted on examination. Note distended stomach with very little gas in lower abdomen. (*b*) Barium study shows dilated duodenum with obstruction and "coil spring," a sign suggestive of duodenal hematoma. (*c*) Finding at surgery after 12 days of conservative treatment was a duodenal hematoma with localized perforation. Note hemostat in area of perforation.

Many cases of duodenal hematoma have had an obscure etiology in the past. However, in recent years, attention has been drawn to the importance of considering child abuse as the possible cause in these cases (17). A recent article by Woolley (18) defines clearly the cause of duodenal hematoma as often due to child abuse. Fifty percent of his reported cases had clear evidence of battering.

The diagnosis of intramural hematoma of the duodenum should be suspected in a child who is vomiting greenish material, has upper abdominal tenderness, and a suggestive mass in this area. The pertinent laboratory studies are a complete blood count, serum amylase, and serum lipase. Blood loss may be significant in this lesion, but seldom demands transfusion; the white blood count is often elevated. Associated pancreatitis is not uncommon; elevated serum amylase and lipase levels have been reported by Woolley (18) and also found in our patients.

The diagnosis of duodenal hematoma is confirmed by radiographic studies. Plain abdominal films may show a distended stomach and duodenum with a paucity of gas in the remaining intestinal tract. A barium study will show varying degrees of obstruction in the area of the ligament of Treitz. Confirming evidence is the "coiled spring" appearance of the barium, which is identical to that seen in intussusception. This is believed to be due to the intramural filling defect that compresses the valvulae conniventes. The management of intramural hematoma of the duodenum in children is now felt to be nonoperative unless there are associated abdominal injuries or in the rare case of duodenal perforation. Some authors (19,20) have recommended operation with drainage of the hematoma but their experience was mainly in adult patients. Recent reports by Holgerson (21) and Woolley (18) on the management of this problem in children have strongly recommended the nonoperative approach.

Once the diagnosis has been confirmed by radiographic studies, nasogastric decompression and intravenous fluids are instituted. Supportive care may necessitate blood transfusion and at times peripheral hyperalimentation. The hematoma will usually resolve within 10 to 14 days with relief of the duodenal obstruction. If obstruction remains after this period of time, operative intervention with evacuation of the hematoma or bypass duodenojejunostomy may be necessary. In the rare case in which perforation occurs, immediate laparotomy with repair of the defect is indicated.

McCort (6) reported intestinal rupture or laceration to be the most common intra-abdominal injury following child abuse. Seven of the 10 cases studied had intestinal lesions. The mortality in these children was 40%, which indicates the seriousness of this lesion. Grosfeld (22) has also reported two cases of intestinal perforation from child abuse with prolonged and severe complications before recovery. Hematoma of the small intestine with obstruction has also been observed as a sequela of child abuse. Eisenstein (23) reported one case and found 11 similar cases in the literature.

These children clinically have abdominal pain, vomiting, and at times shock. The diagnosis is made by radiographic evidence of pneumoperitoneum, hemoperitoneum, and ileus in those cases with perforation, and obstruction in patients with mesenteric hematoma.

The management of these lesions is operative once the patient's general condition is stabilized by supportive care. In patients with obstruction from mesenteric hematoma, simple evacuation of the blood with control of any actively bleeding mesenteric vessels suffices. In those children with perforations of the intestine, simple closure may be possible, but at times resection of the involved bowel is necessary.

PANCREATIC INJURY

Acute pancreatitis in childhood is a rare disease but when present is most likely due to blunt abdominal trauma. Because of the serious nature of this disorder, child abuse should always be considered as the cause of the trauma, particularly in the younger child. The first report of pancreatitis from child abuse was by Hartley (24) and more recently by Slovis (25). The pancreatitis may be a solitary manifestation or may be seen in conjunction with damage to other adjacent upper abdominal organs such as the duodenum, kidney, liver, or spleen. Failure to recognize the possibility that the pancreatitis may be the result of battering exposes the child to unnecessary subsequent risk. Consequently, any child presenting with pancreatitis should have radiographic studies of the long bones, a search for cutaneous manifestations of battering, and investigation of the home situation before discharge from the hospital.

Following pancreatic trauma, hemorrhage and ductal laceration occurs resulting in the release of amylase and lipase into the peritoneal cavity. The activated enzymes produce a hemorrhagic necrotizing chemical peritonitis with a large outpouring of fluid into the peritoneal cavity. The pancreatitis may resolve with supportive management alone or can progress to an acute pancreatic abscess or chronic pseudocyst.

The diagnosis of acute pancreatitis should be suspected in the child who has evidence of abdominal trauma with peritonitis without frank intra-abdominal hemorrhage or pneumoperitoneum. The diagnosis is confirmed by an elevated serum amylase and lipase and by high levels of these enzymes found in fluid obtained by abdominal paracentesis. The increased amylase and lipase content in the serum is believed to be due to direct liberation of the enzymes into the blood stream or by lymphatic absorption from the peritoneal fluid. The serum calcium often drops to levels below normal by the fifth day following injury. The mechanism of this abnormality is the result of calcium being bound to the areas of fat necrosis.

The radiologic manifestations of acute pancreatitis are those related to the local trauma and, second, to the skeletal system. Abdominal and chest roentgenograms may show localized ileus in the area of the pancreas and pleural fluid usually in the left side as the result of diaphragmatic irritation. A contrast study of the duodenum will show widening of the duodenal loop as a result of the edematous head of the pancreas. The bony lesions in pancreatitis as described by Slovis (26) consist of intramedullary necrosis and new bone formation. These lesions may be difficult to differentiate from leukemia, sickle cell infarction, or metastatic disease. Those cases of pancreatitis due to child abuse often will have the classic skeletal findings as described by Caffey (1).

Once major injury to other intra-abdominal organs has been ruled out and the diagnosis of pancreatitis confirmed, initial treatment should be supportive to combat the effects of the peritonitis. Nasogastric decompression is instituted and the shock that is usually manifested from the outpouring of fluid into the peritoneal cavity is treated with blood, plasma, and intravenous fluids. Becker (27) has advocated the conservative management of traumatic pancreatitis and described the successful outcome of six children treated in this manner. If the child shows progression of his disease, this often intimates major pancreatic duct injury and laparotomy should be performed with repair of the duct if possible or otherwise resection of the pancreas distal to the injury.

At times, the pancreatitis may be confined to the lesser sac forming an acute pancreatic abscess. When this occurs surgical drainage is indicated with the placement of a sump-type tube to allow for continual drainage of the pancreatic enzymes. This tube should be left in place until there is no further drainage. Occasionally the pancreatic inflammatory process is localized by the adjacent organs and over several weeks time, a fibrous capsule is formed resulting in a pancreatic pseudocyst. This manifestation of acute pancreatitis becomes apparent approximately two to three weeks following the injury by the appearance of a painful upper abdominal mass. The management of this problem is marsupilization of the cyst to either the stomach or duodenum or by a Roux-en-Y anastomosis to the small intestine.

LIVER INJURY

Liver injury secondary to blunt trauma carries a significant mortality even with the improved methods of management described in the past decade. As pointed out by Walt (28) this may be due to the inappropriate interpretation of animal experimentation on liver trauma as well as an uncritical assessment of the management of liver injury to improve further the end result. Death is generally due to uncontrolled hemorrhage or multiple organ system damage. Liver injury following child battering has been described by O'Neill, McCort, Touloukian, Grosfeld, and Perry (5–7,22,29). The mode of injury to the liver, described by Haller (12), is usually due to a crushing force that forces the liver against the vertebral column and lower bony thorax. Decelerating forces may also result in shearing of the round ligament at its attachment to the liver with resultant laceration downward deep into the liver.

Aldrete (30) has recently proposed a gross pathologic classification of liver injuries in order to understand better and manage more efficiently patients with this potentially lethal disease (Table 2).

Table 2. Classification of Hepatic Injuries

I.	Simple laceration with capsular tear and minimal hemorrhage
II.	Moderate laceration with active and significant bleeding
III.	Intraparenchymal hematoma
IV.	Large lacerations with transection of identifiable intrahepatic branches of hepatic artery, portal vein, hepatic vein or bile duct, but amenable to suture repair
V.	Large laceration with transection of identifiable intrahepatic branches of hepatic artery, portal vein, hepatic vein or bile duct necessitating resection of a portion of hepatic parenchyma
VI.	Large lacerations associated with injury of the retrohepatic veins and vena cava with massive hemorrhage

SOURCE: Aldrete, J.S., Halpern, N.B., Ward, S., et al.: Factors determining the mortality and morbidity in hepatic injuries. Analysis of 108 cases. *Ann. Surg.* 189:466–474. 1979.

The clinical presentation of liver trauma may vary from that of apparent benign abdominal pain to profound shock. The injury is frequently seen in association with major damage to other organ systems. As in other forms of abdominal trauma, the first priority is stabilization of vital signs with replacement of blood volume loss and control of the airway if necessary. Once this has been accomplished and intraperitoneal hemorrhage has been confirmed by physical signs and abdominal paracentesis, definitive studies should be undertaken. Radioisotope liver and spleen scan, using technetium sulfur colloid, or abdominal CT scan are the two most acceptable radiologic studies available. If major hemorrhage occurs that will not allow stabilization of the patient's condition by replacement therapy, immediate laparotomy is indicated.

The majority of liver injuries that will be encountered are Types I and II previously mentioned in the classification by Aldrete (30). The lacerations can be easily sutured to control hemorrhage or at times need no suturing. Drainage of the area is generally recommended. Recovery from this type of injury is prompt and without complication.

The Type III or intraparenchymal hematoma is an uncommon type of liver injury. Those hematomas that are larger than 5 or 6 cm in diameter should be opened with evacuation of the blood and ligation of the severed vessels or biliary ducts. The area is again drained as in Type I and II injuries.

The Type IV lesions with large lacerations involving the intrahepatic vessels, but with minimal devitalized liver tissue, are of greater risk to the patient and demand prompt surgical care. These are best treated by suture ligation of the damaged vessels and bile ducts with drainage. At times Avitene, a microfibrillar collagen hemostatic compound, is of value in controlling hemorrhage deep within the liver where the sutures are difficult to place. Debridement of devitalized liver tissue is also indicated.

Aldrete's Type V lesion with major lacerations of liver substance that involve transected vessels and bile ducts as well as large segments of devitalized liver most often demand resection of major segments or a lobe of the liver. Hemostasis is often difficult to obtain and it may be necessary to isolate the blood supply to the liver by cross-clamping the portal vein and hepatic artery at the foramen of Winslow. If hepatic vein bleeding is troublesome, this may be controlled by clamping the aorta and the vena cava above the renal veins and in the suprahepatic area. To perform this maneuver, the incision must be extended into the chest usually by median sternotomy as described by Yellen (31).

The Type VI lesion is described as lacerations involving the vena cava or hepatic veins where they enter the inferior vena cava. This lesion, like the Type V, has a significant mortality and often must be treated by vascular isolation and repair of these major structures or if this is impossible by resection of the involved liver tissue.

Major complications following surgery are continued hemorrhage, subphrenic abscess, biliary fistula, and liver failure. Postoperative hemorrhage is usually secondary to defects in coagulation from the large amounts of infused bank blood and respond to fresh frozen plasma. Subphrenic abscess occurs due to the large residual dead space remaining following major liver resection and the necrosis of liver tissue when incomplete debridement has occurred. The best preventive measure is the careful excision of all necrotic liver tissue, the use of antibiotics, and judicious use of drains and sump tubes. Biliary fistula occurs when unrecognized intrahepatic bile ducts are not ligated, but the drainage generally ceases spontaneously in 7 to 10 days. Liver failure is usually temporary with the rising bilirubin falling to within normal range within 1 week.

The mortality from liver trauma is still significantly high. It is related to involvement of other organ systems or major lacerations of the liver involving large portions of the liver and major vessels supplying this organ (Fig. 4). An aggressive planned approach to correcting the pathology will help lower the mortality rate.

RETROPERITONEAL BLOOD VESSEL INJURY

Lacerations of the retroperitoneal blood vessels may occur from blunt trauma as the result of shearing of the lumbar vessels from the aorta or inferior vena cava. This hemorrhage is usually confined to the closed retroperitoneal space, which tamponades the blood and resolves without surgical intervention. Occasionally, if bleeding is excessive, the pressure ruptures the posterior peritoneum resulting in free bleeding into the peritoneal cavity. When signs of this bleeding occur, immediate laparotomy and control of the hemorrhage are necessary.

SPLENIC INJURY

The spleen is probably the most common intra-abdominal organ injured following blunt abdominal trauma in children. This structure, although well protected by the lower thoracic cage, is susceptible to injury because of its marked vascularity and the fragile nature of its capsule. Decelerating forces will cause shearing of the splenic attachments resulting in capsular tears or damage to the splenic vessels either in the pedicle or short gastric vessels. Crushing forces also may play a role in splenic injury as the greater elasticity of the child's

Figure 4. Deep lacerations of the liver with hemoperitoneum found at autopsy.

ribs results in the spleen being crushed by the lower thoracic cage. This elasticity of the child's ribs also explains why rib fractures are seldom seen in association with splenic trauma in children. While splenic injury is seen frequently in blunt abdominal trauma, there is little mention of child abuse as being one of the causes. However, because of the serious consequences of unrecognized splenic rupture, this entitiy should be considered in any child with suspected child abuse and abdominal pain.

Abdominal pain that is most severe in the left upper quadrant is suggestive of splenic injury. Referred pain in the left supraclavicular area due to the irritation of blood under the dome of the diaphragm is a confirmatory symptom. A physical examination will reveal a distended tender abdomen with muscle spasm most marked in the left upper quadrant. A mass may also be palpated in this area. Bowel sounds are either depressed or absent. Peritoneal lavage may confirm the impression of intraperitoneal hemorrhage. However, if blood is not obtained, this should not be considered as absolute evidence that there is no intra-abdominal hemorrhage.

Laboratory studies of value are a complete blood count and a urinalysis. An initial low hemoglobin and hematocrit value implies hemorrhage, but of more importance are serial determinations that reveal decreasing values. A leukocytosis with levels as high as 20,000 is often seen, but is not diagnostic of intraperitoneal hemorrhage as shown by Williams (32). Urinalysis is important to rule out coincidental renal trauma. Because of the anatomical proximity of the left kidney and spleen, concomitant injury to these two organs frequently occurs. The presence of hematuria on urinalysis in suspected splenic injury should mandate an infusion intravenous pyelogram before any definitive treatment of the splenic trauma.

Radiographic studies are usually diagnostic in confirming damage to the spleen. The abdominal roentgenogram may show a left upper quadrant mass that pushes the stomach medially and the colon downward. If there is air in the stomach the "saw tooth" sign may be noted, which is a serrated appearance along the greater curvature of the stomach in the area of the attachments of the short gastric vessels. The technetium sulfur colloid radioisotope scan is of most value in confirming the diagnosis of ruptured spleen. This scan also has the added advantage of evaluating an unsuspected laceration of the liver. The CT scan is also becoming a valuable adjunct in diagnosis, particularly when the isotope study is not available. On rare occasions, selective splenic arteriography may be of value in aiding in the diagnosis. This procedure, however, should be reserved for the occasional case in which the simpler diagnostic radiographic studies are not confirmatory.

The management of splenic trauma in children has undergone considerable alteration in the past decade. Unlike the adult, the child is at serious risk from overwhelming infection following splenectomy. The 1952 report by King and Shumaker (33) of fulminant sepsis in five splenectomized infants alerted physicians to this life-threatening complication of splenectomy. More recent reports have confirmed this initial observation. Singer (34), in reviewing almost 2,800 cases of splenectomy, found a 2% mortality and over a 4% morbidity due to sepsis. A recent review by Krivit (35) has also emphasized this risk to children.

While pneumococcal infection has been the most common offending organism, meningococcus, H. influenza, staphylococcus, and E. coli are also seen. With the development of a polyvalent pneumococcal vaccine and the use of prophylactic penicillin following splenectomy, the risk of overwhelming post-splenectomy sepsis has decreased. But there is still the ever present danger of this syndrome from bacteria not susceptible to this prophylaxis.

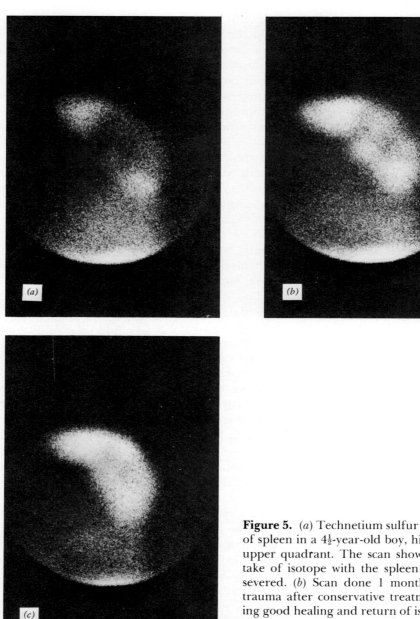

Figure 5. (*a*) Technetium sulfur colloid scan of spleen in a 4½-year-old boy, hit in the left upper quadrant. The scan shows poor up-take of isotope with the spleen completely severed. (*b*) Scan done 1 month following trauma after conservative treatment, show-ing good healing and return of isotope pick-up by spleen. (*c*) Scan done 2 months after injury, which shows a normal spleen scan.

Because of this ever present threat to children, particularly children under 6 years of age, pediatric surgeons no longer feel that splenectomy is mandatory in the presence of a damaged spleen. The 1971 report of Douglas and Simpson (36) stimulated other pediatric surgeons to investigate the conservative management of splenic trauma and confirm their conclusion that many children with lacerated spleens may be managed successfully without splenectomy. Recent reports describe further refinements in the management of the ruptured spleen in which suture of the laceration or partial splenectomy has been carried out with success (37–40).

With this background the accepted management of splenic trauma should be directed toward saving the entire spleen or at least as much splenic tissue as possible (Fig. 5). Once the diagnosis has been made and the hypovolemia corrected, the child is carefully observed with frequent abdominal examinations, vital signs, and serial hematocrits. If the child's condition remains stable, careful observation with bed rest is continued for 2 weeks. Following this the child may go home, but activity should be restricted for another 2 weeks. Should the patient show continuing evidence of bleeding, laparotomy is indicated. Suturing of the laceration may be all that is necessary, but at times partial splenectomy must be performed in order to control the hemorrhage. Avitene, a relatively new hemostatic agent, has been found to be of help in curbing the bleeding when used locally on the raw splenic surface. In the rare case, total splenectomy may be necessary. If this occurs, prophylactic penicillin and polyvalent pneumococcal vaccine should be instituted in the immediate postoperative period. The parents should also be warned about the possibility of overwhelming infection and instructed in the early recognition of this possibility.

CONCLUSION

Abdominal and thoracic trauma in children are common disease entities with appreciable morbidity and mortality. Child abuse plays a significant role in the etiology of these lesions and should always be suspected. Consequently, children with other stigmata of child abuse, particularly head injury, should be screened for evidence of unsuspected thoracic and abdominal trauma. Intra-abdominal injuries following child battering often involve multiple organs with profound pathology.

REFERENCES

1. Caffey J: Multiple fractures in long bones of infants suffering from chronic subdural hematoma. *AJR* 56:163, 1946.
2. Silverman FN: Roentgen manifestations of unrecognized skeletal trauma in infants. *AJR* 69:413, 1953.
3. Kempe CH, Silverman FN, Steele BF, et al: The battered child syndrome. *JAMA* 181:17, 1962.
4. Fontana VJ, Donovan D, Wong RJ: The maltreatment syndrome in children. *N Engl J Med* 269:1389, 1963.

5. O'Neill JA Jr, Meacham WF, Griffin JP, et al: Patterns of injury in the battered child syndrome. *J Trauma* 13:332, 1973.

6. McCort J, Vaudagna J: Visceral injuries in battered children. *Radiology* 82:424, 1964.

7. Touloukian RJ: Abdominal visceral injuries in battered children. *Pediatrics* 42:642, 1968.

8. Thomas PS: Rib fractures in infancy. *Ann Radiol* 20:115, 1977.

9. Morse TS: Renal injuries. *Pediatr Clin North Am* 22:379, 1975.

10. Sinclair MC, Moore TC: Major surgery for abdominal and thoracic trauma in childhood and adolescence. *J. Pediatr Surg* 9:155, 1974.

11. Talbert JL, Rodgers BM: Acute abdominal injuries in children. *Pediatr Ann* 5:36–37, 39–42, 44, 46, 49, 51, 54, 56, 58, 60–62, 65, 67, 70, 1976.

12. Haller JA Jr: Injuries of the gastrointestinal tract in children. Notes on Recognition and Management. *Clin Pediatr* 5:476, 1966.

13. Cass AS: Management of renal injuries in the severely injured patient. *J Trauma* 12:516, 1972.

14. Morse TS: Infusion pyelography in the evaluation of renal injuries in children. *J Trauma* 6:693, 1966.

15. Philippart AI: Blunt abdominal trauma in childhood. *Surg Clin North Am* 57(1):151, 1977.

16. Siemens RA, Fulton RL: Gastric rupture as a result of blunt trauma. *Am Surgeon* 43(4):229, 1977.

17. Maull KI: Selective management of post traumatic obstructing intramural hematoma of the duodenum. *Surg Gynecol Obstet* 146:221, 1978.

18. Woolley MM: Duodenal hematoma in infancy and childhood. Changing etiology and changing treatment. *Am J Surg* 136:8, 1978.

19. Hughes CE: Intramural hematoma of the gastrointestinal tract. *Am J Surg* 133:276, 1977.

20. Margolis IB, Carnazzo AJ, Finn MP: Intramural hematoma of the duodenum. *Am J Surg* 132:779, 1976.

21. Holgerson LO: Non-operative treatment of duodenal hematomata in childhood. *Surg* 12(1):11, 1977.

22. Grosfeld JL: Surgical aspects of child abuse (Trauma-X). *Pediatr Ann* 45(10):113, 1976.

23. Eisenstein EM: Jejunal hematoma: An unusual manifestation of the battered child syndrome. *Clin Pediatr* 4:436, 1965.

24. Hartley RC: Pancreatitis under the age of five years: A report of three cases. *J Pediatr Surg* 2:419, 1967.

25. Slovis TL: Hemangiomas of the liver in infants. Review of diagnosis, treatment and course. *AJR* 123(4):791, 1975.

26. Slovis TL: Pancreatitis and the battered child syndrome. Report of two cases with skeletal involvement. *AJR* 125(2):456, 1975.

27. Becker WF: Traumatic Pancreatitis. *Am Surgeon* 20:525, 1954.

28. Walt AJ: The mythology of hepatic trauma—or babel revisited. *Am J Surg* 135(1):12, 1978.

29. Perry JF, Venters HD: Childhood deaths due to injury. *Surgery* 62:620, 1967.

30. Aldrete JS, Halpern NB, Ward S, et al: Factors determining the mortality and morbidity in hepatic injuries. Analysis of 108 cases. *Ann Surg* 189:466, 1979.

31. Yellen AE, Chaffee CB, Donovan AJ: Vascular isolation in treatment of juxtahepatic venous injuries. *Arch Surg* 102:566, 1971.

32. Williams RD, Yurko AA Jr: Controversial aspects of diagnosis and management of blunt abdominal trauma. *Am J Surg* 111:477, 1966.

33. King H, Shumacher HB Jr: Splenic Studies; susceptibility to infection after splenectomy performed in infancy. *Ann Surg* 136:239, 1952.

34. Singer DB: Postsplenectomy sepsis, in Rosenberg HS, Bolande RP (eds): *Perspectives in Pediatric Pathology*. Chicago, Yearbook Medical Publishers, 1973, p 285.

35. Krivit W: Overwhelming postsplenectomy infection. *Am J Hematol* 2:193, 1977.

36. Douglas GJ, Simpson JS: The conservative management of splenic trauma, *J Pediatr Surg* 6:565, 1971.
37. Hendren WH, Kim SH: Trauma of the spleen and liver in children. *Pediatr Clin North Am* 22:349, 1975.
38. LaMura J, Chung-Fat SP, San Filippo JA: Splenorrhaphy for the treatment of splenic rupture in infants and children. *Surgery* 81:497, 1977.
39. Mishalory HG: Repair of the ruptured spleen. *J Pediatr Surg* 9:175, 1974.
40. Sherman NJ, Asch MJ: Conservative surgery for splenic injuries. *Pediatrics* 61:267, 1978.

10
Burns as a Manifestation of Child Abuse

Theodore C. Jewett, Jr.
Norman S. Ellerstein

Burns as a form of child abuse had received little attention until recently in spite of the voluminous literature on other aspects of child abuse. In 1965 Gillespie (1) published the first article entirely devoted to the subject of burns as a form of abuse. Soft tissue injuries have been found to be the most common physical manifestation of child abuse. Both O'Neill (2) and Lauer (3) in their reviews found that approximately three quarters of their cases had some form of soft tissue injuries, many of which were burns. Gillespie (1) reported a 100% incidence of other types of soft tissue injuries in association with inflicted burns. Other manifestations frequently seen are those involving the central nervous system, bones, and malnutrition. It becomes apparent that it is most important for the physician to be alert to the fact that any child who has thermal injuries be appraised as a possible case of child abuse. The incidence of child abuse caused by thermal injury varies. In a study of 712 abused children, Lenoski (4) reported that 6% had thermal injuries; Ofodile (5) reported 9 of 23 (39%) burn admissions to be secondary to child abuse. Ayoub and Pfiefer (6) stressed that inflicted burns place a child in grave danger of permanent injury or death. Maintaining a high index of suspicion for abuse is important in evaluating burned children. Recognition of a burned child as being abused is the first step in protecting him from further maltreatment.

CLINICAL ASPECTS

The history and physical examination are the most important factors in alerting the physician to the possibility that the burn may be due to child abuse. The actual injury may be minor or result in permanent disfiguration or physical impairment. Even children with minor burns must be evaluated for the possibility of maltreatment in order to protect them from subsequent injury.

The demographic data on children with inflicted burns is similar to that found in other forms of child maltreatment. Both Gillespie (1) and Ofodile (5) found the average age of their cases to be under 24 months. Self-initiated burns are uncommon during infancy because of the child's limitations of movement. Even when the child begins to walk he is usually unable to reach the boiling water on the stove or experiment with the electrical appliances on the kitchen counter. Two studies indicate that boys are more likely than girls to be the victims of child abuse by thermal injuries. Feldman (7) reports that abusive scalds are twice as frequent in boys. In the study by Stone (8), 20 of 26 burned abused children were boys. As in other forms of child abuse the infliction of thermal injuries is not confined to the lower socioeconomic groups. Gillespie (1) points out in his study that the problem is not limited to economically destitute or culturally deprived individuals. However, Feldman (7) shows that incidence of abusive scald injuries is higher in the lower socioeconomic groups. Hernandez-Denton (9) reported an interesting ethnic difference in the manifestation of abuse in Puerto Rican children in the United States. Of the physically abused children he reviewed, 36% had burns as their primary injury, an unsually high incidence.

As in all cases evaluated by the physician, a detailed history of the events leading up to the burn should be obtained. The environmental circumstances surrounding the incident should be specifically noted. The people, objects, times, and distances should be detailed. For example, in scalds the depth of the water in the bathtub or other container, the location of the vessel containing the scalding liquid, the estimated temperature of the water, and the chronologic sequence of the events before, during, and after the burn should be documented. A detailed history of the child's development is needed to determine if the victim was developmentally mature enough to have self-initiated the accident. A history of prior failure-to-thrive, hospitalizations, burns, and accidents in the child being evaluated and in his siblings might elicit a pattern of repeated trauma. A carefully obtained history will usually allow the physician to decide if the burn was caused by accident, neglect, or direct abuse.

If there is delay in seeking medical attention, the possibility of abuse or neglect should be explored. Feldman (7) reported that 70% of scalded abused children experienced a delay of at least 2 hours in seeking medical care. If the burn appears older than the alleged day of the accident, the inconsistency might be an expression of ambivalence about seeking medical care and risking exposure of the incident as abusive. If the parents state that there was no witness to the accident, or they have no idea how the burns could have occurred, abuse should be suspected. Similarly, if the burn was attributed to the actions of a sibling or baby-sitter, suspicion should be aroused. Most importantly, if the history of how the burn occurred is inconsistent with the physical examination of the burn, abuse or neglect as a cause should be highly suspected. In addition, if the history changes on subsequent tellings, or if different people provide conflicting histories, cover-up of the accurate history is likely.

To further determine the likelihood of maltreatment in the assessment of the burned child, a detailed physical examination is mandatory. This should include not only the burned areas, but a total examination of the child. If other injuries suggestive of abuse, such as fractures, multiple hematomas, scars, or evidence of growth failure, are present, the probability of abuse increases. In the study by Ayoub and Pfiefer (6), most of the maltreated burned children had evidence of other trauma in addition to the burn. If the child being evaluated has burns in varying stages of healing or scars from old burns, special attention should be paid to the possibility of abuse or neglect. The extent of the burn, that is, the percentage of surface area involved, bears no consistent relationship to the likelihood of abuse; a burn of any size may be abusive. Both Stone (8) and Ayoub (6) reported that in their cases of maltreated children, the mean area of body surface involved was 16%. However, 19% of the patients reviewed by Stone and 17% of the children reviewed by Ayoub died secondarily to their burns. Several authors emphasize the high incidence of burns to the buttocks and perineum in abused children (Fig. 1) (1,8,10). Any child with burns in these areas should be considered abused unless otherwise proven.

If the physician can determine the mechanism of the burning, he can usually make an assessment of the likelihood of abuse. By comparing the probable mechanism with the history given by the parents and the developmental skills of the child, he can determine if the burn was caused by accident, was self-initiated by the child, or was inflicted. Lenoski (4) and others describe basic patterns of burns seen in abused children. *Immersion burns* are produced when a child is dipped into a hot liquid. The burn is uniform in all areas exposed to the hot liquid, and there is a line of demarcation indicating which area of skin was exposed to the hot liquid and which was not (Fig. 2). Commonly, burns to the hands or feet are symmetrical and may be full thickness in depth, suggesting that the extremities were held in the hot liquid and allowed to burn for a period of time. "Stocking" or "glove" distributions are examples of immersion burns. Satellite or noncontiguous burns are not usually present, as the child is not able to splash when being held by the abuser. In a small number of immersion

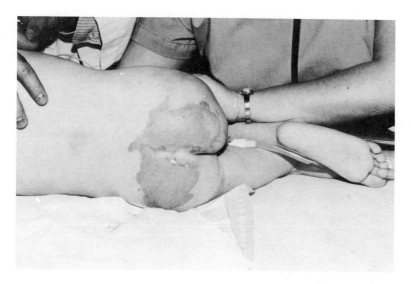

Figure 1. Second degree burn on buttocks of 6-year-old boy who presented with severe head trauma and fractured arm.

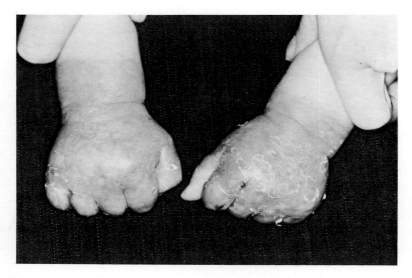

Figure 2. Immersion burns on the hands of an infant with a "glove" distribution; definitely abusive. (From Ford RJ, Smistek BS and Glass JT: Photography of suspected child abuse and maltreatment. *Biomedical Communications*, July, 1975.)

burns, there is an area of skin within the total burn area that is spared from injury. The area of sparing results when the child's body is compressed against the sides or bottom of the vessel containing the hot liquid. The area of skin compressed against the vessel is exposed to the hot liquid for a shorter period of time and, therefore, is less severely burned than the surrounding areas that are in constant contact with the hot liquid. A child may suffer an immersion burn, but have flexion areas of his body spared from burning. This results when a certain part of the body, such as the hip, is in flexion when the child is dipped into the hot liquid (Fig. 3). In flexion areas, two surfaces of skin press against each other preventing the hot liquid from entering that area. Therefore, the child with an extensive immersion burn may have several nonburned areas of skin. *Splash burns* occur when a liquid is thrown at or poured onto the child. In these cases the depth of the burn may be less than that seen in immersion burns. The liquid is in contact with the skin for a shorter period of time, and the liquid cools as it stays in contact with the relatively cooler skin and air. The burns may not be uniform in depth, and they may occur in noncontiguous areas of the body (Figs. 4 and 5). *Contact burns* results when an object is placed directly on the skin and causes a burn, usually at least second degree in depth. The configuration of the burn depicts the implement used to cause it. "Grid" burns are caused when a child is seated on or held against a heating grate or other object that brands the child with its configuration (Fig. 6). Cigarette burns are a type of contact burn in which the round shape of the cigarette tip is seen on the skin.

The most frequent cause of burns in abused children is scalding with hot water (1,4–6). The buttocks and perineum are frequently burned areas, but any part of the body may be involved. The location and extent of the burn are not as important as the pattern in determining the probability of abuse.

Occasionally a child may present with burns that, at first appearance, seem to have been inflicted. However, on more careful evaluation the burn proves to be accidental. Five such cases were reported by Schmitt et al. (11). All five children were thought to be abused, but they were accidently burned when their skin came in contact with surfaces heated by the sun. All the children were less than 1 year old and sustained second-degree burns. Three of the children came in contact with vinyl upholstery in cars, one infant was burned by the safety strap on an infant bicycle seat. Another case was reported by Saitz (12), in which a 2½-year-old girl was burned by an automobile seat belt buckle. In all these cases the burning agents were heated by being exposed to direct sunlight. The children were accidently burned when they came in contact with these common objects. These cases illustrate that all possibilities should be

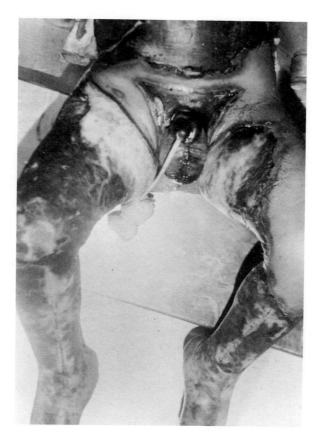

Figure 3. Extensive immersion burns with sparing of parts of the inguinal region because hips were flexed at time of immersion. Note that one knee is not burned; it remained above the surface of the water indicating that the knee was also in flexion. This pattern is pathognomonic of abuse.

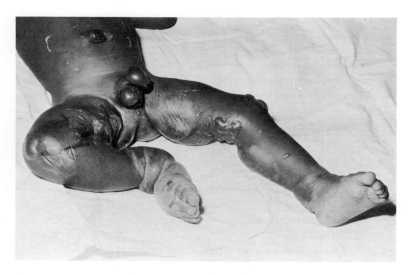

Figure 4. Splash burns. Second degree burns on various noncontiguous parts of the lower body.

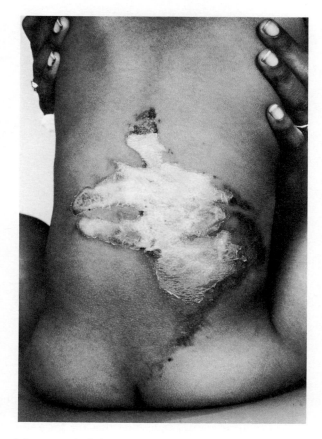

Figure 5. Second degree splash burn without recognizable configuration. This could be accidental.

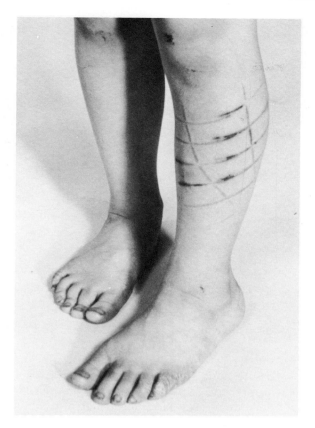

Figure 6. "Grid" burn resulting from contact with a space heater. (From Ellerstein NS: The cutaneous manifestations of child abuse and neglect. *Am. J. Dis. Child.* 133:906, 1979).

explored before a final determination is made as to the cause of a childhood burn.

PATHOPHYSIOLOGY

First-degree burns, namely hyperemia of the skin, are seldom encountered in cases of child abuse. Since abusive burns are purposely inflicted, the child cannot easily remove himself from the thermal exposure that results in a longer contact and consequent deeper burn. Gillespie (1) reported two-thirds of the burns in his cases were second degree and the remaining were third degree. The second-degree burn, in which the upper layers of the dermis are destroyed, but the deeper layers such as the hair follicles remain intact, is manifested by blisters, a weeping skin surface, and hypersensitivity to touch (Figs. 1, 4, and 5). In addition, the erythema blanches with pressure, but returns promptly to a red color when the pressure is released. Third-degree burns are those in which the full thickness of the skin is destroyed (Fig. 7). They are white or

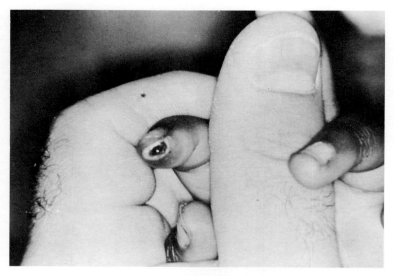

Figure 7. Third degree burn caused by a match flame.

charred in color, nonsensitive to touch and pin prick, and appear as a thick eschar.

The determinants of the depth of a burn are (*1*) the thickness of the child's skin, (*2*) the exposure time, and (*3*) the temperature of the offending substance. The infant's skin is appreciably thinner than that of the older child. Consequently, what may be a superficial second-degree burn in the older child, could well be a deep second or even third-degree burn in the infant. Moritz and Henriques (13) have shown that there is a definite time-temperature relationship. in the determination of the depth of a burn. Using the pig, whose skin corresponds closely to that of the human, and human volunteers, they showed that at a temperature of 44°C (111°F) an exposure time of 6 to 7 hours was necessary to cause a full thickness destruction of the skin. With temperatures exceeding 70°C (158°F) only 1 second of exposure is necessary to cause a third-degree burn. Boiling water, at a temperature of 100°C (212°F), may cool to 70 to 80°C (158–176°F) in transit from the container to the child's skin, but is still hot enough to produce a third-degree burn in only a 1 to 2 second expsure. Since most inflicted burns are caused by hot liquids via either immersion or splash, it is easy to see how only brief skin contact can produce marked injuries. Feldman (7), in a survey of homes, found that the mean tap water temperature was 60°C (142°F). At this temperature, an exposure of less than 10 seconds will cause a third-degree burn. Therefore, it is possible to inflict serious burns on a child with water directly from the tap without additionally heating it on the stove. Liquids being heated, such as coffee, tea, soups, and others are dangerous weapons long before they come to boil. It is important to keep in mind that the experiments of Moritz and Henriques were probably done on adults; most children with inflicted burns are less than 5 years old. The thinner skin of young children may be damaged with lower temperatures and shorter exposure times. However, ethical standards for research prohibit confirmation of this hypothesis for humans.

Sometimes abusing parents will falsely claim that they did not know that the bath water was burning the child because he did not cry out in pain. Moritz and Henriques (13) report that discomfort is felt at a skin surface temperature of about 48°C (118°F). There is no evidence to suggest that a child's skin is less sensitive than an adult's. Therefore, a liquid hot enough to burn the child is also hot enough to cause discomfort for anyone who comes in contact with it.

Chemical burns are not common manifestations of maltreatment, but they have been reported (1). The child may come in contact with the chemical agent in the same ways that he comes in contact with hot liquids, namely, immersion, splash, or being forced to drink the liquid. In chemical injuries, the burn is most likely to be third degree. Hot liquids cool with time, thereby losing their capacity to burn. But chemicals, either acids or alkalies, maintain their tissue destroying ability and continue to damage skin and subcutaneous tissue until the chemical is removed. Electrical burns have not been reported in association with child abuse. Frostbite, another type of thermal injury, can also be the result of abuse. Children may be forced to sit or stand in ice water or snow or forced to remain outdoors in cold weather. Injuries from cold have the potential of being as severe as those caused by heat, but are encountered much less frequently.

TREATMENT

One of the first decisions to be made in the management of the burn patient is whether to hospitalize the child. If the history and physical examination are suggestive of maltreatment, hospital admission is usually the safest way to proceed even if the severity of the burn does not warrant inpatient management. The need for intravenous fluid therapy is the second major criterion for hospitalization.

With the arrival of the child in the emergency suite, all attendants should be wearing masks as the first step in the prevention of future infection. The evaluation and estimation of the extent and depth of the burn should then be determined. First degree, which is merely erythema, is not included in the estimation of the extent of the burn. Second-degree burns generally heal spontaneously within 14 to 21 days if infection does not supervene. Third-degree burns heal only by contracture and epithelialization from the edges or by skin graft. The extent of the burn is estimated the same as an adult's using the "rule of nine," except that the body surface distribution is different in the infant than in the adult. The head of the infant is proportionately larger and the legs smaller than in the adult. An infant's head accounts for 19% of the total body surface, and each leg for 13%, as compared to the adult in which the head is 9% and the legs 18% each (Fig. 8). The remaining portions of the body are comparable. For each year of age over 1, 1% is substracted from the head, and $\frac{1}{2}$% is added to each leg until the patient is over 10 years of age, and then the adult configuration becomes operative.

Body Surface

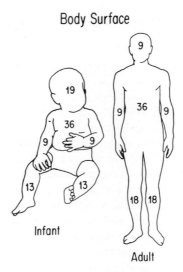

Infant

Adult

Figure 8. Different surface area distributions in infant and adult.

Once the total extent of second and third degree burns is determined, a decision regarding intravenous fluids can be made. The indications for intravenous fluid therapy are the following: (*1*) children under 2 years of age with a second- or third-degree burn of greater than 10% of the body surface; (*2*) patients between 2 and 12 years of age with more than a 15% burn; (*3*) any child with involvement of over 20% of body surface. The modified Evan's formula is a convenient and well-established method for calculating fluid replacement. One cubic centimeter per kilogram of body weight per percentage of body surface burned of crystalloid solution plus an equal volume of colloids is used as replacement during the first 24 hours. Half normal saline is the crystalloid used, and once a urinary output is established, potassium is added to the solution. Colloid can be used either as reconstituted albumin or Plasmanate. Whole blood is not usually necessary during the first 24 to 48 hours, unless the patient has a falling hemoglobin and obvious loss of blood from the burn area or from other concomitant injuries. A maintenance amount of fluid is also added to supply water for insensible loss and urinary output. Maintenance amounts to 1,500 cc/M^2 per day. This entire amount of fluid is calculated and then half of it given during the first 8 hours, and the remaining half during the ensuing 16-hour period. The amount of fluid used in this formula is purely an estimate; other parameters such as the urinary output, which should be monitored by an indwelling Foley catheter, and the hemoglobin-hematocrit response are determinate factors for increasing or decreasing the total amount of fluid necessary. Careful monitoring of vital signs and twice daily weights are also important in determining the response of a patient to the intravenous therapy. All burn formulas are estimates based on the previously observed behavior of many burned children. They merely predict the approximate amount of fluid that will probably be required. An increase in pulse rate, a drop in the pulse pressure, decreasing hourly urine output with high specific gravity, and rising hematocrit are indications for increasing the rate of fluid administration. Obviously, increase in urinary output would intimate decreasing the fluid. Around 36 to 48 hours after the initial burn trauma, a diuresis usually occurs as a result of the third space burn fluid leaving the burn area and entering the intravascular compartment. This should be watched for carefully and fluids rapidly decreased at this time; otherwise, the patient's circulatory system may become overloaded.

The initial management of the burn wound should consist of sterile technique using masks and gowns. Sterile instruments are used for debridement of all bullous lesions that are then covered with sterile nitrofurazone or providone-iodine dressings. The face is treated without dressings using only antibiotic ointment. For extensive third-degree burns, silver sulfadiazine cream or one of the silver nitrate preparations is most effective. The burn area and the nasopharynx should be cultured and the patient stated on penicillin until the cultures show that there is no streptococcus either in the wound or in the patient's nasopharynx. Other than this short course of penicillin, prophylactic antibiotics are generally felt to be contraindicated. Tetanus toxoid is given if indicated. Burn dressings are left in place for 4 or 5 days unless there appears to be an excessive amount of secretion oozing through the dressing or evidence of sepsis. At the initial dressing, the burn area is again examined for depth of burn and the patient then placed in a whirlpool bath for gentle debridement. The goal is to debride the burn of all devitalized tissue as rapidly as possible to allow second-degree burns to heal without intervening infection.

The nutritional aspects of burn management start at the time of the burn trauma. The initial treatment consists of the colloids that are given during the first 48 hours. Once the shock phase is over, careful attention must be paid to the use of whole blood to replace the constant loss of plasma and microscopic red cells from the burn area. This replacement therapy will prevent anemia, which would interfere with the healing of the skin grafts and donor area. At the onset of the burn, a nasogastric tube should be placed in the child's stomach for the first 24 hours, since an ileus often is encountered in serious third degree burns, and vomiting with aspiration is a danger to the child. After 24 hours, clear fluids may be started and, if tolerated, the child is allowed to take a full high caloric diet, rich in protein. A careful calorie count should be kept, and if the oral intake is not adequate, gavage feedings of an elemental high protein tube feeding formula should be added. Adequate calories must be taken by the child to not only supply the basal needs, but also to replace the plasma loss from the burn surface and the extra calories lost from the fever accompanying burns.

Following the successful treatment of the burns, children whose injuries are suspected to be due to child abuse should not be discharged until the home situation has been completely evaluated. A foster home may be a temporizing solution if the child is ready for discharge before a thorough assessment has been completed.

REFERENCES

1. Gillespie RW: The battered child syndrome: Thermal and caustic manifestations. *J Trauma* 5:523, 1965.
2. O'Neill JA, Meacham WF, Griffin PP, et al: Patterns of injury in the battered child syndrome. *J Trauma* 13:332, 1973.
3. Lauer B, TenBroeck E, Grossman M: Battered child syndrome: Review of 130 patients with controls. *Pediatrics* 54:67, 1974.
4. Lenoski EF, Hunter KA: Specific patterns of inflicted burn injuries. *J Trauma* 17:842, 1977.
5. Ofodile F, Norris J, Garnes A: Burns and child abuse. *East Afr Med J* 56:26, 1979.
6. Ayoub C, Pfeifer D: Burns as a manifestation of child abuse and neglect. *Am J Dis Child* 133:910, 1979.
7. Feldman KW, Schaller RT, Feldman JA, et al: Tap water scald burns in children. *Pediatrics* 62:1, 1978.
8. Stone NH, Rinaldo, Humphrey CR, et al: Child abuse by burning. *Surg Clin North Am* 50:1419, 1970.
9. Hernandez-Denton JL: Methods of physical abuse in battered Puerto Rican children treated at Yale New Haven Hospital. *Bol Asoc Méd PR* 70:423, 1978.
10. Keen JH, Lendrum J, Wolman B: Inflicted burns and scalds in children. *Br Med J* 4:268, 1975.
11. Schmitt BD, Gray JD, Britton HL: Car seat burns in infants: Avoding confusion with inflicted burns. *Pediatrics* 62:607, 1978.
12. Saitz EW: Seat belt buckle burn. *Am J Dis Child* 129:1456, 1975.
13. Moritz AR, Henriques FC Jr: Studies of thermal injury: II The relative importance of time and surface temperature in the causation of cutaneous burns. *Am J Pathol* 23:695, 1947.

11
Growth Failure

Charles F. Whitten

The focus in this chapter will be on the relationship between inappropriate mothering and the physical growth and mental and emotional development of children. The relationship will be analyzed largely within the context of failure-to-thrive. *Failure-to-thrive* is defined as a condition in infants in which there is severe growth retardation.

From an etiological standpoint there are three major types of failure-to-thrive: (*1*) *nonorganic*—with a definable cause that is not related to a disease process; (*2*) *organic*—with a definable cause that is related to a disease process; and (*3*) *idiopathic*—with no definable cause. Growth failure from inadequate mothering is a nonorganic type of failure-to-thrive. Associated with the growth failure are varying degrees of intellectual, developmental, and emotional impairment. It is variously known as the maternal deprivation syndrome (1), environmental retardation (2), environmental failure to thrive (3), emotional deprivation (4), as well as psychological deprivation (5). In this discussion the term *maternal deprivation syndrome* will be used.

Since the effects of inappropriate mothering also can be considered within the context of *psychosocial dwarfism* (6) (a condition in older children characterized by severe growth retardation and varying degrees of intellectual, emotional, and behavioral alterations), limited analysis of this syndrome will follow the discussion of the more common maternal deprivation syndrome.

FAILURE-TO-THRIVE

Pathogenesis

Infants who have sustained growth failure from maternal deprivation tend to have the following characteristics: they are below the third percentile for height and weight on standard growth grids; they are retarded in motor, social, and language development; they are withdrawn, lethargic, and apathetic. Less frequently, they exhibit autoerotic behavior, a radar gaze, or an infantile posture (2–10).

The first task in examining the relationship between maternal deprivation and its effects on infants is to answer the question, "How does inadequate mothering lead to impairment of physical growth, social and motor development, and emotional status?"

The first substantive report (11) in the American literature (1915) described a relationship between the handling of infants and their overall well-being. It revealed that in all but one of 10 institutions that were studied where infants were admitted for prolonged care all infants under 2 years of age, except one, died. At a national research meeting discussants of these findings indicated similar outcomes in other American institutions.

The failure of infants to thrive in hospitals was not confined to American institutions; similar reports appeared in European medical journals. "Hospitalism," as the condition was named, was initially and generally attributed to poor nutrition, then later to infections. But, as Bakwin (4) indicated, some pediatricians had suspected that hospitalism was in some way related to the infant's psyche. He noted that Parrot concluded hospitalism was due to a lack of adequate stimulation, that Czerny felt monotony and staring at blank walls and ceilings were important factors, and that Pfaundler observed that when the mother or some sympathetic person took care of the child, severe damage did not take place.

Although the matter of death from living in institutions seemed to have been largely resolved in the intervening years, Spitz (7), in the early 1940s, published a set of observations that highlighted another deleterious aspect of the effects of the type of care provided in institutions on the well-being of infants. Spitz compared the growth and development of four groups of infants. One group lived with their mothers in middle-class homes. A second group lived with their mothers in low socioeconomic homes. A third group lived in an institution but were taken care of by their mothers, who were delinquent and/or retarded. These mothers were under the tutelage and supervision of the nursing staff. A fourth group lived in a foundling home.

The three groups of infants cared for by their mothers received the type of care we traditionally view as good mothering, but the care of the infants in the foundling home was grossly different. They lived in an environment in which they received little stimulation of any kind. From 2 to 3 months of age they were confined to cribs with sheets covering the foot and side railings. The cribs were in partitioned cubicles; thus, the infants were virtually in solitary confinement. Their only human contact occurred during daily visits by the medical staff and during periodic custodial care by the attendants, each of whom was responsible for seven infants. Not even toys were available for self-stimulation.

At the end of the first year of life, the infants cared for by their mothers were within normal limits for growth and development (although the infants from the middle-class homes were more advanced). The infants in the foundling home, however, showed severe growth retardation; they were virtually silent, retarded in their motor development (few could sit alone), withdrawn, apathetic and inactive, and attained low scores on infant intelligence tests.

Although these early descriptions of maternal deprivation only dealt with institutionalized infants, it was later discovered that in certain cases mothers in their own homes treated infants similarly to the way infants had been handled in the foundling home, with similar outcomes (2,3,8).

The observations of Spitz (7) and others stimulated further investigations of the relationship between mothering and development of the child. Babies come into the world with the ability to see, to hear, to feel, to move, to make sounds, etc., and the capacity eventually to handle very complex tasks using these skills. In order for these abilities to develop, they must be used. Obviously, young infants cannot do this on their own. They have virtually no ability to create practice situations. In the first year of life, someone must provide opportunities for the infant to look, to listen, to hear, to touch, to relate to objects and human beings. Thus, in addition to all the other roles that mothers (parents) play for infants, they are the most significant stimulators for the infant's growth and development.

Now, there is an extensive body of literature that clearly indicates that lack of social and sensory stimulation are directly responsible for delays in sitting, standing, walking, and talking, as well as for emotional withdrawal and poor performance on intelligence tests among maternally deprived infants (12–16). This deprivation occurs when the mother or mother-substitute seldom holds, handles, or fondles the infant, when she usually does not keep the baby where the baby can see her, and when she infrequently talks to and plays with her baby in a way typical of most mothers.

Spitz (7) and several later investigators (6,17,18) also attributed the severe growth retardation to inadequate mothering. In general, they postulate that the way the infant is handled initiates emotional mechanisms that interfere with either metabolism and food absorption or endocrine regulation of growth by the hypothalmus, pituitary, or adrenal cortex. In effect, they theorize that although these infants receive sufficient food to grow, there is ineffective metabolism or utilization.

Because of observations that were inconsistent with this concept, Whitten et al. (19) tested this thesis by determining whether maternally deprived infants receiving very little mothering would gain weight at an accelerated rate if their food intakes were adequate. They studied infants who had sustained maternal deprivation in their homes (with the characteristic traits stemming from that type of handling). When those infants were fed as much as they wanted to eat in the hospital, the majority gained weight at an accelerated rate. Their weights improved despite their being handled just as they were presumed to have been handled at home, that is, understimulated and isolated. Furthermore, the amount the infants gained when they were grossly undermothered equaled the amount they gained when placed in a setting where the nurses provided a high level of fondling and handling, plus social contact in the form of talking and playing games. The amount of food eaten under these two types of mothering was also the same.

The few who did not gain rapidly in the understimulating setting had poor appetites. They did not eat enough to permit them to gain at even a normal rate. Their poor appetites, low food intake, and small weight gain persisted during a short period when they were showered with tender loving care and sensory stimulation.

The hospital findings were duplicated in the homes. Some of the infants, after being returned to the care of their mothers, did not sustain the rate of weight gain achieved in the hospital; they acutally returned to their prediagnosis weight level. However, during a 2-week period when food was delivered to the home three times per day and the mothers fed the infants in the presence of the person who delivered the food, the infants again gained weight at an accelerated rate. There was good evidence that there was no significant change in the type of mothering during the period of the home-feeding program.

In all the infants, whether they gained weight in the hospital or in the home appeared to be dependent on whether they ingested enough food, not whether they received enough mothering. The data strongly suggested that maternally deprived infants are underweight because of undereating, which is secondary to not being offered adequate food or not accepting it, not because of some psychologically induced defect in absorption or metabolism.

How then do we explain the growth failure in the infants described by Spitz and others? Although Spitz's studies were published first, sparking a new concern over the devastating effects of the way infants were handled in institutions, about the same time Goldfarb (5,20) conducted a similar study. He too was concerned about the lack of social and sensory stimulation. In the institution he investigated, he reported that babies below 9 months of age were kept singly in separate cubicles. They had brief, hurried contacts with adults when they were cleaned and fed by nurses. During the first year of life, therefore, each child lived in almost complete isolation. During the next 2 years, the experience was only slightly less impoverished. Thus, from the standpoint of social-sensory stimulation of the infants, there appeared to be no basic difference in institutions described by Spitz and Goldfarb.

Yet, Spitz described severe growth retardation while Goldfarb did not even mention the infants' growth status. It is inconceivable that any investigator could write a series of articles on these infants without mentioning their growth status if they were severely undergrown. Hence, it is evident that there is some factor in operation other than insufficient stimulation.

An institutional study conducted in the 1960s suggests the answer. Provence and Lipton (21) have extensively detailed observations on a group of 50 infants who had lived in the same type of environment as described by Spitz and Goldfarb. (The understimulation was proabably not quite as severe.)

The type of effects on the developmental and emotional state of the infants was similar, but initially no comments were made about the growth status. Later, it was learned that the infants were all within the normal range for weight and that the caloric intake was proabably adequate. In their book the authors indicate that special efforts were made to assure adequate food intake. For example, if the infants were asleep at feeding time, they were awakened for feeding. If an infant was crying when the attendant began to prepare the group for feeding, that infant might receive his/her bottle first. Older infants (9–24 mos.) were fed while lying on their backs in the crib until they were 18 months old; then, they were allowed to sit-up in the corner of the crib for feeding. Those who took the longest to feed were fed last. Self-feeding was rare.

Although Spitz did not describe the feeding process, it is reasonable to speculate that the infants in Spitz's study did not grow properly despite the availability of food (whereas Goldfarb's and Provence and Lipton's did) because there was a difference in the staff's concerns over feeding. Spitz specifically states that there were too few caretakers to take care of the infants. It is probable that in Spitz's institution bottles were "propped" and some infants lost them before they were finished feeding; or, some infants might have fallen asleep and not finished eating before the bottle was taken away. Since feeding occurred "on schedule," some babies might not have been hungry enough at the scheduled feeding time to consume all available food; then they would not be given more food when they became hungry.

The concept that growth retardation in maternally deprived infants stems from an inadequate intake of food is supported by an animal study. Kerr et al. (22) have assessed the effects of sensory deprivation on monkeys. They reared the animals in total social isolation, but fed them as much as they wanted to eat. The monkeys exhibited marked behavioral changes consisting of austistic posturing, fear, and absence of social play, but they grew as well as monkeys that had lived in an enriched, stimulating environment.

To summarize this analysis, the best evidence indicates a dual causality for the effects of maternal deprivation on infants. Growth failure is secondary to an inadequate intake of food (undernutrition); the intellectual, developmental, and emotional impairments and alterations are secondary to inadequate social and sensory stimulation.

Although this dual concept is operationally sound from the standpoint of primary causation, it is highly likely that secondarily there is a relationship between undernutrition and mental, as well as social and emotional development. The long-term relationship will be considered later in this chapter. However, what about the immediate effects?

Undernutrition undoubtedly has an effect on physical vigor, motivation, and affect. It is safe to assume that the reduction in muscle mass and tone and the decrease in energy (lack of vigor) experienced by the undernourished infant will affect adversely the infant's ability to develop motor or physical skills. Furthermore, delayed development of motor and physical skills, along with lack of energy, may limit the infant's ability to take advantage of opportunities to develop both socially and cognitively or to perform at "capacity" on mental and developmental tests. The infant may just be too weak or too tired, from undernutrition, to respond to or sustain interest in the stimuli presented by his or her environment. Also, it is possible that the apathy induced by malnutrition may result in less response and stimulation from the mother.

One other issue needs to be dealt with in a consideration of pathogenetic mechanism within the infant: that is, whether there are hormonal changes in the maternally deprived infant. If so, what is the significance of these alterations? This is a pertinent issue because proponents of the concept that the growth failure is secondary to psychosocial factors cite deficiencies in growth hormone response to arginine and insulin stimulation in psychosocial dwarfism as evidence (17). However, this has not been found in maternally deprived infants. The only endocrine changes reported in maternally deprived infants are decreased total and free thyroxine and increased cortisol secretion rate (23,24). These changes cannot be interpreted as causative factors, for they are also found in children with malnutrition from organic causes. Therefore, they are more appropriately viewed as endocrine adaptations to malnutrition.

Etiology

What happens to and in the child has been described. Next to be considered are the reasons why mothers fail to feed and stimulate their infants.

There is limited literature devoted to an analysis of the factors operative in mothers whose infants fit the criteria established for the maternal deprivation syndrome. In addition to the paucity of data, there is another difficulty: the individual authors have not assessed the mothers by the same set of standards. Thus, it is frequently not known whether a finding emphasized by one investigator is present in the mothers described by others.

Leonard et al. (8) (13 cases) described the mothers as unwilling mothers. These mothers did not intend to have babies at the particular times of the conceptions. From a psychological standpoint, not a single mother reported sustained supportive nurturing in her own childhood. Many expressed feelings of inadequacy. They tended to lack the capacity to cope in a constructive way with their stressful life situations. Anxiety and depression were often present, immobilizing them. They were relatively lonely and isolated, with very little adult companionship. The researchers concluded that the mothers were lacking in self-esteem and had difficulty in assessing their baby's needs and their own worth. The mothers needed nurturing to promote their capacity to nurture their baby. From a social standpoint, there were multiple problems in every family, such as poverty, substandard housing with overcrowding, threat of eviction, disorganized and chaotic home life, unemployment, illegitimacy, and seriously disturbed marital relationships.

Since other children had grown and developed satisfactorily (though no documentation was provided), the authors questioned why one particular child had been unable to thrive. They speculated that either complications of the pregnancy and delivery affected the mothers' anticipation and perception of the baby, the baby's personality and temperament affected the way the mother responded to him, or this baby depleted a mother's already overburdened resources.

Glaser et al. (9) (40 cases) stated that "most of the children in our study were members of intact, relatively stable families with steady incomes. The parents were not teenagers overwhelmed by the strangeness of a first baby, but rather adults in their midtwenties with two or three children." They could not consistently assign the growth failure of these children to poverty, family disruption, parental immaturity, or large families.

Coleman and Provence (2) (2 cases) reported that the parents were well educated, with no economic or other social problems; they attributed the deprivation to the mothers' psychological difficulties. The mothers were depressed during the first year of the infants' lives and found no pleasure in taking care of the babies. They specifically stated that these were not unwanted babies.

Barbero and Shaheen (3) (unstated number of cases, four examples cited) found maternal deprivation to be associated with "significant environmental psychosocial disruption." It is of interest that in enumerating the type of disruptions they did not differentiate between psychological and social factors implying a communality and interrelationship. The factors that they found included one or more of the following: "alcoholism, severe financial deprivation, sexual incompatibility or promiscuity, serious parental or family illness, childhood deprivation in mother (or father), physical abuse between parents, high-risk pregnancy and delivery, inexperience in mothercraft, job instability or chronic unemployment, too frequent unplanned or unwanted pregnancies, and considerable strain of the parent with their own families." They noted that although the families often had multiple problems, economic deprivation was not always present.

Patton and Gardner (1) (six cases, including five infants and one 6½-year-old child) indicated that the children were products of grossly disturbed family environments characterized by emotional disorders in the parents, separation of the parents, alcholism, and other unstated socially undesirable behaviors. In one case, they stated the mother had a violent hatred of the infant.

Elmer (25) (five cases) attempted to identify the role of the mother and reported that one mother was apathetic and depressed; another was neurotic with a particular dislike for men; two presumably experienced anxiety about their predicament following desertion by their husbands and depression over the unwanted child; a fifth experienced overwhelming anxiety over a physical defect that was not responsible for the failure-to-thrive.

Evans et al. (26) (40 cases) found some common denominators in their mothers, yet were able to classify them into three profiles. All of the mothers reported that the children were unplanned and unwanted, and all of the families were struggling with economic problems. The mothers in one group were depressed and had had a recent personal loss (such as a death of a mother). Those in a second group had had far more crises, longer standing chronic problems, and the child was viewed as "just one more failure or crises in a wide range of problems with which the family had to cope." In the third group were mothers who were angry and hostile, and it appeared that they had never been able to establish any meaningful relationships.

Fischhoff et al. (27) (12 cases) confined their report to a description of psychiatric evaluations. They found that 10 of the mothers could be diagnosed as having character disorders in that they had varying degrees of a limited ability to perceive and assess accurately the environment, their own needs, or those of their children; a limited ability to adapt to changes in the environment; an adverse affective state; defective objective relationships, and a limited capacity for concern. Further, they indicated that descriptions of the mothers in several of the articles cited in this report were consistent with character disorders. The other two mothers were considered to be psychoneurotic.

Based on these observations, it appears that one or more of the following pathogenic mechanisms are operative in mothers who had not fed and nurtured their infants:

1. The mother's psychic energies are consumed by social problems or environmental stress, creating depression, apathy and/or reducing motivation, perception, or awareness.
2. The mother's psychic energies are consumed by inner conflicts that create depression and/or reduce motivation, perception, and awareness.
3. The mother rejects the infant because the infant was the product of an unwanted pregnancy or because of the infant's physical and behavioral characteristics.
4. The mother never developed an adequate capacity to give affection and nurturing care.

5. The mother lacks the self-esteem necessary to establish a nurturing role or to view the infant as having independent needs.
6. The mother is out of touch with reality (psychotic).

Obviously these are not mutually exclusive factors; more than one may be operative in some mothers. Overall, the data suggest that these mechanisms produce mothers who are either aware that their care is adequate and are not motivated to respond or are not aware of the inadequacy of their care. Stated another way, some mothers do not want to mother their infants and know it, some do not want to and are not aware of it, and some want to but are unable to mobilize the energy that is necessary to fulfill their desire.

One final factor is pertinent. Does the infant contribute to the understimulation? Is there a vulnerable personality type? Maternally deprived infants are characteristically nondemanding. But, is this an adaptation or reaction to the mothers failure to respond to its needs, or is it entirely the result of undernutrition and understimulation? These questions have not yet been answered.

Table 1 provides a schematic overview of this pathogenic model.

Diagnosis

When faced with an undergrown infant, a two-phased diagnostic approach is recommended. The first phase is designed to determine which of two lines of investigation (i.e., nonorganic or organic) should be explored first.

In phase one the physician should take a standard history covering the chief complaint, prenatal period, birth, feeding, growth, development, previous illnesses, and a review of organ systems, perform a physical examination including a neurologic assessment, and obtain the following laboratory tests—hemoglobin, blood urea nitrogen, serum electrolytes, and a urinalysis.

In taking the history the physician should obtain more information than usual, with respect to growth, feeding, and daily activities. The type of information that should be elicited and some typical findings in maternal deprivation are as follows:

1. *Questions to ask about* growth:
   What was the infant's weight at birth and at subsequent weighings? When did the growth failure begin? What has been done about it? What is the mother's explanation for the growth failure?
   Typical findings.
   The infant has not been weighed periodically; the growth failure is not acute; the mother has not sought medical care for the growth problem or did not follow through on the physician's advice. The mother provides an implausible explanation for the growth failure; and the mother does not perceive the growth failure to be a serious problem.
2. *Questions to ask about* feeding:
   What is a typical 24 hour total intake, including the specific foods eaten and the quantities? How does the infant behave when hungry? How long will the infant go without expressing hunger? What is the consistency, frequency,

Table 1. Pathogenesis of Growth Failure Secondary to Maternal Deprivation

	External	Internal
Etiological Factors	Child of unwanted sex Illegitimacy Marital discord Unsupportive husband Too many children Inadequate income Alcoholic spouse No husband Unwanted pregnancy Appearance of child distasteful to mother	Mother inadequately mothered as a child Mother out of touch with reality Psychoneurotic conflict Poor self-esteem Poor ability to relate to persons Limited ability to perceive needs of others Limited capacity for concern Depression
Psychological Effect on Mothering Potential	Unwilling to mother OR Unable to mother OR Unaware of mothering (Quality or quantity)	
Behavior Toward Infant.	Mother provides inadequate foods Mother provides inadequate sensory stimulation	
Effect on Infant	Growth retardation Developmental lags, apathy, low IQ, retarded language Poor appetite, poor food intake, growth retardation	

205

and size of stools? Does the infant sleep through meal times? What type appetite does the infant have? Does the infant spit-up, regurgitate, or vomit? If so, how much?

Typical findings.

The mother describes a voracious appetite and an enormous intake that is not accompanied by spitting-up, vomiting, or frequent voluminous stools. There is a wide descrepancy between the intake and the infant's size. The infant does not demand to be fed when hungry and may sleep through mealtimes.

3. *Questions to ask about* daily activities:

What does the infant do, and how is the infant handled? The mother should be asked to describe, in detail, a typical day on an hour to hour basis including where the infant is, what the infant does, and who is with the infant.

Typical findings.

The infant spends virtually the entire day alone; he has little social or physical interaction with the mother or anyone else.

If the history, physical examination, and limited laboratory tests do not clearly suggest an organic basis for the growth failure and if there is either developmental retardation, autoerotic behavior, alterations in affect, hands-up posture (10), or watchfulness, a provisional diagnosis of maternal deprivation can be made. The history as indicated will invariably contain further evidence in support of the provisional diagnosis. The physician's confidence in a provisional diagnosis arrived at in the above manner can be inappropriately undermined by either of two potential detractors. First, there is a stereotype of the neglecting mother and neglected infant. If the picture is the reverse, that is, a middle class, well-groomed, articulate, and apparently concerned mother, and a clean well-dressed infant, the possibility of maternal deprivation may be summarily dismissed. The former mother-infant combination (the sterotype) is apt to be "worked-up" for maternal deprivation whereas, the latter is afforded an exhaustive search for an obscure metabolic disease. But, it has been adequately documented that the mother's race, educational level, socioeconomic status, etc. cannot be used to exclude the diagnosis. Second, a history of vomiting should not signal the need for an immediate search for organic pathology; this can occur in the maternally deprived infant.

Following the establishment of a provisional diagnosis of maternal deprivation the infant should be admitted to the hospital to confirm the diagnosis through demonstrating significant weight gain with an adequate caloric intake (phase 2). The infant should be placed on a normal age-appropriate diet with the caloric content based on the infant's expected weight for height. The containers should be weighed before and after feeding so that there is an exact measurement of the caloric intake. This is exceedingly important because even in the hospital it is not uncommon for inadequate calories to be offered or false presumptions made about the calories ingested from gross descriptions of whether the infant "ate well." The hospital setting is essential because these mothers cannot be relied on to administer a prescribed diet or to report accurately their infants intakes.

The majority of infants with the maternal deprivation syndrome have retained their appetites, eaten avidly from the beginning of hospitalization, and, if offered adequate calories, shown a significant weight gain in 5 to 7 days. If significant or accelerated weight gain occurs, the diagnosis is confirmed. Usually during this period there are some beginning changes in affect.

The remainder have anorexia and/or vomiting, and their net caloric intake is not sufficient to result in significant weight gain. In any case, the character of the feeding problems is invariably nonorganic, thus sustaining the credibility of the presumptive diagnosis of maternal deprivation.

The rationale for this overall approach is fivefold:

1. The demonstration of accelerated weight gain with normal caloric intake establishes a nonorganic cause.

2. The majority of infants with severe growth failure are suffering from maternal deprivation; therefore, it is economically wasteful to embark of an extensive and expensive laboratory work-up before excluding this possibility.

3. It is unlikely that an infant's overall health status will be compromised by the feeding study if there is no evidence of organic pathology by either history, physical examination, or the obtained laboratory tests.

4. Laboratory studies are usually not of positive value in determining the cause of growth retardation if there is no specific indication from the clinical evaluation (28).

5. An extensive social work evaluation is not critical to the medical diagnosis and can be considered as equivalent to performing an exhaustive battery of laboratory tests without a specific indication. An in-depth assessment of family dynamics can wait until the diagnosis of nonorganic failure to thrive is made.

A common approach is to identify inadequate mothering by establishing a medical diagnosis of the maternal deprivation syndrome. This method probably results in the failure to recognize two groups of infants who have been inadequately mothered, that is, those with a lower than average growth potential and those without growth failure.

The requirement that subjects score below the third percentile for weight and height probably excludes some children who have an equivalent degree of growth failure as those identified. A 15-month-old boy with a growth potential in the fiftieth to seventy-fifth percentile would weigh 11.3 kg (25 lb). If, as a result of maternal deprivation, he weighed 9.7 kg (21 lb, 8 oz) his weight would be in the tenth to twenty-fifth percentile, and he might not be investigated for inadequate mothering. Whereas, if his inherent growth potential was in the tenth to twenty-fifth percentile range with a weight of 9.7 kg, and he only weighed 8.2 kg (18 lb), he would score below the third percentile and thus be investigated for maternal deprivation. Yet, the relative weight deficit (14%) is the same in the two instances. And of course, the degree of underfeeding may not be severe enough to result in a status below the third percentile. Hopefully, the condition in some instances may be detected before the infants growth status deteriorates to the third percentile level. Support for the thesis that the third percentile requirement excludes some maternally deprived infants is found in Lipton et al.'s study (29). All of the infants in the study were maternally deprived but 50% were above the tenth percentile for weight.

We can extend the argument further and conclude that, by focusing on growth failure, we are missing infants who are understimulated. The recognition that growth failure stems simply from an inadequate intake of food should help focus attention on the fact that mothers can inadequately stimulate and relate to their infants while offering them sufficient food. This yields infants with a normal growth status but development retardation and/or affective changes. Thus, just as severe growth failure in infants leads us to suspect maternal deprivation and to initiate a diagnostic process to determine whether the growth failure is from underfeeding; so should the presence of developmental lags or apathy and poor responsiveness (without growth failure) lead us to initiate a diagnostic process to determine whether the infant has been understimulated. The just described diagnostic process can be used with slight modification. In phase one, more stress would be placed on the parental and birth history as it relates to the potential for central nervous system damage and the laboratory tests should include a urine screen for aminoacidurias. In the hospitalization phase, the question to be answered is whether a period of planned, documented stimulation results in an improvement in affect and/or development.

Effort to diagnose maternal deprivation in the absence of growth failure is vital. Although undernutrition threatens the infant's immediate survival, it is far more likely that the child's ability to function effectively in later life will be compromised by the effects of the understimulation on emotional and mental development than by the effects of undernutrition on his/her physical status. Early recognition, diagnosis, and intervention are important because deaths have been reported and, of course, infants stand a better chance of recovery with respect to growth, intellectual capacity, and emotional status if the process is interrupted early.

Treatment

Although the diagnosis of the maternal deprivation syndrome is relatively simple, it is far more difficult to intervene appropriately. Unfortunately, there are no substantive reports that document management strategies that have achieved the highest priority goal: that of having the deprived infant receive adequate food as well as social and sensory stimulation by the mother on an ongoing basis.

The approach delineated here is based on techniques that are compatible with those contained in an extensive body of literature on how the adverse psychological states, social conditions, and stresses delineated in the pathogenic model should be handled.

In general, there should be an investigation of the social milieu of the family and the psychological status of the mother to determine the specific factors responsible for the mother's behavior. It is not a question of whether there is social pathology (marital discord, inadequate income, unwanted pregnancy, etc.), but whether the social pathology is a factor in the mother's behavior. Social pathology may be the result of or independent of the mother's behavior rather than the cause of it.

Based on the thesis that there is a limit to the duration of maternal deprivation that an infant can take without risking irreversible damage to his/her capacity for growth and development, maternal deprivation must be viewed as a crisis by the health professional and the approach must be planned around a crisis intervention strategy. The crisis intervention implies the need for vigorous, aggressive, and immediate efforts designed to effect maternal care and a stimultaneous attack, where possible, on the social and/or psychological factors responsible for the mother's behavior. The basic strategy of treating mothers who are depriving their infants is to focus on the mother as a person who needs help to feed and stimulate her child adequately. Professionals must assist her by removing whatever situational or psychological barriers that are present, recognizing that they will not be able to change some social and psychological facts about the mother but must be content with helping her to function adequately as a mother in spite of them.

The health professional(s) responsible for providing or coordinating the care must develop an intervention plan for each mother based on the specific etiological factors operative in/on the mothers. To do so the health professional needs to know:

1. The social factors, if any, responsible for the mother's dysfunction.
2. The psychological factors responsible for the mother's dysfunction.
3. The time estimated to achieve meaningful change in the mother's ability to mother.
4. The mother's willingness to participate in the intervention plan.
5. The overall prognosis for achieving adequate mothering.
6. The risk of the child sustaining physical abuse by remaining in the home.
7. The availability of personal and physical resources to implement the various intervention strategies.

Many instances require considerable contact and experience with the mother to determine the etiological factor(s); meanwhile, continuing deprivation may compromise the infant's potential for recovery, so that an intervention plan must be initiated before a complete delineation of the etiology.

Assuming that the initial assessment indicates that it is reasonable to return the infant to the mother, the basic approaches to improve the mother's functioning are covered in the following list.

Efforts should be made to:

1. Eliminate or diminish identified social or environmental stresses through social casework.
2. Lessen the adverse psychological impact of social factors on the mother through counseling and support.
3. Reduce demands on the mother to a level that is within her capacity. (This can be achieved through such means as day-care placement of the infant or provision of a housekeeper or baby-sitter).
4. Provide support, empathy, and training.
5. Resolve or diminish the inner psychic conflict through psychotherapy.

Items 1, 2, 3, and 5 are conventional techniques. Special stress needs to be placed upon item 4. Studies to date indicate that the majority of depriving mothers have a character disorder; these mothers have a limited capacity to perceive and assess their environment, the needs of their children, or their adverse affective state. They also have primitive or defective objective relationships and a limited capacity for concern. Consequently, these mothers need to be provided with emotional support, encouragement, and sympathy; that is, someone to "lean on." They should be shown how to feed, play with, interact with, and care for their infants in a nonthreatening, direct, tutorial relationship (usually with a homemaker or social worker). Such a mother needs help in all phases of her life, since she may not be able to perceive and assess the requirements of her child or herself. The program should extend over a long period of time, because the mother may not learn to comprehend and conceptualize how she functions as a person.

One extremely important factor in the management of this problem is how the mother is approached. In all contacts with the mother, the interventionists must be aware that attitudes and feelings about the mother can play a negative role in the intervention process. From a legal standpoint, mothers who have not adequately mothered their children are guilty of neglect. Furthermore, they evoke hostile feelings, but it is counterproductive to tell the mother that she is guilty of neglect, either verbally or nonverbally. Criticism, condemnation, and accusations, either overt or implied, will alienate her and create a barrier to establishing and maintaining the type of relationship necessary for a successful outcome. Rather she should be approached in a nonjudgmental way with understanding, empathy, and tolerance.

As a part of the plan, every child returned to its mother should have a periodic evaluation to ascertain whether a satisfactory rate of change is occurring in growth, development, behavior, and intellect. In these follow-up sessions the evaluation must not be limited to physical growth. Evidence has been provided that an adequate caloric intake will induce satisfactory weight gain despite an undersirable level of inputs in the other spheres of mothering. Theoretically, at least, mothers can be induced to feed their children without significantly changing their overall functioning with them. In such cases, the physical status of the children might not reflect the quality of the mothering. If they show progress in all areas, we know the mothering has been satisfactory. But, if the improvement in either development or intellect is below normal, we cannot be certain if this means the mothering is now adequate but the original deprivation lowered the potential for achievement, or if the mothering is now adequate but special enriching measures are necessary to achieve the child's psycho-developmental potential, or if the mothering is now adequate but the child's inherent physical growth or intellectual capabilities were lower than the norm. A period of rehospitalization during which adequate food and stimulation are provided can be helpful in determining whether inadequate improvement is attributable to the mother's current handling of the child.

Sometimes, rather than permitting the infant to return to the mother, it is advisable to place the child in a foster home temporarily. Circumstances that justify this approach are:

1. Mother's unwillingness (expressed or demonstrated) to participate in the intervention plan.

2. The quality of mothering and potential for change are such that the child is at risk of starvation or physical abuse before the intervention program improves the situation.

3. Failure of previous substantial efforts to improve the mothering.

While the child is temporarily in the foster home, obviously substantive efforts should be made to redress the factors responsible for the mother's behavior so that when the child is returned to the home the probability of adequate mothering has been enhanced. There are instances in which a deprived infant has been removed from the home, then after a period of time returned through court action initiated by the mother, despite the lack of substantive evidence that her "ability" to mother has improved or that she has even been involved in an intervention program.

Efforts to achieve satisfactory feeding and mothering of the infant by the mother may fail, in which case the second-choice goal must be invoked, that is to achieve adequate feeding, stimulation, and care of the infant by a permanent foster mother. Of course, simple placement in a foster home, if available, is not a panacea; it does not guarantee adequate mothering. A foster mother may not find the infant appealing, may not be a "good" mother, and may not keep the infant permanently. Because all foster mothers cannot be relied on to feed and stimulate the infant adequately, the infant's status after placement requires frequent monitoring just as has been proposed when the infant remains with the mother.

Unfortunately, the decision to remove the infant from the home permanently is less likely to be inspired by the mother's demonstrated inability to respond to therapy than by limited resources for analyzing and attempting to enable her to alter her behavior. There is little evidence to suggest that more than a few mothers have had an adequate course of psychotherapy, adequate supportive casework, or a reduction of the demands on their time. Instead, either no substantive analysis of the causative factors is undertaken or limited efforts are made to resolve the underlying causative factors. The management tends to be primarily one of "confrontation-expectation-surveillance." After the mother is told that the infant's failure to thrive is the result of the quantity and quality of her mothering (confrontation), it is anticipated that she will, with limited help, mobilize herself to deliver adequate care (expectation). The mother is also told to expect follow-up evaluation (surveillance). Frequently when this plan does not work, court action is initiated. It would appear that intervention failures are the result of ill-conceived and inadequate plans, unavailability or disinterest of health care professionals, and the inability to obtain the necessary involvement of some mothers in an intervention plan.

Much emphasis has been placed on the value of a team approach to the treatment of maternal deprivation. Use of teams is optimal but many times not achievable. Maternal deprivation is a nationwide problem, but relatively few institutions or communities have the resources or are organized to provide coordinated teams. Indeed, most institutions, agencies, and communities would be taxed to provide even a single health professional to work with each identified maternally depriving mother on a substantive ongoing basis.

"Substantive ongoing basis" is stressed because of another dimension of the problem. Health professionals who have had direct experience with depriving mothers will attest to how difficult, emotionally depleting, and frustrating it is to work with many of them. These mothers tend to be resistant to treatment and to interference with their life styles, manifested by such behaviors as failure to keep scheduled appointments, or not being home when the worker is scheduled to visit, or, if they are at home, failure to answer the door. If therapy is accepted and cooperation with the plan is achieved, progress in altering their behavior tends to proceed at a slow pace, thereby not evoking sufficiently the positive feedback that assists the professional in maintaining the energy, interest, and motivation to do all that is possible. These factors are vital barriers, particularly if their case loads consist of more than one or two of these mothers.

The described management or treatment model is based on the unproven premise that all that is required for the deprived infant to recover fully from the effects of understimulation and undernutrition is to receive an adequate intake of food and the type of care that the "average mother" provides. Another conceptual model has been proposed. Saran et al. (30) hypothesize that infants who have sustained failure-to-thrive are defective in their ability to use environmental input for the purposes of organization and growth. This failure may result from the deprivation or from an inherent inability to process information or from a combination of both factors. Saran et al. propose a structured psychosocial stimulation program designed to elicit and develop a general response in the child, particularly with regard to vocalization, affect, activity, attending, and even physical appetite. They do not provide data on the effectiveness of this approach; rather, they speculate that remediation requires more than conventional mothering—this is worthy of investigation.

Prognosis and Sequelae

The immediate effects of maternal deprivation on infants' growth and development have been discussed. What about later consequences? What are the sequellae of maternal deprivation? Are they preventable? Are they reversible?

Spitz (31) reexamined some of the previously referred to children who during infancy had been severely deprived of stimulation to determine whether his original assumption that the damage was irreparable could be confirmed. The methodology consisted of visits to the institutions at regular intervals to observe the children, to measure their weights and heights and to quiz the nursing personnel about the children's behavior and activities.

Of the 91 children observed in the original study, 34 had died and 36 were no longer in the institution (23 had returned to their families, 7 had been adopted, 2 had been placed in other institutions, and 4 could not be accounted for). Thus, the follow-up data involved only 21 of the original 91.

Spitz states that after 15 months, these infants had been in a more favorable environment than during early infancy. They were placed on a ward for older children, which was a large room, sunny, without the partitions so they were not isolated from each other and from other environmental stimuli as they had been. Three to five nurses were constantly in the room and they chatted with each other and with the children. The children were also taken out of their cots and placed on the floor, allowing them an opportunity for infinitely more active stimulation than they previously experienced.

At the time of the follow-up, the 21 children ranged in age from 2 years 4 months to 4 years 2 months but only three were within the normal range for weight for 2-year-old children and only two for height. From the standpoint of development, five were incapable of any locomotion, 12 could not eat alone with a spoon, 20 could not dress alone, six were not toilet trained in any way, six could not talk at all, and only one used sentences. He concluded from these data that "not withstanding the improvement in environmental conditions, the process of deterioration has proved to be progressive. It would seem that the unfavorable conditions during the children's first year produces a psychosomatic damage that cannot be repaired by normal measures" (31).

Goldfarb (5) compared groups of children who had been in institutions and grossly deprived (with respect to sensory and social stimulation as previously described) to groups of children whose major life experiences from early infancy had been in foster homes. The children who had been institutionalized were transferred to foster homes at about the age of 3 years. The comparisons of the various groups (a cross-section study) were made when the children were about 3, 6, 8 and 12 years old.

In general, Goldfarb found that the institutionalized children had lower IQ scores (only measured at 3 years); an unusually defective level of ability to conceptualize, with difficulty in organizing a variety of stimuli meaningfully and in abstracting relationships from them; they exhibited concept deficiency expressed in difficulty in learning songs, rhymes, and stories, in achieving time and space concepts, and later in adolescence, in remembering the past in a clear, focused fashion. From an emotional standpoint, Goldfarb concluded that the infant deprivation had resulted in a basic defect in total personality. There was an absence of normal inhibitions, easy distractability, an uninhibited, unreflective response to frustration leading to impulsive reactions and temper displays. Incomprehensible cruelty to other children, foster parents, and animals were frequently observed. "Affect hunger" was evident in the form of indiscriminate demand for affection and attention, which did not seem to influence their ability to form relationships. Finally, there was an absence of normal anxiety following acts of hostility or cruelty.

Elmer and Gregg (32) assessed the growth, intellectual, behavioral, and emotional status of 15 children. The median elapsed time since hospital treatment was 4 years 9 months. Only two of 15 children were functioning reasonably well in all of the areas evaluated. With respect to the specific areas, four of the 15 were below normal status in height and weight, 10 were below normal in intellectual development, and seven were abnormal in behavioral parameters.

Glaser et al. (9) evaluated 40 children from 6 months to 8 years after the hospitalization; the mean was 40.8 months. They stated that one-third had no detectable evidence of physical, emotional, or psychological abnormalities. Of the children, 42.5% were below the third percentile standards for height and/ or weight; six children (15%) were mentally retarded. The IQ scores of the others approximated a normal distribution. Projective tests did not reveal a consistent pattern of emotional disturbance. Through psychiatric evaluation, one child was judged to be psychotic, three had clear evidence of nonpsychotic emotional disorder, and seven children had mild behavior disorders.

Provence and Lipton (21) presented follow-up data on 15 of 75 infants who had been institutionalized from the first month of life and then had been placed in foster homes at varying times, one at 8 months, one at 29 months, and the others between 1 and 2 years. "At the time of placement the retardation in development pervaded all areas that one can measure."

Provence and Lipton indicate that through superficial observation and casual contact the 15 children did not differ markedly from their peers. But, when examined more closely in general there was mild to severe impairment with respect to: "their capacity for forming emotional relationships; aspects of control and modulation of impulse, and in areas in thinking and learning that reflect multiple adaptive and defensive capacities, and the development of flexibility in thought and action." The authors did not view their material as providing definitive answers to the questions about the outcome of institutionalized infants, because this was not their prime purpose and there were flaws in the methodology.

These reports claim that some children who had been maternally deprived during infancy do not show significant deviation from their age peers with respect to growth, mental development, and psychological functioning. In other children an array of adverse consequences are described: retardation in growth; deficits in intellectual performance, the ability to learn, visual-perceptual functioning, and language skills; alterations in learning styles; excessive concreteness of thought; and reductions in the capacity to control and modulate impulses (to defer or postpone immediate gratification and to form deep interpersonal relationships).

Definitive answers to the three questions posed at the beginning of this section cannot be derived from the current literature because:

1. None of the cited studies provide details on the day-to-day handling and feeding of the child after the diagnosis was made. Thus, it is impossible to differentiate between effects that might be attributable to deprivation during infancy from those that might be the result of continuing underfeeding and understimulation in the period between infancy and the follow-up assessment. Indeed, in each of the follow-up studies of infants deprived by their mothers there are infants for whom there is no basis for assuming that the quality or quantity of mothering improved.

2. There is insufficient communality in the assessments of the children with respect to the length of time between the original and the follow-up assessment, the parameters assessed, and the discriminative qualities of the instruments used. For example, Goldfarb's finding of defects in the ability to conceptualize and to form interpersonal relationships is frequently referred to, but no other investigator has reported on this facet.

3. There is virtually no consideration given to three variables that undoubtedly can play a role in whether the effects are lasting (i.e., the infant's age when deprivation began, the duration, and the severity of the deprivation).

4. None of the investigators attempts to factor out the long-term psychosocial effects of understimulation from those factors that might be the result of undernutrition. With one exception, the reported follow-up studies attribute the intellectual, social, and psychological sequelae from maternal deprivation to the damage done by understimulation. Chase and Martin (33) have attempted to ascertain the effects of undernutrition on these parameters. However, the authors attribute the mental and emotional sequelae to undernutrition without considering the effect of understimulation.

5. There are no reports describing efforts to prevent lasting effects, if any, of maternal deprivation.

6. There are no reports describing efforts to remediate the "lasting effects."

The lack of data on the possible long-term effects of undernutrition on mental and psychosocial development in the maternally deprived infant is a critical but understandable void.

Infancy is a very critical time for brain development. Studies of nutritional aspects among undernourished infants and children in developing countries have indicated that undernutrition may play a role in many if not all of the psycho-social-intellectual effects that are seen in the maternally deprived child. But, even in developing countries, where malnutrition is secondary to unavailability of food to the family, investigators have not been able to separate the role of undernutrition from that of environmental factors. Malnutrition may be the primary or even the only factor or it may interact with socio-environmental influences in producing the effects.

Because of the complexity of the relationship between nutrition and development, the questions we have posed about the long-term effects of undernutrition in maternally deprived infants are not likely to be answered from research on maternally deprived infants in the United States. The number of patients available for study is too small, and the ability to control the variables is too limited.

The design of several current studies of protein-calorie malnutrition in developing countries is more likely to provide useful data. For example, in one study, immediately after the diagnosis, one group received adequate nutrition and routine care and the other adequate nutrition as well as programmed extra stimulation. These studies will not provide the complete answers, however, because detailed information on the quality and quantity of social-sensory stimulation before the diagnosis will not be available. Also, the type of understimulation is different. The infants in those studies have sustained protein-calorie malnutrition, whereas the maternally deprived infants in the U. S. have invariably sustained calorie undernutrition. This is an important distinction, given the vital role that protein plays in brain development.

If undernutrition does influence mental and psychosocial development, there are conflicting hypotheses as to the underlying mechanism. According to one concept, undernutrition influences performance directly by interfering with structural and chemical development of the brain, expressed through such structural and biochemical parameters as brain weight, number and size of brain cells, protein and lipid content, cerebral cortical thickness, synaptic numbers, glycolytic metabolism, and neurotransmitter synthesis and metabolism. The other viewpoint is based on the premise that the cause-effect relationship is mediated directly through a decrease in such psychological parameters as learning time, motivation, and maintenance of interest. There is evidence on both sides, but the available data, which are primarily from animal studies, are not sufficiently definitive to resolve the question.

The ability to provide definite answers relative to long-term effects of maternal deprivation requires· prospective study of infants in whom it can be documented that, after the diagnosis in infancy, they were appropriately mothered from that time until the follow-up assessment.

PSYCHOSOCIAL DWARFISM

As indicated in the introduction, inappropriate mothering with resultant growth failure and varying degrees of intellectual, developmental and emotional impairment can also be considered within the context of *psychosocial dwarfism*, a condition occurring in children rather than in infants. This section will be devoted to a brief overview of this condition.

Characteristics

Children with psychosocial dwarfism have sustained adverse mothering and tend to have the following characteristics (34):

1. Severe growth failure (less than the third percentile) for height and weight. The height may be more severely affected than weight particularly in the older child.
2. Delay in skeletal maturation, which is usually consistent with the height age.
3. An appearance of infantilism because the facial features and head size tend to be consistent with the reduced height age.
4. Stereotypic behavior, that is, they are either passive and withdrawn or aggressive and cruel, including self-abusiveness, or they intermittently express both.
5. Delayed, immature, and indistinct speech, night wandering, and severe temper tantrums.
6. Ravenous appetites and bizarre eating habits such as eating from garbage cans.
7. Polydipsia and bizarre drinking habits such as drinking from toilet bowls and drinking rain water.
8. Large, malodorous, and watery stools.
9. Developmental retardation.
10. Deficiencies in growth hormone response to arginine and insulin stimulation, decreased total and free thyroxine, and increased cortisol secretion rates.

Pathogenesis

The discovery of a deficiency in growth hormone responsiveness to arginine in the first children studied led to an interpretation that the dwarfism was secondary to a deficiency in growth hormone (hypopituitarism) (18,35). But, it has been demonstrated subsequently that the growth failure is not responsive to the administration of growth hormone and growth hormone responsiveness returns without any specific therapy (17). Although the studies are very limited, the rapid recovery of growth in weight and height that occurs when the children are removed from the home and fed adequately suggests that the pathogenesis is similar to the maternal deprivation syndrome. Thus, the growth failure is secondary to an inadequate intake of food on a daily basis, and the alterations in affect and behavior result from the mother's adverse handling of the child.

Definitive studies have not been conducted to ascertain the basis for the hypopituitarism, but it is not inconsistent with the effects of chronic starvation.

The feeding and drinking habits seem to be related to the nature of the mother-child interactions. Perhaps it should not be considered to be bizarre behavior when children, whose intake of food and water is severely restricted, resort to raiding garbage cans or drinking from toilet bowls. Nor should it seem strange if their appetites are ravenous (when food is available) or if they drink copiously (when water is available).

With respect to polydipsia and the large malodorous stools that have been reported, neither appear to have a classic organic basis. There are no alterations in renal concentrating ability or in the ability to absorb nutrients as judged by conventional tests for malabsorption.

Although the two conditions have been discussed separately, it is clear that they might represent a continuum with differences in manifestations because of the differences in the way a mother can relate and interact negatively with a child as opposed to her behavior with an infant, the duration of altered mothering, and the options open to a child as opposed to an infant when food and water are restricted.

The primary differences between the *maternal deprivation syndrome* and *psychosocial dwarfism* are:

1. The maternal deprivation syndrome occurs in infants, and psychosocial dwarfism occurs in older children.
2. The effects on behavior in maternal deprivation syndrome are secondary to inadequate mothering whereas in psychosocial dwarfism they are the result of adverse mothering. Basically, it appears that the infant tends to be ignored, whereas there is a constant negative interaction with the older child.
3. Growth hormone responsiveness is normal in the maternal deprivation syndrome and deficient in psychosocial dwarfism.
4. Infants with the maternal deprivation syndrome exhibit voracious appetites; children with psychosocial dwarfism also exhibit voracious appetites accompanied by bizarre eating habits and polydipsia with bizarre drinking habits. Obviously infants could not exhibit the bizarre habits because of their immobility.

5. Infants with maternal deprivation syndrome may or may not have a delay in skeletal maturation, children with psychosocial dwarfism all have a marked delay in skeletal maturation that is consistent with their height age.

6. Infants with maternal deprivation syndrome have normal stools or are even constipated. Children with psychosocial dwarfism may have bulky malodorous stools suggestive of malabsorption.

7. Physical abuse is unusual in the maternal deprivation syndrome but is not uncommon in psychosocial dwarfism. All children with dwarfism should have a skeletal survey.

Diagnosis, Treatment, and Sequelae

The very limited observations to date suggest that the descriptions of diagnosis and treatment, as delineated in the section on the maternal deprivation syndrome, are applicable to psychosocial dwarfism.

There have been no long-term studies to determine the outcome of children with psychosocial dwarfism with respect to their psychosocial and intellectual status. Observations on growth status have been variable, but it is not known whether or not those who have failed to attain the height and weight of their peers have, subsequent to the diagnosis, received adequate nutrition.

CONCLUSION

Clinicians should suspect the maternal deprivation syndrome or psychosocial dwarfism whenever faced with an infant or child respectively with growth failure and a history of adequate or voracious appetite, irrespective of the socioeconomic status of the family, the apparent "normalcy" of the mother-infant/child relationship, and the adequacy of mothering as obtained from the mother's history.

The suspicions should lead to a presumptive diagnosis of maternal deprivation/psychosocial dwarfism if there are no specific indicators or an organic cause in the history or physical findings and no abnormalities in the routine laboratory tests.

With a presumptive diagnosis of maternal deprivation/psychosocial dwarfism the infant/child should be hospitalized for trial feeding test during which an adequate, measured diet is provided. Accelerated weight gain within several weeks confirms the diagnosis.

The treatment or management is difficult and requires the identification and alteration of the specific aspects of the inadequate or adverse mothering and the psychosocial factors that spawned the inappropriate maternal behavior. Continuous monitoring of the "mothering" and the child's growth and development is essential.

REFERENCES

1. Patton RC, Gardner LI: Influence of family environment on growth: the syndrome of "maternal deprivation." *Pediatrics* 30:927, 1962.

2. Coleman RW, Provence S: Environmental retardation (hospitalism) in infants living in families. *Pediatrics* 19:285, 1957.

3. Barbero GJ, Shaheen E: Environmental failure to thrive: a clinical view. *J Pediatr* 71:639, 1967.

4. Bakwin H: Emotional deprivation in infants. *J Pediatr* 34:512, 1949.

5. Goldfarb W: Effects of psychological deprivation in infancy and subsequent stimulation. *Am J Psychiatry* 102:18, 1945.

6. Thompson RG, Parra A, Schultz RB, et al: Endocrine evaluation in patients with psycho-social dwarfism. *Am Fed Clin Res* 17:592, 1969.

7. Spitz RA: Hospitalism. *Psychoanal Stud Child* 1:53, 1945.

8. Leonard MF, Rhymes JP, Solnit AJ: Failure to thrive in infants. *Am J Dis Child* 111:600, 1966.

9. Glaser HH, Heagarty MC, Bullard DM, et al: Physical and psychological development of children with early failure to thrive. *J Pediatr* 73:690, 1968.

10. Krieger I, Sargent DS: A postural sign in the sensory deprivation syndrome. *J Pediatr* 70:332, 1967.

11. Chapin HD: A plea for accurate statistics in infants institutions. *J Am Pediatr Soc* 27:180, 1915.

12. Bowlby J: Maternal care and mental health. *World Health Organization Series Monograph Series*, Publication 2, 1951.

13. Ainsworth MD: The effects of maternal deprivation: a review of findings and controversy in the context of research strategy. *World Health Organization Papers*, Publication 14, 97:1962.

14. Deprivation of maternal care: a reassessment of its effects. *Geneva, World Health Organization, Public Health Papers* 14:1962.

15. Casler L: Maternal deprivation: a critical review of the literature. *Soc Res Child Dev* 26:80, 1961.

16. Yarrow LJ: Maternal deprivation: toward an empirical and conceptual revolution. *Psychol Bull* 58:459, 1961.

17. Powell GF, Brasel JA, Raiti S, et al: Emotional deprivation and growth retardation stimulating idiopathic hypopituitarism. II. Endocrinologic evaluation of the syndrome. *N Engl J Med* 276:1279, 1967.

18. Silver HK, Finkelstein M: Deprivation dwarfism. *J Pediatr* 70:317, 1967.

19. Whitten CF, Pettit MG, Fischhoff J: Evidence that growth failure from maternal deprivation is secondary to undereating. *JAMA* 209:1675, 1969.

20. Goldfarb W: Psychological privation in infancy and subsequent adjustment. *Am J Orthopsychiatry* 15:247, 1945.

21. Provence SA and Lipton RC (eds): *Infants in Institutions.* New York, International Universal Press Inc, 1962, p 147.

22. Kerr GR, Chanrove AS, Harlow HF: Environmental deprivation: its effect on the growth of infant monkeys. *J Pediatr* 75:833, 1969.

23. Krieger I, Good M: Adrenocortical and thyroid function in the deprivation syndrome. *Am J Dis Child* 120:95, 1970.

24. Krieger I, Mellinger RC: Pituitary function in the deprivation syndrome. *J Pediatr* 79:216, 1971.

25. Elmer E: Failure to thrive: role of the mother. *Pediatrics* 25:717, 1960.

26. Evans S, Reinhart J, Succop R: Failure to thrive: a study of 45 children and their families. *J Am Acad Child Psychiatry* 11:440, 1972.

27. Fischhoff J, Whitten CF, Pettit MG: A psychiatric study of mothers of infants with growth failure secondary to maternal deprivation. *J Pediatr* 79:209, 1971.

28. Sills RH: Failure to thrive: the role of clinical and laboratory evaluation. *Am J Dis Child* 132:967, 1978.

29. Hufton IW, Oates RK: Non-organic failure to thrive: a long-term follow-up. *Pediatrics* 59:73, 1977.

30. Saran BG, Hatcher RP: The psychological treatment of hospitalized children with failure to thrive. *Pediatr Nurs* 10, 1975.

31. Spitz RA: Hospitalism: a follow-up report. *Psychoanal Study Child* 2:113, 1946.

32. Elmer E, Gregg G: Later results of the "failure to thrive" syndrome. *Clin Pediatr* 8:584, 1969. 1969.

33. Chase HP, Martin HP: Undernutrition and child development. *N Engl J Med* 282:933, 1970.

34. Krieger I: Food restriction as a form of child abuse in ten cases of psychosocial deprivation dwarfism. *Clin Pediatr* 13:127, 1974.

35. Powell GF, Brasel JA, Blizzard RM: Emotional deprivation and growth retardation simulating idiopathic hypopituitarism. I. Clinical evaluation of the syndrome. *N Engl J Med* 276:1271, 1967.

12
Dermatologic Manifestations of Child Abuse and Neglect

Norman S. Ellerstein

The importance of the cutaneous manifestations of child maltreatment is twofold: first, the skin is the most common site of physical manifestations of child abuse and neglect; second, it is an area where the effects of child maltreatment can be observed by people not in the health professions. Relatives, neighbors, school teachers, social workers, and others can observe objective evidence of abuse and neglect. The physician must be able to differentiate maltreatment-associated cutaneous findings from those produced by accident or disease.

Dermatologic lesions are also important because they are easily documented by photographs. Thereby, they can serve as dramatic proof of the child's mistreatment. Photographs of injured children can be very persuasive in depicting the extent to which a child has suffered. It may be difficult for family court judges or others to visualize the extent of a child's injury from laboratory reports, x-ray films or verbal or written descriptions. However, when confronted with a photograph of a bruised or burned child, there is instant recognition of the problem at hand.

Soft tissue trauma, usually manifested by cutaneous signs, is often the earliest manifestation of physical child abuse (1). As such, the recognition of the cutaneous finding as being representative of maltreatment could be vital in the prevention of further trauma to the child.

PHYSICAL ABUSE

The most obvious and dramatic examples of child abuse are the result of intentional physical trauma to the child. Soft tissue injuries (ecchymoses, hematomas, abrasions, and contusions) are the most common injuries that physically abused children will have (1–3). Since these types of injuries are

221

common in both abused and nonabused children, the physician must be able to decide which of the injuries were intentional and which were accidental. Pascoe et al. (3) have shown that lacerations are more likely to occur by accident than by intention. The location of the soft tissue injury on the child's body has significance in determining how the injury was caused. Injuries to bony prominences of the trunk and extremities as well as injuries to the head and periorbital area are as likely to be caused by accident as by abuse (3). However, injuries to the genitals, buttocks, cheeks, thighs, neck, and back are more likely to have been caused by abuse than by accident (2–4). Injuries to shins, knees, elbows, and hands should not necessarily raise suspicion of abuse because these areas are frequently accidentally injured in childhood.

In addition to the location, the age of the soft tissue injury is another important criterion in determining the cause of the injury. Bruises in different stages of healing are likely to have occurred at different times. If the history states that only a single accident occurred, and injuries of varying ages are present, intentional injury must be suspected; a discrepancy between the historical and physical findings is one of the cardinal signs of abuse.

Bruises can be morphologically similar to the implement used to inflict the trauma (2,4). For example, the imprint of a belt buckle or hand may be clearly seen on the child's skin.

The most common example of this type of injury is the "loop" mark, which is caused by a flexible object such as an electric cord or clothesline being folded over and used to strike the child (Fig. 1). Multiple curvilinear loop marks on a child are pathognomonic of abuse. The loop mark or other implement-made marks may be an ecchymosis, laceration, burn, or scar. Circumferential marks around the ankles, arms, or neck probably indicate that the child was forcibly restrained by being tied or shackled to a fixed object (Fig. 2). The marks may be rope burns or abrasions if the restraint was recent or scars indicating past restraint.

Burns are a common manifestation of physical abuse and are discussed in Chapter 10. Human bite marks are usually pathognomonic of intentional trauma and are discussed in Chapter 8.

Hair loss can be seen in several different forms of child maltreatment. Traumatic alopecia results when parents pull out their child's hair, as the hair provides a convenient handle with which to seize the child (Fig. 3). This type of injury is analogous to the orthopedic problems of metaphyseal injuries as seen when an extremity is twisted or wrenched. Subgaleal hematoma in children is usually the result of hairpull. The subgaleal hematoma occurs when there is sufficient abrupt traction on the hair to induce scalp and calvarial separation at the aponeurotic junction. Subgaleal hematoma in a child should be attributed to intentional trauma, unless a specific documented cause is otherwise proven (5).

Occasionally a child has unusual dermatologic findings for which there is no obvious cause. Because some of these signs resemble trauma, a diagnosis of child abuse is entertained. Cultural or religious practices may have caused the cutaneous abnormalities and may not represent maltreatment. Yeatman et al. (6) have reported finding linear petechial and purpuric lesions on the backs of Vietnamese children. They report that children with symptoms such as fever

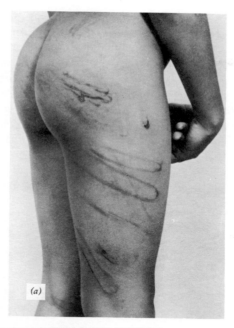

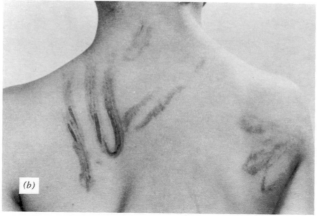

Figure 1. Loop marks are pathognomonic of intentional trauma. They are caused by a cordlike object, such as a belt, clothesline, or electric cord, being folded and used to strike the child.

or chills are massaged with coins on their back until petechia or purpura occur. The linear lesions produced by this cultural practice resemble those caused by abuse. Sandler and Hanes (7) report that "cupping" can produce abusivelike injuries to children. Cupping is an ancient remedy used for various maladies and is still practiced by some Mexican-American families. They describe how in this folk practice a small amount of alcohol is ignited in a cup which is then placed on the child's skin, sometimes causing a burn. These examples of skin findings that imitate abuse emphasize the importance of exploring all possible etiological explanations.

When a pattern of cutaneous or other medical findings cannot be explained by known pathophysiological mechanisms, the possibility of child maltreatment must be explored. Kohl et al. (8) report the case of a child who was being evaluated for immune deficiency because of recurrent bacterial infections of her skin and soft tissues. In their case, the child was repeatedly infected because her mother was injecting fecal material into her skin and was withholding antibiotic therapy. There was no evidence of a primary immunologic abnormality. It must be constantly kept in mind that bizarre human behavior may explain apparent medical mysteries. As in the case reported by Kohl et al. and others, common problems such as child maltreatment are found more frequently than rarer diseases such as immune deficiency.

Another unusual manifestation of child abuse is the baby who presents as a

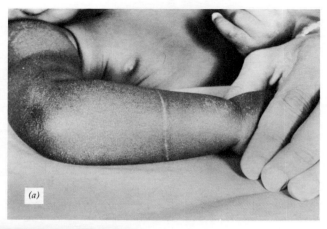

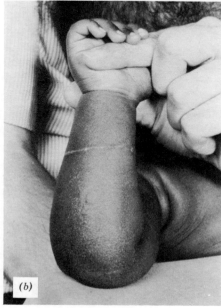

Figure 2. Circumferential restraint mark around the arm of a 7-month-old infant.

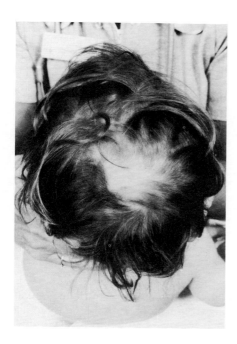

Figure 3. Area of hair loss in a pattern consistent with traumatic alopecia.

"near-miss" sudden infant death syndrome. Berger (9) has presented two cases of "near-miss" SIDS in which the infants were suffocated by their mothers. The only physical manifestations besides cyanosis and apnea were bleeding gums and pinch marks on the alae nasi. Before SIDS was clearly delineated as a distinct problem, many parents were falsely accused of killing their infants. In more recent years the diagnosis of child abuse has been considered less frequently in apneic children. But, as Berger points out, intentional suffocation does occur.

NEGLECT

There are many different kinds of neglect (See Chap. 16). Medical neglect, the failure to seek medical attention for a child with a health problem, can lead to deterioration of a dermatologic problem. A child may present to a physician with a severe skin problem for which most parents would have sought medical attention before the process had reached such an advanced stage. The presence of abscesses, fissures, lymph node enlargement, or necrotic tissue is usually evidence that the illness has been present for a long enough period of time for a parent to have sought medical attention for his child. If common dermatologic problems such as impetigo, eczema, scabies, pediculosis, or seborrhea have not responded to the prescribed treatment, noncompliance with medical recommendations should be suspected. If the physician is confident that his diagnosis and therapeutic recommendations are correct and the problem is not improving, failure of the parent to administer the prescribed treatment is likely.

Physical neglect, failure of a parent to provide for a child's basic physical

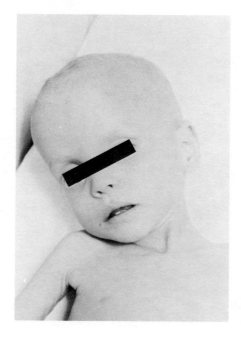

Figure 4. Very scant hair growth in an infant suffering from malnutrition secondary to maternal deprivation (failure-to-thrive syndrome).

needs, may also have cutaneous manifestations. Feces and dirt may be present on the child's skin, under his nails, or on his clothing. If a child has a multiple rat or dog bites, he may have been left unattended for lengthy periods of time. Inadequate bathing may lead to repeated skin infection. If a child has frostbite, the physician should question the adequacy of the protective clothing and the length of time the child was left outside in cold weather.

The failure-to-thrive syndrome due to maternal deprivation is a form of neglect in which the child suffers from severe emotional and physical neglect by his parents (For a full discussion of this problem see Chap. 11). The infant exhibits marked growth failure, especially in the first year of life. Externally the child appears to be malnourished and has marked loss of subcutaneous tissue. Sometimes many of the findings of the physically neglected child are also present in the failure-to-thrive child. Nutritional hair loss may be seen in children with severe malnutrition (Fig. 4). Hair is composed almost entirely of fibrous protein (10). If dietary protein requirements are not met, hair growth slows or may stop completely. The diameter of the hair shaft decreases, the growth of new hair stops, and the color usually lightens in dark haired children (11). Clinically the children appear to have generalized thin short hair. Not all malnourished children exhibit hair loss.

SEXUAL ABUSE

The recognition of childhood sexual abuse has increased in the last several years (See Chap. 13 for a full discussion of this problem). Children may acquire sexually transmitted diseases from their contact with an infected adult or another child. Both boys and girls are sexually misused and may demonstrate the dermatologic findings associated with venereal diseases (12). Gonorrhea is one of the most common sexually transmitted diseases. Disseminated gonorrhea may produce gonococcal skin lesions (13) representing cutaneous septic emboli. They are small tender papules 1 to 2 mm in diameter, often on an erythematous or hemorrhagic base. The papules may be vesicular or pustular in appearance and occur more commonly on the extremities than on the trunk (Fig. 5).

Syphilis may be acquired by a child through contact with an infected person. The chancre is usually the first cutaneous lesion, appearing 18 to 21 days following exposure. Initially the chancre is a small red papule or superficial erosion that progresses in a few weeks to a round or oval, indurated painless ulcer. Chancres usually occur on the penis, labia, vagina, cervix, mouth, or anus (Fig. 6). The chancre will generally disappear with or without treatment. It is followed by the generalized nonpruritic rash of secondary syphilis that usually involves the palms and the soles. This rash will disappear in about 6

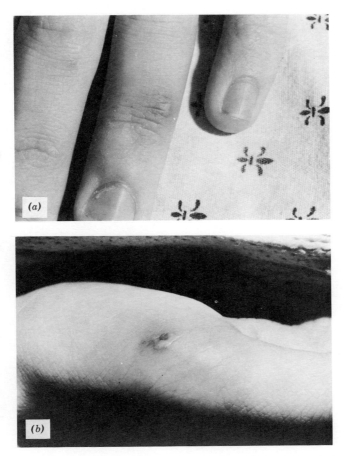

Figure 5. Gonococcal skin lesions representing systemic infection. (*a*) A papule on a finger. (*b*) A hemorrhagic lesion on the side of the hand. (Courtesy of Howard S. Faden, M.D., Buffalo, New York.)

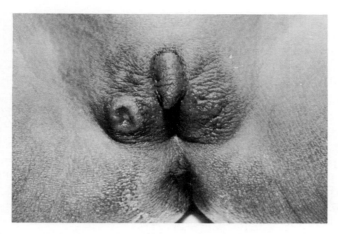

Figure 6. A chancre of primary syphilis on the labia of a 2-year-old girl. (From Rasmussen JE: Bacterial infections and venereal disease. *Pediatric Annals* 5:82, 1976.)

weeks (14). Secondary syphilis has many varied skin manifestations (Fig. 7). Of course, infants with cutaneous manifestations of congenital syphilis are not necessarily abused. Therefore, it is important to be able to differentiate the cutaneous lesions of primary and secondary syphilis from those of congenital syphilis.

Condyloma acuminata has been reported in children (15–17). There is no reason to believe that this disease is acquired by children in other than a venereal mode. Condyloma acuminata, sometimes called venereal warts, are small pinpoint projections that multiply to form a large vegetating cluster (Fig. 8). In children these have been reported in the perianal, urethral, and vaginal areas.

Chancroid, lymphogranuloma venereum, and granuloma inguinale are ve-

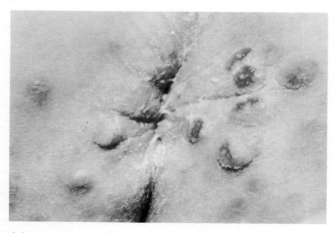

Figure 7. Condylomata lata, a skin manifestation of secondary syphilis, in the perianal area of a 6-year-old girl. (From Rasmussen JE: Bacterial infections and venereal disease. *Pediatric Annals* 5:82, 1976.)

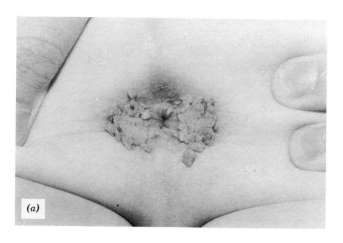

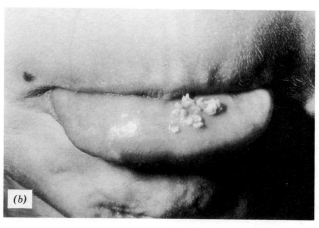

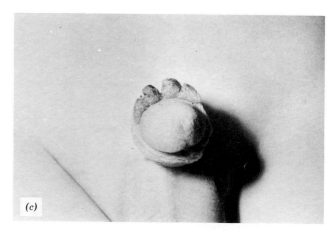

Figure 8. Condyloma acuminata (venereal warts) in three different children. (*a*) in the perianal area, (*b*) on the tongue, and (*c*) on the penis. (Courtesy of James E. Rasmussen, M.D., Ann Arbor, Michigan.)

229

nereal diseases with cutaneous manifestations, but are not as common as the diseases mentioned above. However, there is no evidence to suggest that children cannot acquire any sexually transmitted disease. Furthermore, sexual abuse is a common enough problem to be considered in the differential diagnosis of any child with a venereal disease.

EMOTIONAL DISTURBANCES

The types of cutaneous findings already discussed in this chapter are the direct results of abuse or neglect of the child. Dermatologic abnormalities may also be caused by psychological problems secondary to abuse or neglect. Frequently, the emotional and psychological sequellae of child maltreatment have a more devastating effect on the life of the child than do the physical manifestations of maltreatment (18). The skin is an easily available and commonly used site for self-inflicted trauma in both adults and children with psychological problems (19). Self-mutilation is not pathognomonic of child maltreatment, but many behavioral and personality problems seen in adults and children are the result of recognized or unrecognized child abuse. The psychological trauma that accompanies most cases of physical or emotional abuse may be manifested by self-inflicted sucking, scratching, head banging, rubbing, or biting; all have recognizable cutaneous patterns.

Trichotillomania in children, is usually a minor self-limited problem. However, when self-inflicted hair loss is severe and persistent, it is likely that problems in family dynamics exist (Fig. 9) (20). Some have gone so far as to state that severe trichotillomania in children can be the result of emotional

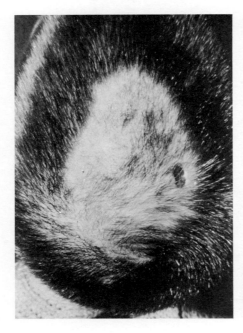

Figure 9. Trichotillomania that has progressed to the point where a psychological evaluation is warranted. (Courtesy of James E. Rasmussen, M.D., Ann Arbor, Michigan.)

deprivation of the child by his mother in the early years of life (21). Finding trichotillomania or other manifestations of self-mutilation in children should not immediately lead the physician to report the child as abused. However, a psychological evaluation and assessment of family dynamics is warranted.

REFERENCES

1. O'Neill JA, Meacham WF, Griffin PP, et al: Patterns of injury in the battered child syndrome. *J Trauma* 13:332, 1973.
2. Ellerstein NS: The cutaneous manifestations of child abuse and neglect. *Am J Dis Child* 133:906, 1979.
3. Pascoe JM, Hildebrandt HM, Tarrier A, et al: Patterns of skin injury in nonaccidental and accidental injury. *Pediatrics* 64:245, 1979.
4. Sussman SJ: Skin manifestations of the battered-child syndrome. *J Pediatr* 72:99, 1968.
5. Hamlin H: Subgaleal hematoma caused by hair-pull. *JAMA* 204:339, 1968.
6. Yeatman GW, Shaw C, Barlow MJ, et al: Pseudobattering in Vietnamese children. *Pediatrics* 58:616, 1976.
7. Sandler AP, Haynes V: Nonaccidental trauma and medical folk belief: a case of cupping. *Pediatrics* 61:921, 1978.
8. Kohl S, Pickering LK, Dupree E: Child abuse presenting as immunodeficiency disease. *J Pediatr* 93:466, 1978.
9. Berger D: Child abuse simulating "near-miss" sudden infant death syndrome. *J Pediatr* 95:544, 1979.
10. Price VH: Disorders of the hair in children. *Pediatr Clin North Am* 25:305, 1978.
11. Sims RT: Hair growth as an index of protein synthesis, *Br J Dermatol* 80:337, 1968.
12. Ellerstein NS, Canavan JW: Sexual abuse in boys. *Am J Dis Child* 134:255, 1980.
13. Grossman M, Drutz OJ: Venereal disease in children. *Adv Pediatr* 21:97, 1974.
14. Domonkos AN: *Andrew's Diseases of the Skin*, ed 6. Philadelphia, WB Saunders, 1971, pp 420–434.
15. Storrs FJ: Spread of Condyloma Accuminata to infants and children. *Arch Dermatol* 113:1294, 1977.
16. Misinberg DT, Rudick DH: Urethral Condyloma Accuminata in male children. *Pediatrics* 57:571, 1976.
17. Seidel J, Zonana J, Totten E: Condylomata Accuminata as a sign of sexual abuse in children. *J Pediatr* 95:553, 1979.
18. Martin HP: *The Abused Child: A Multidisciplinary Approach to Developmental Issues and Treatment.* Cambridge, Ballinger Publishing Co, 1976.
19. Whitlock FA: Self-inflicted and related dermatoses, in *Psychophysiological Aspects of Skin Disease.* London, WB Saunders, 1976, pp 99.
20. Orentreich N: Disorders of the hair and scalp in childhood, *Pediatr Clin North Am* 18:953, 1971.
21. Mannino FV, Delgado RA: Trichotillomania in children: a review. *Am J Psychiatry* 126:505, 1969.

13
Sexual Child Abuse

J. William Canavan

Sexual abuse of children is an emotion-charged, confusing problem. Those activities that are considered sexual abuse today may have appeared as acceptable behavior at different points in the history of both eastern and western cultures. In recent times, it has been the exception rather than the rule to find exact agreement in medical, legal, or social circles as to what constitutes sexual abuse. The personal taboos of the patient and his family, health care personnel, social workers, and the public at large have protected sexual abuse from the close objective scrutiny its gravity demands. Only in the late 1970s has it gained the recognition nonsexual child abuse received two decades earlier (1). Thus, our knowledge of the subject is quite incomplete.

DEFINITIONS

It is useful to provide some definitions early in the discussion of such a topic. However, even definitions are not readily agreed on where matters of sexual abuse are concerned. There is some consensus in medical circles as to what constitutes *sexual abuse* in general. Dr. C. Henry Kempe defines it as "the involvement of dependent, developmentally immature children and adolescents in sexual activities that they do not fully comprehend, to which they are unable to give informed consent, or that violate the social taboos of family roles" (1). Drs. Brant and Tisza speak of *sexual misuse* as "exposure of a child to sexual stimulation inappropriate for the child's age, level of psychosexual development, and role in the family" (2). For the most part the two versions agree with each other. Problems arise in trying to apply the definitions to individual cases. The authors of the latter definition qualify their statement saying:

> We use the appearance of physical behavior symptoms in the child and evidence of family dysfunction as criteria for determining the appropriateness of the stimulation and recognize that which is "inappropriate" may vary according to the family and ethnic or socio-cultural context. (2)

In one recent review, the complexity hidden in such a definition was further underscored:

> Variation in regional and local views on child sexual abuse and differences between civil and criminal legal definitions and practices also complicates efforts to define,

233

identify, compile, and study known cases to compare findings from different investigators on childhood sexual abuse. (3)

Agreements are less likely on the categories or forms of sexual behavior between child and adult that can be considered abusive to the child. (3)

Put another way, when does a "harmless pat on the bottom" become child abuse?

"Abuse" or "trauma" is automatically assumed in child sexual experiences, especially in the earlier years, whether coercion or assault has been used or not. (3)

Sexual abuse may occur as a variety of forms of activities. It may simply occur as *molestation*, which involves touching or kissing the child in some manner. Molestation may also be considered to involve voyeurism and exhibitionism. Molestation may include displaying photography to the child. The abuse may take the form of the child undergoing oral intercourse, anal intercourse, or vaginal intercourse. A combination of the various forms of abuse may be employed. Two other applications of sexual abuse are the use of children and adolescents as objects of pornographic photography and for prostitution. Sexual abuse may occur in conjunction with nonsexual abuse or may be found where nonsexual child abuse has been present in the past. The sexual child abuse may arise as the result of incest, pedophilia, or as one aspect of attempts at sexual gratification that at other times involves the sexual abuse of adults. *Pedophilia* is defined as "an intense craving for young children" (4). This is applied in a sexual context. Pedophilia may overlap with incest; that is, a pedophilic may have an incestuous relationship with his own child as well as other children. Both the adult perpetrators of incest with juveniles and pedophiles in general may employ any combination of the sexual activities described above.

Two additional terms require definition: *sodomy* and *rape*. *Sodomy* is defined as mouth-genital or genital-anal contact between humans (4). *Sodomy* as a term is more commonly used in the latter context. The definition of rape varies somewhat within the medical profession as well as between the medical and legal professions. For medical purposes, *rape* is attempted or successful penetration of the vagina or labia with the use of force or threat of force. Whenever possible it is preferable to avoid confusing terminology and adhere to descriptive anatomical terminology. For example, it is clearer to speak of penile penetration of the anus or penile penetration of the vagina than to speak of sodomy or rape. This descriptive approach can be employed in lieu of other nebulous sexual abuse terminology, too. Instead of saying the child was molested, it may be simpler to say what happened to the child. Such an approach not only is much more lucid but also does not presume the judgment implied in the typically employed terminology of sexual abuse.

DEMOGRAPHY/INCIDENCE

The term *sexual child abuse* often evokes a stereotypic image of a stranger, a "dirty old man," luring and then brutalizing little girls. Indeed, an overwhelming percentage of the perpetrators of such abuse are men. However, in a 1969 study parents either perpetrated or condoned the offense in 72% of the cases

(5). A more recent study notes a parent or guardian as the perpetrator in 80% of the cases (6). The mean age of the perpetrator is relatively young, reported as 28 years old in one study (7), 33 years old in another in which the age range was 18 to 67 years (8). Girls constitute the majority of victims. In one recent study girls accounted for 88% of the victims (7). While boys are a relatively small fraction, they are significant as was pointed out in a study in which they constituted 11% of victims (9). Victims, in that study, ranged in age from 0.3 years upward. The mean age has been quoted fairly uniformly at approximately 10 years of age (7,9). The one-time assault of a child by a stranger is more likely to take place in the summer, although year-round occurrence is certainly reported. Most incidents occur in afternoon or evening hours (10). Statistics for the more chronic or recurrent intrafamilial problems are neither available nor meaningful; that is, incest is not comparable to the isolated incident.

Efforts to record cases and to estimate the incidence of sexual abuse are relatively new and insufficiently uniform. They are often tied to child abuse statistics, which are subject to imprecision. They are thus offered haltingly as "12.1% of all validated 'abuse' and 3.2% of all (combined) validated 'abuse' and 'neglect' cases" (3). In one epidemiologic study, sexual abuse of children under 16 years of age accounted for a third of reported sexual offenses in all age groups of victims including adults and children. (7).

PEDOPHILIA

Pedophiles were essentially described above as adults or adolescents with a preference for sexual relationships with children. The pedophile is usually a man but can be a woman. The pedophile is usually consistent in his choice of juvenile partners; that is, he or she usually picks a child of the same age and·sex each time and performs the same particular sexual activity each time. The relationship may be heterosexual or homosexual. Thus a pedophile may have a heterosexual predilection for prepubescent subjects and another person may have a heterosexual relationship with subjects who are at least pubescent. Likewise there may be a homosexual tendency for the prepubescent or another person with an inclination to those of the same sex whose development is pubescent or beyond (11). Pedophiles can also be classified as either fixated or regressed, and this gives some insight to the mechanisms at work in producing a pedophilic act. This typing of pedophiles is discussed thoroughly by Groth (12).

A *fixated pedophile* is a person in whom an aspect of his psychosocial development has arrested such that the objects of his social and sexual interests do not continue to advance in age as he does. Groth describes him:

A fixated offender is a person who has, from adolescence, been sexually attracted, primarily or exclusively to significantly younger people, and this experience has persisted throughout his life, regardless of what other sexual experiences he has had. (12)

Groth also points out that the fixated pedophile avoids socialization with his chronological peers. He may accept "sexual involvement with a chronological peer but he does not initiate it and it remains secondary to his preference for significantly younger, juvenile partners. The fixated pedophile does not find his pedophilic desires . . . disturbing . . ." and he experiences no sense of guilt for his aberrant activities (12). However, he is inclined also to have a poor self-image. The fixated pedophile is in sharp contrast to the *regressed pedophile*. According to Groth:

> Regression is defined as a temporary or permanent appearance of primitive behavior after more mature forms of expression have been attained. . . .
>
> A regressed child offender is a person who originally preferred peers or adult partners for sexual gratification. However, when these adult relationships become conflictual in some important respect, the adult became replaced by the child as the focus of this person's sexual interest and desires. (12)

The regressed pedophile also has a sense of his own inadequacy. He has carried on appropriate social and sexual relationships with adults or chronological peers. He is often married. In fact, it is often the marriage that provides the stress to which he cannot adapt and thus seeks the involvement with a child. He may well continue his social and sexual relationships with his chronological peers concommitantly. He does feel guilt or remorse for his pedophilic acts and has a better chance of being rehabilitated (12).

INCEST

As another term with multiple interpretations, *incest* is perhaps best defined as "any sexual relations (i.e., activities) between various combinations of 'legal' relatives" (13). Incest accounts for 70 to 80% of all child sexual abuse, which in turn accounts for 3 to 8.8% of all child abuse. The most common form is brother-sister incest, which is cited as five times as common as the next most frequent type, father-daughter incest (13). Mother-son incest is rare. Father-son incest is rarer still. Other combinations of relatives in incestuous relationships have been reported (13). While brother-sister incest is likely the most common type, it is transient and reputed to be typically without sequelae (13). In contrast the second most common type, father-daughter incest is taken most seriously and is the most often reported. It also involves frequent and serious sequelae. It has its effects on not just one, or even two, but three people. Authors speak of the "father-daughter-mother triad" (13) that is, "a domineering and patriarchal father, a passive and ineffectual mother, and a daughter who may have actively encouraged the father's sexual advances or at least not resisted them. The mother colluded by pushing the daughter into becoming the central female figure in the household. The incestuous interaction often continued over a period of years and in some instances eventually included younger female siblings." (13). The family is often a loosely organized one in which family roles are blurred. The other typical family, the "classic" family type involved in this problem, is the opposite extreme—so tightly knit that extrafamilial social relationships are lacking for family members. This latter family is usually unknown to social agencies while the former is usually well known for a variety of social problems, but perhaps not for incest. In the very beginning of the problem the daughter may have felt obliged to indulge her father to keep the family together in a setting where the father's sexual relationship with the mother had been lacking. The mother's role is not a minor one. The mother may not only choose not to interfere with the father-daughter relationionship but also may choose to aid and abet that process by encouraging the daughter to submit herself as her duty to her family. The mother may also facilitate the process by minimizing her presence perhaps even absenting herself in the form of taking a job that keeps her away from home in the evening hours. It is the desire to keep the family intact and to protect the family breadwinner that causes the child and other family members to foster the relationship in the first place and not to come forth and speak up to social agencies, educators, or health caretakers about the problem. If the child victim or another family member does come forward to disclose the incestuous situation, other family members pressure the "traitor" to retract his charge and not to give testimony using the threat of family dissolution if the family secret is revealed.

The disorganized family group profile implies that incestuous relationships predominate in the lower socioeconomic class. However, incest actually transcends social strata. It appears in all social classes, although some classes may be better able than others to hide the problem. Peters describes a 14-year-old runaway who had been forced to have intercourse over the three previous years with her father who preached a "strict fundamental religion, including sexual abstinence" (10). Kempe mentions a judge and a college-educated computer programmer as fathers involved in incestuous relationships (1).

A person may be involved in incest as one aspect of his pedophilia; that is, he may sexually abuse his own children as well as those of others (13). In some settings it is possible to think of incest as one aspect of pedophilia.

SEQUELAE OF SEXUAL CHILD ABUSE

The sequelae of sexual abuse of children are physical and psychological. A victim of sexual assault may have either, neither, or both types of effects. The physical after-effects are trauma, infection, and pregnancy. Traumatic lesions may be genital or nongenital. Nongenital lesions may arise from the sexual episode itself or from the broader picture of nonsexual child abuse. Such nongenital lesions may range from trivial superficial lesions to soft tissue injuries to fractures and severe internal injuries with serious consequences for life and limb. Genital lesions may occur on the breasts, the anus or perianal area, and the perineum—in particular the labia and the vagina. The lesions may be present in any combination of abrasions, hematomas, and lacerations. The latter may demand immediate detection and repair.

Aside from infections of such injuries, a number of other infections may occur. As noted above many pedophiles will have sexual relationships with adults or chronological peers as well as their juvenile victims. That is, some pedophiles have had opportunities to exchange venereal diseases with their chronological peers and later pass those infections on to the children and adolescents they abuse. Grossman and Drutz (14) note the "much more open and permissive approach to sex, widespread availability and use of the 'pill' and intrauterine devices for contraception, and the common belief that venereal diseases can be treated fairly easily and without serious sequelae have all played a part in the spectacular rise in the incidence of these infections." They note that syphilis, gonorrhea, herpetic type 2 infections of the genitalia, group B beta-streptococcus infections, chancroid, lymphopathia venereum, lymphogran-uloma inguinale, Trichomonas infection, inclusion blenorrhea, pubic lice, and scabies may all be sexually transmitted to children. Chlamydial infections of the mucus membranes of the GU tract may also occur (15). Again, early detection and treatment is desirable not only to minimize the physical disease and epidemiologic impact, but also to prevent symptomatic disease and procedures that may serve to amplify the psychological after-effects of the sexual assault.

Another physical effect of sexual abuse is pregnancy. This too has its own psychological sequelae that may compound those of the sexual abuse itself. The problems of adolescent pregnancies are well known and cited elsewhere. Pregnancies resulting from incestuous relationships further compound the aftermath. Nakashima and Zakus (13) reviewed studies of "offspring of inces-tuous unions" and decided these ". . . studies clearly demonstrate that the children of incest suffer from higher infant mortality, severe congenital malformations, and lowered intelligence levels." They felt that this was due not only to the "genetic risks of such close inbreeding" but also that adolescent mothers came from "chaotic families with disturbed members and distorted relationships."

The degree of psychological sequelae of sexual child abuse depends on several determinants: the offender's characteristics, the victim, the offence, and the reactions of family members, health care personnel, and workers from the various social services. Whether the offender was a man or woman and how close he was in age to the victim will all have a bearing on the impact on the child. The closer the offender's relationship to the victim the more probable are psychological sequelae. The age and level of development of the victim will bear on how he or she is affected (16). In general, the impact on the victim is worse with increasing age. Preschool children do better than preadolescents who not only view adults less as unquestionable authority figures but are more sexually aware and have a sense of right and wrong. This may render preadolescents confused and having a greater sense of guilt (13). The teenage years provide a relatively chaotic background for an episode thus heightening its impact because teenagers' sexual and emotional development may not be keeping pace with their physical development. They are ripe to have the most critical reactions. The sex of the victim bears on the outcome of the assault episode; Kempe notes that "boys do much worse than girls" (1). The level of intelligence and emotional stability of the victim will affect the episode's impact. Pascoe (16) also points out that the impact on the victim will vary with the nature of the act and the degree of participation of the child. The last aspect will interplay with the victim's age and development. The child's reaction to violently forced rape is likely to be more severe than the response to "nontouch-ing" acts such as exhibiting pornography or nonforced acts such as fondling. An isolated incident will usually have a different, lighter impact than chronic recurring activity. The reactions of others in the child's life to the episode of sexual abuse are important. The child's family's reactions are of twofold importance. Their reactions are important because they may require as much or more help than the victim. Like the child, the family members' stability at the time of the assault episode will affect their reactions. The reaction of family members as well as those of health caretakers and social service personnel are equally important in that they easily influence the child's reactions and their eventual outcome. A visibly distraught parent may magnify a child's response to the sexual assault. Gruff insensitivity among medical personnel may add to an already ugly situation for the child.

A relatively nonviolent assault episode that had made little impression on the child may be seen by that same child in a more significant perspective after a tactless history-taking session or an indelicate approach to the physical examination.

The psychological effects on the child of the sexual episode can be divided into an acute phase and chronic phase. Immediately following the incident, the victim is fearful, uncertain about whom to trust, angry, and may feel guilt that is heightened by any physical pleasure experienced during the sexual activity. In the days to several weeks following, the victim attempts to deal with the anxiety these feelings produce. Simrel, Berg, and Thomas (17) describe "a constant series of adaptive maneuvers and problem-solving activities," undertaken for that purpose, that is, to deal with these activities and the feelings with which they are associated. In other words, it is an attempt to maintain stability or equilibrium. If the victim cannot deal with those stresses in such a problem-solving and/or adaptive manner, the unresolved situation constitutes a "crisis state" (17,18). The crisis state can last several weeks. It begins with the stress, heightened tension. The victim draws on his usual coping mechanisms. When these fail "emergency problem-solving behavior are brought into play in an attempt to . . . re-establish some kind of equilibrium," which "may be better than, the same as, or worse than the pre-crisis level of functioning" (17). If efforts to deal with the stress are not successful then "the stress will continue, and mal-adaptive solutions may be chosen" (17). Nakashima and Zakus (13) describe "acting out behavior" including "school truancy, arson, dealing in heroin, thefts, sexual promiscuity and illegitimate pregnancies." A chronic after-effect may be thus realized; its degree of intensity is variable. A victim may sustain (1) depression that may be attended by suicide attempts, (2) guilt and a negative self-image that may prompt sexual promiscuity and prostitution in particular, (3) difficulty in relationships with others, men in particular, to the point of sexual dysfunction including frigidity (19). Not to be forgotten is the tendency for the abused later to become abusers themselves, perhaps to carry on the only way of life they know. As a long-term effect this is not restricted to women. Glueck (11) notes a study in which "almost half" of the pedophilics had been victims of sexual abuse, typically "some type of sexual contact with the mother."

It is the role of all professionals involved in the care of the child to intervene in the crisis state. It is the goal of such interventions to help the child and often the child's family members to "regain the level of functioning they maintained before the crisis" (17). It is also a goal to prevent further sexual abuse of the child. To achieve the first goal, it is often up to the professional to provide support to the child or adolescent victim. While some families readily support the victim in his or her time of need, other family members may require every bit as much support themselves thus compounding the professionals' task. In addition to being supportive, the professional is important in assisting the victim as well as his family in the problem-solving process that brings about a solution to the crisis. In such a manner undesirable chronic after-effects can be prevented.

UNRECOGNIZED SEXUAL ABUSE

For every child presented to the police, his physician, or other care facility as a victim of sexual abuse, it is estimated there are at least two unrecognized cases. Such estimates are admittedly crude due to the very nature of the problem. These numbers are commonly derived from interviews with adults many years after they were victimized as children. The interviews' common denominator is that these adults were either referred for psychoemotional or antisocial problems or sought help for such problems. In the process of interviewing patients, a history of being sexually abused as a child would sometimes surface. The problems for which adults were interviewed often traced back to their premature sexual experiences. Thus the problems in question represented chronic psychological sequelae of being a sexually abused child or adolescent. The adults' problems varied widely including prostitution, frigidity, anxiety neuroses, and pedophilia. That a large proportion of cases of child sexual abuse remain hidden reflects several factors: the victim, the offender, the victim's family, and society. The victim may be fearful of the disclosure process and the potential anxiety associated with it. The victim may feel too much shame about what has happened to reveal the facts. The victim may feel some guilt arising from the sexual nature of the relationship. The victim may fear the perpetrator's reprisals for revealing the situation particularly if force or threat of force was employed to achieve the sexual act. The victim may fear disruption of his family and home life if the perpetrator is a household member. The victim may fear harm will come to that member of the household. If the victim's family is aware of the episode, family members may choose not to reveal it and may pressure the victim not to reveal it out of a sense of shame or guilt or out of a fear of disruption of the family. Society's representatives in police, educational, health care, and social agencies often fail to look for sexual abuse including situations that should prompt evaluation.

Victims of unrecognized sexual abuse will on occasion have other complaints. These complaints derive from after-effects of sexual abuse. Victims may come to the attention of the police, educators, social agencies, or health care facilities for psychological problems manifested as runaways, school problems, depression, anxiety neuroses, and "acting out" antisocial behaviors such as theft, drug abuse, and sexual promiscuity. Physical symptoms may develop as a result of psychological problems or as a manifestation of one of the organic sequelae of sexual abuse. Thus the psychological aftermath may be expressed in acting out behavior such as promiscuity that in turn may result in pregnancy. The victim then may present for care only as a pregnant teenager without allusion to the underlying problem. Other organic symptoms may be psychosomatic representations of the psychological aftermath including abdominal pain, perineal discomfort, enuresis, and encopresis. Still other organic symptoms may result directly from the organic diseases that sexual abuse may produce. Thus a victim may present as a pregnant adolescent or with either genital or nongenital trauma that may appear accidental. A victim may be diagnosed as having a venereal disease but give a history only suggestive of innocent nonvenereal transmission. A patient may present with a vaginal discharge that turns out on evaluation to be gonorrhea or *Trichomonas vaginalis*; likewise symptoms of urethritis and proctitis may appear.

The manner of transmission of venereal disease to children has been the subject of some debate. The controversy in particular has revolved around gonorrhea. Authors have postulated nonvenereal routes of transmission especially in the relatively close environment of a family household (20). There is some evidence indicating that nonvenereal transmission of *N. gonorrheae* is possible, but the weight of the evidence suggests that the overwhelming percentage of cases of gonorrhea in children is venereal in origin (21). Therefore, when children are found to have gonococcal disease it is prudent to assume venereal transmission and evaluate the child's case with an exhaustively thorough approach. Virtually all cases will be found to have venereal transmission.

The interviewer or examiner should not find much comfort in the absence of positive physical findings in a patient with specific or nonspecific complaints referable to sexual child abuse. In overt cases of sexual abuse it can be expected to find a higher percentage of physical findings than in unrecognized cases since need for treatment of the physical after-effects may have been the motivating force for overtly seeking care. And yet only half of those children with overt presentations have positive physical findings (9). A smaller percentage can be expected in unrecognized cases. Therefore, more than half of unrecognized cases of sexual abuse will have no physical findings to give them away.

RECOGNITION OF SEXUAL ABUSE

Physicians' offices, social agencies, and health care facilities unfortunately contribute disproportionately low percentages of reports of sexual abuse cases compared to law enforcement agencies. Yet many sexual abuse victims and their families visit these facilities seeking care for symptoms that are in fact sequelae of sexual abuse. Sexual abuse is rarely considered in the differential diagnosis of the symptoms. Only rarely does the child receive evaluation for the possibility of sexual abuse (8,22).

Recognition of sexual abuse requires a high "index of suspicion." Child care workers, social case workers, physicians, and nurses must be prepared to consider the possibility of sexual abuse when patients present with problems known to be potential manifestations or results of sexual child abuse. More than one child has been part of an incestuous relationship for years while the physician who regularly cared for the child remained unaware of the problem. In addition to a knowledge of the general problem of sexual abuse, sensitivity to the problem of the victim and the victim's family is required. Table 1 summarizes indicators that should alert the examiner to the possibility of sexual abuse.

Table 1. Indications of Sexual Child Abuse

A history of sexual assault reported[a]
 By the victim or the victim's family or the offender or others
 Whether volunteered or elicited in process of investigating a medical problem
A history of nonsexual child abuse
A history of venereal disease in childhood or adolescence[a]
Nonspecific symptoms in preschool children
 Failure-to-thrive
 Excess clinging behavior
 Sleep disturbance
 Encopresis
 Enuresis
 Abdominal pain
 Changes in behavior
 Changes in appetite
 Vomiting
 Speech problems
 Nail biting
 Thumb sucking
Nonspecific symptoms in school age children
 Sleep disturbance
 Changes in appetite
 Decrease in school performance
 Truancy
 Fear states
  anxiety, depression, phobias, obsession, tics, conversion hysteria
Nonspecific symptoms in adolescents
 Antisocial behavior
 Truancy
 Loss of self-esteem
 Depression
 Psychosomatic complaints
 Abdominal pain
 Assume mother's roles
 Drug abuse
 Promiscuity
 Prostitution
 Runaway
 Changes in appetite
Excessive parental concern over medical complaints of the child
Physical exam suggesting nonsexual child abuse
Physical exam revealing genital or perineal trauma[a]
Physical exam or laboratory findings of venereal disease in child or adolescent[a]
Physical exam revealing foreign body in vagina, rectum, or urethra
Physical exam revealing sperm in rectum, vagina, or vulva/perineum[a]
Sperm on clothing[a]
Blood on clothing
Adolescent pregnancy

SOURCE: Adapted from Pascoe DJ: Management of sexually abused children. *Pediatr Ann* 8:309, 1979.

[a] More likely to indicate sexual abuse

MEDICAL HISTORY

In an emotionally charged topic fraught with subjectivity as is the case with sexual abuse of children and adolescents, it is important to establish an accurate data base. Such information will have implications for more than the courtroom. It will be pivotal in determining what other steps are taken to evaluate the patient as well as what treatment and follow-up are begun. For example, different measures must be taken in the case of a 12-year-old girl who was recurrently forced to participate in intercourse with her father at home as opposed to a girl of similar age raped or molested in a city park by a total stranger. In the process of determining where who did what to whom it is easy to fall into a brusque "third-degree" manner of interrogation of the victim and family. An abrupt approach certainly will not establish the rapport necessary to obtain a candid and thorough account of the victim's experiences. Of paramount importance is the effect such an approach will have on the child and family members. Evidence of a gruff attitude on the part of the history-taker will serve as a continuation of the abusive process thus amplifying the negative effects the sexual abuse itself has had on the patient. Similarly, the professional must employ sufficient self-discipline to control his or her own reactions to a possibly repulsive situation. As a person from whom authority and support are expected, revealing personal feelings may magnify the situation and enhance the victim's reactions. Sensitivity, support, and assistance in the problem-solving process must be employed from the start. The history interview itself is thus an opportunity to let the child ventilate his feelings. It is also an opportunity to explain to the child about potential physical and emotional after-effects and possibly allay fears and guilt.

Ideally, all persons concerned should be interviewed including the offender, if possible, the victim, the victim's family or household members, and any other witnesses. For court purposes most accusations by a child require corroboration by an adult or through evidence. However, it has been unequivocally stated that children do not give graphic descriptions of sexual activities as a matter of fantasy but only if they have seen or been involved in such activities. Therefore, when a child describes details of sexual activity, even if there is no supporting evidence, he should be believed. In cases in which the perpetrator was a stranger, family members will often be supportive of a child who has a complaint or history to give. If the perpetrator is a family member or friend, various family members may press the child to withhold his history or to alter it. These pressures may later bring the victim to deny his original story. All such efforts are usually directed at hiding the problem and thus attempt to protect a specific family member or the integrity of the family as a whole. Thus, in the very cases in which it is most difficult to achieve, it is desirable to establish a rapport with the child victim and interview him alone. It may be a useful adjunct to have the child draw a picture of the events that occurred during the episode (23). Doll play is another approach (12). Adult members corroborating testimony is useful but not always obtainable. Interviewing any assailant, be he previously known to the victim or not, may be important for achieving an appropriate understanding of the case.

Many specific facts can be learned from a carefully conducted interview. Just what occurred will affect the examination, treatment, and follow-up. The identity of the perpetrator, or at least his description, may be learned. Where the child was located when he was vulnerable is very important as is the location of the actual abuse. When the activity occurred should not only include the time and date of a single episode but whether the episode was an isolated event or just one of a series of recurring episodes. When the most recent event occurred will bear on the significance of the physical examination and the various specimens collected for laboratory analysis. The details of the sexual activity are taken to determine the appropriate tests as well as treatment for the victim. Was there exhibitionism, voyeurism, or exposure to pornography? Was there touching or kissing? Was there successful or attempted penetration of the victim's mouth, rectum, or vagina? Were foreign bodies employed? Was there force or threat of force? Was there threat of retaliation for reporting the episode? Were there other victims and what was their involvement? Were there any witnesses? Was there nongenital child abuse?

What symptoms have resulted from the episode? Is there abdominal pain, or rectal, urethral, or vaginal symptoms? Is there urinary urgency, frequency, hematuria, or dysuria? Is there bleeding of the rectum, vagina, or perineum? Are there contusions, lacerations, abrasions of the mouth, rectum, vagina, vulva, or nongenital areas? Is there urethral or vaginal discharge? Has the victim urinated, eaten, brushed his teeth, bathed, douched, or changed clothes since the most recent sexual activity and thus altered the physical findings?

Gynecological history, especially menstrual history, is relevant particularly in cases in which there is history of attempted or successful vaginal penetration. Has menarche occurred? When was the last normal menstrual period? Is the patient already pregnant? Has the patient been pregnant in the past? Developmental history and age are important in assessing the psychological impact on the child. Similarly, a history of mental retardation or psychoemotional problems is relevant. Are there prior or current medical problems to consider that might interplay with either organic or psychological sequelae?

PHYSICAL EXAMINATION

Child victims often have no positive findings on physical or laboratory examination. This may reflect the lack of necessity for the perpetrator to apply physical force to achieve his goal because the child is often familiar with him and thus relatively compliant. When positive physical findings do occur, they are important for two reasons. First, they may require treatment, and second, they are an important objective corroboration of the child's testimony. A thorough physical examination is a must regardless of the amount of time elapsed since the last sexual contact. The examination is preferably done at the time of presentation although the patient rarely may have an emotional reaction that justifies postponing it, but as briefly as possible. As in the other aspects of the victim's management, the exam technique should be gentle and sensitive to the patient's feelings not only to obtain a good exam but also to avoid enhancing the negative effects of the sexual activity. The examination should be conducted with the same privacy accorded any other patient. It is attuned to findings of sexual abuse.

Collection of evidence and laboratory specimens may accompany the physical examination. Young children are often more successfully examined in their parent's lap while older children and adolescents often want their parents to leave the room. It is appropriate to allay the child's fears by explaining each part of the examination before actually performing it.

Beginning the examination with nongenital areas allows the subsequent examination of the genitalia, anus, and rectum to appear as just another part of the exam. Again, this represents an effort to minimize the psychological after-effects of the sexual abuse. A thorough nongenital examination is useful in itself to uncover injuries reflecting nonsexual child abuse. After ruling out emergency situations, such as active bleeding and serious injuries, a complete routine physical examination is performed. At the onset the general appearance of the child is noted. Particular attention is paid to the victim's emotional status. An area often overlooked is what kind of clothing the victim is wearing noting the type and style as well as the presence of tears, dirt, blood, and semen (24).

Body surfaces are examined in search of evidence of injury. Abrasions, excoriations, erythema, swelling, ecchymoses, hematomas, lacerations, scars, and bony deformities are to be noted. One particular lesion occurring in sexual activity is the bite mark that may occur on genital or nongenital surfaces (25). Evidence of traumatic injuries warrants a radiographic skeletal survey for old and new fractures. A developmental examination is performed.

The genital examination addresses not only the genitalia but also the breasts, the rectum, and the mouth. In some cases bargaining with the patient will achieve adequate cooperation for a good examination. In other cases sedation and, failing that, examination under anesthesia may be necessary (26). Examination under anesthesia should only be considered in cases in which positive findings are likely to be found on a pelvic exam. Allowing the patient to see and touch the examination instruments alleviates some fears, as does allowing the patient to assist in the examination. For example, the patient of adequate age may be asked to separate the labia (26). Throughout the genital examination the presence and stage of development of anatomical structures should be noted. The mons veneris, buttocks, thighs, and surfaces of the vulva and perineum (including the perianal area) should be inspected for the presence of blood, dirt, semen, and foreign objects as well as lesions of trauma. Similar examination of the labia majora, labia minora, urethral meatus, and clitoris continues as the labia are separated. The examiner determines whether or not the hymen is present and whether or not it is intact. If the hymen is present is there evidence of injury? Does the injury appear to be old or recent? Much is made of the legal significance of the hymen. And yet its condition is equivocal. A relatively elastic hymen may allow penile penetration without injury. At the other extreme the normal hymen may be innocently traumatized and exhibit injuries from a number of nonsexual childhood activities. Most hymens are perforated or absent at the time of menarche without the presence of sexual abuse. The vaginal walls and cervix are examined for soft tissue injuries. In smaller children, a vaginoscope (26) may replace the vaginal speculum. Ano-rectal examination is important especially in boys since the anus represents the largest perineal orifice in the male child (9). After longstanding recurrent penetrations an episode may leave no physical signs. Initial episodes, however, may produce a shearing force sufficient to injure vessels at the anal verge, which is the narrowest diameter of the orifice in girls and boys (27). On examination, swelling, laceration, or hematoma of the anal verge may be evident. Other lesions may include perianal abrasions, erythema, lacerations, or ecchymoses. The mouth rarely exhibits positive physical signs relative to its frequency as a target organ. This is attributed to its relatively large diameter. The breasts are examined for injuries in the same manner applied to other body surfaces. As the genital examination progresses, laboratory specimens appropriate to that structure and history may be collected.

LABORATORY SPECIMENS

At the time of the physical examination, ideally as soon after the most recent episode as possible, wet mount slide specimens should be collected from the mouth, rectum, and vagina for immediate microscopic examination by the examining physician to look for spermatozoa. Swabs of the mouth, urethra, vagina, and cervix should be considered and appropriate cultures begun by immediate direct plating on Thayer–Martin medium to isolate the fastidious gonococcus bacterium. From the same sites smears on microscope slides can be made for Gram stain in search for evidence of gonorrhea. Likewise, wet mount microscope slide preparations of vaginal secretions should be examined for the presence of *Trichomonas*. Serologic specimens for complement fixation are useful for diagnosis of Chlamydial mucosal infections as well as lymphogranuloma venereum (15). Local secretions may be collected for identification of immune globulin G antibodies or for culture of the organism itself in special cell lines. Blood should be drawn for a serologic test for syphilis. Some sources advocate a serologic test for syphilis one month after presentation. A pregnancy test may be necessary depending on the history. Blood or urine specimens for toxicologic investigation may be appropriate if the history warrants. Other specimens to be gathered are described in the following section.

EVIDENCE COLLECTION

Evidence collection is an aspect of the evaluation of a sexual abuse case. Like the physical examination, lab work, and adult witnesses hard evidence may provide a source of corroboration of the child victim's testimony. It is important that such evidence be collected promptly to prevent loss or claims of contamination thus rendering it questionable. At the same time the collection of physical evidence, like the history intake and physical examination, must be done with sensitivity to the child's feelings. Collected evidence may be useful in confronting the family of the victim particularly in incest cases (12). The following evidence collection has been described by Pascoe (16).

Clothing should be inspected for hair and other debris. Fingernail clippings or scrapings should be collected. The patient's hair, pubic hair in particular, should be combed for foreign hair. Suspected areas of the victim's body may be scanned for semen fluorescence with a Wood's lamp. As indicated in the accounts of the episode the mouth, rectum, vagina, or cervix should be swabbed and dry smears made for microscopic exam for the presence of spermatozoa. Wet mounts from the mouth, rectum, vagina or cervix of secretions should be promptly studied to determine the motility of the sperm. Swabs from the same sites should be obtained and air-dried for acid-phosphatase detection as a reflection of prostatic secretion indicative of the presence of semen. Semen specimens for ABO semen typing should be collected. A blood specimen should be collected from the patient for grouping and typing. Medical photography of the genital lesions should be done if visible evidence of trauma is present. (16)

The specimens to be collected and the method of collection is described in Table 2 modified after Pascoe (16).

REPORTING SEXUAL ABUSE

When a child or adolescent presents or is recognized as a victim of sexual abuse, that visit should be only the first step in management of his case. It is not a problem that can be successfully dealt with in a one-time appointment in a physician's office, emergency room, principal's office, or social agency. Follow-

Table 2. Specimen Collection in Cases of Sexual Abuse

Clothing   Have child disrobe on a white sheet. Collect clothing, debris, hair, leaves, and other materials. Place in a bag, seal, and label.

Fingernails   Scrape from beneath the nails or clip the nails; place scrapings or clippings in a specimen container. Keep specimens for the left and right hand separate. Label accordingly.

Pubic or other hair   Retrieve suspected foreign hairs. Place in an envelope and indicate where found. Normal pubic or scalp hair may be plucked at this time and saved for use in comparisons.

Wood's lamp   If body areas appear to have traces of semen, scan with a Wood's lamp. Semen, if present, will fluoresce with a characteristic dark green color. Record semen locations. Cut, label, and preserve any pubic hairs that show traces of semen.

Sperm motility   Collect suspicious material from the vaginal vault or the posterior fornix using a cotton swab or glass dropper. Place a drop of the material on a slide; cover with a cover slip and examine under high dry power for motile sperm.

Sperm identification   Swab all suspicious areas with separate applicators (mouth, anus, labia, vagina, cervix, etc.). Smear swab onto two slides and air-dry both. Preserve a swab in 1 cc of normal saline. Label specimens.

Acid phophatase   Using cotton swabs, collect specimens from any suspicious areas. Air-dry swabs; place in tubes; cover and label. Place an additional swab in buffered albumen. Label specimen.

ABO semen typing   Using a cotton swab, obtain specimens from suspicious areas. The best specimens of semen traces are obtained from areas that are not contaminated by the patient's own secretions. Label.

Medical photography   Photograph all genital lesions if visible evidence of trauma is present. Likewise nongenital lesions.

Nonsexual child abuse procedures   Radiographic skeletal survey, prothrombin time, partial thromboplastin time, platelet count. . . .

SOURCE: Adapted from Pascoe DJ: Management of sexually abused children. *Pediatr Ann* 8:315, 1979.

up is necessary. Therefore, reporting the case to the appropriate agency is mandatory. At the moment of recognition, the professional newly aware of the situation may be the child's only advocate. To not report a case of sexual assault of a child or adolescent is to condone it and become a passive accomplice of the abuser. In all of the United States sexual abuse of a child is a crime and thus requires reporting. In many states, a specific statute requires that sexual child abuse be reported like all other child abuse. In those areas, failure to do so is itself punishable. In most communities, sexual child abuse is reported to the same agencies and by the same procedure as physical nonsexual child abuse. In reporting abuse, care should be taken to not confuse the specific child protective service agency with other social service agencies.

TREATMENT

Treatment of sexual child abuse reflects the physical and psychological needs of the victim and his family. Early treatment should emphasize opportunities for the child to ventilate his feelings or anxieties regarding the events in question. The child needs reassurance about physical after-effects, about his guilt feelings, and specifically about fears that he might be punished. He may need positive reinforcement as well as help in the problem-solving process as noted in the discussion of sequelae. Parents likewise should be reassured regarding after-effects and where possible included in the child's care so that the child may ventilate his feelings at home and receive assistance in the problem-solving process.

The 70 to 80% of sexual child abuse cases that are incest require a number of additional specific measures. As Nakashima and Zakus (13) point out, incest represents a variety of psychosocial diseases at both the individual and family levels; incest is a symptom of abnormal family forces. Treatment must approach each of those levels. To treat one person but not the other members of the father-daughter-mother triad mentioned above will only result in resumption of family behavior patterns present before the disclosure of the incest. Wide-ranging degrees of success of treatment of incest have been described (29,30). Success has been measured by the ability to have children live in the family home. The greatest degree of success appears to come from a broad treatment program (31). Such a program involves not only counseling of the child, the father, the mother, and other child victims as individuals but also counseling the "sides" of the incestuous triangle: father-daughter, mother-daughter, and marital counseling. Family counseling is appropriate in such a program, too. Placement of the child victim or victims outside the home may be necessary as may be the placement of the father in a jail or psychiatric hospital. Attention to other family problems such as unemployment and inadequate housing may be necessary. These treatment modalities may occur in a number of combinations or sequences. They involve a variety of agencies (31).

The "classic" tightly knit incestuous family has more of its own resources than the disorganized family and has overall better prospects for successful therapy although members of both family types may be resistant to treatment (31).

Nakashima and Zakus (31) provide prognostic indicators of successful therapy:

1. The members of the triad must give up their denial of the incestuous relationship.
2. The father must accept his responsibility as the adult parent figure for the incest.
3. The mother must be willing to protect the child from any further incestuous involvement.
4. The parents must have some hope and wish for restoring their marital sexual relationship.
5. The members of the triad must be able to focus on family interactions other than the sexual activity.
6. The members of the triad must have some recognition of their distorted roles and some wish to change these.

Evaluation of physical status will often reveal traumatic genital lesions some of which will require surgical intervention. Nongenital lesions may also be present and require surgical care. In either case tetanus immunization status should be reviewed and updated if necessary. Of those girls who become pregnant as a result of such an episode, some will opt for abortion. Others will choose to carry the baby to term and thus require careful obstetric attention as a pregnant adolescent is at high risk for obstetric and perinatal complications. Treatment of demonstrated venereal disease is appropriate. Also, some authors (16) recommend very strongly that prophylaxis be employed for gonorrhea with the added benefit that it is likely to also eradicate an innoculum of syphilis. Diethylstilbestrol or ethinyl estradiol may be indicated to prevent conception if the history indicates that a female victim may be fertile but not already pregnant (16,28).

FOLLOW-UP

Follow-up after initial presentation reflects the sequelae of sexual abuse of children and adolescents. For physical effects of sexual abuse, initial surgical care of traumatic lesions will require follow-up to ensure proper healing and to handle wound infections if they occur. Venereal diseases require treatment of contacts as well as a follow-up examination or cultures. In some cases a laboratory diagnosis of pregnancy will be made. These, as well as those pregnancies known at the time of presentation, require thorough repeated medical visits as high risk pregnancies. Laboratory reports that return subsequent to presentation may bear diagnoses such as syphilis, obviously requiring treatment. The child or adolescent's psychological aftermath will, as noted, require support in his crisis and assistance in the problem-solving process. The victim may require special support during medical attention and legal processes.

As discussed in the treatment section, the victim's family members may require follow-up themselves. Even family members with only one victim and no perpetrator in their midst may require support and crisis counseling. The victim's siblings as well as other children in an extended household may have been victims themselves and thus require physical and psychological evaluation and treatment as well. If a family or household member has been the perpetrator, he also requires physical and psychological treatment, which may be of primary importance to what legal steps are being entertained. The fate of the family as a whole must be considered. What spontaneous disruption of the family integrity will take place? What socioeconomic provisions will have to be made for housing, employment, and income? Will the victim or perpetrator need to be removed from the home immediately or after attempts at treatment? What will be the disposition of the victim and other children in the household? Are they better off continuing in the home? Can the perpetrator be left in the home? Have the appropriate police and child protection agencies been notified? Obviously, much of the follow-up of physical effects requires attention by a physician in a health care facility, usually a hospital. Much of the psychological support and assistance can be provided by rape advocate teams and crisis counseling services.

Such a multidisciplinary approach is necessary but chaos may easily ensue. A coordinator is necessary. While such a role may fall by default to a member of one of the disciplines involved in the child's care, a coordinating agency is preferable. A child protective services department is present in many communities to give direction and organization to both immediate steps and follow-up care.

REFERENCES

1. Kempe CH: Sexual abuse, another hidden pediatric problem. *Pediatrics* 62:382, 1978.
2. Brant RST, Tisza VF: The sexually misused child. *Am J Orthopsychiatry* 47:80, 1977.
3. Greenberg NH: The epidemiology of childhood sexual abuse. *Pediatr Ann* 8:289, 1978.
4. *Dorland's Illustrated Medical Dictionary.* Philadelphia, WB Saunders Co, 1965, p. 1400.
5. deFrancis V: *Protecting the Child Victim of Sex Crimes.* American Humane Association, Denver, 1969.
6. Sgroi SM: Sexual molestation of children. *Child Today*, May–June:18, 1975.
7. Jaffe AC, Dynneson RN, ten Bensel RW: Sexual abuse of children. *Am J Dis Child* 129:689, 1975.
8. Swanson DW: Adult sexual abuse of children. *Dis Nervous System* 29:677, 1968.
9. Ellerstein NS, Canavan JW: Sexual abuse of boys. *Am J Dis Child* 134:255, 1980.
10. Peters JJ: Children who are victims of sexual assault and the psychology of offenders. *Am J Psychother* 30:398, 1976.
11. Glueck RC: Pedophilia, in Slovenko R (ed): *Sexual Behavior and the Law.* Springfield, Illinois, Charles C Thomas, Publisher, 1965, pp 539.
12. Groth AN: Patterns of Sexual Assault against Children and Adolescents, in Borgen AW, Groth AN, Holmstrom LC, et al (eds): *Sexual Assault of Children and Adolescents.* Lexington, Mass, Lexington Books, 1978.
13. Nakashima II, Zakus GE: Incest. Review and clinical experience. *Pediatrics* 60:696, 1977.
14. Grossman M, Drutz DJ: Venereal disease in children. *Adv Pediatr* 21:97, 1974.
15. Klein JR: Update: Adolescent gynecology. *Pediatr Clin North Am* 27:146, 1980.
16. Pascoe DJ: Management of sexually abused children. *Pediatr Ann* 8:309, 1979.

17. Simrel K, Berg R, Thomas J: Crisis management of sexually abused children. *Pediatr Ann* 8:317, 1979.

18. Rapoport L: Crisis intervention as a mode of treatment, in Roberts RW, Nee RH (eds): *Theories of Social Casework*. Chicago, University of Chicago Press, 1970, pp 267.

19. Tsai M, Wagner NN: Therapy groups for women sexually molested as children. *Arch Sex Behav* 7:417, 1978.

20. Shore WB, Winkelstein JA: Non-venereal transmission of gonococcal infections to children. *J Pediatr* 79:661, 1971.

21. Folland DS, Burke RE, Hinman AR, et al: Gonorrhea in pre-adolescent children. An inquiry into source of infection and mode of transmission. *Pediatrics* 60:153, 1977.

22. Orr DP: Limitations of emergency room evaluations of sexually abused children. *Am J Dis Child* 132:873, 1978.

23. Gorline LL, Ray MM: Examining and caring for the child who has been sexually assaulted. *Am J Maternal Child Nurs* 4:110, 1979.

24. Breen JL, Grenwald E, Gregori CA: The molested young female. *Pediatr Clin North Am* 19:717, 1972.

25. Levine LJ: Bite mark evidence. *Dent Clin North Am* 21:145, 1977.

26. Capraro VJ: Gynecologic examination in children and adolescents. *Pediatr Clin North Am* 91:511, 1972.

27. Paul DM: The medical examination in sexual offences against children. *Med Sci Law* 17:251, 1977.

28. Tilelli JA, Turek D, Jaffe AC: Sexual abuse of children. *N Engl J Med* 302:319, 1980.

29. Molnar G, Cameron P: Incest syndrome: observations in a general hospital psychiatric unit. *Can Psychiatr Assoc J* 20:373, 1975.

30. Giarreto H: The treatment of father-daughter incest: a psychosocial approach. *Child Today* 5:2, 1976.

31. Nakashima II, Zakus G: Incestuous families. *Pediatr Ann* 8:300, 1979.

14
Radiology of the Skeletal System

Leonard E. Swischuk

Since Caffey's original description of children with subdural hematomas and unexplained fractures (1), the roentgenographic findings in the battered-child syndrome have become well-known (2–6). Of these, the most pathognomonic is the healing epiphyseal-metaphyseal fracture, and this is especially true in young infants where this type of injury seldom is seen other than in the battered-child syndrome. These injuries, of course, are exclusive to children and result from shearing forces across the epiphyseal-metaphyseal junction. In older children, such forces are common in everyday injuries, but in infants, they are most often encountered with the twisting or jiggling occurring in the battered-child syndrome. The young infant who might fall on the out-stretched extremity is more likely to sustain a metaphyseal cortical buckle (torus) fracture, for this is the weakest part of the bone. As the child grows older, the cortex becomes stronger and the epiphyseal-metaphyseal junction becomes the relatively weaker of the two regions.

However, as pathognomonic as these epiphyseal-metaphyseal fractures are, it must be added that they probably occur in only 50% of cases (7–9). Indeed, many battered infants show no evidence of skeletal injury at all, and those who do, often demonstrate innocuous appearing transverse or spiral fractures of the midshafts of the long bones. To be sure, these fractures are probably as common as the epiphyseal-metaphyseal injuries (8), but are not at all pathognomonic of the battered child. Because of this, knowledge as to which fractures are the most significant and how they are likely to have been sustained is important. Indeed, it is not the injury itself so much which enables diagnosis, but rather the lack of correlation between: (*1*) the type of injury observed, (*2*) the known mechanism required for its production, and (*3*) the proported mechanism of its production.

THE ROLE OF RADIOLOGY

The primary role of radiology is to detect occult or subtle injuries and to confirm known injuries. In terms of the skeleton, a complete bone survey is

253

required, for many of these injuries are "relatively silent" and detected only by the roentgenographic bone survey. This is especially true of healing fractures. Isotope bone surveys also can be used to locate the fractures, but are less useful for they yield relatively nonspecific information. There is no question, of course, that they can pinpoint areas of bone abnormality and detect fractures invisible on the roentgenogram, but they cannot differentiate between infection, tumor, and trauma.

MECHANISMS OF INJURY AND ROENTGENOGRAPHIC APPEARANCES OF THE FRACTURES

Different mechanisms lead to different bone and joint injuries, and it is important to appreciate just which mechanisms result in which injuries. The reason for this is that the diagnosis of the battered-child syndrome depends on the discrepancy between alleged mechanisms of injury and mechanisms actually responsible. Basically, these mechanisms include: (1) direct blows, (2) twisting forces, (3) shaking, and (4) squeezing.

Direct Blow Injuries

Direct blows to the extremities usually result in transverse or spiral diaphyseal fractures (Fig. 1). These fractures, although quite common, are not pathognomonic of the battered-child syndrome. On the other hand, under certain circumstances, they can rouse suspicions. For example, a transverse fracture of a long bone in a 3-month-old baby is a much more suspicious injury than the same fracture in a 6 year old. The 3-month-old baby simply is not developed enough to self-initiate such an injury. This may prompt a bone survey, whereupon other fractures may come to light (Fig. 2). Alone, however, these fractures must be assessed with caution, even though they account for approximately 50% of the fractures seen in abused children (8).

A direct blow to the clavicle results in a midshaft fracture, and in the battered-child syndrome, this fracture is quite common (Fig. 3a). However, because this fracture also is common in the pediatric population at large, it has little diagnostic specificity. Direct blows to the scapula also can result in nonspecific linear or stellate fractures (Fig. 3b). Because these fractures are relatively uncommon in infants and young children, their presence should cause suspicion. The same pertains to the uncommon sternal fracture resulting from a direct blow (Fig. 3c).

Direct blows to the face produce a variety of facial and mandibular fractures, and direct blows to the calvarium produce linear, curvilinear, or depressed fractures (see Fig. 2b). Often such fractures are associated with intracranial injury, and CT scanning is the best modality for its demonstration (10,11). It also is important to note that these intracranial injuries can occur in the absence of skull fractures and that the calvarium may appear entirely normal in some patients. In others, spreading of the calvarial sutures due to increased intracranial pressure can provide a clue to the presence of an underlying problem (Fig. 1c).

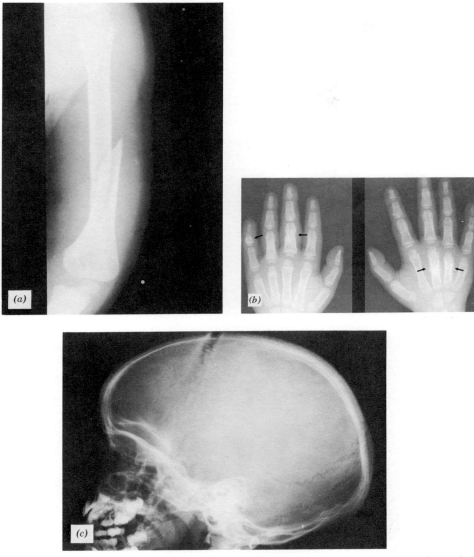

Figure 1. Battered-child syndrome: injuries from direct blows. (*a*) Note the spiral fracture of the humerus. (*b*) Numerous fractures, some older than others, are present in the small bones of both hands (arrows). (*c*) Note spread sutures indicating increased intracranial pressure. This was secondary to a subdural hematoma. This patient did not demonstrate any classic epiphyseal-metaphyseal fractures.

Direct blows to the abdomen result in visceral injuries, while direct blows to the chest result in rib fractures, and occasionally, associated findings such as pleural effusions, hemothorax, pneumothorax, and pulmonary contusion. Most commonly, however, rib fractures alone are the problem and result from squeezing of the thorax. These fractures occur bilaterally and are discussed later.

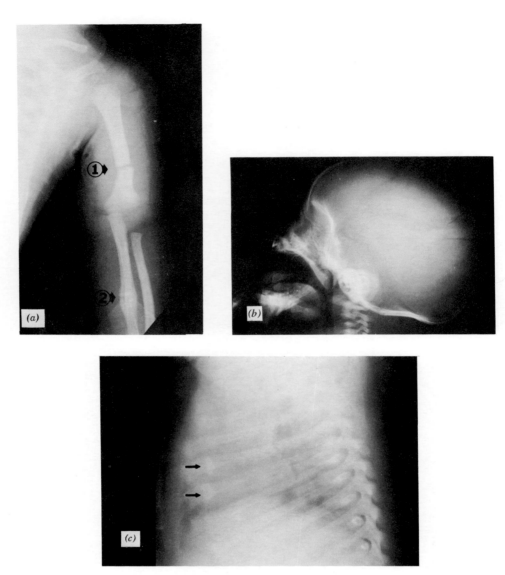

Figure 2. Battered-child syndrome: transverse fracture as a signal of other injury. (*a*) Note the innocuous-appearing transverse fracture through the upper humerus (1). The mother brought this infant in because he would not move his arm. However, another older fracture was seen in the midshaft of the radius (2). This prompted a bone survey, and the other arm demonstrated typical epiphyseal-metaphyseal fractures. Similar fractures were seen in the left tibia and fibula. (*b*) Radiograph of the skull demonstrates a number of fractures and spread sutures. (*c*) Lateral view of the chest demonstrates exaggerated cupping of the anterior aspect of some of the ribs (arrows), characteristic of costochondral separations.

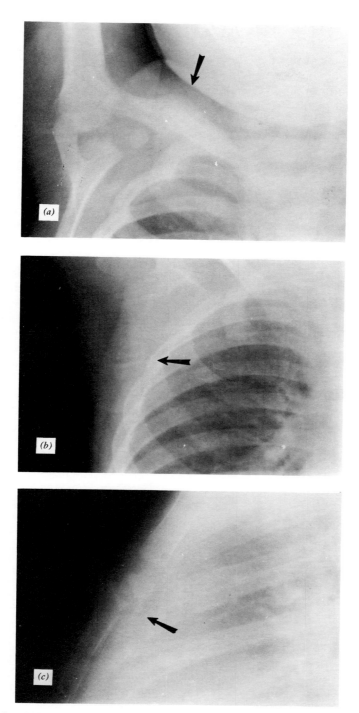

Figure 3. Direct blow injuries: other than long bones. (*a*) Typical healing midclavicular fracture (arrow). (*b*) Transverse fracture through the scapula (arrow). (*c*) Displaced fracture of the sternum (arrow).

Twisting Force Induced Injuries

Twisting forces applied to the extremity can result in spiral fractures of the long bone shaft (Fig. 1). Such forces exist commonly outside the battered-child syndrome and in the tibia result in the so-called "toddler's" spiral fracture (Fig. 4). This fracture also occurs often in the battered-child syndrome, but of course, has no diagnostic specificity. On the other hand, this type of tibial fracture might be treated with more suspicion than a spiral fracture in another bone, for it is a relatively common injury in battered children. The other fracture resulting from twisting forces is the epiphyseal-metaphyseal fracture, and it is this fracture which is the most pathognomonic of the battered-child syndrome. The epiphyseal-metaphyseal junction is one of the weakest parts of the long bones, and because of this, it is easy for the shearing forces produced by twisting or jiggling to cause separation of the epiphysis from the metaphysis. Similar injuries also can result when the child is shaken violently and the extremities are allowed to dangle and lash back and forth.

In the initial stages, epiphyseal-metaphyseal injuries often manifest in nothing more than soft tissue swelling around the fracture site (Fig. 5). In other cases, a small avulsed metaphyseal, or occasionally, epiphyseal, fragment can provide a clue to the presence of the injury (Fig. 6a), but often, it is not until healing occurs that the fractures become clearly apparent. With healing, callus formation is abundant, periosteal new bone deposition often profound (Figs. 5b, 6b), and in some cases, changes are so striking that systemic diseases such as scurvy, leukemia, or congenital lues are first considered (Fig. 7).

Bleeding into the adjacent joint is not uncommonly associated with these epiphyseal-metaphyseal injuries, and in the hip or shoulder, widening of the

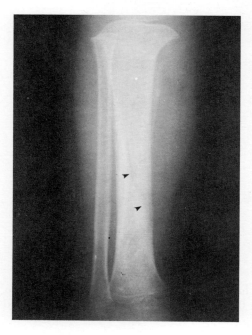

Figure 4. Spiral ("toddler's") fracture of the tibia. First note early periosteal new bone deposition around the tibial shaft. Then note the spiral fracture (arrows). This type of fracture is not pathognomonic of the battered-child syndrome, but it commonly occurs in the syndrome.

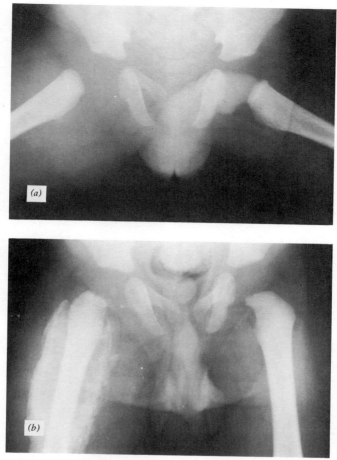

Figure 5. Battered-child syndrome: early soft tissue findings. (*a*) First note that the soft tissues around the right hip are thickened and whiter than those on the left. This indicates soft tissue edema. Next note that the joint space is much wider than the one on the left. This finding indicates bleeding into the joint and an underlying epiphyseal-metaphyseal fracture should be suspected. (*b*) Two weeks later, note marked periosteal new bone deposition around the right femoral shaft and proximal healing changes.

joint space is the hallmark of such bleeding (Fig. 5). When either of these joint spaces is widened and surrounding soft tissue swelling is present, it can be assumed that an epiphyseal-metaphyseal injury has been sustained. In the remaining joints, joint space widening does not occur for the ligaments are too strong to allow distraction of the bone. Rather, there is distortion of adjacent fat pads. In the knee, accumulation of fluid in the suprapatellar bursa causes compression of the suprapatellar fat pad against the femur and posterior displacement of the popliteal fat pad (12). In the ankle, there is outward displacement of the anterior and posterior juxtacapsular fat pads (12), whereas in the wrist, generalized swelling around the joint is seen.

Twisting or jiggling forces can produce injuries similar to those seen at the

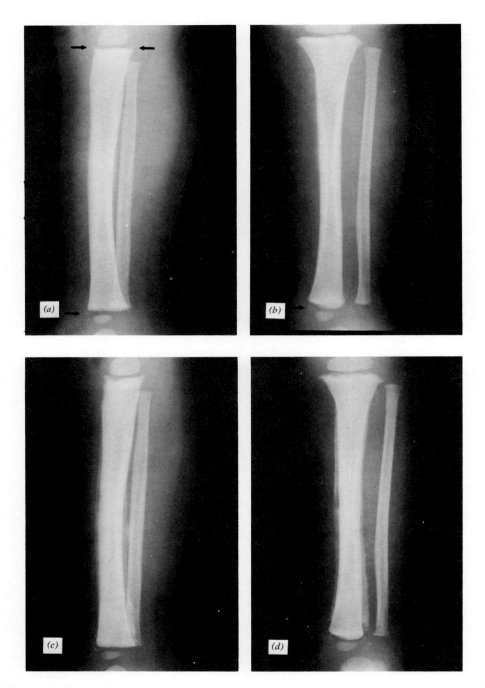

Figure 6. Battered-child syndrome: epiphyseal-metaphyseal fractures. (*a*) Minimal changes are seen, but small avulsion or corner fractures are present proximally and distally in the tibia (arrows). (*b*) Frontal view demonstrates the distal fragment (arrow) only. (*c*) There is clear-cut evidence of healing of these suspected fractures $2\frac{1}{2}$ weeks later. Periosteal new bone deposition is seen and the corner fractures are more readily visible. (*d*) Similar findings on frontal view.

260

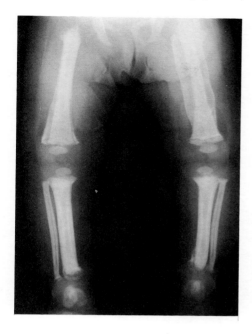

Figure 7. Battered-child syndrome: changes mimicking systemic bone disease. Note epiphyseal-metaphyseal fractures at the ends of all of the long bones. Periosteal new bone deposition is profound in some areas, and this together with metaphyseal fragmentation can cause a suspision of such conditions as leukemia, scurvy, rickets, etc.

epiphyseal-metaphyseal long bone junctions in certain other bones. Indeed, some of these are as pathognomonic as are the long bone injuries and, for the most part, include fragmentation fractures of the distal end of the clavicle, fragmentation of the acromial process of the scapula, and separation (with widening and cupping) of the costochondral junctions of the ribs. In any of these cases, the fractures are more readily apparent when healing occurs, for callus formation draws attention to their presence (Fig. 8).

Shaking Injuries

Shaking injuries result when the infant is grasped around the torso and shaken violently back and forth or when one extremity is violently shaken. Under such circumstances, it is readily apparent how the shaken extremity, or the dangling extremities in a shaken infant, are subject to injury (i.e., epiphyseal-metaphyseal fractures), but it is less well appreciated that the calvarial contents also can be injured, indeed, it has been suggested that as the head bobbles back and forth, subdural hematomas can result (5). In addition, violent shaking can lead to retinal hemorrhages (3,13,14) and spinal injury (8,15). In some cases, frank dislocations of the spine occur, while in others, hyperflexion of the spine leads to compression fractures and/or anterior notching (Fig. 9).

Squeezing Injuries

Squeezing of the infant usually involves the thorax, and rib fractures are the result. These fractures occur at points of maximal stress (i.e., posteriorly, laterally, and anteriorly at the costochondral junctions), and in addition, they often are bilateral (Fig. 10). Indeed, in the end, it is the bilaterality that makes them most significant. Underlying intrathoracic visceral injury also can result from severe squeezing.

Multiplicity of Fractures

A classic feature of the battered-child syndrome is "multiple fractures at different stages of healing." However, there are those infants in whom only one fracture is seen, but this point notwithstanding, multiplicity of injuries and fractures appearing in different stages of healing, still are the most suggestive radiographic features of the battered-child syndrome.

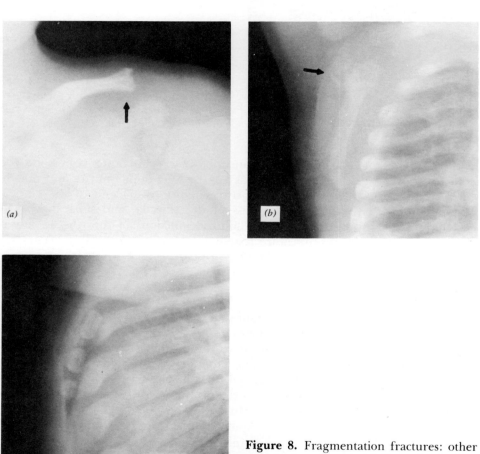

Figure 8. Fragmentation fractures: other than in long bones. (*a*) Note the healing fragmentation fracture of the distal clavicle (arrow). (*b*) Note irregular fragmentation of the acromial process of the scapula (arrow). (*c*) Note extreme cupping and flaring of the rib ends. This is typical of the healing phase of a costochondral separation.

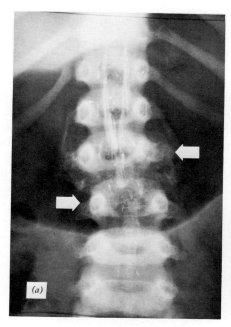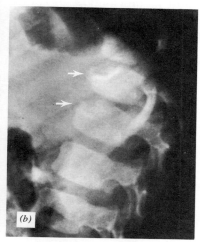

Figure 9. Battered-child syndrome: spine trauma. (*a*) Note abundant callus formation and calcified hematoma around the dislocated lumbar spine (arrows). (*b*) Another infant demonstrating notch defects (arrows) and associated intervertebral disc space narrowing. The notches result from hyperflexion of the spine and may or may not be associated with extrusion of the nucleus pulposus anteriorly. This latter problem results in the disc space narrowing.

Miscellaneous Injuries

The foregoing mechanisms of injury and the resulting fractures are the usual ones encountered in the battered-child syndrome. Occasionally, however, tendon avulsions, periosteal avulsions, and other bizarre injuries can be encountered (Fig. 11). In addition, in older children, multiple injuries to the small bones of the hands can be seen (Fig. 1*b*), and of course, ordinary cortical buckle or torus fractures of the extremities also can be seen in the battered-child syndrome. Finally, it might be noted that any injury that can occur accidentally also may be the result of intentional trauma.

DATING THE FRACTURE

Dating a fracture is most important, for in this way, important discrepancies between historical data and that yielded by the radiographic appearance of the fracture may be detected. Furthermore, many times fractures in different stages of healing are seen, and this being the case, multiple episodes of injury can be documented. In these cases, it is of the utmost importance to determine just when the different injuries occurred, but while it is relatively easy to date a fracture in its early stages, it is more difficult later on.

In dating a fracture, look for: (*1*) soft tissue changes, (*2*) visibility of a fracture line, (*3*) calcification of callus, and (*4*) ossification of newly laid periosteal bone. Soft tissue changes, of course, occur early and consist of edema and/or fluid-blood accumulations in the joint space. Immediately after a fracture, blood and exudate pour out between the ends of the broken bone, and as this involves the soft tissues, edema and swelling result. After 4 or 5 days, granulation tissue forms at the fracture site and then osteoblasts from the adjacent bone form osteoid. This osteoid forms callus, and the callus is the natural splint for the fracture. Calcification of the callus does not occur for about 10 to 14 days after injury, and consequently, in the early stages, it is invisible roentgenograph-

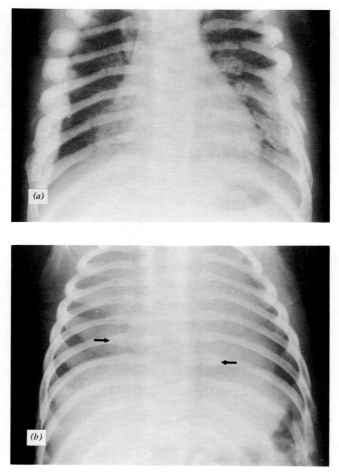

Figure 10. Rib fractures. (*a*) An infant demonstrating numerous fresh and healing rib fractures. (*b*) Old healed posterior rib fractures produce bulbous expansion of the posterior ribs (arrows). This patient also has expansion of the costochondral junctions, best seen on the lower right and fresh fractures in the lower left. Also see Figure 2*c*.

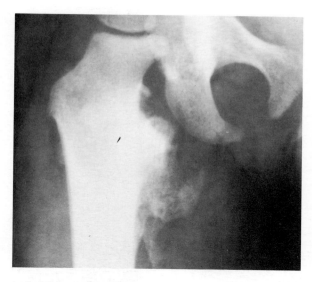

Figure 11. Battered-child syndrome: miscellaneous injury. Note abundant callus formation secondary to avulsion of the iliopsoas muscle from the lesser trochanter.

ically. At about 10 to 14 days, faint, hazy calcification occurs, but astute inspection is required for its identification. Later, calcification becomes more profound, and in some cases, is very exuberant.

In most instances, a fracture line is visible, but it should be noted that in some cases, a clear-cut fracture line never is seen. In these cases, the fracture is hairline, and even during healing, often remains invisible. On the other hand, in some cases, and in all instances where a fracture line is visible initially, bone resorption along the fracture line edges occurs within a few days and enhances its visualization. With epiphyseal-metaphyseal fractures, since the fracture line occurs through the growth plate (physis), bone resorption occurs along the adjacent epiphyseal and metaphyseal edges. The resulting picture can be quite bizarre with alternating radiolucent and radiodense areas visible. Generally, a fracture line in the shaft of a long bone remains visible from 4 to 8 weeks.

The last feature of fracture healing to be evaluated is periosteal new bone deposition. With any fracture, bleeding under the periosteum causes its elevation and displacement away from the cortex. However, there is no roentgenographic evidence that this has occurred until 10 to 14 days has passed. It is at this point that osteoblasts from the deep layer of the periosteum deposit a strip of new bone, just under the elevated periosteum, and parallel to the old cortex. Progressively, this stripe of new bone becomes thicker, and eventually fuses with the old cortex.

Zero to 10 Days

Calcified callus and periosteal new bone deposition are not seen for at least 10 days after the injury. Depending on just how recent the injury is, soft tissue

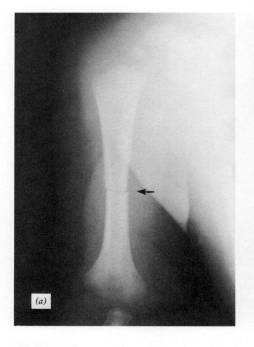

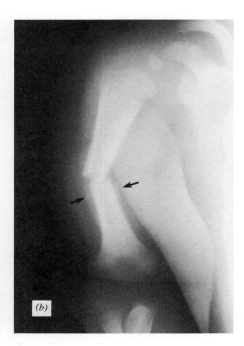

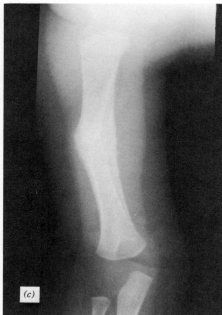

Figure 12. Transverse fracture: healing stages. (*a*) *At 2 to 3 days.* Note the fresh transverse humeral fracture (arrow). (*b*) At *12 days*, early periosteal new bone deposition is seen (arrows). (*c*) At *6 weeks.* Note that periosteal new bone is extensive, callus formation is marked, and that the fracture line has almost disappeared. However, a radiolucent space between the periosteal new bone and the old cortex still exists.

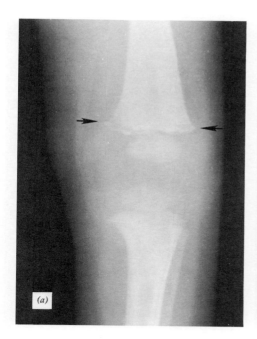

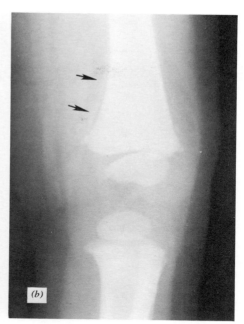

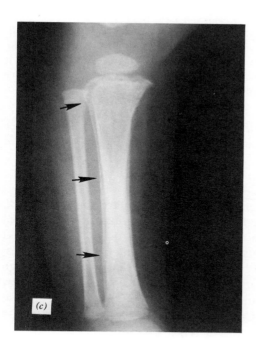

Figure 13. Epiphyseal-metaphyseal fractures: stages of healing. (*a*) *Fresh fracture— under 10 days.* Note rarefaction of the bone underneath the epiphyseal plate. For other early injuries, see Figures. 5 and 6. (*b*) *Ten days to 2 weeks.* Note early periosteal new bone deposition (arrows). (*c*) *Two to 4 weeks.* Note more pronounced periosteal new bone deposition and epiphyseal-metaphyseal changes (arrows) characteristic of this stage of healing.

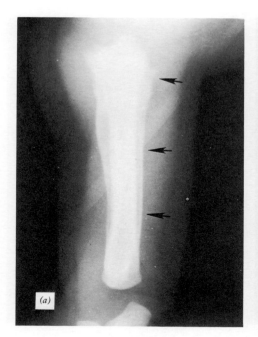 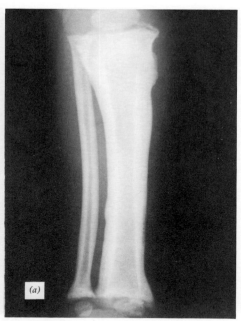

Figure 14. Epiphyseal-metaphyseal fractures: later stages of healing. (*a*) *Four to 8 weeks.* Note the more mature appearance of the periosteal new bone (arrows). The space between it and the cortex is disappearing slowly and changes around the epiphyseal-metaphyseal junction are maturing. (*b*) *Twelve weeks and over.* With more maturation, the periosteal new bone becomes thicker and the space between it and the old cortex is obliterated. The new cortex now appears grossly thickened and uneven. The entire bone (tibia) is involved and the overall contour is somewhat lumpy.

edema may be extensive (Fig. 5). Overall, however, between 0 and 10 days after injury, roentgenographic signs of bone healing are absent (Figs. 5, 12, 13).

Ten Days to 8 Weeks

After 10 to 14 days, periosteal new bone deposition becomes evident (Figs. 12, 13), and resorption of bone along the fracture line, or epiphyseal-metaphyseal junction occurs (Figs. 12, 13). At the same time, callus formation can be detected as faint, hazy calcification of the callus. With epiphyseal-metaphyseal injuries, avulsed metaphyseal fragments often become more clearly visible at this stage (Figs. 5, 6, 12), and toward the end of the 8-week period, the periosteal new bone stripe becomes even thicker. However, it still remains separate from the cortex of the bone. In the meantime, callus calcification progresses and in some cases becomes quite exuberant and flocculent (Figs. 12, 13).

Over 8 Weeks

The periosteal new bone stripe becomes even thicker after 8 weeks, and with time, more closely apposed to the shaft of the bone (Fig. 14). Eventually, it

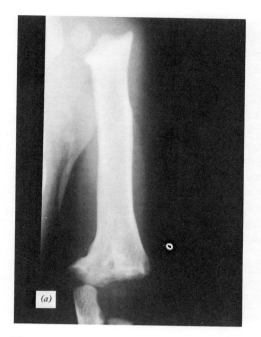 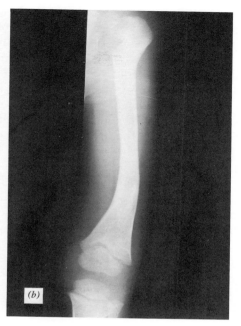

Figure 15. Old deformities. (*a*) Note the lumpy, markedly deformed humerus. Both metaphyseal regions are quite irregular and reflect the aftermath of old epiphyseal-metaphyseal injuries. Irregularity of the shaft is due to old periosteal new bone deposition. (*b*) Another patient demonstrating bowing deformities, epiphyseal-metaphyseal growth disturbances resulting in tilting of the upper tibial epiphyseal-metaphyseal junction and scalloping abnormalities of both the distal and proximal femoral metaphyses. Also note the irregular cortex of the femur.

blends completely with the old cortex, and at the same time, any callus present begins to remodel and become incorporated into the shaft of the long bone. Fracture lines previously visible tend to become obliterated, and eventually, there may be nothing more than subtle bumps along the bones at the site of old callus formation, areas of thickened cortex where periosteal new bone had been deposited, or residual bending deformities and epiphyseal-metaphyseal growth disturbances (Fig. 15).

DIFFERENTIAL DIAGNOSIS

Often the appearance of the healing epiphyseal-metaphyseal fractures in the battered-child syndrome causes consideration of some underlying hematologic, metabolic, or dysplastic bone disorder (Fig. 7). For the most part, however, these possibilities can be discounted when it is recalled that in most cases, the bones of a battered child are normal in contour and "healthy appearing," except for the fact that they are fractured. In other words, there is no evidence of bone destruction, dysplasia, or modeling error. If fracturing is due to some underlying pathologic condition of the bones, such changes usually are present

(Fig. 16). In some battered infants, however, demineralization of the bones can occur (i.e., a few of these infants also are neglected and malnourished), but usually the bones are relatively well mineralized.

Epiphyseal-metaphyseal fractures, virtually indistinguishable from those seen in the battered-child syndrome, commonly occur in the newborn infant (Fig. 17). They are most likely to be seen with breech deliveries and to the unwary, can pose a significant problem. However, as an aid to this dilemma, it has been stated that if an infant, 11 days or older, demonstrates a fracture that shows no signs of healing, the injury should be considered one sustained after birth (16). The reason for this is that fractures sustained during delivery usually show periosteal new bone deposition and callus formation by 7 to 11 days (16).

In older children, epiphyseal-metaphyseal fractures similar to those encountered in the battered-child syndrome can be seen in the congenital insensitivity to pain syndrome (a very rare disease), and in infants with underlying neurogenic or muscular disease. Patients with congenital insensitivity to pain

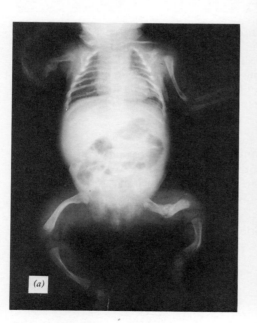
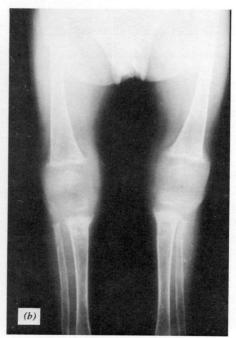

Figure 16. Differential diagnosis of battered-child syndrome. (*a*) Osteogenesis imperfecta. Note numerous fractures and bending deformities of the long bones. Also note the dysplastic appearing, thin ribs showing numerous fractures. Clearly the fractures are secondary to some generalized bony abnormality. (*b*) Epiphyseal-metaphyseal changes in this infant might be misinterpreted for those of a battered child. However, note that the bones are extensively demineralized, the cortices quite poorly formed, and the epiphyses very shaggy around their periphery. This patient had severe rickets.

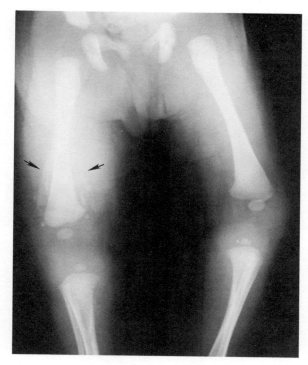

Figure 17. Birth injuries mimicking battered-child injuries. Note extensive periosteal new bone deposition (arrows) secondary to an epiphyseal-metaphyseal fracture. Note the bony fragments in the distal femur. This was a breech-delivered infant.

may be difficult to differentiate from those truly battered, but the problem in children with underlying neuromuscular or neurogenic disease is not so difficult.

FAILURE-TO-THRIVE OR DEPRIVATIONAL DWARFISM

For the most part, these patients are neglected infants, and are more a problem of failure-to-thrive. In some cases, battering and deprivation occur together, but frequently they occur separately. Deprivational (psychosocial) dwarfs present with short stature, a picture not unlike that seen with hypopituitarism (17–19). Indeed, these infants may suffer a transient lack of growth hormone, but once they are removed from their deprived environment, the deficiency resolves rapidly and brisk growth results. The brain partakes in this vigorous catchup phenomenon; because of this, intracranial pressure increases and a spreading of the calvarial sutures is seen (20–23). Such a spread is easier to see in the young infant, but also occurs in the older child. In the older child, it may take longer to appear. All of these patients also demonstrate a delay in bone age and multiple growth arrest lines (Fig. 18), a finding that serves to differentiate them from patients with true hypopituitarism (24).

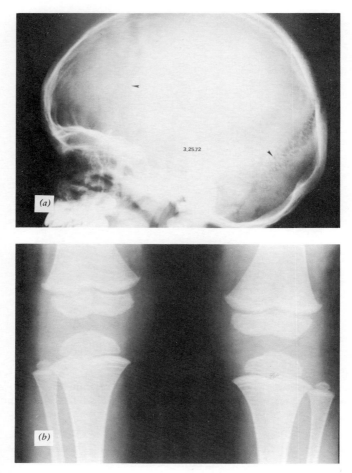

Figure 18. Deprivational or psychosocial dwarfism. (*a*) Skull film demonstrating spreading of sutures. This is due to catch-up growth of the brain. Nine months later the skull was normal. (*b*) Same patient demonstrating numerous growth arrest lines in the distal femurs and proximal tibias.

REFERENCES

1. Caffey J: Multiple fractures in long bones of child suffering from chronic subdural hematoma. *AJR* 56:163, 1946.
2. Caffey J: The parent-infant traumatic stress syndrome (Caffey-Kempe syndrome) (battered babe syndrome). *Am J Roentgenol Rad Ther Nucl Med* 114:217, 1972.
3. Caffey J: The whiplash shaken infant syndrome: manual shaking by the extremities with whiplash-induced intracranial and intraocular bleedings, linked with residual permanent brain damage and mental retardation. *Pediatrics* 54:396, 1974.
4. Kempe CH, Silverman FN, Steel J, et al: Battered child syndrome. *JAMA* 181:17, 1962.
5. Lauer B, Ten Broeck E, Grossman M: Battered child syndrome: review of 130 patients with controls. *Pediatrics* 54:67, 1974.
6. Silverman FN: Unrecognized trauma in infants, the battered child syndrome, and the syndrome of ambroise tardieu. Rigler lecture. *Radiology* 104:337, 1972.

7. Akbarnia B, Torg JS, Kirkpatrick J, et al: Manifestations of the battered child syndrome. *J Bone Jt Surg* 56:1159, 1974.

8. Kogutt MS, Swischuk LE, Fagan CJ: Patterns of injury and significance of uncommon fractures in the battered child syndrome. *AJR* 121:143, 1974.

9. O'Neill JA Jr, Meacham W, Griffin P, et al: Patterns of injury in the battered child syndrome. *J Trauma* 13:332, 1973.

10. Ellison PH, Tsai FY, Largent JA: Computed tomography in child abuse and cerebral contusion. *Pediatrics* 62:151, 1978.

11. Zimmerman RA, Bilaniuk LT, Bruce D, et al: Computed tomography of craniocerebral injury in the abused child. *Radiology* 130:687, 1979.

12. Hayden CK Jr, Swischuk LE: Para-articular soft tissue changes in infections and trauma of the lower extremity in children. *AJR* 134:307, 1980.

13. Mushin AS: Ocular damage in the battered baby syndrome. *Br Med J* 3:403, 1971.

14. Tomasi LG, Rosman NP: Purtscher's retinopathy in the battered child syndrome. *Am J Dis Child* 129:1335, 1975.

15. Swischuk LE: Spine and spinal cord trauma in the battered child syndrome. *Radiology* 92:733, 1969.

16. Cumming WA: Neonatal skeletal fractures: birth trauma or child abuse? *J Can Assoc Radiol* 30:30, 1979.

17. Money J: The syndrome of abuse dwarfism (psychosocial dwarfism or reversible hyposomatotropism). *Am J Dis Child* 131:508, 1977.

18. Powell GF, Brasel JA, Blizzard RM: Emotional deprivation and growth retardation simulating idiopathic hypopituitarism. I. Clinical evaluation of the syndrome. *N Engl J Med* 276:1271, 1967.

19. Silver HK, Finkelstein M: Deprivation dwarfism. *J Pediatr* 70:317, 1967.

20. Afshani E, Osman M, Girdany BR: Widening of cranial sutures in children with deprivation dwarfism. *Radiology* 109:141, 1973.

21. Capitanio MA, Kirkpatrick JA: Widening of the cranial sutures. A roetngen observation during periods of accelerated growth in patients treated for deprivation dwarfism. *Radiology* 92:53, 1969.

22. De Levie M, Nogrady MB: Rapid brain growth upon restoration of adequate nutrition causing false radiologic evidence of increased intracranial pressure. *J Pediatr* 76:523, 1970.

23. Gloebl HJ, Capitano MA, Kirkpatrick JA: Radiographic findings in children with psychosocial dwarfism. *Pediatr Radiol* 4:83, 1976.

24. Hernandez RJ, Poznanski AK, Hopwood NJ, et al: Incidence of growth lines in psychosocial dwarfs and idiopathic hypopituitarism. *AJR* 131:477, 1978.

15
Radiology of Internal Injuries

Jerald P. Kuhn

SPECTRUM OF INJURIES

Internal injuries were not originally recognized as part of the spectrum of child abuse, but since the descriptions in the 1960s by McCort (1) and Eisenstein (2) there has been increased recognition of the frequency and severity of visceral injury as important manifestations of the child abuse syndrome.

Gastrointestinal Tract and Mesentery

Touloukian (3) and Gornall (4) have emphasized the high frequency of central upper intestinal injuries caused by application of a shearing force occurring when a child is hit in the abdomen and a fixed loop of bowel is compressed between the abdominal wall and the spine. The most common of these injuries is an intramural hematoma of the duodenum or jejunum, which may present clinically as a silent lesion or with a myriad of abdominal signs (5,6). The loop of bowel may perforate either intraperitoneally or retroperitoneally. In older children these injuries may be accidental from direct trauma such as a blow against the handlebar of a bicycle; but when they occur in children under the age of 3, they should be viewed with great suspicion as having been inflicted by another person. Chylous ascites is another complication of mesenteric injury, which has been reported as a late sequellae (7).

Damage to other hollow organs is less common although gastric perforation has been reported (8). Rarely perforation of the colon has been seen either secondary to violent external trauma or in one case secondary to the administration of a lye enema.

Pancreas and Biliary Tree

Trauma is the most common cause of pancreatitis in children; it often accompanies duodenal injury (9,10,11). Pancreatitis may be complicated by the development of bone necrosis, ascites, extrapancreatic fluid collections, or pseudocysts of the pancreas (12,13). Pena (14) reported 13 children with pancreatic trauma, nine of whom developed pseudocysts. Three children all under the age of 3 were battered. Slovis (15) reported three battered children with pancreatic pseudocysts diagnosed by ultrasound. Jaundice can occur from pancreatitis or from direct injury to the hepatobiliary tree, and rupture of the common bile duct as well as rupture of the left hepatic duct have been reported (16).

Liver

The liver is frequently injured in battered children, and the mortality of hepatic injury is high. Camps (17) reported 19 liver injuries in 100 fatally battered children; Touloukian (18) had one fatality in five cases; McCort (1) and Gornall (4) each had two cases with one fatal injury. Simpson (19) reported two fatal cases and, in a study of 32 children with liver trauma of all types, Suson (20) found four cases due to battering, one of which was fatal. The liver has also been injured by direct needle perforation (21).

Kidney and Spleen

In the 100 fatal injuries studied by Camps (17), six renal and three splenic injuries were noted. Although these injuries are frequent in other forms of blunt abdominal trauma, they seem to be less common than intestinal injuries in battered children (3).

THE ROLE OF RADIOLOGY

Radiology plays two roles in child abuse. The first is to detect a lesion that might not be suspected clinically and to alert the referring physician to the possibility of child abuse. Second, the radiologist may be called on to examine the patient suspected of being injured in an effort to determine accurately the presence and extent of injury that is suspected clinically.

In all radiologic examinations, it is important for the radiologist to have an accurate history and to be aware of pertinent physical findings. Often an appreciation of a discrepancy between the history and the radiologic findings may be the key to suspecting child abuse. Furthermore, with the multiple imaging procedures that are now available, consultation with the radiologist is mandatory for the clinician to determine which studies will be most efficacious.

SELECTION OF THE RADIOLOGIC EXAMINATION

Usually, plain films are done first and serve as screening tests to direct further investigations. Diagnostic clues seen in the skeletal radiographs which might be indicative of child abuse are presented in the chapter on radiology of the skeletal system. Significant findings in plain films of the chest and abdomen are discussed in the section on radiologic assessment of organ injury in this chapter.

Conventional noninvasive contrast studies of the gastrointestinal and genitourinary tracts are indicated in investigation of suspected injury to these organs.

Angiography is considered to be an invasive diagnostic technique and is now generally reserved for assessment of damage to the vascular tree. Study of the vascular anatomy gives a significant amount of indirect information about an injured organ but much of this information can also be gained from radionuclide scanning, computed tomography (CT), and ultrasound studies that are less expensive and less invasive.

Noninvasive Techniques

Radionuclide Scanning

Radionuclide imaging techniques require an intravenous injection of a small amount of a radioactively tagged pharmaceutical. The half-life of the radioactive material is short and the amount of radiation to which the patient is exposed is generally equal to or less than that used in conventional radiographic contrast studies. The organ of interest is imaged on a gamma camera allowing rapid serial images to be made. Blood flow studies are thus possible, and depending on which radiopharmaceutical is used, images of organs are obtained. Anatomical resolution is less than with other techniques (Fig. 1), but more physiological information such as blood flow and function of the organ is obtained. The cost is generally higher than that for conventional studies and ultrasound but less than for computerized tomography.

Diagnostic Ultrasound

Diagnostic ultrasound has come into extensive use since 1970. Using a highly focused sound beam rather than ionizing or x-radiation, rapid distinction can

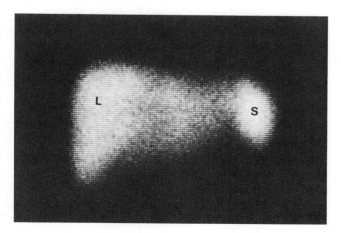

Figure 1. Radionuclide scan of the liver and spleen shows the liver (L) and the spleen (S) as areas accumulating radioisotope. The thinner area of the left lobe over the spine shows less radioactive uptake than does the larger right lobe of the liver.

be made between cystic and solid structures. Cystic structures are acoustically homogeneous and produce no internal echoes and therefore appear on an ultrasound study as clear or sonolucent areas. Solid structures have variable patterns of internal echoes (Fig. 2). The ultrasound study produces a picture of a section of tissue depending on which way the transducer is moved; therefore, the radiologist may produce a transverse (axial) or longitudinal tissue section. Virtually any plane of view is possible.

This tomographic capability is a drawback as well as an advantage because the abdomen is not imaged as a whole. Ultrasound is limited further because the sound beam does not pass through gas or bony structures; therefore, some areas of the body are difficult or impossible to image clearly. The technique is highly dependent on the skill of the examiner but equipment costs are less than for computed tomography or radionuclide scanning.

Computed Tomography

Computed tomography (CT) is the newest and most powerful imaging tool available to the diagnostic radiologist. A highly focused x-ray beam is passed through the patient from multiple points and detected by a series of sensors arranged in a circle around the patient. The computer analyzes the relative densities from each sensor and constructs an axial tomographic section of startling clarity (Fig. 3a,b). The significance of this tool is just becoming known, but its inventors were awarded the Nobel Prize in Medicine in 1979, indicating its already great contribution to medical diagnosis.

Computed tomography has proven to be of clinical value in children with a variety of abdominal abnormalities. Using computed tomography, medical personnel are better able to define the normal and pathologic anatomy in a three-dimensional perspective and thus establish diagnoses not previously possible.

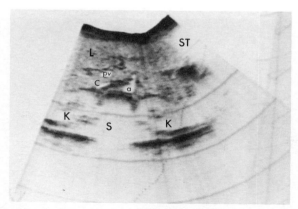

Figure 2. Ultrasound study of the normal liver shows the spine (S) flanked by the two kidneys (K). Vascular structures are sonolucent. Seen in this section are the aorta (A), vena cava (C), and portal vein (PV). Note that the liver (L) has a different textural pattern from the normal kidneys. Note also that on this section, which shows the central portion of the liver clearly, the peripheral portions are not well seen due to the tomographic nature of the ultrasound study. The stomach (ST) is indicated.

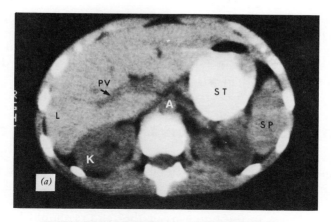

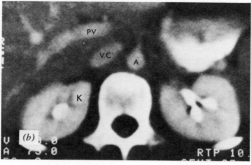

Figure 3. (*a*) CT section of normal liver, noncontrast enhanced. Opaque media is seen in the stomach (ST). Note that the bony structure of the spine is better seen than on the ultrasound study. The kidneys (K) are clearly seen on either side of the spine. The liver (L) is denser than the kidneys and the vascular structures aorta (A) and portal vein (PV). Spleen (SP) is indicated. (*b*) Magnified view of the same area after injection of contrast material shows more clearly the vascular structures. Vena cava (VC) is now visible. The kidneys (K) have enhanced to a greater degree than has the normal liver tissue so that they now appear whiter than the liver.

Using computed tomography it is possible to measure tissue densities. Water density fluid can be distinguished from fresh blood, and these, in turn, can be separated from solid organs. Areas of hemorrhage in organs can be detected.

Despite its many advantages, computed tomography has significant limitations. As in all imaging techniques except diagnostic ultrasound, ionizing radiation is necessary. In general, the radiation from computed tomography is not much greater than that of conventional examinations. Furthermore, the exposure in CT examinations is sharply limited to the area examined so that there is less scattered radiation to critical organs such as the thyroid, the lens, and the gonads. Further limitations of CT include the fact that the examination is generally limited to the axial view, making evaluation of longitudinal structures such as the vena cáva or the ureters somewhat difficult. Thin structures such as the diaphragm that are parallel to the axial plane are not as well imaged as they would be in the longitudinal plane. Artifacts may be produced from high density structures, particularly if there is motion. There are also limitations that are imposed by the nature of pediatric patient himself. The most important of these limitations is the small size of the structures examined and the fact that many of the structures are not surrounded by body fat, making delineation of anatomy less satisfactory than it is in the adult patient.

CONVENTIONAL RADIOGRAPHIC FINDINGS IN ABDOMINAL TRAUMA

Plain film evaluation for abdominal injury should include a frontal chest radiograph and supine, left lateral decubitus, and cross-table lateral views of the abdomen. Thin, poorly developed soft tissues may be noted in a neglected or abused child. A large food- and fluid-filled stomach may also be seen (22). Metaphyseal fractures in the humerus or the femurs should be searched for. Careful observation of soft tissue detail can permit the diagnosis of a fatty liver occurring in a child suffering from nutritional neglect. The radiographic findings of fatty liver have been summarized by Yousefazdeh (23). This diagnosis is possible because the abnormal liver is more radiolucent than normal liver tissue because of an increased amount of fat. If enough fatty replacement occurs, this change in density becomes visible even on a plain radiograph. If the suspicion of a fatty liver is raised on a plain radiographic study, the diagnosis can be confirmed by a CT scan where the liver density can be accurately measured (Fig. 4).

The findings of abdominal trauma on plain radiographic examination are limited by being nonspecific but, none the less, should be carefully searched for as they may provide the first clue to a serious injury. Pneumoperitoneum strongly suggests a perforated viscus. Free intraperitoneal air can be best appreciated subdiaphragmatically on an upright chest radiograph or in the left lateral decubitus position. More subtle findings are those of the central radiolucency outlining the falciform ligament as seen on the supine radiographs (Fig. 5).

Free fluid in the peritoneal cavity is harder to appreciate than is free air, and the radiographic findings are less well known. Classic obvious findings include central displacement of bowel loops separated by fluid and bulging flanks. This

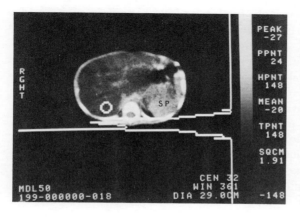

Figure 4. CT scan showing a fatty liver. The cursor is placed over the posterior portion of the right lobe of the liver and has measured the mean density of the liver at −27 Hounsfield units, indicating its fatty nature. Note that the liver is blacker (more radiolucent) than it normally is. The vessels are seen in this non-enhanced study as areas of increased density in the liver because of the low density of the fatty liver.

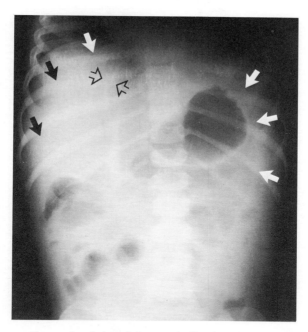

Figure 5. Supine radiograph of the abdomen indicating free intraperitoneal air. The air has accumulated anteriorly in this supine film; its interfaces outlined by the arrows are seen laterally. The two central open arrows outline air on either side of the falciform ligament that is seen as a curvilinear white structure.

degree of fluid, however, is usually obvious clinically. Of more importance is the ability of the radiologist to detect smaller amounts of fluid. Jorulf (24) in a monograph on roentgen diagnosis of intraperitoneal fluid suggests that with careful technique it is possible to detect as little as 25 cc of free intraperitoneal fluid. The signs of intraperitoneal and extraperitoneal fluid collections have been tabulated in Whalen's book (25). Those that seem useful in children include: the dog-ear sign in the pelvis, loss of visualization of the inferior angle of the liver, and displacement of the colon medially away from the flank stripe (Fig. 6). These findings should be searched for carefully on the initial radiographic study.

If the plain film study is equivocal for the presence of fluid, the examination may be supplemented by either ultrasound or CT scan to establish a firm diagnosis of the presence or absence of fluid.

A mass can be suspected on plain film examination if normal gas shadows are disturbed, displaced, or effaced. Studies to be done after a mass is detected might include contrast studies of the gastrointestinal or genitourinary tracts, computed tomography, or ultrasound. A mass associated with a partial or complete small bowel obstruction should lead to suspicion of an intramural hematoma of the bowel. Pancreatic pseudocysts may also present as masses related to trauma but are often appreciated only after opacification of the bowel or after performing CT or ultrasound tests.

The findings of bowel obstruction are well known, but in the context of child

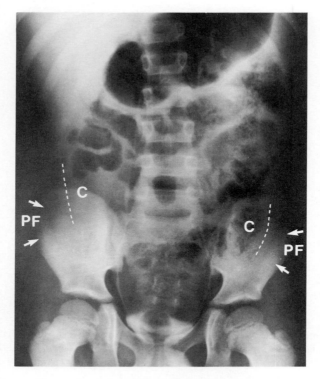

Figure 6. Supine radiograph of the abdomen showing free intraperitoneal fluid. The peritoneal fat or flank stripe is outlined bilaterally on both sides (PF). The colon (C) is displaced medially from its normal position immediately next to the peritoneal fat. This indicates the presence of fluid in the paracolic rescesses.

abuse, a bowel obstruction should raise a possibility of an intramural hematoma or severe mesenteric injury.

RADIOLOGIC ASSESSMENT OF SPECIFIC INJURY

In the past, radiology has been of limited value after the plain film examination and many children have been subjected to exploratory laparatomy solely to determine the presence and extent of injury. With the advent of nuclear medicine, angiography, and especially computed tomography and ultrasound, exploratory surgery may be avoided in many cases because radiologic techniques are now capable of detecting extent of injury to most abdominal organs using noninvasive procedures.

Gastrointestinal Injury

Gastric perforation resulting from child abuse has been reported (8). Pneumoperitoneum can result. It is thought that this injury most likely occurs when the child is struck after recently eating when the stomach is still distended.

Pneumoperitoneum is an indication for surgery, but if desired by the surgeon, water-soluble contrast material can be administered orally to localize the perforation, which usually occurs on the anterior gastric wall.

Far more common in abused children is duodenal injury, either with or without associated pancreatic injury. The duodenum may either be compressed against the vertebral column or sheared, resulting in tearing of the rich submucosal and subserosal vascular plexus within the duodenal wall. The hematoma thus formed may gradually increase in size due to breakdown of hemoglobin in the clot that produces an increase is osmotic pressure and, therefore, an accumulation of fluid (26). This may either partly or completely obstruct the duodenum, block the common bile duct, or block the common pancreatic duct. Severe damage to the mesentery ranging from hematoma to avulsion can occur with a blow to the midabdomen.

Plain radiographic findings may show partial or complete obstruction of the duodenum usually in the proximal portion (Fig. 7). Occasionally, the hematoma may be large enough to appear as a mass, especially if it involves the jejunum or mesentery (Fig. 8). Other findings as described with pancreatic injury may be present. Contrast examination can provide a definite diagnosis. A water-soluble contrast agent should be used first if perforation is suspected clinically or radiologically or if a CT examination is to follow. The classic roentgen appearance of intramural hematoma was first described by Felson (27) and includes a coil-spring mucosal appearance, an intramural mass, and duodenal obstruction (Fig. 9).

Ultrasound can be used to follow the size of the hematoma especially if there is a mesenteric component (28). The ultrasonic appearance of the hematoma

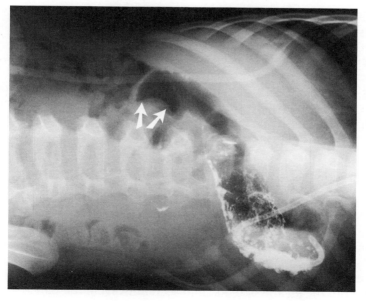

Figure 7. Decubitus abdominal radiograph showing duodenal dilatation and a small mass (arrows) extending into the lumen of the duodenum.

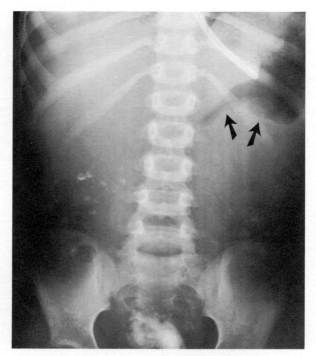

Figure 8. Gasless abdomen with a mass (arrows) extending into the antral region of the stomach in this patient who had a large jejunal hematoma.

depends on the age of the injury (Fig. 10). Usually, a cystic or sonolucent lesion due to fresh, unclotted, or homogeneously clotted blood can be seen. Once lysis and fragmentation of the clot occur, the mass becomes more complex and fluid-fluid levels and septa may be seen (28).

Ultrasound can also aid in the evaluation of associated pancreatic injury (15).

CT will also detect mesenteric hematomas with the appearance of the lesion depending on the age of the injury and the density of the surrounding structures. Fresh blood may appear either as increased or decreased density depending on the density of the viscera surrounding it. As the hematoma ages, its relative density diminishes.

Pancreatic Injuries

Pancreatic injuries often escape early detection in children. Some children are subjected to surgery for other conditions before the correct diagnosis is made (9). Abdominal pain, bilious vomiting, signs of inflammation, and increased serum amylase are usually present. Trauma is the most common cause of pancreatitis in early childhood. Pancreatitis may be complicated by sepsis, shock, and late development of pseudocysts. Pseudocysts are masses of necrotic tissue that result from the escape of blood and secretions from the pancreas dissecting into the lesser sac, peritoneum or retroperitoneum, or even, on occasion, into the mediastinum (29). Plain film examination can lead the radiologist to suspect

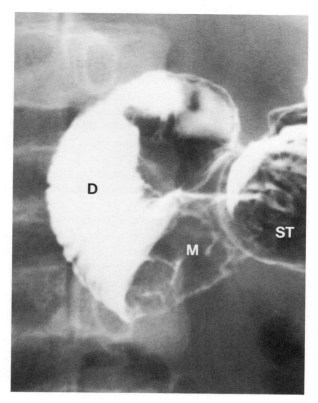

Figure 9. Spot radiograph from an upper gastrointestinal series. The duodenum (D) is dilated. There is a typical filling defect from a duodenal hematoma presenting as a mass (M) causing duodenal obstruction.

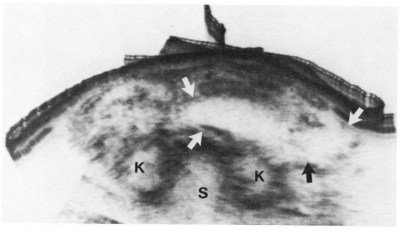

Figure 10. Ultrasound of mesenteric hematoma. The hematoma is outlined as a sonolucent (white) area anterior to the left kidney and extending across the midline.

a diagnosis of either pancreatitis or pseudocyst formation. Twenty-percent of patients are said to present with a pleural effusion (30). Localized ileus, often in the form of a dilated duodenum and the "colon cut-off sign," are highly suggestive signs of pancreatitis (12). Free intraperitoneal fluid may be present. There may be an increased space between the stomach and transverse colon.

Contrast studies of the upper gastrointestinal tract are useful for evaluation of the indirect signs of pancreatitis or associated duodenal injury. The following signs of pancreaticoduodenal injury have been described (12): (1) coarsened duodenal mucosa; (2) localized paralytic ileus with cut-off of opaque material; (3) intramural duodenal mass; (4) widening of the duodenal loop; (5) reversed "3" sign of Forstburg; (6) mass impinging on the stomach or bowel; and (7) rupture of the duodenum or jejunum with contrast leakage or pneumoperitoneum.

Ultrasound and computed tomography are now important modalities to visualize the normal and abnormal pancreas. Ultrasound is especially suitable in the young pediatric patient without much body fat. Despite the superb studies sometimes obtained, however, often in the injured patient the localized ileus hampers a complete examination. A common approach is to use ultrasound first, because of the lack of radiation. If a complete evaluation is not possible, CT is then performed. After opacification of the small bowel with dilute gastrografin and intravenous injection of contrast material, computed tomography can usually offer complete evaluation of all organs. In addition to the pancreas, the liver, spleen, and kidneys can be studied to rule out injury to these structures. Extrapancreatic fluid collections are easily recognized as is minimal dilatation of either the intrahepatic or extrahepatic biliary tree (Fig. 11). Formation and evolution of pseudocysts can be assessed. Surgery can be reserved for the child with appropriate clinical signs rather than being performed only to exclude serious hidden injury.

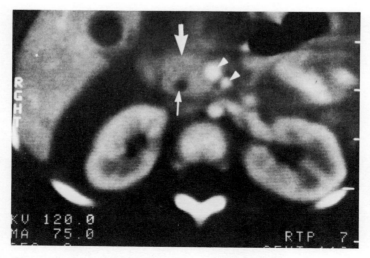

Figure 11. CT scan outlines a dilated common bile duct (small arrow). The head of the pancreas is indicated by the large arrow and small arrowheads point to the superior mesenteric artery and vein. Note the fluid collection indicating extrapancreatic fluid between the liver and the kidney (dark area).

Liver Injuries

Plain radiographic examination is limited to detecting gross alterations in the liver size and shape. Detection of blood in the peritoneal cavity is possible as described, and this finding should raise the possibility of liver injury. Radionuclide imaging of the liver is a reliable method of detecting intrahepatic trauma (31) but is limited by being relatively organ-specific (no information is gained about other intra-abdominal organs except the liver and spleen), by having relatively poor anatomical definition, and by being unable to detect intraperitoneal blood.

Ultrasound has been used to detect intrahepatic hematomas, but this examination is highly examiner dependent, may be difficult to perform in an acutely uncomfortable child, and is significantly interfered with by bones and gas, making complete evaluation of the organ difficult. Ultrasound is especially well suited to following the progress of a known liver injury rather than making initial evaluation.

CT is the best available technique for study of serious liver trauma (Fig. 12a,b). The advantages of CT include exquisite anatomical detail, organ specificity, lack of need for transducer contact, and ability to detect intraperitoneal bleeding. Bones and gas do not interfere with the CT image. Access to body scanners with a short scan time is currently limited but this situation should improve with passage of time.

On computed tomography, liver hematomas and lacerations are seen as low-density areas in the liver but are better visualized after a bolus injection of intravenous contrast material of the type used in excretory urography (32). Injury can be accurately assessed, the presence of free blood determined, and appropriate therapy undertaken. If conservative management is feasible, serial scans show progression of healing. Ultrasound may well be used to follow the course of healing as an alternative to CT.

In hospitals where CT is available, angiography plays little role in the evaluation of liver trauma unless there is an associated tumor, vascular malformation, or severe bleeding. Occasionally, if a partial hepatic resection is contemplated by the surgeon, he may desire a preoperative angiogram.

Splenic Injuries

Splenic injuries are considerably less common in child abuse than in other forms of blunt abdominal trauma (33). Plain film diagnosis is neither specific nor sensitive, but rib fractures, pneumothorax, elevation of the left hemidiaphragm, enlargement of the spleen shadow, and signs of free intraperitoneal blood should be searched for. As in liver imaging, ultrasound and radionuclide scanning provide noninvasive methods of diagnosis of splenic hematoma with the radionuclide scan being preferred as the spleen can be difficult to image with ultrasound because of its position beneath the ribs. Radionuclide studies have been reported to be both accurate and sensitive for detection of splenic injury (34); contour defects can suggest a diagnosis of splenic laceration or subcapsular hematoma. An accessory spleen can cause a false-positive finding, and multiple views are necessary to decrease the incidence of false negative

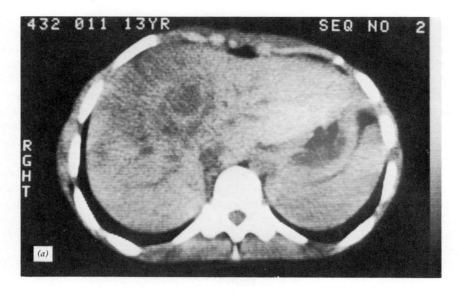

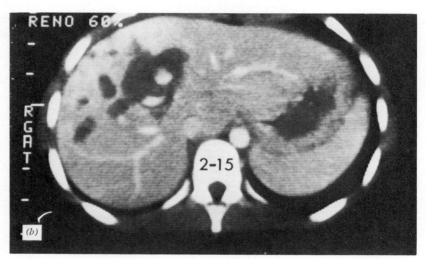

Figure 12. (*a*) Nonenhanced CT liver scan. This 13-year-old girl has a large hepatic hematoma, which is seen as a radiolucent or dark area in the central portion of the liver primarily in the right lobe. (*b*) After contrast enhancement the area of the hematoma is much more dramatically outlined.

examinations. The liver is visualized and liver injuries can be studied at the same time but other organs are not routinely seen by the radionuclide study.

Splenic angiography has been considered the most accurate diagnostic test in splenic trauma (35), but it is time consuming, expensive, and invasive. Computed tomographic imaging shows considerable promise in the evaluation of splenic injury. Five patients with splenic laceration and hemoperitoneum were diagnosed successfully in one recent series (36). Berger and Kuhn (32) have recently reported their experience with successful diagnosis of splenic injury. The patient must be able to suspend respiration momentarily to diminish artifacts from the ribs. An intravenous contrast material injection is necessary, but if a technically good examination is obtained the spleen can be quite accurately evaluated as can its neighboring organs (Fig. 13).

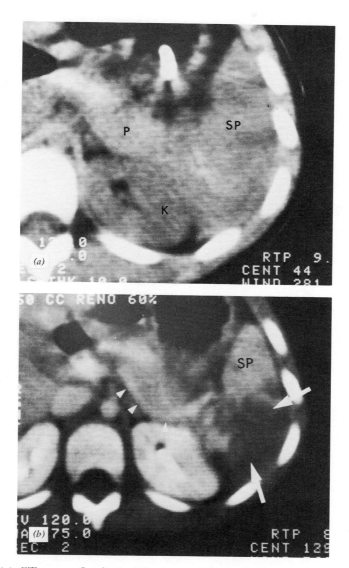

Figure 13. (*a*) CT scan of splenic injury, nonenhanced. The kidney (K), tail of the pancreas (P), and spleen (SP) are clearly seen. The outline of the spleen is poorly seen but it is difficult to say with certainty that there is a splenic injury. (*b*) After injection of contrast material, a low-density area in the posterior portion of the spleen indicating a large intrasplenic hematoma is outlined by the large arrows. Arrowheads indicate the splenic vein.

Renal Injuries

Renal injury as a result of child abuse is not common but may occur following a blow to the back or the abdomen. Discovery of hematuria should prompt radiologic investigation. Plain film findings are nonspecific but may show blurring of the psoas margins or splinting of the vertebral column toward the injured side. Enlargement or blurring of the renal outline may be seen. Fractures of the lower rib cage are a clue to upper abdominal trauma.

The basic radiologic test to assess renal injury is the excretory urogram and the findings of renal trauma have been reviewed by many authors (37–40).

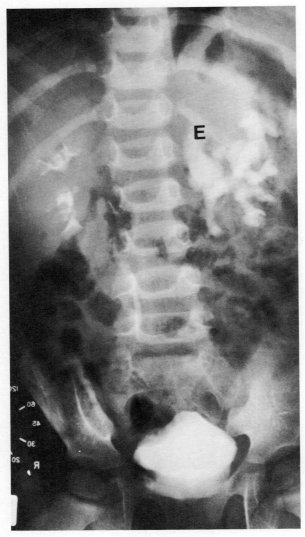

Figure 14. Intravenous urogram in an injured girl. Note the extravasation of contrast material (E) from the upper pole of the kidney, indicating calyceal damage.

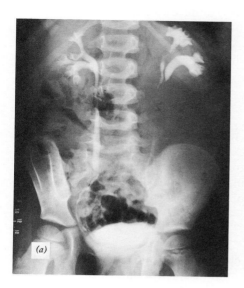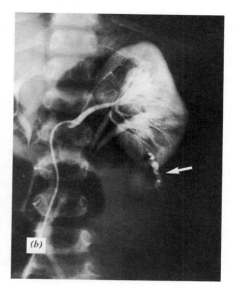

Figure 15. (*a*) Intravenous urogram showing superolateral displacement of the left kidney by a large mass presumably a perirenal hematoma. (*b*) Angiogram performed because of continued bleeding. Selective angiogram shows extravasation of contrast material from a puncture wound in the lower pole of the kidney in this patient who was stabbed with a pair of scissors.

Young (37) in a review of 44 childhood renal injuries divided the radiographic findings and extent of injury into minor, major, and critical categories. *Minor injuries* included contusion and laceration confined to the kidney and were associated with x-ray findings of diminished opacification of the renal parenchyma and pelvocalyceal spasm. He defined *major injuries* as those in which contrast material was seen beyond the renal capsule and/or the pelvocalyceal system (Figs. 14, 15). These radiographic findings were generally associated with a laceration extending into these regions and frequently included a perirenal hematoma. *Critical injuries* may show no radiographic function or markedly diminished opacification. Extravasation of contrast material may or may not be present. Renal angiography is necessary in these cases to delineate possible vascular pedicle damage.

Rarely, the urogram may show a prolonged nephrogram with delayed pelvocalyceal opacification. This can occur in children who have suffered from renal injury, shock, dehydration, and rarely, with myoglobinuria from muscle damage and resultant acute tubular blockage (41,42,43).

Radionuclide scanning, especially when performed with early blood pool imaging, can give valuable information about renal vascularity and damage even though the anatomical detail is less than on the radiographic studies. Ultrasound can be especially useful in diagnosing perirenal collections of blood or urine that are difficult to see on urography or on the radionuclide scan (44). Berger and Kuhn (32) have reported the use of CT scanning in childhood renal injury. They feel that if CT is available, it provides the best assessment of renal injury, the degree of which is usually underestimated on the urogram (Fig. 16). CT documents most accurately the presence and extent of renal injury thereby allowing optimal care to be given. Additionally, CT is not organ-specific, and instances of liver and splenic injury have been seen when it was thought that only the kidneys had been injured.

Other Genitourinary Injuries

Injury to the remainder of the genitourinary tract occurs occasionally in abused children often as a result of sexual abuse. Radiologic investigation is generally not needed in these cases but voiding cystourethrography can assess damage to the bladder and urethra. Using ultrasound, the radiologist can study the uterus and ovaries in children. Contrast studies of the vagina can be done if necessary.

Thoracic Trauma

Radiologic evidence of trauma to the chest most often is manifest by rib fractures, which may occur bilaterally, symmetrically, and posteriorly. Rib fractures can be difficult to see on conventional radiographic studies, and radionuclide scanning may provide a more sensitive means of diagnosing these

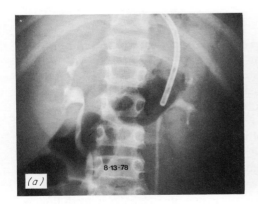

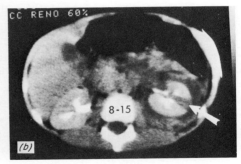

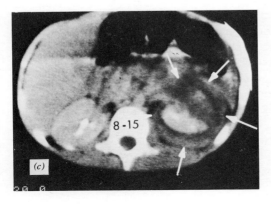

Figure 16. (*a*) IVP showing slight straightening of the left ureter and indistinctness of the upper pole of the left kidney, findings thought to be consistent with minor renal injury. (*b*) CT in the same patient shows a large upper pole laceration seen as a wedge-shaped low-density area (arrow). (*c*) CT at a slightly different level shows the large perirenal hematoma associated with marked renal laceration in this patient whose urogram significantly underestimated the degree of renal injury.

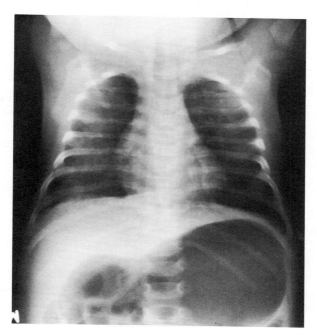

Figure 17. Chest radiograph in an injured infant. Bilateral vague alveolar densities are seen peripherally in both lungs. These are of nonspecific nature and could be pulmonary edema or pneumonia but because of the history of trauma, contusion was suspected.

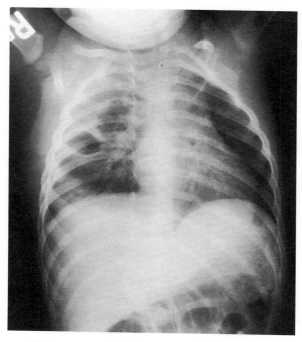

Figure 18. Chest radiograph in a patient with known pulmonary contusion who developed two large pneumatoceles in the traumatized area of the right lung.

lesions (45). Fractures of differing ages, of course, are highly suggestive of child abuse.

Pulmonary contusion can occur from trauma to the chest, but this condition generally presents radiologically as patchy alveolar densities that are difficult to distinguish on a chest x-ray from pneumonia (Fig. 17). The clinical findings may aid in the distinction. Post-traumatic pneumatoceles may develop (Fig. 18). If the trauma is severe enough, pneumothorax, hydrothorax, transsection of the trachea or one of the main stem bronchi, or even extensive cardiac damage may occur. These conditions generally require emergency surgical intervention rather than further radiologic studies.

SUMMARY

The radiologist plays a key role in the evaluation and management of the abused child. It is important that good communication exists between the referring physician and the radiologist both to optimize radiologic interpretation and to direct most appropriately the proper radiologic investigation to assess specific organ injury. The use of the new imaging modalities, radionuclide scanning, ultrasound, and CT scanning, have greatly broadened the ability of the radiologist to establish noninvasively the presence of extensive internal injury.

REFERENCES

1. McCort J, Vaudagna J: Visceral injuries in battered children. *Radiology* 82:424, 1964.
2. Eisenstein EN, Delta BG, Clifford JH: Jejunal hematoma: An unusual manifestation of the battered child syndrome. *Clin Pediatr* 4:436, 1965.
3. Touloukian RJ: Abdominal visceral injuries in battered children. *Pediatrics* 42:642, 1968.
4. Gornall P, Ahmed S, Jolleys A, et al: Intra-abdominal injuries in the battered baby syndrome. *Arch Dis Child* 47:211, 1972.
5. Mahboubi S, Kaufman JH: Intramural duodenal hematoma in children. *Gastrointestinal Radiol* 1:167, 1976.
6. Stewart DR, Byrd C, Schuster SR: Intramural hematomas of the alimentary tract in children. *Surgery* 68:550, 1970.
7. Boysen BE: Chylous ascites: Manifestation of the battered child syndrome. *Am J Dis Child* 129:1138, 1975.
8. Schechner SA, Ehrlich FE: Gastric perforation in child abuse. *J Trauma* 14:723, 1974.
9. Grosfeld JL, Cooney D: Pancreatic and gastrointestinal trauma in children. *Pediatr Clin North Am* 22:365, 1965.
10. Tank ES, Eraklis AJ, Gross RE: Blunt abdominal trauma in infancy and childhood. *J Trauma* 8:439, 1968.
11. Silverman A, Roy CC, Cozzetto F: *Pediatric clinical gastroenterology.* St. Louis, CV Mosby Co, 1971, p 470.
12. Young LW: Pancreatic and/or duodenal injury from blunt trauma in childhood. *Ann Radiol* 18:377, 1975.
13. Slovis TL, Berdon WE, Haller JO, et al: Pancreatitis in the battered child syndrome. *AJR* 125:456, 1975.
14. Pena SDJ, Medovy H: Child abuse and traumatic pseudocyst of the pancreas. *J Pediatr* 83:1026, 1973.

15. Slovis TS, VonBerg VJ, Mikelic V: Sonography in the diagnosis and management of pancreatic pseudocysts and effusions in childhood. *Radiology* 135:153, 1980.

16. Beau A, Prévot J, Mourot M: Rupture tramatique du canal hepatique gauche. *Ann de Chirurgie Infantile* 12:47, 1971.

17. Camps FE: Injuries sustained by children from violence, in FE Camps (ed): *Recent Advances in Forensic Pathology.* London, Churchill Livingstone, 1969, p 129.

18. Touloukian RJ: Abdominal trauma in childhood. *Surg Gynecol Obstet* 127:561, 1968.

19. Simpson K: Battered babies: Conviction for murder. *Br Med J* 1:393, 1965.

20. Suson EM, Klotz D Jr, Kottmeier PK: Liver trauma in children. *J Pediatr Surg* 10:411, 1975.

21. Stone RK, Harewitz A, Sanfilippo JA, et al: Needle perforation of the liver in an abused infant. *Clin Pediatr* 15:958, 1976.

22. Franken EA, Fox M, Smith JA, et al: Acute gastric dilatation in neglected children. *AJR* 130:297, 1978.

23. Yousefazdeh DK, Loupetin A, Jackson JH: The radiographic signs of fatty liver. *Radiology* 131:351, 1979.

24. Jorulf H: Roentgen diagnosis of intraperitoneal fluid. *Acta Radiologica*, suppl 343, Stockholm, 1975, p 85.

25. Whalen JP: *Radiology of the Abdomen: Anatomic Basis.* Philadelphia, Lea & Febiger, 1976.

26. Mahour GH, Woolley MM, Gans SL, et al: Duodenal hematoma in infancy and childhood. *J Pediatr Surg* 6:153, 1971.

27. Felson B, Levin EJ: Intramural hematoma of the duodenum: Diagnostic roentgen sign. *Radiology* 63:823, 1954.

28. Fon GT, Hunter TB, Haber K: Utility of ultrasound for diagnosis of mesenteric hematoma. *AJR* 134:381, 1980.

29. Kirchner SG, Heller RM, Smith CW: Pancreatic pseudocyst of the mediastinum. *Radiology* 123:37, 1977.

30. Warshaw A: Inflammatory masses following acute pancreatitis. *Surg Clin North Amer* 54:621, 1974.

31. Gilday DL, Alderson PO: Scintigraphic evaluation of liver and spleen injury. *Semin Nucl Med* 4:357, 1974.

32. Berger PE, Kuhn JP: Computed tomography in the evaluation of blunt abdominal trauma. *AJR* 136:105, 1981.

33. Touloukian RJ: Battered children with abdominal trauma. *General Practitioner* XL(6):106, 1969.

34. Lutzger L, Loenigsberg M, Meng CH, et al: The role of radionuclide imaging in spleen trauma. *Radiology* 110:419, 1974.

35. Reuter SR, Redman HC: *Gastrointestinal Radiology.* Philadelphia, WB Saunders Co, 1972, p 145.

36. Mall JC, Kaiser JA: CT diagnosis of splenic laceration. *AJR* 134:265, 1980.

37. Young LW, Wood BP, Linke CA: Renal injury from blunt trauma in childhood. *Ann Radiol* 18:359, 1975.

38. Witten DM, Myers GH Jr, Utz DC: *Emmett's Clinical Urography*, ed 4. Philadelphia, WB Saunders Co, 1977, vol. 3, p 1767.

39. Elkin M, Meng CH, DeParedes RG: Roentgenographic evaluation of renal trauma with emphasis on renal angiography. *AJR* 98:1, 1966.

40. MacPherson R, Dexter A: Pediatric renal trauma. *J Can Assoc Radiol* 22:10, 1971.

41. Rubin BE, Schliftman R: The striated nephrogram in renal contusion. *Urol Radiol* 1:119, 1979.

42. Korobkin M: The nephrogram of hemorrhagic hypotension. *AJR* 114:673, 1972.

43. Rosenberg H: Children's Hospital of Philadelphia, Pa. Personal Communication.

44. Kaye CJ, Rosenfield AT, Armm M: Gray scale ultrasonography in the evaluation of renal trauma. *Radiology* 134:461, 1980.

45. Ash JM, Gilday DL: Child abuse syndrome: Nuclear medicine detection of occult bone trauma. Scientific Paper. Presented at meeting of Society for Pediatric Radiology, Salt Lake City, Utah, April 1980.

16
Child Neglect

Barton D. Schmitt

Child neglect can be defined as the adverse consequences of inadequate or negligent parenting. Child neglect is much more common than child abuse. Child neglect is usually unintentional or inadvertent. When neglect is deliberate and very severe, the term deprivation is commonly applied. The types of child neglect discussed in this chapter are medical care neglect, safety neglect, emotional deprivation, educational neglect, and physical neglect. Nutritional neglect is covered in Chapter 11.

MEDICAL CARE NEGLECT

Medical care neglect is the type of neglect most likely to involve physicians. Both medical care neglect and safety neglect carry the potential for a fatal outcome unless intervention is vigorous and timely. Medical care neglect will be discussed as it pertains to serious acute illness, life-threatening chronic illnesses, disabling or handicapping chronic illnesses, fatal illnesses, and well child care.

Serious Acute Illnesses

A court order to hospitalize and treat a child is needed when an emergency exists that the parents will not acknowledge. This situation occurs most often when working with a Jehovah's Witness family who believes infusion of blood products transgresses the laws of God. A court order to treat allows the physician to provide the jaundiced newborn with an exchange transfusion and thereby prevent the long-term complications of kernicterus. Likewise, the life of a bleeding child in shock may be saved. Often these parents seem relieved that the decision has been taken out of their hands with the judicial authority intervening on behalf of their child. Certainly the child's right to live must override the parents' constitutional right to religious freedom. In recent years this same religious problem also has arisen around the need for transfusions in childhood cancer victims. Frankel et al. (1) found that hemoglobin levels as low as 3 g/100 ml could be tolerated in many patients without difficulty, and that the need for transfusions could sometimes be averted.

A court order to treat may also be needed to hospitalize a seriously ill child from any faith. Examples include children with dehydration or possible septicemia. Some parents refuse procedures such as lumbar punctures despite careful explanation. Obviously a child who is febrile and has a bulging fontanelle requires a spinal tap to rule out meningitis. When parents steadfastly refuse to sign a consent form under such circumstances, the court must intervene. Diseases that endanger the public safety also can evoke a court order if the parents refuse treatment. An example of this would be a diphtheria outbreak where the parents of culture-positive children refuse to have their children take antibiotics. Since these refusals are usually based on anxiety rather than anger, a major effort must be directed at identifying and nullifying the parents' specific concern about the procedure, treatment, or hospitalization. For good results, attempts should be made to include both parents in this decision-making process as early as possible.

Life-Threatening Chronic Diseases

Some children with chronic diseases experience frequent exacerbations or even emergencies, because their parents ignore medical recommendations for home treatment. Examples are children with asthma or diabetes mellitus who do not receive their medications in the prescribed fashion. Some children with asthma are brought to the emergency room only when their respiratory distress is so severe that immediate admission to an intensive care unit is required. Other children have serious deterioration in their health because the parents are noncompliant with the treatment program. Examples are children with congenital hypothyroidism who do not grow because they do not receive their thyroid medication or children with phenylketonuria who are not kept on an adequate diet to permit normal mental development. These conditions cry out for intervention. Most juvenile court judges will act on behalf of children who have life-threatening diseases and who are not receiving adequate therapy. Although parents are free to become martyrs themselves, they cannot be permitted to make martyrs of their children. After comprehensive evaluation, some children also will be noted to be emotionally rejected by their parents and foster care is needed.

A recent case illustrates the pitfalls of court-ordered medication for a chronic disorder. The family of a 12-year-old boy with grand mal seizures refused on religious grounds to treat the child. The case was heard by the juvenile court and the family was ordered to administer the anticonvulsants. When surveillance of this family diminished, they abruptly discontinued the medication. The boy went into severe status epilepticus for more than 6 hours without medical care. He sustained a permanent hemiparesis from hypoxic brain damage. Although this case can be analyzed in several ways, clearly drugs with serious withdrawl reactions (namely, anticonvulsants) should not be court-ordered unless the child is in a controlled setting.

Disabling or Handicapping Chronic Diseases

Although courts are somewhat hesitant about intervening on behalf of children with disfiguring or disabling diseases, they usually can be swayed by an appropriate review of the risks and benefits of surgery. Children with congenital glaucoma, cogenital cataracts, and severe strabismus will eventually develop blindness or suppression amblyopia in the involved eye if surgery is not performed. Children with a congenitally dislocated hip will eventually acquire a permanent hip abnormality and limp if treatment is not permitted. Children with certain congenital heart diseases will develop irreversible pulmonary hypertension if corrective surgery is delayed beyond a specific age. Although most parents eventually can be persuaded of the need for surgery in these conditions, those parents who persist in their refusal will need to be taken to court. A much more difficult question relates to parents who refuse physical therapy, occupational therapy, or speech therapy for their child. Parents of children with mild to moderate developmental delays probably should not be taken to court. However, in those children with a neurologic deficit that is proven rather than potential and therapy is known to be beneficial, treatment should be mandated (e.g., a child with a hearing loss.)

Fatal Diseases

The place of court intervention in potentially fatal diseases is much more complex. If the disease is clearly incurable (e.g., widespread cancer) the parents' wishes regarding nonintervention, whether on religious or philosophic grounds, should be respected. If the surgery that is being offered will be only palliative, the family should have the final decision on whether or not it is performed. In children where modern medicine has nothing hopeful to offer, the parents' desire to try unproven therapy (for example Laetrile) should be supported or at least tolerated. However, in the child with the early diagnosis of a treatable malignancy, where the present treatment regimen offers at least a fair cure rate, and where the parents refuse such treatment, a court order may be necessary to initiate treatment.

The medical situation of ultimate complexity is one involving a defective newborn who has a prognosis of almost certain mental retardation and who also has a life-threatening condition during the neonatal period. An example of this would be a child with trisomy 21 who has duodenal atresia or severe congenital heart disease with congestive heart failure. The best results occur when the family, their religious advisor, and the primary physician discuss openly the alternatives and come to a conclusion that is supported by the ward staff and other consulting physicians. When a child protective service agency and court overrules parents who have refused treatment of their child in such a situation, this action usually leads to a bitter experience for all concerned.

Well Child Care

We cannot hold all parents accountable for meeting the optimal standards of well child care as set forth by the American Academy of Pediatrics (2). However, health professionals do need some minimal standards of well child care for which they hold all parents responsible, so that no child in this country is allowed to go through the first 5 years of his life without receiving any medical attention. These standards may vary from community to community. Immunizations have proven to be effective at saving lifes. In some states, laws now require all students entering school to have their immunizations up to date or the child will be temporarily excluded from the classroom. Families with religious beliefs that preclude immunization are given special consideration. This type of law sets an automatic endpoint of 5 years after which all children must be fully immunized. Cantwell (3) recommends that the basic series of 4 DPTs, 3 OPVs, and the other live virus vaccines that normally should have been completed by 18 months of age have a cut off point at 2 years of age, after which time immunization neglect should be considered.

Since the nutritional status of a child is of vital importance during the first year of life, two visits to a health care setting during this period would be considered a minimal requirement by most prudent physicians. The first visit should occur by 2 months of age. Medical care neglect can also be considered present if a child with a visual impairment is not brought to an eye care specialist for evaluation, even after several referrals. Another example would be the child with multiple painful dental caries who is not taken to the dentist despite the efforts of school personnel to arrange dental appointments. Overall, the subject of well child care neglect remains in a state of debate.

Intervention

All types of medical care neglect should be handled with the utmost patience and diplomacy by the physician. Except for the rare situation that is an acute emergency, the physician or social worker can usually initiate a stepwise approach to the problem. First he should make certain that any financial or transportation barriers are eliminated. The parents can often be helped to gain funding from Medicaid, the Crippled Children's fund, local charitable organizations, or special parents' groups. Second, several attempts should be made to clarify any questions the parents might have about their child's treatment needs. An informed consent must include the following: a description of the risks without treatment, the risks of treatment itself (i.e., confirmation that the procedure is relatively safe), and the expected outcome with treatment. Many families will need a chance to go home and think over what has been discussed rather than making an immediate decision. Third, the physician must show evidence that he has attempted to work through a trusted intermediary of the family. This person may be a relative, friend, or member of the clergy. In some cases an interpreter is necessary to overcome language barriers. Fourth, if the family still persists in their decision to refuse the recommended treatment, the physician should give the family and their trusted intermediary one warning that if they do not change their mind, he is obligated by law to refer the case to the juvenile courts. Finally, if the required treatment continues to be refused, a court order will be sought. In the more severe cases the child may also need to be placed in a foster home both before and after treatment. On a practical level, if these steps are followed, court orders are rarely necessary.

SAFETY NEGLECT

Some accidents are clearly due to a complete disregard for the child's safety. To keep this subject in perspective, true accidents, suspicious accidents, and repeated accidents must also be considered.

True Accidents

Although most accidents are due to a breach in safety and theoretically could have been prevented, the interruption of the event would have required unusual prediction and timing on the part of the parent. Such chance events are considered true or legitimate accidents. In these situations the normal parent is already filled with self-recrimination, and reporting these accidents to child protective services does nothing but accentuate this guilt. Other potential side-effects of the indiscriminate reporting of accidents are acute depression, suicide, hostility toward the medical staff, or decreased visiting patterns by the parents. The physician would do best to use an educational approach rather than a punitive approach in true accidents. Every child has some "preventable" accidents. According to Janesky and Bartlett (4), burns may be the most preventable accident (91% being preventable). Since these injuries cause great suffering for the child and his parents, major anticipatory guidance should be directed here.

Safety Neglect

Safety neglect can be defined as a situation where an injury occurs because of gross lack of supervision. These situations usually involve children under 3 years of age, because by this age, most children develop a safety awareness and an active interest in their own self-preservation. Parents must supervise their children carefully in these early years; the highest mortality from accidents occurs during the first year of life. Beyond age 3 most children have a certain degree of freedom that can lead to some legitimate accidents. Gross lack of supervision would include leaving the young child in the home without sitters or unsupervised to roam the neighborhood. Another type of safety neglect is a hazardous home environment. Prudent parents realize they must totally control the safety of the child's environment during the first 3 or 4 years of life. Leaving poisons, caustics, knives, or guns within easy reach of children is clearly negligent. Repeated dog bites by the family dog also represents a dangerous home environment. Another factor that should concern the physician investigating a case for safety neglect is the parent who shows a lack of concern. An example is the child who has already fallen off a sofa, and in the office setting the mother leaves the same child unguarded on the examining table. Such an action should indicate that this particular child is at risk for additional accidents. Serious injuries resulting from gross safety neglect should be reported to the child protective services agency for ongoing family supervision. These criteria for safety neglect are found in less than 1% of accidents.

A recent case in our community demonstrates the caution required before reporting a case as safety neglect. Three preschool children suffered smoke inhalation in a fire in their home, and one of the children died. The mother had left the children for 30 minutes to walk her fourth child to school because he had been beaten up on his way to school the previous day. The mother was accused of child neglect. The case was given heavy coverage in the press, and the mother decompensated and required psychiatric care.

Suspicious Accidents

Just because the parents provide an explanation for a child's injury does not mean that the explanation is true. Although many abusive parents will not invent a story of an accident to cover up injuries they have inflicted, some will. The physician must be well versed in the nature of age appropriate accidents so he can detect the ones that are questionable. Gregg and Elmer (5) point out the dilemmas of separating accidents from abuse in young infants. Suspicious accidents must be reported to the protective service agency for a complete investigation. For example, a 2-year-old boy was examined with a burn on his right buttock that allegedly occurred when he fell onto the stove while trying to get cookies out of a kitchen cabinet. A home evaluation found it was impossible for the boy to have sustained the injury as described. In addition, the relatives were concerned about previous nonaccidental trauma in this child.

Repeated Accidents

When a family has children with repeated accidents, other family problems are usually present. Since supervision usually decreases during times of stress, the association between accidents and family crises is not surprising. The parents of some accidentally injured children do not visit their child in the hospital which may indicate their lack of concern for the injured child. Nonaccidental trauma should be reconsidered in these children since accidents are also more common in abusive homes (6). Overall, repeated accidents are usually a clue to a mentally disturbed child, a temporary crisis, or a chronically crisis-ridden family. The genuineness of the accident and the lack of fault on the part of the family does not mean that the family with many accidents is not in need of referral to various community resources.

EMOTIONAL DEPRIVATION

The signs of emotional deprivation or maternal deprivation in young infants are well known (7). These children are withdrawn, listless, or immobile. The facial expression of a deprived child is unhappy; smiling or cooing is difficult or impossible to elicit. If they cling to their mothers, eye contact and playful interactions are wanting. Speech delays and gross motor delays leading to a false diagnosis of mental retardation are common. This deprivation picture was first described in infants being raised in orphanages or hospitals. The reaction was attributed to the absence of a mothering figure. Later, the same syndrome was described secondary to the loss of a mothering figure through death or prolonged separation. In 1957 Coleman and Provence (8) observed that this same syndrome could occur in babies who were living at home with their parents. Haka-Ikse (9) reported similar behaviors in babies being raised by mothers with severe depression. Many of these children will also have evidence of failure-to-thrive and physical neglect. These parents need major psychiatric help. These babies need supplemental mothering and stimulation programs through a nursery school, day-care center, or foster home.

The manifestations of emotional abuse and neglect in older children are rather nonspecific. The children may be aggressive, unduly fearful, or withdrawn and depressed. A chaotic environment may breed profoundly hyperactive children. Proving these cases in court is extremely difficult at this time. The practical approach is to refer to these problems as medical care neglect of a psychiatric illness. A psychiatrist or psychologist is needed to examine the child and document the presence of severely disturbed behaviors. In addition, it must be carefully documented that the parents have refused therapy for their child on at least two occasions. The psychiatrist must be encouraged to give a prognosis for the child without therapy. Most of these children become nonfunctioning, noncoping adults. In a sense the neglect of the child's psychiatric illness is very similar to the neglect of an incapacitating physical disorder. Usually there children will need to be taken out of the home to profit from psychotherapy. Their pathology is too advanced to change without introducing a predictable, consistent, and caring environment. In a community in which the court is not convinced by the previous argument, mild physical abuse will eventually occur in most of these children, thereby allowing the child protective service unit to intervene and bring more easily documented evidence before the court.

EDUCATIONAL NEGLECT

Laws to guarantee school attendance for children have been in effect for a long time. Cantwell (3) notes that nonattendance in excess of 25 days should be viewed as symptomatic of family disorganization serious enough to warrant reporting and intervention. Some children are kept home from school to babysit for siblings, perform chores, or meet their parents' abnormal emotional needs. Other children have a severe school phobia for which the parents are unwilling to seek treatment. If parents do not respond appropriately to counseling about improving their child's school attendance, reporting the situation to child protective services and a full investigation is required. A good school experience may be the only major positive influence in an abused child's environment.

PHYSICAL NEGLECT

Physical neglect includes children who are living under conditions of inadequate food, clothing, and shelter. Children who come to school hungry or with no provision for lunch may be included here. The first time this happens the parent should be warned by the school principal to pay more attention to their child's diet. If this admonition does not bring improvement, the case should be reported to the child protective service agency. A visit to the home may disclose inadequate or spoiled food.

The most common example of the child with physical neglect is one who smells of urine or dirty feet. Such a child is teased or even ostracized by his peer group (e.g., no one will sit near him). Acute management can include helping the child wash himself at school. If this type of hygiene neglect is not corrected after the parents have been notified to have their child bathe at least twice a week, they should be reported to the proper authorities. Milder cases of repeatedly unkempt clothes or a dirty face should probably not be reported unless only one child in a family is so treated. In this instance, the specific child needs to be reported to find out if he is being scapegoated and rejected by the family. Another situation worthy of attention is a home so filthy that it doesn't comply with environmental sanitation laws (e.g., a home strewn with garbage or human and animal waste). An investigation in such a case will usually uncover a very depressed or withdrawn parent living in that home. In general the best criterion for deciding to report a case of physical neglect is if the neglect has caused harm to or problems for the child.

EXCESSIVE REPORTING OF NEGLECT

Case finding and reporting of neglect (especially physical neglect) has become overzealous in some communities. To be poor, out of work, living in marginal housing, and also accused of child neglect for conditions over which the person has no control is unjust. The following conditions are prone to overreporting. The first four items are subtypes of physical neglect.

- Clothing neglect: Examples are wearing torn pants, wearing cast-off clothing, or not having a raincoat or gloves.
- Nutritional neglect: Examples are eating unbalanced meals, eating too many "junk foods," or cultural food preferences. Even skipping breakfast can be normal if it's the child's choice. We must remember that approximately one third of adults prefer not to eat breakfast.
- Hygiene neglect: Examples are coming to school with a dirty face, dirty hair, or dirty clothing. If the child is not malodorous and the problem is periodic, it is probably of minimal importance.
- Home environment neglect: Mildly unsanitary homes are quite common. We should not be over critical of housekeeping below standards, such as poorly washed dishes or a house that is covered with dog hair and needs vacuuming.
- Cultural deprivation or intellectual stimulation neglect: This term is often directed at families whose children allegedly are not talked to enough or presented with sufficient creative toys. All too often this term is applied to children with developmental delays due to normal variation or prematurity.
- Safety neglect: Many normal accidents are called safety neglect to the detriment of the parents, for example, blaming the parents for burns that occur on space heaters despite numerous precautions the parents have taken. On a practical level, some unsafe environments cannot be changed.
- Minor acute illness neglect: Insect bites, lice, scabies, and impetigo occur in children from all socioeconomic groups. Often parents are blamed for diaper rashes and cradle cap. Parents may be criticized because they have not given their child antipyretics before bringing them to the physician for a fever. Parents may be blamed for not coming to the clinic soon enough for an ear infection that they did not know existed.

Including these categories in child abuse and neglect investigations will dilute the efforts of child protection units in responding to more serious cases and also lose them the respect of certain constituents of their community. We live in an imperfect world. Neglect is easily confused with poverty, ignorance, or parents who are overwhelmed by other problems. Some ethnic groups have defined neglect as "a failure to live up to the white middle classes' standards." For this reason neglect should not be reported automatically to the child protective service unit. Instead the family should be offered help, especially financial assistance. Only if the family refuses services for their children, should the child neglect laws be implemented.

THE EVALUATION OF NEGLECT

Several types of neglect usually occur together in the same child. When a child is reported because of neglect, he deserves a complete evaluation and careful documentation of the findings. The following steps can be taken:

- Medical examination: At a minimum the child deserves a body surface examination to exclude the possibility of concomitant nonaccidental trauma. Obviously his height and weight should be plotted to rule out the presence of failure-to-thrive.
- Medical record review: The child's medical record should be examined for his immunization status, missed appointment rate, and any serious accidents that the child has sustained. Sometimes a child with repeated dangerous accidents has been overlooked. Any public health nurse reports that are available should also be reviewed.
- Day-care report or school report: Inquiries should be made at the school as to the child's attendance, school performance, and general behavior status. Special attention should be paid to the amount of lunch provided for the child and also whether he comments on missing breakfast. If the child attends preschool, a standardized development screening test should be administered (e.g., the Denver Developmental Screening Test).
- Family assessment: The child protective service unit should evaluate both parents. Investigation of serious neglect cases often uncovers a depressed parent or one who is addicted to drugs or alcohol. Relatives should be contacted regarding their concerns about the parents' ability to provide for the children.
- Home visit: A home visit is the only way to be certain the child does not live in a markedly unsanitary or hazardous environment. The case worker will provide this information.

TREATMENT OF NEGLECT

The treatment approach to neglectful families should depend on the cause. If the neglect is due to erroneous thinking on the parents' part, in most cases the parents will respond to an educational approach. More commonly, the parents are exhausted, pessimistic, needy people without any helpful extended family or support network. Most of these parents will accept intervention when it is provided on an outreach basis. These parents need public health nurses, case workers, and lay therapists who visit in the home. Any material assistance is usually appreciated (e.g., homemaker services, food stamps, or unemployment compensation). Frequent visits with a sensitive and flexible primary physician are helpful. These appointments for medical care and transportation could be arranged by a family advocate. To counteract the deleterious effects of emotional neglect, the younger children usually need a stimulation program in a therapeutic nursery school or preschool. If the neglect has occurred because the caretakers have serious mental illness (for example alcoholism or depression), the parent needs referral for individual psychotherapy, group therapy, or both. If the neglect has been willful or sadistic, the parents probably are unconcerned about their child and long-term foster placement will be necessary. Eventually voluntary relinquishment or permanent termination of parental rights may need to be sought. This step can usually be achieved only if the failure of the parents to respond to various treatment programs has been carefully documented.

REFERENCES

1. Frankel LS, Damme CJ, Van Eys JV: Childhood cancer and the Jehovah's Witness faith. *J Pediatr* 60:6, 1977.
2. American Academy of Pediatrics: *Standards of Child Health Care* ed 3. Evanston, Ill, 1977.
3. Cantwell HB: *Standards of Child Neglect*. Denver, Colo, Denver Department of Social Services, 1978.
4. Janesky C, Bartlett GS: Serious preventable injuries as a manifestation of child neglect, abstracted. *Ambulatory Pediatric Association*, 1979.
5. Gregg GS, Elmer E: Infant injuries: accident or abuse? *J Pediatr* 44:3, 1969.
6. Newberger EH, Reed RB, Daniel JH, et al: Pediatric social illness: toward an etiologic classification. *J Pediatr* 60:2, 1977.
7. Bakwin H: Emotional deprivation in infants. *J Pediatr* 35:512, 1949.
8. Coleman RW, Provence S: Environmental retardation (hospitalism) in infants living in families. *J Pediatr* 19:285, 1957.
9. Haka-Ikse K: Child development as an index of maternal mental illness. *J Pediatr* 55:310, 1975.

17
Poisonings and Child Abuse

James J. Kresel
Frederick H. Lovejoy, Jr.

The intent of this chapter is to examine the relationship existing between chemicals (mainly drugs) and child abuse. Although the deliberate poisoning of a child is not common, it is an area containing documented fatalities. Less clearly documented is the frequency of preventable childhood injury associated with an adult who abuses drugs. This person appears more apt to injure a child physically (1) and also more likely to provide an environment deficient both in safety and in that quality of parenting behavior considered necessary for optimal child development.

There is a dilemma of boundries when child abuse and poisonings are viewed concomitantly. This chapter will address that dilemma by focusing on four areas. The first area deals briefly with accidental ingestions. Although accidental ingestions are not customarily considered to fall within the scope of child abuse, there exists both environmental and host characteristics of this population that provide a working framework from which to consider other aspects of childhood poisoning.

Second, the intentional poisoning of children is considered. This section is addressed primarily from a literature perspective; however, it is possible that the frequency of routine parental medication of children, coupled with environmental factors, may escalate into a toxicologic episode.

Third, the concept of safety neglect is discussed. The absence of safety in the home is clearly responsible for a vast number of calls to poison centers, and its relationship to child abuse is worthy of careful investigation.

Finally, the role of the poison center is explored; especially its potential for child advocacy within two areas: namely, its ability to identify safety neglect environments, and as a follow-up, its potential to generate an "ingestion-at-risk list." Included will be programs currently in use at the Massachusetts Poison Control System that specifically address the poison repeater. It is felt that this population may live in what may be considered an environment of safety neglect. Such programs are designed to identify that environment and to provide educational interventions that may reduce the possibility of an ingestion occurring again.

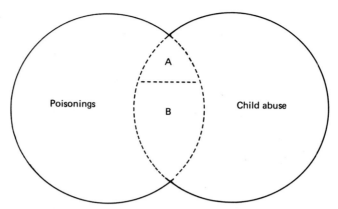

Figure 1. Possible overlap of the populations of poisoned and abused children. (A) Acts of Commission (intentional poisoning) (B) Acts of Omission (safety neglect).

ACCIDENTAL INGESTIONS: ETIOLOGICAL CONSIDERATIONS

Virtually all ingestions in children under 5 years of age are viewed as accidents. These events are thus not considered child abuse. Conceptually, the accidental ingestion can be visualized as an interaction involving an environmental situation, an accessible agent, and a susceptible host. However, environmental factors such as stress, marital discord, and family illness are associated both with ingestions (2) and child abuse (3). The existence of these disrupting factors within the home clearly places these children "at risk" for either or both events. However, the boundry between the accidental ingestion and the genesis of what may be considered child abuse is often difficult to define.

Statistics from the Massachusetts Poison Control System indicate that of approximately 50,000 calls received annually, greater than 60% involve children less than 5 years of age (4). The age distribution of childhood ingestions simulates the age at which most cases of physical child abuse occur. Current estimates are that two-thirds of all cases of physical child abuse occur in children 3 years of age or younger (5). As such, it is not unreasonable to suggest that these populations overlap; in fact, at any particular time, they may well be the same. It is important to emphasize that accidental ingestions should not universally be viewed as child abuse. However, because of similar environmental and host factors, the potential overlap of these populations bears consideration. Schematically, this overlap is represented in Figure 1.

While the percentage distribution of either the intentional ingestion or the safety neglect environment is speculative, there is similarity of host demographics. Of major importance is the potential for developing programs aimed at this fertile population. Child advocates in many disciplines have an opportunity for intervention, especially within the safety neglect environment.

INTENTIONAL POISONING: ACTS OF COMMISSION

In the original description of the battered-child syndrome, Kempe et al. (6) called attention to the fact that parents may assault a child by giving a deliberate drug overdose. This form of abuse is seldom reported, often difficult to diagnose, and probably more common than currently recognized.

Meadow (7) reported a case in which a child was deliberately given a 20 g dose of sodium chloride. The child later died from extreme hypernatremia. A similar case also involving sodium chloride has been reported by Feldman (8). Related cases have been described in which the diuretics furosemide and chlorthalidone and the opiate dihydrocodeine were purposely administered (9), as well as cases involving amobarbital, secobarbital, and a phenothiazine (10).

In one unusual case, a 3-year-old girl was deliberately poisoned repeatedly with chloral hydrate during hospitalization (11). The child had lapsed into coma on four occassions after receiving a gastrostomy feeding from her mother. Exploration of family dynamics revealed that the father's affection was directed primarily toward the daughter while the mother was continually belittled. This eventually led to the mother deliberately poisoning the child. Similar situations, which have been labeled the Medea complex, have been reported (12).

It is felt the majority of intentionally drugged children do not receive a sufficient dose to cause toxic symptoms and thus their poisoning is not reported. What is more apt to occur is a situation in which an adult deliberately sedates a crying or "bothersome" child. Literature evidence in support of this concept does not exist; however, the ease with which sedative drugs are prescribed suggests that this probably occurs. In addition, parents who are continually denied sleep may well pressure a pediatrician to prescribe hypnotic drugs for their child so that they may sleep.

The pivotal concept is not that administering prescribed depressant drugs to children (especially infants) is inherently bad, but in defining the point at which this practice threatens the child. In fact, this medication practice certainly has therapeutic usefulness, especially in treating cases such as colic. In addition, it is felt that sedating a crying child may also reduce a stressful environment for a potentially abusive family. Little literature evidence supports this practice, however, medicating for this purpose is common; and of major importance, it represents a clear risk-benefit issue. In families where this practice occurs, all medical personnel must be cautious, if not at times suspicious, so that an excessive frequency and quantity of drug use does not emerge.

SAFETY NEGLECT: ACTS OF OMISSION

While beaten, malnourished, and sexually molested children represent acts of commission usually labeled abuse, the failure to provide adequate safety (maltreatment by omission) accounts for most accidental poisonings. The improper storage of medications and chemicals (such as bleach, charcoal lighter fluid, furniture polish, etc.) represents safety neglect and is related to a number of home situations well recognized as risk factors for both child abuse and poisonings. Sibert (13) has reviewed a number of factors associated with childhood ingestions. Although these factors are reported in poisoning literature, they concur with those associated with child abuse. For example, he notes that a stressful home environment, recent moving, illness, marital discord, and death of a family member are events that often precede or are concomitant with the ingestion episode. Similarly, Newberger and Hyde (14) noted that marital stress and its related problems are clearly associated with child abuse. One such related problem is parental drug abuse.

Parents abusing drugs (including alcohol) are less likely to exercise adequate safety precautions. The absence of this safety factor can be considered a pharmacologically induced act of omission. Of particular note with respect to this omission are addicted parents, such as those enrolled in methadone maintenance programs. The magnitude of this problem is large. For example, approximately 185,000 doses of methadone were dispensed in Boston in 1978 (15). Lee et al. (16) have reported poisonings from methadone that occurred as a result of the child's presumed attraction to the dispensing vehicle (an orange-flavored Tang solution). Compounding this flavor stimulus is the fact that the dispensing containers lacked safety closures, despite safety legislation. Methadone deaths have also been reported by others and have been at least partially attributable to the lack of safety caps (17). It appears that flavoring, host factors, inadequate packaging, and inadequate attention to safe storage all contributed to the poisoning event. In addition, families with an alcohol-addicted parent (18) and those where the mother is addicted to amphetamines (19) have been shown to be both more neglectful as well as physically abusive of their children.

In one series of studies, Behling (20) demonstrated a relationship between alcoholism and child abuse. In his study of abused children, 69% had one or both parents diagnosed as either suffering from alcoholism or as being alcohol abusers. It should be expected that as social and psychological problems within family environments magnify, together with increasing alcohol consumption, so too does the likelihood of an ingestion that may be attributed to safety neglect. At present, behavior-modifying drugs are often prescribed to correct or at least abate these stressful situations; however, the value of their use is questionable.

Diazepam (Valium) is the leading prescription drug sold in the United States (21). In addition, diazepam is the most commonly ingested prescription medication reported to the Massachusetts Poison Control System ranking second only to aspirin products. Alcohol-containing substances rank fourth. Although diazepam is intended to ameliorate the stress of living, there is growing evidence that its intented pharmacologic effect is modified by such environmental factors as group interaction (22). Animal data suggest an increase in aggressive behavior following continuous chlordiazepoxide (a benzodiazepine related to diazepam) administration (23). In human situations, Salzman (24) observed that normal individuals demonstrated increased hostile behavior when given benzodiazepines; however, that behavior was only observed in a group setting and only when frustration was introduced into the environment. Additional evidence exists that benzodiazepines and alcohol produce disinhibition and consequently facilitate the release of hostility and aggression (25). Lynch et al. (1) reported that a high percentage of families referred for actual or threatened child abuse are ingesting drugs at those times of crises. In this study they describe how mothers having been "tranquilized" instead of feeling less anxious actually experienced open aggression toward the child.

Considering the enormous drug use in the United States, it is reasonable that the availability of drugs paired with the frustration-stimulus of the crying baby may yield violence. Additionally, parents have been known to intentionally sedate the crying child. Physicians must be hesitant in prescribing tranquilizers for parents who have difficulty coping with their children. In addition, they can never be too cautious in prescribing sedatives for the children.

THE ROLE OF THE POISON CENTER

Since the first poison center originated in Chicago in 1953, their numbers have grown to well over 650. At present they provide vast management information, however their potential for influencing child care has gone virtually untapped. Poison centers have the potential to evolve into an arm of the child advocacy team. Support for this concept has developed mainly because the "at risk" group with respect to poisonings shares many of the environmental factors associated with the "at risk" group with respect to abuse and neglect.

Further, repetitive poisoning occurs in approximately 25–30% of all ingestions reported (4). These data concur with previous studies (26). Environmental factors associated with repeat ingestions are clearly those associated with child abuse (3,13). It thus becomes possible that poison centers monitoring and computerizing ingestion data would be able to identify poison repeaters and develop an ingestion at risk list. Such a repeater screening program is currently in progress at the Massachusetts Poison Control System. The aim is to identify those children possibly residing in what might be a safety neglect environment and initiate educational intervention regarding drug and chemical storage.

Poison repeaters, in addition to being clearly at risk for a repeat ingestion, may reside in homes where parents possess one or more characteristics associated with child maltreatment. Safety neglect, as related to repeat ingestions, affords poison centers an opportunity for expanded poison prevention education.

A cross-tabulation and compilation of the Massachusetts Poison Control System statistics for 1978 has recently been completed. A section of this program addresses the poison repeater and provides baseline data from which trends in repeat poisonings can be analyzed.

Figure 2 shows the number of repeat ingestions reported during 1978 for children from ages one through five years for each sex. The mean age of poison repeaters was 24.1 months. This approximates the average age of maltreated children. The data observed for the 2-year-old group suggest that boys may be repeat ingestors more often than girls.

In interpreting these data, it appears that the repeat ingestor affords the poison center the opportunity to expand its role into the child protection area. The overall safety neglect concept is particularly relevant for poison repeaters and intervention programs aimed at that group have been established. At present, the Massachusetts Poison Control System tabulates repeater data for ingestions of selected drugs. Current plans are in progress in which home visits to this repeater population will be conducted. Included in this visit are educational materials designed to improve the environmental component of the host-agent-environment triad. Hopefully this program will reduce the repeat poisoning of children.

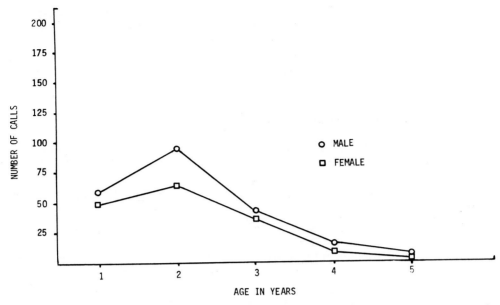

Figure 2. Number of repeat poison calls for each year of age from 1 through 5 for each sex.

CONCLUSION

Poisonings and child maltreatment overlap in several ways. Overt abuse (the intentional poisoning of children) is less common than neglect (the potentially preventable accidental poisoning). Both of these situations are related to a number of environmental factors. Prominent among these is that a child of an alcoholic or drug-abusing parent appears to have a higher probability of being maltreated, either through omission or commission.

It is possible that poison control centers can be instrumental, especially in certain aspects of omission-maltreatment, by identifying "at risk" populations and offering educational intervention.

REFERENCES

1. Lynch MA, Lindsay J, Ounsted C: Tranquillizers causing aggression. *Br Med J* 1:266, 1975.
2. Katz, J: Psychiatric aspects of accidental poisoning in childhood. *Med J Aust* 2:59, 1976.
3. Newberger EH, Reed RB, Daniel JH, et al: Pediatric social illness: Toward an etiologic classification. *Pediatrics* 60:178, 1977.
4. Massachusetts Poison Control System. Annual Statistics, 1978.
5. Schmitt BD, Kempe CH: The pediatrician's role in child abuse and neglect. *Curr Probl Pediatr* 5:3, 1975.
6. Kempe CH, Silverman FN, Steele BF, et al: The battered child syndrome. *JAMA* 181:17, 1962.
7. Meadow R: Munchausen Syndrome by proxy-The hinterland of child abuse. *Lancet* II:343, 1977.

8. Feldman K, Robertson WO: Salt poisoning: Presenting symptom of child abuse. *Vet Human Toxicol* 21:341, 1979.

9. Rogers D, Tripp J, Bentovim A, et al: Non-accidental poisoning: An extended syndrome of child abuse. *Br Med J* 1:793, 1976.

10. Hvizdala EV, Gellady AM: Intentional poisoning of two siblings by prescription drugs. *Clin Pediatr* 17:480, 1978.

11. Lansky LL: An unusual case of childhood chloral hydrate poisoning. *Am J Dis Child* 127:275, 1974.

12. Stern ES: The Medea complex: Mothers homicidal wishes to her child. *J Ment Sci* 94:321, 1948.

13. Sibert Jr R: Stress in families of children who have ingested poisons. *Br Med J* 3:87, 1975.

14. Newberger EH, Hyde JN: Child abuse: Principles and implications of current pediatric practice. *Pediatr Clin North Am* 22:695, 1975.

15. Heffernan S: Personal Communication.

16. Lee KD, Lovejoy Jr FH, Haddow JE: Childhood Methadone intoxication. *Clin Pediatr* 13:66, 1974.

17. Smialek JE, Monforte JR, Aronow R: Methadone deaths in children: A continuing problem. *JAMA* 238:2516, 1977.

18. Mayer J, Black R: Child abuse and neglect in families with an alcohol or opiate addicted parent. *Child Abuse Neg* 1:85, 1977.

19. Billing L, Eriksson M, Larsson G, et al: Occurence of abuse and neglect of children born to amphetamine addicted mothers. *Child Abuse Neg* 3:205, 1979.

20. Behling DW: Alcohol abuse as encountered in 51 instances of reported child abuse. *Clin Pediatr* 18:87, 1979.

21. Anon: Most prescribed drugs. *Drug Topics* 18 May 1979, p 33.

22. Anon: Tranquillizers causing aggression. *Br Med J* 1:113, 1975.

23. Guaitavi AG, Marcucci F, Garattini S: Increased aggression and toxicity in grouped male mice treated with tranquilizing benzodiazepines. *Psychopharmacologia* 19;241, 1971.

24. Salzman C, Kochansky GE, Shader RI, et al: Chlordiazepoxide-induced hostility in a small group setting. *Arch Gen Psychiatry* 31:401, 1974.

25. Gray JA: Drug effects on fear and frustration, in Iverson L, Iverson S, Snyder S (eds): *Handbook Of Psychopharmacology* vol 8, New York, Plenum Press, 1977, p 433.

26. Wehrle PF, DeFreest L, Penhollow J, et al: The epidemiology of accidental poisoning in an urban population. III. The repeater problem of accidental poisoning. *Pediatrics* 27:614, 1961.

18
Photography of the Maltreated Child

Robert J. Ford
Brian S. Smistek

Many medical institutions are becoming involved in evaluating suspected cases of child maltreatment. Many states have enacted laws that not only mandate physician reporting of abuse cases, but also include standard procedures that are to be followed. This puts the physician into a position of being a principle gatherer of medical evidence, as well as the child's medical caregiver.

Skeletal radiographs are routine tools that are diagnostic in nature and may also be used as physical evidence in civil or criminal court. Because photographs are not diagnostic, they may be overlooked for their value in recording trauma. Long after memories have faded, photographs can still graphically represent the severity of the child's initial condition, which words could never portray. The laws of 17 states make reference to taking photographs in suspected cases of abuse. Some states mandate the taking of color photographs in such cases. The vast majority provide for immunity from civil or criminal prosecution for the institution reporting and the person arranging for or taking photographs, if done in good faith. The readers should become familiar with child protection laws within their own state concerning the subject of photographs. A few states do not protect institutions, photographers, or other reporters of child abuse. Surveys of professional medical photographers in the United States and Canada show a general lack of awareness of the statutes that require photographs and provide immunity (1). Photographers fear liability in spite of the existence of statutory immunity and many refuse to take photographs when abuse is suspected.

The information in this chapter should serve to clarify for physicians, medical photographers, and any others involved in child protection issues how to obtain and use photographs in suspected child maltreatment cases.

THE PHOTOGRAPHER

Hospitals that have a medical photographer on staff are best equipped to document properly areas of visible trauma found on child abuse victims.

Members of the photography department should be aware of the proper technical skills necessary to illustrate effectively the abusive injury. Consultation with the responsible medical personnel is required to delineate areas of the body to be photographed.

Should your institution not have a resident medical photographer, there are several options to obtain acceptable photographs. The hospital might enlist the services of a professional free-lance photographer on a contract or fee-for-service basis. Police agencies are frequently very responsive to the needs of abused children and might avail themselves to hospitals in need of documentation in such cases. Law enforcement photographers, however, are not experienced in photographing personal injuries, and child protection agencies may feel that police involvement is threatening to the family. Some hospitals provide equipment for their emergency room staff or housestaff to take their own pictures. This equipment may vary from sophisticated 35 mm cameras and strobes to simplified instant cartridge type cameras.

EQUIPMENT

The professional photographer generally uses a 35 mm single lens reflex camera with studio lighting or electronic flash-on-camera (Figs. 2 and 3). The amateur has a choice of photographic equipment. There are three basic types of compact easy operating cameras that may be considered useful in the photography of abused children. The least expensive and easiest to operate

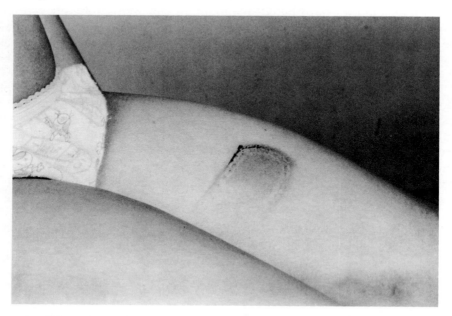

Figure 1. This ecchymosis clearly documents that the trauma was inflicted by a belt. Even the stitching around the border of the belt is visible in the ecchymosis and recorded by the photograph.

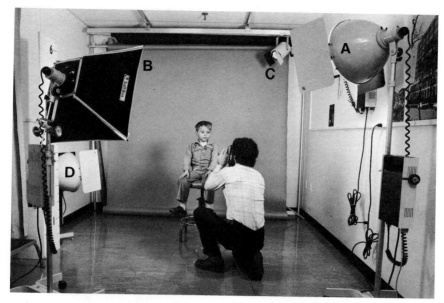

Figure 2. Typical studio lighting. (A) The main light is used to control the three-dimensional quality of the photograph. Its proper use will delineate contours and texture. A diffuser is usually used to soften both the contrast and the shadow areas. (B) The fill-in light is used to light the shadow areas created by the main light so that no detail is hidden. (C) The halo light, a spotlight behind the subject, provides illumination for the hair and shoulders and is important for separating the patient from the background. (D) The background light eliminates disturbing and confusing shadows.

cameras are those of the cartridge-loading flashcube type. This variety of camera accepts 110 or 126 film, uses disposable flashcubes, and is simple to operate. The person taking the picture merely has to frame the subject and snap the picture. Generally lacking focusing control, these cameras serve a limited purpose in proper identification of specific trauma in detail. The instant picture cameras are fundamentally similar to the cartridge-loading type in that they have minimal focusing capabilities and usually produce photographs that lack good resolution and accurate color rendition. In addition to these drawbacks, instant film is relatively expensive and frequently proves to be mechanically troublesome. On the positive side, the above mentioned cameras are basically inexpensive to purchase and maintain. The instant-type cameras are capable of providing a quick photograph that can be compared to the original area of trauma so as to assure the photographer of a reasonable representation of the injury.

The most efficient and expandable type of camera for photography in the emergency room is the 35 mm single lens reflex (SLR). Most SLR cameras are significantly more expensive than instant picture cameras. In comparison to the other types of cameras mentioned, the SLR offers a selection of lenses that enables the photographer to focus from infinity to magnification view. When photographing the patient's face for identification purposes, a 135 mm long focus lens minimizes distortion of features. A supplementary 50 mm macro

Figure 3. On-location flash-on-camera equipment. (A) A 35 mm SLR camera with a cable shutter release. This allows steady holding of the bracket without awkward movements during picture taking. (B) The lenses are interchangeable so that the telephoto lens can be used for facial photos and the normal-macro lens can be used for other views. (C) Electronic flash unit is synchronized with shutter. (D) Several camera brackets are available, this one has a swivel base that allows the camera to be turned in a vertical position.

lens might be considered for use in photographing the patient's full body or for very close focusing capabilities that require more exact attention to details. Flash on or near the camera is second only to studio lighting for proper illumination. Even though flash-on-camera has some limitations (Table 1). the recommendation is still that all nonstudio photographs be taken with flash-on-camera; either flashcube or, in the case of 35 mm cameras, an automatic electronic flash unit.

Black and white film should be avoided because it does not have the capabilities of registering correct densities of light. The least expensive film and processing combination are color slides. They are quickly developed, easy to file, and can be converted to color prints if necessary.

When taking any child abuse photographs, make an effort to position the child against an uncluttered, neutral-colored background. This not only provides

Table 1. Limitations of Flash-on-Camera Lighting[a]

Shiny lesions (blisters, ecchymosis, and some dark skin) may
   reflect and scatter light hiding important detail

Areas of trauma that have texture or are swollen (contusions,
   lacerations, abrasions, blisters) may lose their three-dimensional quality

Subtle colors may wash out by overexposure, especially areas
   nearest to the lens

The flash may not cover all of the area photographed due to
   its location on the camera or bracket; the lighting may "fall
   off" at the edges

Because there is no fill-in light, harsh shadows may hide detail

[a] Even though flash-on-camera has some limitations, it is still the best
choice in lighting for nonstudio photographic situations

a nondistracting setting, but also aids in determining the color quality of the
film type and the processing method.

WHEN SHOULD PHOTOGRAPHS BE TAKEN?

Photographs should be taken only when evidence of suspected abuse or neglect
is visible. Photography should not be used to enhance or exaggerate the trauma
that exists; it must show injuries as realistically as possible. If in doubt as to
when the injury reaches its peak visibility, having the site photographed as soon
as possible would be the best decision. If bruising becomes more apparent later
as the injury matures, then the injury can be rephotographed (Fig. 4).

Handling each case as an emergency is not necessary. In cases of obviously
fading bruises or scabs, timing is less critical. When cases are clearly a medical

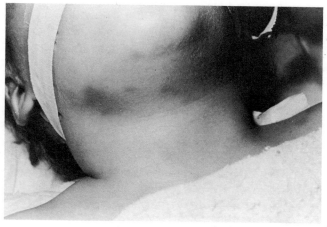

Figure 4. On day of hospital admission, this strangled child's neck was relatively free of
bruises. The following day obvious bruising was visible and was documented by
photography.

emergency (burns, lacerations, sexual abuse, or when surgery is required) pictures should be taken immediately, before extensive medical treatment is performed. If malnutrition as part of the failure-to-thrive syndrome is to be shown, photographs should be taken before treatment is begun and after the child has gained weight.

If your institution has a medical photography staff and handles a substantial number of child abuse cases, they should consider the possibility of being on-call for emergency cases. A remote pager will permit easy contact with the photographer. Caution should be taken against the tendency to misuse this service, since not all cases need be handled on an emergency basis. If a case comes in after the photography department's normal working hours, perhaps the parent or social worker can bring the child in the next day if the injury will still be visible. This is a decision made by the examining physician.

PAPERWORK, LIGHTING, AND LENSES

For the physician to convey to the photographer what parts of the body need to be photographed, a photograph requisition form is recommended. The requisition form should contain an outline drawing of the entire body in the four cardinal anatomic positions (AP, PA, right and left laterals), a series of drawings of the head, and standard information, such as the patient's name, hospital number, birth date, and date of photography. There should be a space for the requesting physician to sign his name and room on the form for specific instructions to be written. The physician can circle the line drawings on the requisition form to indicate the areas of the body that he wishes to have photographed. In court the requisition form can be useful in establishing a "chain of evidence" as to the events surrounding the documentation of the abusive event.

If the photographs are being taken to document specific injuries as part of an evaluation of a possibly abused child, consent forms are generally unnecessary. Furthermore, the parents of the maltreated child may not be interested in signing anything, especially permission to document the injuries on their child. If a recognizable feature, such as the face, of a patient is to be used in a publication, a written release must be obtained from the parent, legal guardian, and the patient, if he is old enough.

One of the most important elements in successful photography is lighting. There is no single aspect that more directly effects the quality and, therefore, the usefulness of a medicolegal photograph. It can show texture, color, depth, and contours. If lighting is done improperly, it can hide details in a shadow, wash out bruises, and misrepresent the evidence. If a professional photographer is taking the pictures, photographing the patient in the studio provides the best lighting possibilities (Fig. 2). Bruises should be lit with a main light and with a fill-in light at a 45° angle to reduce reflection. A more direct lighting would mask the details of a bruise (Fig. 5). A large reflection will obscure the area that needs to be shown. Abrasions, lacerations, and scabs require the main light to show texture by "glancing" the light across the skin at a low angle. Diffused

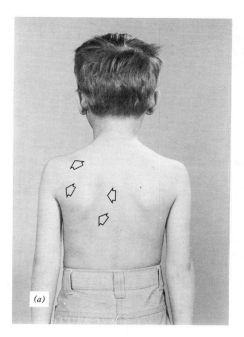 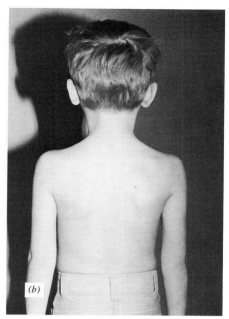

Figure 5. (*a*) A subtle bruise is shown in this studio lighted photograph. The arrows outline the affected area. (*b*) The flash-on-camera technique has washed out most of the detail.

lighting may not show the texture as well as the raw flash lighting. If the patient cannot be transferred to the photography studio and bedside photography is necessary, a flash attached to the camera is recommended (Fig. 3). A ring flash attachment gives the best overall lighting for photographing specific lesions. The flash should be aimed directly at the child and not at an angle to the area being photographed. If flashcubes are used, the camera and flash must be within 8–10 ft of the subject; beyond this distance flashcubes are ineffective.

As a matter of routine, two sets of camera original slides should be taken. Color slides do not have a negative from which they are made. The film that goes through the camera becomes the slide, which is returned after processing. Having two sets prevents the accidental loss of vital documented evidence. One set may be sent to court while one is retained in the photography department or medical record department. Duplicates of slides should never be submitted in court. It is inherent in the duplication process that contrast and, many times, color will shift. Duplicates may be acceptable for instructional purposes, but not for court. The photographer should also vary the exposure slightly to ensure that at least one set of photos are of optimal exposure. Photos for legal purposes must be of high quality. There is no reason to be miserly when shooting film. Film is inexpensive compared to the value of accurate and reliable pictures.

A facial photograph should be taken of every photographed child suspected of being abused whether or not facial trauma is present. This will provide proof that the child in question was indeed photographed, and this view can be introduced into evidence as identification. It is essential that a long focus (telephoto) lens be used for facial identification photos. If taken with a conventional lens at a distance of less than 5 ft, the features will become distorted and the picture may not be admitted as evidence. On 35 mm cameras, lenses ranging from 90 mm to 150 mm can be used for facial photographs; a 135 mm lens is probably the best choice. For most of the other views to be taken, a macro (or close-up) lens should be used. These range from 50 mm to 135 mm.

Not too large an area should be photographed at one time. Full body photographs may show the overall condition of the patient, but details will be too small to be seen. As a rule, nothing larger than the back, torso, or extremities should be taken at one time. It is equally important not to take too much of a close-up without including a body landmark (Fig. 6). The best method to follow where extreme close-ups are necessary is to take another photograph at a greater distance that includes some point of reference and size. A technically excellent photograph may not be admitted as evidence if it does not establish both the scale and anatomical location of trauma.

Once processed and crossmatched to the physician's original request form, the slides or prints should contain somewhere on their surface, the patient's full name, hospital number, and the date the pictures were taken (Fig. 7). Each patient's slides should be stored in clear plastic sheets designed to minimize handling of the slide itself.

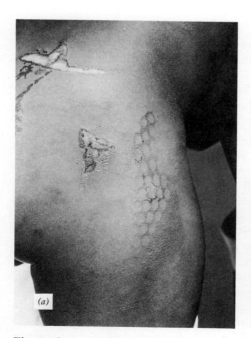
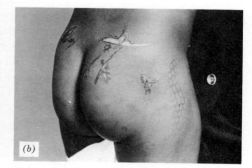

Figure 6. (*a*) Although this closeup photograph shows the grid and other burns, it is difficult to determine its location and size. (*b*) By taking another picture farther away, a landmark makes it less confusing. (From Ellerstein NS: The cutaneous manifestations of child abuse and neglect. *Am J. Dis. Child.* 133:908, 1979.)

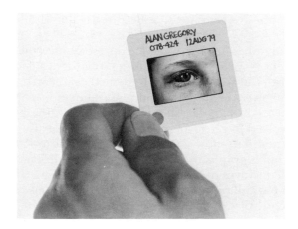

Figure 7. Each slide should be marked with the patient's name, hospital identification number, and date the photo was taken. On the lower left-hand corner the "thumbspot" orients the picture correctly as it is held. If put into a slide projector, this spot must be in the upper right-hand position (as viewed from behind the projector).

PATIENT RELATIONS

When a possibly abused child requires photographs, it is recommended that the photographer should introduce himself to the child and explain that a series of pictures must be taken. Tell the child in advance that there may be a need to undress. Gentle coaxing from a parent or assistant may help to persuade the resistent child to consent to your requirements. Be supportive of the child and attempt to establish good rapport. Avoid unnecessary fast movements that may frighten and intimidate. Explain the basic functions of your task and try to position the child to your needs without undue physical contact, unless of course, the child reaches out for attention or support. Areas concealed by skin folds, creases, and hair should be carefully examined. They may reveal injuries overlooked by the examining physician. Infants and toddlers are customarily best photographed while being held in someones arms, on their lap, or by supporting them under the axilla so that the entire body is suspended and easily rotated. Refrain from asking questions that may induce fear or apprehension in the child. Limit the time a patient has to be undressed. For older children and adolescents, it is advisable to have someone of the patient's sex in the room. Should a child have to be photographed outside the studio, be sure to minimize clutter and distracting objects from the picture. When the photo session is finished, thank the child for his or her cooperation and notify the physician that the photographs have been taken.

PREPARING PHOTOGRAPHS FOR COURT

There are certain to be occasions when photographs of abused children will be called as evidence in juvenile, family, or criminal court. It is important that these pictures be clearly and accurately identified as being those of the child represented in the court proceedings. The prints or slides must be plainly illustrative of the injury in question. Consequently, it is recommended that all consideration be given to accurate recording of detail, including a visual reinforcement in the form of anatomical landmarks that further explain the location of small areas of trauma. As an aid to determining the size of the injury, it is advisable to position an adhesive centimeter scale directly above or below the injury.

Care should be taken when releasing photographs to legal representatives or employees of social service agencies. A plan for establishing photographic release policies should be discussed with the hospital's attorneys, medical records director, and others who may be involved in handling and dissemination of hospital documents. A copy of any procedural policy should then be forwarded to the agencies that are generally involved in retrieving medical records for use in court. The requestor should be required to show some accepted identification or a court subpoena when collecting photographs for use outside the institution. This policy should guarantee that the pictures do not fall into the wrong hands and that the person signing for them has full responsibility for their safekeeping and return to the child's medical record file.

PHOTOGRAPHS IN COURT

Photographs to be used in court must meet certain criteria in order to be admitted as evidence. Photographs will be received into evidence if they are relevant to the issue and are properly verified (2). Pictures that are ruled inadmissible because of technical errors (out of focus, distorted, unidentifiable, too dark, etc.) are of no value (3). If several photographs are successfully challenged and not permitted as evidence, it may have at least a psychological effect in reducing the credibility of other evidence.

In the verification process, a witness is called to lay the groundwork for introducing a photograph into evidence. It may be the photographer or another witness who has seen the patient, such as the attending physician. They are asked to identify the photograph and to give specific information (as to when, where, etc. it was taken); then they are asked to state whether it is a true and fair representation of the patient's condition at the time the photographs were taken. If the witness answers affirmatively, the pictures are then formally offered into evidence. The judge must then decide its relevancy. Judges have broad discretion on the admissibility of evidence. If he or she feels that its prejudicial value outweighs its relevancy, the photographs may be excluded. In most cases, prejudicial photographs are those that would be considered grue-some. Regardless of how repulsive a picture may be, if duly verified and relevant in its depiction of fact, it should be admissible.

In cases that proceed to trial, it is likely that the person taking the photographs will be called on to verify them. The photographer may be asked his or her qualifications or, at the very least, some technical questions about cameras, lenses, film, exposure, processing, etc. It is best to be prepared before appearing in court. A pretrial conference with the prosecuting attorney should be held to discuss the photographs and your qualifications. The nonprofessional should not claim that he is a photographic expert. Expert status implies that the witness is knowledgeable about photographic chemistry, optics, and properties of light. If you are a professional photographer, your testimony should be limited to the photographs. Give no medical opinion unless, of course, you are qualified to do so.

PHOTO COSTS

Photographer's time, equipment, and supplies for abuse photography place additional costs on institutional operations. In some states photographs are allowed to be taken "at public expense." In such cases, the hospital is reimbursed directly by the state or county social service agency that requests the photographs. This type of compensation plan, if available to you, should be investigated at the time of a policy planning session with the appropriate government agencies. A written agreement on established reimbursement for photographs should then be prepared. The reparations could be made on a fee-for-service or retainer basis.

The establishment of standard photographic documentation of abused children may prompt a substantial increase in the number of requests for photographs. This should be seriously considered before initiating any policy in which the institution itself is responsible for expenses involved in photographic coverage.

SUMMARY OF RECOMMENDATIONS

A written policy regarding photographs of child abuse evidence should be formed. For accuracy and consistency, a medical photographer or free-lance professional should, when possible, be called on to document these cases. If this is not practical, attempt to establish an agreement with a law enforcement agency or a social service department to handle photographic coverage. If the photography is to be done by nonprofessionals, such as the emergency department staff, an easy operating camera and flash should be made available in a specific location.

Strive to achieve properly executed photographs that represent the child's condition accurately. Photograph the face of the child for direct reference identity. Document any small areas of trauma by including a landmark to establish both size and location of the injury. Take at least two pictures with different lens openings to ensure proper exposure, and make two views of each site so one set may be retained in the hospital file. Keep the background neutral in color and uncluttered in appearance. Use only color film with proper light sources.

Maintain a filing system that best suits quick retrieval and safe storage of the photographs. Establish policies regarding distribution of photographs in order to protect the child and the institution.

REFERENCES

1. Ford RJ, Smistek BS, Glass JT: Photography of suspected child abuse and maltreatment. *Biomedical Communications* 3:12, 1975.
2. Flower MS: Photographs in the courtroom "Getting it straight between you and your professional photographer." *North Kentucky State Law Forum* 2:184, 1974.
3. Scott CC: *Photographic Evidence*, ed 2. St Paul, Minn, West Publishing Co, 1969.

19
Medical Testimony

Hunter C. Leake, III
Reid F. Holbrook

Regardless of how astute and conscientious a physician is in the identification of child abuse and the management of resultant injuries, and no matter how concerned the physician is for the safety of the child, proper presentation of the medical facts in court is frequently the key function that enables help to be provided for the child and his family. Neither physicians, social workers, psychologists, nor any other professional or layperson dealing in child advocacy has the legal ability to mandate changes in a child's care or custody. In this country, only juvenile or family courts have that ability. If a physician becomes convinced that a child's health and future growth and development are at risk, then it becomes incumbent on the physician to present compelling evidence to the court to achieve an improved environment for the child. It is the physician's responsibility to gather, organize, and present to the court facts of a given child abuse case in a manner that will enable the court to make a decision that is in the best interest of the child. Failure to present data because "I'm too busy with my practice" or "I don't want to get involved," or a sloppy, poorly thought out presentation of the facts may condemn the child to further maltreatment.

Because learning to present medical testimony is absent from medical school curricula, and physicians subsequently have little opportunity to become skilled in such presentations, it is hoped that this chapter will serve as a pragmatic outline that will enable physicians to give testimony that will be useful to the court and beneficial to the child.

WHEN CHILD ABUSE IS SUSPECTED OR DIAGNOSED

Recording the Data

Much of the mechanics of what the physician should do and what should happen to the child when abuse is suspected is covered in other chapters. The first two sections of this chapter will of necessity repeat at least some of those mechanics in order to emphasize the legal implications of those actions and to point out what will and will not make accurate medical testimony. The clear and concise presentation of hard data will be most beneficial to the abused child and facilitate the court's rendering a decision that will be in the best interest of the child and his or her family.

Regardless of whether the physician's first contact with the child is in an office, a clinic, or an emergency room of a hospital, it is important to document in the history section of the medical record:

1. The time lapse between the occurrence of the injury and the caretaker's seeking medical help
2. The appropriateness of the caretaker's actions from the time of injury to presentation at the medical facility
3. The caretaker's affect regarding the child's injury
4. His or her affect toward the child
5. Whether the injuries or problems noted are commensurate with the narration of how they occurred
6. Whether the story changes with subsequent repetitions of how the injuries occurred

A case presentation will illustrate these points:

> A 13-month-old child appeared in the emergency room of a medical center at 8:00 AM with his right lower extremity in a splint. The mother was unconcerned about the child's welfare to the point that she remained in the waiting room during the initial history taking (from the maternal grandmother) and physical exam. When she was brought into the examining room, she showed annoyance and impatience at having to answer questions and made no effort to comfort her son. The mother stated that her child was lying on her bed at approximately 10:00 PM the previous evening when she left the room for a few minutes. She heard the child cry and returned to her bedroom to find that the child's leg had slipped between the outside frame of the bed and the box spring. She picked up the child, who then stopped crying, and thought nothing more of the incident. Then, 20 minutes later as the mother was changing the child's diaper, she noted a swelling in the area of the right midthigh. She put the child in a car and drove past several hospitals, including one children's hospital, to a Veteran's Administration hospital located across town from her home. There the child's leg was splinted; the mother was told the leg was broken, and since the VA hospital did not care for children, the mother was told she should take the child to the children's hospital or the medical center. Instead of going immediately to another hospital, the mother went home, went to bed, and presented in the ER of the medical center the following morning, only at the urging of the child's maternal grandmother. The grandmother's narration differs in that she said the child was at her home and not the mother's. Examination and subsequent x-ray revealed a fracture at the juncture of the middle and proximal third of the shaft of the right femur with minimal displacement. The child had brusies of different ages on his face and buttocks that the mother said he acquired as a result of falling off the bed onto a carpeted floor three days earlier. He had only received one immunization because the mother said she lacked money to take the child to a physician and also had transportation problems.

In the above case there was a delay in seeking medical help, the mother's drive across town to a VA hospital, and her subsequent return home rather than to a facility that could care for her child; all were clearly inappropriate. The mother was not at all upset that the child's thigh was broken, nor did she make any effort to console her child during the examination. Most importantly, the fracture could not have occurred solely as a result of his leg being caught between a bed frame and box spring, nor do bruises of different ages result from a 3-ft fall onto a carpeted floor. The immunizations not being current and the mother's implausible explanation as to why point to a neglectful in addition to an abusive environment.

Another important mother-child interaction to note in older children, approximately 18 months and above, is the phenomenon of "role reversal;" and its occurrence should be documented in the medical record. If the physician observes that a mother ignores her child's distress, and if that mother subsequently exhibits grief or emotional upset and was consoled by her child, then this should be recorded in the chart as "role reversal." The physician should chart this only if he sees it happen. To record it on the basis of a nurse's or someone else's observation will relegate it into the category of hearsay testimony, which will not be admitted into evidence.

In addition to carefully describing all trauma, bruises, burns, lacerations, electric cord marks, rope burns, etc., it is essential to obtain color photographs of the child as soon as possible after the medical and protective legal needs of the child have been met. These photographs, as well as x-ray films and other laboratory data, must be collected as soon as the child is admitted and the results documented in the chart. With respect to bruising, screening coagulation studies such as a partial thromboplastin time, prothrombin time, a platelet count, a bleeding time, fibrinogen level, and a careful past history, family history, and drug history should be obtained in order to rule out a medical defect that could account for bruises occurring other than as a result of trauma. If a caretaker or relative mentions that the child "bruises easily" or states that it is a specific characteristic of the child and/or other family members, then other evaluative tests should be ordered; a hematology consult might be helpful. The goal is to be able to state in court that there is no evidence to support the notion that there is a hereditary or medical reason to account for the bruises on the body.

If the history, physicial exam, and laboratory data all point to an abused or neglected child, or one whose environment is antithetical to his growth and development, then definitive steps must be taken to protect him. In some cases, hospitalization may suffice, but to make absolutely sure the parents or legal guardians do not take the child out of the hospital against medical advice, an Order of Temporary Custody, in some states referred to as an Instanta Order, must be obtained from the family or juvenile court. Depending on the local custom and/or the mechanics set up for reporting, this is accomplished either by the physician notifying the child protection agency, which, in turn, obtains the order, or by the physician contacting the court directly. This order removes legal custody from the parents and entrusts it to the state. This order will stay in effect for varying amounts of time depending on the laws of the state, but usually holds until the evidence that brought about the order can be reviewed and a decision made regarding its continuance. The physician may or may not be involved in this decision, and the reader is encouraged to check with the juvenile or family court in his county to learn the usual and customary procedures. Usually, the order can be given over the phone so that in the event of hostile parents and/or a pressing medical need, the child's safety would not be jeopardized by waiting for an exchange of letters. Once the written order is in hand, it should be placed in the child's hospital chart to become a permanent part of his medical record. When asking for an Order of Temporary Custody, it is important to stress those findings that led the physician to conclude that the child was at risk. It is best to err on the conservative side and obtain an unnecessary order rather than allow a child to return to an unsafe environment and risk additional damage or death.

Discussion with Parent or Legal Guardian

Once the order has been obtained and the child's safety assured, it is then appropriate to discuss your findings and the order with the parents. Occasionally, this can be done without a telephone order, but if there is the slightest concern that the parents might leave the hospital against medical advice once they have been told that the physician suspects abuse or neglect, then it is imperative first to obtain the temporary custody change. The physician must then discuss with the parents why this was done to maintain an honest and open relationship with them. This can be a very anxiety-generating situation for the physician unless he is aware of his responsibility as a child advocate, knows the laws of his state, and recognizes that he does not have the power to put children in foster homes or sever parental rights. The physician will be more sure of himself and in a better position to deal openly with the parents if he points out that as a member of the medical profession he is obligated to protect children from what he perceives to be an unsafe environment. Furthermore, most states have laws that require many professionals (not just physicians) to report unsafe child environments to the proper authorities; and, indeed, failure to do so could result in misdemeanor charges being brought against the offender. Another important point to remember is the limits of the physician's power. He presents medical evidence in court together with data from others, such as social workers, court workers, nurses, and psychologists who are also involved in the child's welfare. After review of all the data, the court, and not the physician, makes a decision with respect to the child's placement and guardian.

With the above information in mind, the physician can approach the parents and point out that based on the extent of the child's injuries and the story of how they occurred, it is necessary to report the case and perhaps seek protective custody. The implications of these actions should be carefully explained. Then outline the plan to hospitalize the child until his medical problems, if any, are resolved and/or the child protection agency and the court have made a decision with respect to the current safety of the child's environment. Be careful not to insinuate or directly state that you feel the parents, boyfriend, babysitter, or others committed the abuse. Point out that you are not a detective or police officer and your responsibility is not to determine exactly how the injury or neglect occurred. Rather, your responsibility is to recognize those situations in which a child's safety may be in jeopardy and take steps to protect the child until a definitive decision is made regarding the true nature of his environment. This usually brings about anger and resentment from the parents as well as accusations that the physician is trying to take the child away from them.

Occasionally, threats of violence will be made toward the physician. If this occurs, it is recommended that the physician remain calm, empathize with the parents' feelings, and point out your professional and legal responsibilities to the child. Emphasize that you have no power to make custodial decisions, but rather, you are mandated by law to report certain types of biosocial situations. Be quick to point out that environments that appear to be adverse or unsafe on first glance can later be judged satisfactory after more careful scrutiny.

Rather than reacting with anger when notified of the necessity to report and subsequent hospitalization, some parents react with great relief and behave as though a great weight has been lifted from their shoulders, which, indeed, it may have been. This can be a good sign with respect to future working relationships with the parent. But occasionally feelings can change; a parent who was initially grateful may after a 24-hour period of reflection become hostile and noncommunicative.

Next, it is important to anticipate and explain the sequence of events that will happen both to the parents and child. After the medical reasons, if any, for hospitalization are explained, give the parent an estimate of how long hospitalization will be medically indicated. Then, based on the laws of the state, explain the procedures with respect to detention hearings, if any, and let them know when the formal hearing will take place. Following this, it should be recommended that the parents seek legal counsel in order to help prepare for their appearance at the child's hearing. Then explain that other professionals such as social workers, psychologists, court workers, psychiatrists, physical therapists, and others will be talking to, testing, and examining the child and the parents. Others who have had caretaking responsibilities for the child may also be contacted. It is also important to urge the parents to be as cooperative as possible during subsequent interviews and testing (1).

All of the above discussion should be documented in the medical record as well as the parents' reaction to your assessment. This is important so it is clear that you have not acted out of malice toward the parent and that your actions were based on what you thought was in the best interest of both the child and his family. Practically speaking, most parents of abused or neglected children do not harbor warm feelings of gratitude toward the reporting physician because they were reported to protective services by him. However, it is felt that honesty, straightforward explanations of what can be expected, and continued communication with the parents during hospitalization stand the best chance of facilitating rapport and an ongoing relationship with the parents regardless of the disposition of the case.

DURING THE CHILD'S HOSPITALIZATION

Preparation of the Medical Report to the Court

Depending on the practices in your community, you may be able to report a case of child abuse and not be called on to submit a subsequent and substantiating medical report. In other jurisdictions, a medical report may be mandatory to enforce an Order of Temporary Custody for the detention hearing, if there is one, and for the formal hearing to determine custody. In the event you are called on to write a report, it is suggested that certain guidelines be followed. Your goal should be to present information in a clear, concise, and understandable form so as to allow the courts to understand your concerns for the child and thereby, in concert with data from other sources, to make the best decision for the child and his family.

The report should be a lay interpretation of your admission history, physical examination laboratory data, and initial interaction with the parent and child. Medical jargon should be avoided, but if technical terms are used, a brief explanation should ensue. After the information is offered, it should be summarized and an explanation given as to why the physician feels neglect and/or abuse has taken place. This should be followed by the physician's reasons for obtaining an Order of Temporary Custody and, finally, what the physician recommends to the court. If, in the physician's mind, there is sufficient evidence to recommend severance of parental rights, then the physician should state that in unequivocal terms. On the other hand, if there is room for doubt and/or the family is viewed initially as one that would respond to therapy and make the home safe for the child's eventual return, then the physician should also make those thoughts known to the court. The following is an example based on the semifactual case presented earlier in the chapter.

The Honorable John J. Doe
Smith County Juvenile Court
1234 Main Street
Kansas City, Kansas 66103

Dear Judge Doe:

On July 8, 1980 at 8:00 AM, Danny Jones, a 13-month-old Caucasian male, was brought into the Medical Center emergency room with his right thigh in a splint and accompanied by his maternal grandmother and his mother. Initially, the mother would not come into the examining room but elected to remain in the waiting area. The grandmother said that she had the child at her home, where he spends most of his time, on the evening of July 7. She heard him cry out, went into a bedroom, and found his leg caught between the bed frame and box spring. Later, she noted swelling in the involved leg and called the mother to take the child to the hospital. The mother was then coaxed into the examining room and she stated that the child was lying on her bed at about 10:00 PM on the evening of July 7 in her home (not the grandmother's) when she left the room for a moment to go to the bathroom. She heard the child cry and returned to find that his leg had slipped between the frame and box spring of her bed. She picked the child up and he promptly stopped crying. She thought no more of the incident until approximately a half-hour later when she changed his diaper prior to putting him to bed. She noted a swelling in his right thigh and took him to the emergency room of the Veteran's Administration hospital where his leg was splinted, and she was directed to another facility that cared for children. She went home from the VA and did not seek further care for her son until the following morning at the urging of the child's grandmother.

Examination and subsequent x-rays demonstrated a complete break in the middle of the right thigh bone and bruises of varying ages on the child's face and buttocks. The mother stated these occurred as a result of a fall from her bed onto a carpeted floor three days earlier. The child had not had an immunization since he was two months old, and the mother explained that she had neither the money nor transportation to obtain this important health maintenance for her son.

Additional laboratory studies failed to offer a medical reason for the peculiar distribution of bruising found only on the face and buttocks.

The differing accounts of how the injury occurred, the inappropriate initial selection of a medical facility and the inordinate delay in seeking definitive care, the broken bone and bruises unable to be explained on the basis of the mother's account, and her unconcern and negative affect toward her son as noted by multiple observers in the emergency room, all lead me to conclude that this child has been a victim of child abuse. Because of this belief, I have asked for and received a Temporary Order of Custody and the child is currently hospitalized on the pediatric service of the Medical Center with his leg in traction prior to casting. I anticipate that he will need to be in the hospital for approximately two weeks and remain in a cast for six weeks. I expect that his bruises and his broken bone will heal without residual damage.

At this point, I recommend a full-scale investigation of the child's environment by court workers and social workers from Social Rehabilitative Services, and that the mother and grandmother undergo psychiatric and psychological evaluation to shed some light on their parenting abilities. If these findings indicate a hostile environment that is antithetical to the child's healthy growth and development, then I recommend complete severance of the mother and grandmother's parental rights and placement of the child in a foster home until he can be legally adopted by competent parents.

If you have questions or need additional information, please do not hesitate to contact me.

Sincerely,

Documentation During Hospitalization

In some instances, a letter similar to the one above will be all that is required from the physician. However, in less blatant cases, careful documentation of the change, if any, of the child's affect during hospitalization is crucial. If the child is initially withdrawn, irritable, nonresponsive to affection, and shows developmental delay in some areas, it is important to document any positive changes that occur as a result of the child's being in a supportive nurturing hospital environment. Again, remember that you must have observed these changes in order to testify in court that they, in fact, did occur. To say that nurses have noted an improvement in the child's affect will be dismissed as hearsay evidence.

Also important is documentation of the number of trips the parents make to visit their child as well as documentation of the interaction between child and parent, and parent and physician. This information can be introduced in court and can be very helpful to a judge who is wrestling with what will be the best disposition for the child and his family.

Disposition Meeting Before the Child's Discharge

In order for all those who plan to testify in court to have a clear picture of what has transpired, a predischarge conference should be held. It is important that each witness understand the findings and interpretations of the other's data before testifying in court. If there are disagreements, these should be resolved so the court is not faced with conflicting information. These inconsistencies can be picked apart by defense attorneys with the potential result of having a child returned to an unsafe environment. If the data generated as a result of admission to the hospital support the opinion that the child's environment is safe for his return, then a concensus should be reached and this communicated to the court during individual testimony.

Finally, those who will testify should be careful to keep their findings confidential and not discuss their data or their testimony before the hearing with anyone other than those professionals directly involved in the case. This information may get to the press or to others involved in the case, such as defense attorneys, and possibly have an undesirable effect on the court's decision.

PREPARATION FOR THE HEARING

Historical Perspective

Discussion of preparation for the hearing requires a brief review of the basis on which a physician is entitled to appear in court and testify to or provide an opinion concerning a child and whether or not he or she is the victim of child abuse.

In Great Britain, before the founding of this country, those laws that were written as a result of a judge and/or jury decision after hearing testimony at a trial, as opposed to those laws enacted by Parliament, were known as British Common Law. As a result of this body of law, every witness was prohibited from giving his opinions, surmises, or conjectures and could testify only to those events or occurrences that he or she actually observed. The deduction process, drawing conclusions from the observed facts, was a function only permitted by the trier of facts (judge or jury) and not that of an ordinary witness. Beginning in the 19th century and as a result of an increasing complexity in our society, this rule became liberalized so that those witnesses with a particular expertise in an area, for example, science, medicine, engineering, could testify as to their opinions. Gradually, the practice of allowing experts to testify as to matters within their expertise grew. However, a limit was correspondingly placed on what opinions the experts could express; the expert could not testify by opinion on the very issue before the jury. Even this limitation has been gradually eroded, first, by use of the hypothetical question, but more recently, by modification of the rules and evidence.

Today, in this country, an expert witness may testify to the "ultimate issue" (the issue to be decided by the trier of fact, or has the child been abused?) The recent Federal Rules of Evidence provide as follows:

> Testimony in the form of an opinion or inference otherwise admissible is not objectionable because it embraces an ultimate issue to be decided by the trier of fact. (2)

This rule is not novel, and in nearly every jurisdiction in the United States, those persons who by virtue of their special knowledge, skill, training, experience, or education may testify in opinion form to the ultimate issue. The experts that most frequently appear and testify are physicians. Permitting them to form and express an opinion, after a proper data base has been established, that a particular child is abused or neglected is permissible.

Regarding the term *expert witness*, any physician qualifies as an expert witness simply by virtue of his medical degree. That degree, regardless of how recently acquired, qualifies him to admit data into evidence as an expert. Therefore, no physician should be hesitant to testify because he feels he is not an expert. The real issue is one of admissibility versus credibility. As a physician, a witness is permitted to offer testimony as an expert, but how credible he or she is can depend on experience in the field and definitely on the witness' conduct on the witness stand. If a physician (expert witness) is confronted with a patient who is jaundiced, nauseated, has lost his taste for food and cigarettes, has right upper quadrant pain, hepatomegaly, markedly elevated liver enzymes, and a history of having pricked his finger with a needle contaminated with Hepatitis A virus, it is suspected that the physician would not hesitate to state and perhaps even testify that the patient has, at the very least, some sort of liver disease. The physician is "expert" enough to have made that diagnosis and it is hoped that he would not refuse to comment on the patient's condition simply because he was not as experienced or "credible" with regard to liver disease as a hepatologist. Correspondingly, if the expert witness were presented with a marasmic, filthy, developmentally delayed, underimmunized child with multiple old and new healing fractures, it is anticipated that the physician would not refuse to testify that the child had been abused.

There are physicians more credible in their individual fields than the "average" physician, but they are no more *expert* with regard to giving testimony than any physician who cares for patients.

Prior Communication with the Prosecuting Attorney

Considering the gravity of the issue involved, it would be extremely improvident for the examining physician and prosecuting attorney not to meet and confer in order to prepare for presentation of testimony in a hearing to determine whether or not a child is maltreated. In most situations prosecuting attorneys are conscientious enough to initiate pretrial hearing conferences in order to determine what the evidence is and what the examining physician's testimony will be. In those situations where a case is pending and no initiative has been made by the prosecuting attorney, it becomes the responsibility of the physician to initiate the contact.

It is important for the examining physician to remember that many prosecuting attorneys have had little experience in medicolegal areas. Physicians should exercise a certain amount of patience in educating these attorneys about the case, examination procedures, and hospital routine. At a minimum, one conference in advance of the hearing should be held with the prosecuting attorney to review the case. The physician should encourage the prosecuting attorney to meet with him in his office or at the hospital so that the entire medical record and any other x-ray films, photographs, laboratory studies, or consultant reports will be immediately available for review and discussion.

Assuming you have a novice prosecutor, it is incumbent on the examining physician to explain the purpose of the medical record and the need for its admissibility (which of necessity must be a complete and correct copy) in evidence during the hearing. It should be pointed out that the medical record is a compilation of written orders by physicians, observations by physicians and nursing personnel, consultants' findings, reports of laboratory results, and other diagnostic studies. The expert witness must point out to the prosecuting attorney those findings (usually the objective findings contained in the admission note) that are most condemning to the respondents in the forthcoming proceedings. Further, in those types of cases where psychological child abuse, malnutrition, or malnurturing of a child is the issue, consultant reports or significant laboratory studies need to be pointed out to the prosecutor and explained in detail. The explanation of a clinical chart in layman's terms so the prosecutor can understand its importance is imperative because it is the job of the prosecutor to present these data to the judge hearing the case.

Frequently, a prosecutor, through inexperience, will not have had a prior opportunity to examine a medical expert witness. Accordingly, it may be as important for you to explain to him the method and order of proof necessary to place before the court for consideration of the necessary facts and data on which to predicate an opinion. Ordinarily, most experienced counsel will commence the examination of an expert witness by placing before the court his or her background, training, education and experience, that is, the witness' qualifications. Accordingly, it will be helpful to counsel if you can supply him with a current *curriculum vitae* or resumé so that he will be familiar with and know what your qualifications are.

The next area of discussion with the prosecutor should concern the evidence that is supportive of his case and the evidence that is either neutral or nonsupportive. It is important for the prosecutor to know potential weaknesses for his case as well as strong points. It is here that it is particularly important for the physician to detail the principle reasons in support of his conclusion that the child in question has been abused. When the prosecutor understands the foundation of your opinion, it is frequently worthwhile to discuss candidly any weaknesses that may exist in your opinion. For example, in the case cited above, if the photographs of the bruises were of poor quality and did not adequately or clearly demonstrate the differing ages of the bruises, then this ought to be brought to the prosecutor's attention. Also, it is worthwhile to point out to the prosecutor the areas where a knowledgeable defense counsel might attack your opinion or conclusion. Finally, it is during this first meeting that you try to develop a line of questioning or order of questioning from the prosecutor to you. It is crucial, once you take the witness stand, to know the sequence of questions that you will be asked in order to present in an orderly and organized manner the medical circumstances and opinion concerning the child. It is equally important for the prosecutor to know in the same orderly manner the responses and answers that he will be receiving to his questions. It is hoped that before the trial any unique or unusual evidentiary issues can be raised by the prosecutor and discussed with his witness. The physician should also explain what audio-visual materials may be necessary for a proper presentation of the case. Any still photographs that are taken should be made part of the chart in order that they can be received in evidence as part of the medical records of the hospital. However, it may be necessary that the person who took the photographs, if it is not the examining physician, be present in court to lay a proper foundation for the admission of the photos. If 35 mm slides are used, arrangements need to be made for a projector and screen. If x-ray films or other radiologic evidence needs to be presented, the prosecutor must be so advised and arrangements made to have a view box present in court. Discussing these kinds of issues with the prosecutor during the initial meeting will obviate many of the problems that are frequently encountered when the aforedescribed communication is absent (3).

Following this first and more lengthy meeting, it is also important that the examining physician and the prosecutor have a brief meeting immediately before the hearing and in many cases as much as 30 to 60 minutes before the actual presentation of the testimony. Here, a final review can be made of the order of questions and answers and any other details that need to be resolved. Frequently, the prosecutor can alert the physician to likely avenues of attack by defense counsel. The degree of pretrial coordination obviously will depend on the nature and gravity of the case. There will be only one occasion for the judge to hear the evidence and make his decision. Since it may be the only chance the involved child has to survive, the communication between physician and attorney is crucial.

Prior Communication with the Defense Attorney

Communication with defense counsel or counsel appointed to represent any party whose interests are adverse to that of the prosecutors is an issue that should be handled carefully by the medical expert witness. Ordinarily, and as stated earlier, an expert witness is permitted to testify to the ultimate issue by virtue of his special skill, training, education, and experience. Accordingly, he comes to the court house cloaked with the mantle of neutrality. It follows that any lawyer representing any party in the proceedings should be permitted to interview and discuss the case with the examining physician. Some prosecuting attorneys, however, view the examining physician as "their" witness and view with reluctance any pretrial conversations or interviews with defense counsel, and particularly any meeting where the prosecuting attorney is not also in attendance. When the first pretrial conference is conducted with the prosecuting attorney, the physician should determine the local protocol or applicable rules with respect to speaking to other counsel.

An additional problem is created by virtue of the establishment of a physician-patient relationship. Growing out of this relationship is the privilege that is enjoyed by the patient, not the physician, that his or her treating physician will not disclose or discuss with another any communications that occurred between the physician and his patient or the nature of the treatment provided or accorded to the patient by the physician. Since the child or children involved are usually minors and the parent or guardian is the only person to whom the physician can legally disclose or discuss the child's case, discussion with others may present a breach of the privilege when the prosecuting attorney appears to discuss the case without an authorization from the concerned parent. This privilege is normally statutory and you will nearly always find, in addition to the privilege, a statutory waiver thereof in the event litigation, civil or criminal, exists that concerns the medical care and treatment of the child. Ordinarily, and in this context, the privilege enjoyed by the patient is waived, and the physician is free to discuss care, treatment, and management of the patient with interested parties. Therefore, the physician should not fail to testify in a child abuse case or fail to disclose information to a child protection agency on a child from his or her patient population because he or she feels to do so would be a breech of patient confidentiality; it would not! It may well be, however, that any conversation with defense counsel cannot take place without the presentation of a duly acknowledged authorization to release medical information signed by one or both parents. Physicians who are required to testify or participate in a proceeding where a claim is being made that a child has been maltreated should carefully review with their personal attorney, hospital attorney, or the prosecuting attorney the law of their particular jurisdiction before having discussions about a patient's care.

If there are no objections by the prosecuting attorney and no physician-patient relationship is being violated, then discussion of the case with defense counsel is permissible. The medical expert may wish to establish and is entitled to establish a certain protocol governing these discussions. The physician may require payment or even prepayment of a professional fee for the time it takes to discuss the case with defense counsel or counsel for other related parties. Also, the physician may establish, absent some unusual procedure or rules in a given jurisdiction, the location where the interview may take place, that is, the hospital, medical office, or some other location of convenience. Finally, the physician has the privilege to refuse to provide or give written statements or electronically recorded statements. Ordinarily, it is unwise to give a written or electronically recorded statement of a view or opinion of the case since there exists the possibility that the recording can be edited or modified to convey an inaccurate position. If the physician chooses to discuss the case with defense counsel, he should be very matter-of-fact in his presentation of findings, not indicating any preconceived notion or position about the merits of a given case.

Preparation of the Data Base

The most important thing a physician can do to prepare for a hearing where the issue is a possibly maltreated child is to prepare properly the data base. The goal at the hearing is to present a clear and concise picture of the medical condition of a child and the cause of his condition. Tangible evidence other than the medical record may be very helpful in showing the court the condition of an infant when first injured, whereas the hearing may take place weeks or months later.

Photographs are essential to the proper presentation of a battered-child case. Any photograph is better than none. It is hoped that the institution or facility where the child is hospitalized will have some photographic capability. It may even be necessary to request that a local commercial photographer come to the hospital on short notice for the purpose of recording photographically any bruise, swelling, burn, laceration, or other physical manifestation of child abuse.

When photographs are taken, record in the progress notes the date and time the photographs are taken, the number of photographs, and the photographer's name.

Fundamental to the initial examination of a suspected battered child is a radiographic examination. Because injuries inflicted by abusive parents can appear in a bizarre form, a most comprehensive radiographic examination is needed.

In cases where the physician is required to deal with the malnourished, malnurtured, or psychologically abused child, care should be exercised to ensure that consultant reports contain the necessary language and findings to support the ultimate conclusion. For example, if psychological abuse is suspected and referral made to a clinical psychologist or child psychiatrist, be sure the examiner to whom the patient is referred details specifically the results of the examination in a manner that will allow for clear interpretation by the court.

TESTIFYING AT THE HEARING

Credibility (believability) of witnesses is often judged on their demeanor and appearance in the courtroom. Exceptionally learned and knowledgeable people have been completely ineffective as witnesses simply because their lack of preparation and inappropriate demeanor had been exploited by opposing counsel. The personal confidence necessary to be effective is best achieved by prehearing preparation. The fact that a witness is well prepared during the hearing will become obvious to all present. Defense counsel or other opposing counsel, while observing your testimony, will quietly be making decisions in their own mind about the extent of their cross-examination. The fact that the medical expert is well prepared to discuss his case frequently discourages vigorous cross-examination by experienced defense counsel. Personal appearance and demeanor should present the physician as a modest or conservative professional dressed in a business suit or dress (do not wear a white smock or scrub suit) bearing an air of neutrality and prepared to present efficiently medical facts and conclusions concerning a patient. Before the hearing begins, it is preferable to have already placed in the courtroom any trial aids such as an x-ray view box, a 35 mm slide projector, or a screen. When called to the witness stand, the expert witness should carry with him nothing more than his personal office notes or records, or possibly the medical record. X-ray films and photographs should have previously been delivered to the prosecuting attorney; this may vary from jurisdiction to jurisdication. Avoid, if possible, lumbering to the witness stand loaded down with weighty files, large manila folders containing x-ray films and other paraphernalia. Additional time spent in coordinating the appearance in court with the prosecuting attorney and use of heretofore mentioned trial aids is well worth the benefits in appearance to all parties.

The expert witness should not be startled after being called to the stand if one or more counsel requests the "rule" be enforced. Nearly every jurisdiction in the United States has a provision that requires that once a hearing begins, and if the rule is invoked, no witness can discuss with any other witness what his or her testimony will be or has been. The rule only applies during that period of time that the hearing is in actual progress and does not preclude any witness from discussing with his or her counsel what the testimony is to be. If during a recess the prosecuting attorney desires to discuss with you a subject that needs to be developed further on a redirect examination, it is perfectly permissible to discuss this with him.

When the examining physician is called to testify, he or she will ordinarily be required to approach the bench or witness stand area to be sworn by the judge or court clerk. In this regard, a medical expert witness is required to be placed under oath like all other witnesses, and whether the oath is administered by the judge or other court personnel will vary from jurisdiction to jurisdiction.

When the physician takes the witness stand, he or she will first observe multiple counsel tables and counsel sitting with their respective clients. There is no particular protocol for seating. One table is not always reserved for the prosecution another for the patient's parents, and another for the *guardian ad litem*. Accordingly, as each counsel proceeds to examine you, he will frequently identify himself and his client. It may be worthwhile for the expert witness to make a diagram of the location of counsel table, note the name of the counsel at each table, and whom they represent. If this can be done before testifying, it will serve to orient the expert witness concerning who will be asking the questions. In the courtroom, in addition to the judge, you will generally find court workers such as juvenile probation officers or social workers. You may find them seated separately from the attorneys or with the prosecuting attorney or parents. Occasionally, they may be seated at a separate table. In addition, there will be a table where the respondent parents and their counsel are seated. It is not unusual to find parents who are separated or divorced and having interest adverse to one another in this particular hearing. Under these circumstances, each will have separate counsel and likely be seated at separate counsel tables. In most jurisdications, an attorney is appointed as *guardian ad litem* (and may be known in other jurisdications as guardians of the person, petitioner's counsel, respondent's counsel) to represent the interest of the child. He may be seated at a separate counsel table or, on some occasions, seated at the same counsel table with the prosecuting attorney. He frequently will view the interest of his client to be identical to the interest of the state in that he may be seeking the court to rule the child to be dependent and/or neglected and parental rights severed either temporarily or permanently. Even though the *guardian ad litem*'s client's interest may be the same or similar to that of the state or the prosecuting attorney, he nonetheless has an opportunity and frequently will cross-examine the expert witness. It is possible in some jurisdictions to find counsel for another party, such as a boyfriend or a girlfriend of a parent of the abused child. If the issue at the hearing goes beyond the question of whether or not the child is battered and includes imposition of criminal sanctions against a parent, boyfriend, or girlfriend, then they will be present in court and represented by counsel. This is not the rule in the majority of the jurisdictions, however.

The rules of procedure will dictate which lawyer begins to examine first. Generally, since you will be the witness called by a prosecuting attorney, he has the privilege of examining the medical expert first, and this is known as direct examination. All other examination by other counsel is known as cross-examination. Following the prosecuting attorney's examination, the court ordinarily will permit examination by the counsel representing the parents, then examination by counsel who is the *guardian ad litem*.

Witnesses are called for the purpose of stating under oath what they have seen or observed about an issue that is under consideration by the court. Accordingly, counsel representing parties who have an interest in the litigation are entitled to examine them (ask questions) and elicit answers that relate to the issue in question. In a child maltreatment case, the examining physician is normally a witness called by the prosecutor who represents the interest of the county or state and will, therefore, be regarded as a state or government witness. Notwithstanding, the expert witness has certain rights as a witness (4).

Generally, hearings involving abused children are conducted in a civilized manner and the examining physician is not subjected to name-calling, harassment, or other inappropriate forms of conduct by adverse counsel. The presiding judge will usually be intolerant of this type of conduct. If the doctor is of the opinion that opposing counsel's conduct amounts to name calling or harassment, he may simply mention to the court those things stated by counsel that are offensive, and frequently the trial or hearing judge will admonish counsel to cease this kind of behavior. In addition, a witness is absolutely entitled to be asked a question that he or she understands. It is the duty of the examining counsel to frame or so phrase his question so that the witness understands it. In the event the witness does not, he should simply state "I do not understand the question" or "Would you rephrase the question." A trial judge will not require a witness to answer a question he or she does not understand. Questions that are compound, vague, or convoluted may also be asked. These questions may be the result of lack of ability by counsel to examine appropriately a witness or may be intentional. A witness has no obligation to respond and can simply advise the counsel that the question is vague and it is not understood. If the question is compound, two or more questions wrapped into one, you may wish to ask counsel which part of the question he wants answered first. Once a response of this kind is provided, the hearing judge or trial judge will admonish the examiner to rephrase his question. Convoluted questions or questions that contain a "shift in premise" are dangerous for the expert witness. A defense attorney may attempt to ask questions that shift emphasis from the case at hand to findings or cases reported in the literature in an attempt to draw an exact parallel between the two. This may unjustifiably strengthen the case for the defense because the two cases may differ substantially; but the defense attorney has only illuminated the similarities. The expert witness should point out to the examiner the shift in premise and advise that the question cannot be answered for that reason. Again, a trial judge will normally admonish counsel to rephrase the question in order to make it a proper one.

The abstract question technique of examining a witness is frequently employed. It amounts to a technique whereby examining counsel will ask a series of general or abstract questions about patient management or treatment and then begin to engage in questions specifically related to the case at hand. The expert witness must again be alert to the point where counsel will try to subtly shift the questions from abstract to the specific case at hand. When the expert observes the shift, he should then inquire of opposing counsel whether this is a general or abstract question, or is he now shifting to the specific case at hand.

Frequently, examining counsel will be chagrined when unmasked in this form, and the court, although permitting an answer to the question, will be on notice that counsel has been unsuccessful in his examining technique.

Narrow questions that mandate a yes or no answer have historically been difficult for medical experts to respond to properly. Because the rules of evidence generally permit wide latitude in both direct and cross-examination, the expert witness should understand that he can give a complete answer regardless of how the question was phrased. Accordingly, the expert is not confined to answer questions on a yes or no basis. Any question so framed may be expanded on by the expert, but only if the expert advises the examining counsel that the question cannot be answered on a yes or no basis. A skillful cross-examiner will try to frame his questions to preclude the expert from giving expansive or narrative type answers. He employs this technique to prevent the expert from further damaging, via his testimony, his client's case. Direct examination is that which is conducted by counsel who calls the particular witness. Generally, all evidence and testimony is admissible provided it is relevant to the issue before the court. Hopefully, during the pretrial conference, the prosecuting attorney will indicate to the expert the kind of cross-examination he or she may expect.

Cross-examination is permitted in the adversary system so that an attorney who represents a person against whom the expert's testimony is directed can test, through a questioning process, the substantiating value of the witness' testimony. Cross-examination generally must be confined to those subjects elicited during direct examination. Generally, the cross-examiner should not be permitted to go beyond those areas that were not developed during direct. If the court does permit this, the witness may be at a disadvantage. If the disadvantage becomes substantial, it may be necessary for the witness to state to the court and examining counsel that he is not prepared to respond to questions in this area or that responses will necessarily have to be qualified. This may be a tactic for the witness that is preferable to attempts to answer questions about which the witness has had no preparation. Hopefully, the prosecuting attorney's objections to excursions beyond the direct examination will be sustained.

Following cross-examination, further questioning is always permitted and may be conducted by the prosecuting attorney who initially called the expert. This examination must be confined to those areas covered by counsel during cross-examination. It is only permitted to clarify any matters discussed during cross-examination and may not be utilized as a technique to expand the scope of the original direct examination. In other words, if the subject wasn't covered during the original direct examination, it is not permissible to develop it for the first time on redirect.

The expert witness who presents himself best conveys an image of confidence and knowledge of his subject matter. Courtesy to counsel and the court is important even though opposing counsel may not be. Some attorneys mistakenly believe that if they are demonstrative in court and accuse the witness of certain improprieties, they are effective; but they seldom are. It is tempting for an expert witness to respond in kind to this type of conduct, but that too is rarely effective. The best expert witness presents an image of being able to discuss quietly and calmly, but firmly, the medical findings and conclusions in the face of an antagonistic counsel. Cool discussion of the issues concerning an abused child, even though in an emotionally charged setting, is exceedingly effective. Becoming argumentative with counsel ultimately conveys to the trial judge or hearing examiner that you are becoming an advocate for the state's case. Although in a sense you are an advocate for the state's case, and particularly an advocate for the child, it is important to maintain the posture of neutrality. Becoming angry on the witness stand is fatal. That is a frequent objective of a skillful examiner because that counsel knows that if a witness becomes angry, he loses his objectivity and his credibility. The angry witness is ripe for making an inconsistent statement that can be very damaging to the state's case. It is important to be restrained, disciplined, and not permit anger or any other emotion to cloud your judgment and objectivity while on the witness stand.

Expert witnesses who testify for the first time frequently do not understand they are entitled to refer to notes, records, and other tangible evidence while on the witness stand. This is perfectly permissible and appropriate. It would be foolhardy, for an expert witness to try and commit to memory an entire medical chart. A frequent trick question of a witness by a skillful examiner applies to the reference to the medical chart. Opposing counsel may ask the expert why he cannot simply describe a child's condition without having to refer to written materials. Of course, the purpose of the question is to make the witness feel that he is incompetent or less than knowledgeable about the case. One response would be to simply state that you consider this hearing and the welfare of the child to be a matter of grave concern to you as well as the child. Accordingly, you wish to be as accurate in your testimony as possible and have, therefore, taken notes on important points to avoid error. The expert must rely on written documents due to the complexities of the medical data.

CONCLUSION

The testimony of the examining physician in many situations will be the evidence that persuades a trial judge that a child has been abused. Rarely are there eyewitnesses to parents or others abusing their children. Therefore, the only remaining objective basis on which a judge can decide that the child was abused is the conclusion or opinion of the medical expert witness. Again, the medical expert, although theoretically a neutral in the courtroom, must be the advocate for the child because the one occasion in court may be the child's last chance to avoid becoming a fatal victim of child abuse.

REFERENCES

1. Leake HC, Smith D: Preparing for and testifying in a child abuse case. *Clin Pediatr* 16:1057, 1977.
2. *Federal Rules of Civil Procedure*, Rule 704. Title XXVII US Code.
3. Ladd M, Carlson RL: *Cases and Materials on Evidence.* Chicago, Callaghan and Company, 1972.
4. Danner D: *Medical Expert Witnesses—Using Them Effectively at Trial.* New York, Law Journal Seminars Press, Inc, 1970.

Index